WOMEN IN SOCIETY
A Feminist List edited by
Jo Campling

Editorial Advisory Group

Phillida Bunckle, *Victoria University, Wellington, New Zealand;* Miriam David, *South Bank University;* Leonore Davidoff, *University of Essex;* Janet Finch, *University of Lancaster;* Jalna Hanmer, *University of Bradford;* Beverley Kingston, *University of New South Wales, Australia;* Hilary Land, *University of Bristol;* Diana Leonard, *University of London Institute of Education;* Suan Londsdale, *South Bank University;* Jean O'Barr, *Duke University, North Caroline, USA;* Arlene Tigar McLaren, *Simon Fraser University, British Columbia, Canada;* Jill Roe, *Macquarie University, Australia;* Hilary Rose, *University of Bradford;* Susan Sellars, *Centre D'Etudes Feminines, Universite de Paris;* Pat Thane, *Goldsmiths' College, University of London;* Clare Ungerson, *University of Kent at Canterbury;* Judy Walkowitz, *Rutgers University, New Jersey, USA.*

The last 20 years have seen an explosion of publishing by, about and for women. This new list is designed to make a particular contribution to this continuing process by commissioning and publishing books which consolidate and advance feminist research and debate in key areas in a form suitable for students, academics and researchers but also accessible to a broader general readership.

As far as possible, books will adopt an international perspective incorporating comparative material from a range of countries where this is illuminating. Above all they will be interdisciplinary, aiming to put women's studies and feminist discussion firmly on the agenda in subject-areas as disparate as law, literature, art and social policy.

WOMEN IN SOCIETY
A Feminist List edited by Jo Campling

Published

Christy Adair **Women and Dance: sylphs and sirens**
Sheila Allen and Carol Wolkowitz **Homeworking: myths and realities**
Niamh Baker **Happily Ever After? Women's fiction in post-war Britain**
Ros Ballaster, Margaret Beetham, Elizabeth Frazer and Sandra Hebron **Women's Worlds: ideology, femininity and the woman's magazine**
Jenny Beale **Women in Ireland: voices of change**
Jennifer Breen **In Her Own Write: twentieth-century women's fiction**
Valerie Bryson **Feminist Political Theory: an introduction**
Ruth Carter and Gill Kirkup **Women in Engineering**
Joan Chandler **Women without Husbands: an exploration of the margins of marriage**
Angela Coyle and Jane Skinner **Women and Work: positive action for change**
Gillian Dalley **Ideologies of Caring: rethinking community and collectivism**
Leonore Davidoff and Belinda Westover (editors) **Our Work, Our Lives, Our Words: women's history and women's work**
Emily Driver and Audrey Droisen (*editors*) **Child Sexual Abuse: a feminist reader**
Elizabeth Ettorre **Women and Substance Use**
Lesley Ferris **Acting Women: images of women in theatre**
Diana Gittins **The Family in Question: changing households and familiar ideologies**
Eileen Green, Diana Woodward and Sandra Hebron **Women's Leisure, What Leisure?**
Tuula Gordon **Feminist Mothers**
Frances Heidensohn **Women and Crime**
Ursula King **Women and Spirituality: voices of protest and promise**
Muthoni Likimani (*Introductory Essay by Jean O'Barr*) **Passbook Number F.47927: women and Mau Mau in Kenya**
Jo Little, Linda Peake and Pat Richardson (*editors*) **Women in Cities: gender and the urban environment**
Susan Lonsdale **Women and Disability**
Sharon Macdonald, Pat Holden and Shirley Ardener (*editors*) **Images of Women in Peace and War: cross-cultural and historical perspectives**
Mavis Maclean **Surviving Divorce: women's resources after separation**
Shelley Pennington and Belinda Westover **A Hidden Workforce: homeworkers in England, 1850–1985**
Vicky Randall **Women and Politics: an international perspective (2nd edn)**
Diane Richardson **Women, Motherhood and Childrearing**
Rosemary Ridd and Helen Callaway (*editors*) **Caught up in p. + Conflict: women's response to political strife**
Susan Sellers **Language and Sexual Difference: feminist writing in France**
Patricia Spallone **Beyond Conception: the new politics of reproduction**
Taking Liberties Collective **Learning the Hard Way: women's oppression and men's education**
Clare Ungerson (*editor*) **Women and Social Policy: a reader**
Kitty Warnock **Land Before Honour: Palestinian women in the Occupied Territories**
Annie Woodhouse **Fantastic Women: sex, gender and transvestism**

Forthcoming

Eileen Aird and Judy Lown **Education for Autonomy: processes of change in women's education**
Maria Brenton **Women and Old Age**
Joan Busfield **Women and Mental Health**
Tuula Gordon **Single Women**
Frances Gray **Women and Laughter**
Annie Hudson **Troublesome Girls: adolescence, femininity and the state**
Ruth Lister **Women and Citizenship**

Women and Politics

An International Perspective

SECOND EDITION

First published 1982 by
THE MACMILLAN PRESS LTD
Houndmills, Basingstoke, Hampshire RG21 2XS
and London
Companies and representatives
throughout the world

ISBN 0–333–44896–0 hardcover
ISBN 0–333–44897–9 paperback

A catalogue record for this book is available
from the British Library.

Printed in Hong Kong

Second edition 1987
Reprinted 1991, 1993

Series Standing Order

If you would like to receive future titles in this series as they are published, you can
make use of our standing order facility. To place a standing order please contact your
bookseller or, in case of difficulty,write to us at the address below with your name
and address and the name of the series. Please state with which title you wish to
begin your standing order. (If you live outside the United Kingdom we may not have
the rights for your area, in which case we will forward your order to the publisher
concerned.)

Customer Services Department, Macmillan Distribution Ltd
Houndmills, Basingstoke, Hampshire RG21 2XS, England

To my Mother

Contents

Preface to the First Edition

At one time convention tended to define women and politics as mutually exclusive, occupying different spheres. Politics was understood as a public activity dominated by men and requiring typically masculine characteristics. Women were identified above all with the private world of the family and domestic life.

Two generations of feminists dating from the mid-nineteenth century and the early 1960s have challenged this view. Both have contributed to important changes in attitudes and have, in their turn, moved issues such as women's suffrage, and abortion, rape and equal pay into the arena of public debate and conflict.

Feminism has shed new light on the relationship between women and politics both by pointing to the structural features of political life which have tended to exclude women from positions of power, and by recovering from oblivion a hidden history of women's involvement in political action. (Political action is broadly defined here to include indirect influence and informal or 'anti-system' activities.) Most important of all, feminism has helped us to see that politics and policies have always, directly or indirectly, affected women's life options through, for instance, prohibitions on birth control, confirmation of fathers' and husbands' authority, or the absence of effective protection or redress for women against rape.

Women's involvement in politics, the impact of politics on women, the politics of women's social position, and the politics of feminism have become widely debated issues and given rise to an extensive and rapidly growing but disparate literature. Much of this lies unambiguously inside the boundaries of political science, centring on women's political participation and, less frequently, on the politics of feminist issues. Some is historical or anthropological; some is less easily classified but sits loosely within other academic disciplines. Last but by no means least are the relevant writings issuing directly from the women's movement.

The primary objective of this book is to familiarise readers with the broad character and concerns of this literature, and to point to sources for further reading. But this is not simply an extended review. In the first place the literature is too vast for such an enterprise to be comprehensively and fairly undertaken. In the second, it would not be particularly useful.

Instead, I have identified a number of themes that are, or should be, central upon which to organise the discussion. This means I have not attempted to reproduce each author's argument, although I hope I have not misrepresented them either, but have concentrated on analysis, whether empirical or theoretical, that helps to clarify and explain these themes.

Finally, in so far as I am offering an interpretation, I should declare my own political sympathies. This book is written from a feminist perspective. The various meanings of the term 'feminist' are discussed in the introduction; here it simply connotes, first, the belief that women share a common oppression, and, second, a commitment to its eradication. Although the approach of this book is academic rather than polemical, I hope that the kinds of questions it asks will be of relevance to debate and strategy within the feminist movement as well as to students of politics.

Many people have helped in the writing of this book, either direcly through their information or advice or indirectly through their moral support. But specifically I should like to thank the following: Joanna Chambers, Judith Evans, David Ewens, Jane Hall, Jill Hills, Joni Lovenduski, my father (Charles Madge), Elizabeth Meehan, June Wyer and Robin Theobald. Thanks are especially due to Jill Hills and Elizabeth Meehan for letting me read the drafts of their respective manuscripts, to Chris Fowler for his typing, George Osborn for his assistance with the index, and Steven Kennedy for his patient and extremely helpful editing. As is customary to say, any faults of fact or interpretation remain my sole responsibility.

London 1982   VICKY RANDALL

Preface to the Second Edition

It is perhaps as well that I did not realise quite how much work would be entailed in writing a revised edition of *Women and Politics* at the outset, or I might not have undertaken such a challenging but rewarding project. On the one hand since 1982 the relevant literature seems to have grown almost exponentially. On the other not only have the key debates become more sophisticated, been recast in different terms or even superseded, but the empirically ascertainable situation of women has continued to change and more information about it has become available.

Even more than when writing the first edition, I have felt it was neither possible nor desirable to produce a comprehensive coverage. I have concentrated instead on tracing what seem to me the most important 'factual' developments and related developments in analysis and argument. I have largely kept to my original framework but this has been modified to allow a wider comparative perspective where possible and in particular more reference to the experience of Third World women. This reflects both the greater availability of such material and the growth of international awareness in the women's movement.

The trends that such a study, five years on, reveals in the world of women and politics are in some ways quite encouraging. I had not fully realised till compelled to investigate systematically just how much steady if unspectacular progress there has been in women's rates of representation in both summit political bodies and those political arenas and related occupations that feed into them (with the obvious and striking exception of women's apparently un-budgetable 4 or 5 per cent in the British House of Commons and the US Congress). It could also be argued that feminist activists have learned from experience more about what policy changes to pursue and how tactically to get these changes adopted. And we can see feminist ideas taking firmer root outside the core of established Western democracies. Yet in other ways feminism in the 1980s appears to be struggling against the tide of recession and political reaction. Instead of being able to push on with an agenda for radical change in gender relations, we are busy defending the victories that we once regarded as mere preliminaries and even driven back to old issues like the need for some kind of state-subsidised childcare provision. One thing is clear to me: the feminist perspective is at least as relevant now as in the 1960s, or five years ago, to an adequate political understanding and, conversely, feminists need more than ever to grasp and make use of the science, and the art, of politics.

Once more I owe thanks to all those who assisted me in different ways, but most particularly to Sally Kenny, Mary Ladky, Joni Lovenduski, Elizabeth Meehan, Pippa Norris, June Nugent and Donley Studlar.

London 1987   VICKY RANDALL

Introduction

Political science and feminism have a lot to learn from each other. Not only has feminism encouraged political science to pay greater and more careful attention to the rather more than half of the world's population who are women. It can also contribute to a fuller understanding both of individual political systems and of politics itself. On the other hand, feminists can learn from political science the importance, for women, of public politics and the state, and the ways in which women and feminists can more effectively influence policy-making.

Up to the 1960s, at least, and the resurgence of feminism, political science had very little to say about women. One obvious reason for this neglect is that the profession of political science was, as it still is, overwhelmingly male-dominated, whether the criterion is numbers, positions in the hierarchy or output. As Lovenduski suggests, a further reason was the intellectual character of the discipline. A harmful split developed, and became particularly pronounced in the immediate post-war years, between 'scientific' empiricism on the one hand and overtly normative political theory on the other. Worse still, from women's point of view, assisted by the expansion of American political science empiricism emerged as the dominant paradigm. Given the limited observable role of women in the political arena, they were unlikely to be selected for study, except in the area of voting behaviour (Lovenduski, 1981). Two further features of this dominant approach help to explain its neglect of women: concentration upon conventional, even constitutional, political behaviour and emphasis on the 'input' rather than the 'output' or policy side of the political process.

When political scientists did discuss women, as feminist critics have pointed out, their interpretation was often sexist. Sexism in

1

political science, as in other social sciences, has mainly taken the following forms: first, omission of women as subject matter, although they may be subsumed under such generalities as 'humanity', 'mankind' or 'man'; second, discussion of women, when they are mentioned, in terms of their significance for men rather than in their own right; finally, the assumption that the male and female nature differ and that male nature is superior, or at least 'normal'.

Neglect of women is obviously more a failure of those political scientists who did not refer to women at all. However, even when male political scientists confidently generalised about women's political behaviour, it was on the basis of surprisingly limited discussion and evidence. A solitary but honourable exception must be Maurice Duverger, who wrote his sympathetic study of *The Political Role of Women* as early as 1955. Illustrations of the other two aspects of sexism are not hard to find. The most often quoted and blatantly sexist passage occurs in Lane's *Political Life*, where he writes:

> It is too seldom remembered in the American society that working girls and career women, and women who insistently serve the community in volunteer capacities, and women with extracurricular interests of an absorbing kind are often borrowing their time and attention and capacity for relaxed play and love from their children to whom it rightfully belongs. As Kardiner points out, the rise in juvenile delinquency (and, he says, homosexuality) is partly to be attributed to the feminist movement and what it did to the American mother (Lane, 1959, p. 355).

Today we can consult a number of feminist critiques of the treatment of women in the major political science textbooks of the 1950s and 1960s. These will be discussed more fully in subsequent chapters, but it is still worth underlining at this point just how extensive, but also insidious, sexism in political science has been. Sometimes it is unmistakable, as in the passage from Lane. At other times it is less easy to detect. Sexist assumptions lead to interpretations of evidence that only seem unwarranted upon reflection, for instance the suggestion that women as voters are fickle and personalise politics. Such assumptions may be unconscious, but when authors, in the words of Bourque and Grossholtz, 'fudge the footnotes', citing other authors out of context or occasionally with no basis at all, their innocence is in doubt (Bourque and Grossholtz, 1974, p. 227). Perhaps more serious is the intrusion of sexist assumptions into the research methods, where 'facts' about female political attitudes or behaviour are elicited, and thus into the very evidence itself. A survey question may prompt a sexist reply, as in the notorious 1936 Gallup Poll question, 'Would you vote for a woman for President, if she was qualified in every other respect?' (Wells and Smeal, 1974, p. 56). Or a question may be inappropriate for the attitude it purports to measure, as when Greenstein took the answers to questions about war as evidence that boys are more interested than girls in politics (Greenstein, 1965). Still more insidious is the subtle cueing that emerges from questionnaires in which 'Politics is portrayed as a male only world, by the use of the male gender, the pictures chosen and the limited and sterotyped choices of answers provided' (Iglitzin, 1974, p. 33).

Since the late 1960s, much has been done to rectify the sexist bias of political science, not least because of the growth of studies by female political scientists, influenced by reviving feminism. Although there is still a tendency to compartmentalise discussion of women in politics – the guest lecture, the separate conference panel, a section in the chapter on minorities, the token article, and specialised studies by women's political scientists – we can no longer complain that women's political behaviour is being ignored. Almost the reverse. Chapters 2 and 3 will explore this flourishing literature. While its coverage still leaves major questions unanswered it undoubtedly represents a tremendous advance.

Yet this literature has still to be integrated into mainstream, or as O'Brien (1981) calls it, 'male-stream' political science and its implications for a general understanding of political institutions and processes remain largely unrecognised. This book, for example, examines in Chapters 2 and 3 the factors that determine women's political participation. As Lovenduski and Hills suggest (1981b, pp. 4–5), such findings, especially when they take account of cross-cultural variations, could make a valuable contribution to a more general theory of participation. Meehan similarly argues 'The innovatory directions in the discipline which appear both to invite and to require a feminist perspective are those which seek to explain the informal processes that deprive other subordinate classes or groups of access to formal decision-making institutions' (Meehan, 1986, p. 120).

Still more fundamentally, it has been argued that feminism, at least radical feminism, requires a reconceptualisation of politics itself. Later in this chapter I shall consider the meaning, or meanings, of politics, including those offered by feminists. I shall point out that radical feminists were not the first to claim that 'the personal is political', and shall suggest that this perception should be used to supplement rather than replace prevailing notions of politics. None the less, the particular experience of women who become feminists enables them to ask searching questions which, at the least, must deepen our present understanding of what politics is.

If political science needs the lens of feminism to correct for sexist distortion, then feminists should not be too chary of the wisdom of 'bourgeois, male chauvinist' political science. In the nineteenth century, many feminists condemned the ruthlessness and corruption of public politics, though this was partly in order to argue the need for their own edifying participation. More recently radical feminists have regarded the public political sphere with, at best, extreme ambivalence. Although they have implicitly through their campaigns and latterly more explicitly recognised the possibility of influencing state policies, they have simultaneously mistrusted conventional participation, fearing, with some justification, both 'co-option' into male-dominated élites and the contagion of male patterns of organisational hierarchy. The radical feminists' critique of 'power politics' is not only telling, it is also probably a major reason for the continuing appeal of radical feminist ideas to younger or less 'established' women.

Even so, I shall argue here that feminists *have* to involve themselves in conventional politics, as well as campaigns of protest. Chapter 4 will trace the ways in which public policies have subordinated women's interests to those of men and the state, so long as feminists were unable to modify them. Chapter 6 will show what feminists have been able to achieve through co-ordinated action to influence public policy. Lest this sound too complacent, let me emphasise that it will not be enough for more women to acquire political office, since, as we shall see, female politicians are not necessarily feminist. Nor am I suggesting that legislation, judicial decisions and administrative measures can on their own improve women's status. On the contrary, constant feminist pressure and vigilance is needed to ensure their effective implementation. I am simply arguing that public politics is a tool, however imperfect, for modifying relationships within society, and feminists cannot afford to ignore it. Political science can help them to put that tool to the best use.

What is feminism?

There are two rather different ways to look at feminism. One is simply to define it, as it has defined itself, historically. The other, more controversial, approach is to identify what are or should be its guiding principles.

Taking the first approach, feminism can be seen as a wide and changing movement, seeking in various ways to raise women's social status. Though there have probably always been individual feminists in this sense, and feminist writings are found at least as far back as medieval France and seventeenth-century England, feminism as a self-conscious movement with some elements of organisation emerged in the 1840s in the United States and Britain. Its history during the remainder of the nineteenth century was complex, as Chapter 5 will describe, and it certainly did not focus exclusively on the suffrage question. However it is generally agreed that winning the vote (in 1918 in Britain and 1920 in the United States) paradoxically weakened and divided the movement. Though militant feminism never went under completely, this was the heyday of 'reasonable feminism', based on the premise that the main battle had been won and women could now enjoy their new rights and equal status (Wilson, 1980). Women's growing uneasiness, what Friedan called 'the problem that has no name', was apparent by the 1950s (Friedan, 1963, p. 13). But it was the 1960s that witnessed a dramatic revival of more militant feminism which has been dubbed feminism's 'second wave'. Chronologically this began in America in the mid-1960s, with the organisation of a feminist lobby to exploit the new possibilities of legislation favourable to women. The real impetus, though, and the distinctive character of this second wave, stems from the emergence of radical feminism in the late 1960s. It was out of radical feminism that the new slogan of 'women's liberation' came, with its emphasis on women uniting to liberate themselves, and which was then adopted by much of the wider movement. It was the radical feminists who posed the questions and established the new practices against which other feminist groupings examined and redefined their own positions. This does not mean, however, that radical feminism has dominated the movement. On the contrary, feminism defined in this historical fashion now embraces a vast assortment of individuals and groups, extending beyond Western Europe and the old Commonwealth countries to many parts of the so-called 'Third World', whose social backgrounds, practical interests and theoretical orientations vary enormously, may indeed conflict.

Which is why the question arises: should they all be seen as feminist, or must we adopt an alternative definition of feminism, including only those who adhere to certain basic principles? Feminists themselves will give different answers to this question according to their own analysis of women's oppression and how to overcome it. Over the last ten to fifteen years, in keeping with developments in the movement, such analyses have moreover become increasingly differentiated even if there has also been refinement and cross-fertilisation of ideas. But we can get some purchase on the present diversity by tracing it back to the three main tendencies in the movement as it emerged from the late 1960s. (I should incidentally stress here that normally I shall use labels, such as 'radical feminist', 'Marxist feminist', to describe how women situate themselves.)

The first tendency, radical feminism, has been defined by its insistence that sex is the fundamental division in society to which all other differences, such as social class or race, are merely secondary. Radical feminists have argued that, apart perhaps from an ancient era of 'matriarchy', there has always been a sexual division of labour underpinning and reinforced by systematic male dominance or 'patriarchy'. Although their explanations for male dominance have varied, most have emphasised the physical dimension of men's control over women. From this analysis have followed certain crucial implications for strategy. On the one hand, since men are the enemy who will not willingly surrender their power over women, there must be no compromise with them. The system of male dominance must be overthrown by some kind of revolution; it cannot be reformed. By the same token, men cannot be accepted as allies. Radical feminists insist on political 'separatism'. On the other hand, since all women share a basic oppression, all women are potentially 'sisters'. Radical feminists have tended to focus on issues bringing out the physical or sexual aspect of male dominance, such as abortion or rape, which are intended to appeal to a shared experience and unite women rather than dividing them.

Conflicting tendencies within radical feminism itself, discernible from the start, have become increasingly apparent. As Chapter 5 will show more fully, the debates and groupings within this broad approach have formed around a complex and shifting set of questions. But at the risk of oversimplifying, these can be reduced to three major issues. Usually the first of these to emerge, chronologically, has concerned the relationship between feminist politics and personal sexual conduct. Initially lesbian women while drawn to the movements in significant numbers were regarded by other feminists with some ambivalence. Increasingly however the strand of radical feminism, variously called political lesbianism or radicalesbianism, has come to insist the separatism be extended to sexual relations themselves, as the most fundamental site of women's oppression and to accuse heterosexual feminists of being 'male-identified'. Pushed on the defensive, opponents of this line have tended to emphasise the need for women to determine their own sexuality and for choice.

The second argument has been about the nature of sex differences. If to begin with there was some doubt as to whether physical or social factors best explained differences between the sexes, radical feminists tended to agree that they were potentially irrelevant and to favour, at least by implication, an androgynous model for a future society. As they came to investigate alleged sex differences, many began to accept that such differences existed, whether historically induced or innate. The 'pro-woman' position went further in attributing to women special or even superior qualities. This notion of a recoverable and distinctive woman's nature, often linked to female sexuality and ability to create life, has exercised a particular fascination in America and France. Its critics have in turn pointed out the dangers of its 'essentialism'.

These two issues have linked up with a third, concerning political strategy. Both insistence on a separate sexuality and the pro-woman orientation have led some women to concentrate on creating their own subculture or space, whether in terms of lifestyle or in terms of theoretical inquiry. Other radical feminists, often describing themselves as 'revolutionary feminists' have attacked this as a withdrawal into an exclusive cul-de-sac of 'cultural feminism' which claims to be revolutionary but is ultimately reformist and élitist.

The second main tendency has been Marxist or socialist feminism. This was particularly strong at the outset within the British women's liberation movement where women in socialist parties and groups were among the first to respond to and shape feminism's revival. Marxist feminists, typically, have started from Marxist premises and sought to reconcile these theoretically and in their political activities with the insights of radical feminism. Initially it was often these insights that had to do the adapting to a somewhat rigid and traditional Marxist framework. Increasingly, as Marxist political theory itself diversified and became less deterministic and as Marxist feminists recognised its inadequacies for analysing women's oppression, they broke new ground searching for a more satisfactory fusion of the two perspectives. Though still insistent upon the primacy of the class struggle they accepted that the struggle between the sexes could not be reduced to its parameters, but had a history of its own and would not automatically disappear with the overthrow of capitalism. In seeking to explain women's oppression, they explored the notion of reproduction and issues around the role and autonomy of ideology. By the mid-1970s Marxist feminism appeared to be losing ground to radical feminism, within the movement, though Marxist feminists continued to produce much of the best theoretical analysis. Improving fortunes of the Left in Britain and in France, together with recession, subsequently encouraged the revival of a socialist feminist current now more concerned with immediate questions of political tactics, how best to work with left-wing parties and trade unions and the role of autonomous women's organisations.

Radical and Marxist feminists have in common a 'revolutionary' platform and self-image. Although they do not entirely discount, and indeed have often campaigned for, reforms within the existing 'system', they generally regard these as palliatives, at best as providing women with greater leverage for an eventual revolution. By contrast, both tendencies have been inclined to lump together the feminists who do not fall into either camp as 'reformists' or 'liberals'. This is not altogether helpful, since it obscures important differences between such feminists. As a residual category, reformist feminists do not necessarily see themselves as sharing a common orientation within feminism, though in the US a liberal feminist perspective has been particularly explicit and successful. Some reformist feminists come close to the revolutionary position in their recognition of the need for radical social change before women can be 'liberated', and in their emphasis on women organising separately. At an opposite extreme, others see women as suffering only a minor and temporary handicap and look for the remedy to equal rights legislation, achieved through low-profile lobbying on a largely individual basis. But this is not the only dimension of variation. Reformist feminists are divided by the same questions which divide radical and Marxist feminists. Like Marxist feminists, some emphasise economic aspects of women's oppression, while others share the radical feminist stress on its physical basis. Some even tend towards the pro-woman position which in the absence of a revolutionary commitment can produce the rather conservative argument that women bring special 'maternal' qualities of caring and sympathy to public life, as well as, most recently, a rediscovery of the importance of the family as the site in which moral and caring capacities are fostered and preserved.

There are therefore at least two main dimensions along which contemporary feminists are ranged with any number of possible positions between their four poles. Lately feminist assumptions, and in particular, radical feminism, have come under challenge from women in non-white minorities within Western countries and from Third World countries, for a presumed 'universalism' which fails to recognise the variety of forms women's oppression can take and specifically for white women's connivance in racist attitudes and policies, towards their supposed sisters. Though such arguments cannot yet be said to amount to a distinct feminist theory or approach (Jaggar, 1983), they have contributed to a greater awareness of the issue of racism but also of the significance of historical and cultural variations in the experience of women.

This brings us back to the initial question whether all these strands can be called feminist. Radical feminists have either claimed exclusive right to the designation or at least denied it to reformist feminists. 'Radicalesbians' and 'pro-woman' radical feminists have argued that only they are the true feminists, and so on.

The meaning of feminism must ultimately depend on the context in which it is being discussed. Since this book is concerned with women as a whole, feminism will be understood in its widest, historic sense. This does not, however, extend to including as feminists the men who have so described themselves. While otherwise adhering to the broadest definition we should not lose sight of the profound divisions within contemporary feminism. Their implications for the coherence of feminism as a doctrine and its success as a movement will be examined in chapters to follow.

What is politics?

As with feminism, so with politics, there is no overall agreement on definitions. In different eras and different societies and even from one political thinker to another, the nature and scope of politics have been viewed very differently. In this sense, as Wolin writes, politics is 'created' not given (Wolin, 1960, p. 5). Conceptions of politics reflect the values of those who hold them. In other words, definitions of politics are themselves inevitably political.

However, most seem to share certain common assumptions about the kind of situation that gives rise to politics. Politics is recognised to be social; it has little meaning for the solitary inhabitant of a desert island. It arises in situations where resources, in the broadest sense of the term, are limited and there is, at least potentially, conflict of interest or opinion as to how they should be distributed. At a minimum, politics is about how people influence the distribution of resources.

But beyond this point of fairly widespread agreement, interpretations diverge. First of all, they differ on what politics essentially is. Simplifying, we may say that there are at present two main and contrasting views. One, the more traditional, sees politics as an *activity*. It is conscious, deliberate participation in the process by which resources are allocated amongst people. The alternative view, which has become influential more recently, tends to equate politics with the *articulation*, or working out of *relationships* within an already given 'power structure'. In so far as Marxist theory provides a consistent conception of politics, it takes this form, though with an emphasis on class struggle (Miliband, 1977, pp. 6–7). But this approach is not confined to Marxism. If politics is the dynamic of power relationships within society, it does not need to be either conscious or deliberate. It embraces the slave's 'conditioned' and unthinking acceptance of his bondage and the drunken driver who accidentally runs over the President. So our first question must be whether politics is to be understood as a distinctive and deliberate activity or more broadly as the working out of social power relationships.

The second question is: 'Where does politics occur?' Those who see politics as the articulation of power relations in theory recognise no boundary separating it from social life as a whole. Those who perceive politics as an activity, however, are more divided. Traditionally this view has implied that there is a distinctive 'public' political arena. Politics has been seen as the process by which members of a community – in the sense of a relatively self-sufficient group of people – decide on matters deemed to be of common, or public concern. This public political sphere has been contrasted with a private realm, in which and about which, by definition, there is no politics. Of course, the scope of the public arena has varied and, with the recent growth of government intervention and the state's direct responsibilities, it has expanded enormously. But according to this view an apolitical private sphere remains. Most crucially for feminism, this private sphere centres upon family life which still defines and limits most women's wider social role. Some political scientists, while still understanding politics as activity, have questioned its confinement to a specific public arena, arguing that it can be found in ostensibly private institutions, such as business corporations, universities and even the family.

In theory, therefore, many political scientists, including some who define politics as an activity, see it as virtually ubiquitous. Yet this apparent openmindedness is misleading. For in practice political science of whatever theoretical disposition, tends to concentrate on community-level politics. In the context of modern societies, this means the processes surrounding the operations of government or the state. Even those political scientists who reject the concept of a distinct public arena for politics have so little to say about family relationships that they seem tacitly to condone their relegation to a private apolitical sphere.

This is the context of theoretical approaches and of emphasis in practice within which we should next examine what feminism has had to say about politics. In fact, nineteenth-century feminists and many contemporary feminists have not really questioned prevailing notions of politics. It is the radical feminists who have recognised it as an important issue for feminism and stimulated new thinking about it within the wider women's movement.

Firstly, radical feminism rejects the definition of politics as an activity. The pioneer, in this respect, was Kate Millett. In *Sexual Politics*, she refers to politics as 'power-structured relationships, arrangements whereby one group of persons is controlled by another' (Millett, 1972, p. 23). Subsequent radical feminist writers have implicitly followed this approach, though with little explicit discussion, because it accords with their experience of male dominance as *systematic*, reliant on conditioning and the diffuse threat of violence, as well as on conscious actions. Some feminist political theorists have been unhappy with this conception of politics, however. Both McWilliams, and Boals, have warned lest, in depicting politics exclusively as power relationships, its more deliberate and potentially creative aspect is lost sight of (McWilliams, 1974; Boals, 1975).

There is a second feature of radical feminism's approach to politics which is more important and, in the way it has been applied, much more original. Radical feminism has attacked the notion of a distinctive political arena, and the public-private split that goes with it. The reasons for such an attack are easy to see. It reflects the lessons women learned as student radicals in the 1960s and then applied to their own situation. Many American radical feminists owed their political education in particular to the civil rights campaign. It was here that they learned 'the personal is political'. As McWilliams wrote:

> The 'We Shall Overcome' era saw the most striking conversion of private to political issues: where one sat on a bus, whom one married, in whose company one ate, where one swam, slept and urinated became questions of public policy. Women in . . . radical organisations were expected to see the political nature of private things in relation to blacks but not in relation to themselves. Not surprisingly, they soon made the transfer (McWilliams, 1974, p. 160).

If the convention of a private sphere had obscured the extent to which blacks as a group were oppressed and capable through concerted political action of changing their situation, how much more had it mystified the subordination of women. Accordingly radical feminists spoke not only of 'personal politics' but also of 'sexual politics', 'the politics of housework' and so on, challenging the orthodox assignment of these issues to the realm of private choice.

Influenced by radical feminism, many women political scientists have elaborated this critique of the public-private divide, condemning it both on ideological and on factual grounds. Elshtain, for instance, traces the way in which it has been used in successive eras to legitimise women's exclusion from public politics. Thus Aristotle upheld the public political sphere as that in which the highest good was or should be realised. Since he believed that women, along with slaves and children, possessed only limited capacity for good and reason, he concluded that they were unfit to participate in politics. Much later, political thinkers came to contrast the *immorality* of the public political sphere with the purity of the private. But again, they insisted that this domestic haven of morality could only be preserved if women were protected from the corrupting world of public politics. Whether politics was viewed as moral or as immoral, an argument was always at hand to support women's confinement to a private world that kept them from it (Elshtain, 1981). At the same time, governments have cited the privacy of the family as grounds for not interfering with a man's treatment of his wife, even when he beats or rapes her. Dahl and Snare describe this as the 'coercion of privacy' (Dahl and Snare, 1978). Not only has the public–private dichotomy been used to legitimise practices oppressive to women and to trivialise women's participation in public life when it occurs, but it has not necessarily accorded with the facts of social or political life. Feminist anthropologists have rightly stressed that in many primitive societies such a division is scarcely in evidence, while others have shown how in advanced industrial societies public and private spheres are increasingly fused. Even in societies where the convention is strongly established it need not prevent governments from outlawing contraception and abortion and so denying women's most intimate 'right to choose'. Siltanen and Stanworth also point out that the equation of the public sphere with politics firstly obscures the extent to which many matters occurring in public space, for instance sexual harassment at work or even the operation of the 'free' market, have not been deemed political and second exaggerates by implication the part of the ordinary public in political decision-making (Siltanen and Stanworth, 1984).

So, given these differing conceptions of politics and feminists' criticisms of them, what is the approach to be adopted in this book? It is constrained by its intentions. On the one hand, it is directed to political scientists and is also attempting to show feminists that they can learn from mainstream political science. To that extent it must follow political science's present emphasis upon public policy-making and government. On the other hand, since this book is concerned to point up the theoretical and practical shortcomings of the treatment of women by political science, it must also encompass a broader notion of what politics is, or could be.

Accordingly, the emphasis will be upon politics as an activity, both women's participation in public politics and the impact of policy-making upon women. But in order to explain how women influence and are affected by the social allocation of resources, we shall also need to consider politics in its broader sense of social power relationships. The following chapter in particular will examine the system of male dominance that shapes women's relationships with politics, as a deliberate activity.

Secondly, and despite the cogency of feminist criticism, I shall not completely discard the public-private distinction. This is because it refers to a convention that, however regrettably, does influence political practice and in particular the relationship between women and politics. I shall try to show the negative implications for women of this conception of politics: how it has been used to reinforce and justify male dominance and women's exclusion from public power, and the inconsistencies in its application. I shall also stress the complex interdependence in practice of public and private spheres, as well as the wide variation in the rigidity of the distinction and in the relative scope of the two domains through time and between societies. Used in this manner, the dichotomy provides a useful analytical tool, as Stacey and Price have shown in their account of the changes in British women's political participation (Stacey and Price, 1981). At the same time a focus upon public politics is insufficient. We need to know about the politics of sexuality, the family, 'culture' and economic life. This 'politics of everyday life' indeed must be our starting-point, and is the subject of Chapter 1.

1
Women's place in society

Is male dominance universal? Have men exercised disproportionate power over women in all known societies to date? Many feminists say that they have. Their grounds are partly intuitive; they have discovered their own oppression by looking inwards, and particularly by reflecting together on their personal experience in 'consciousness-raising' sessions. This has enabled them to detect male dominance in other contexts. They have also arrived at this position through deductive reasoning. For instance, Firestone's identification of the causes of patriarchy in relations of reproduction implies that patriarchy will prevail until there are radical changes in reproductive 'technology' (Firestone, 1970). Some of feminism's opponents have similarly argued that male dominance is universal. Indeed, Goldberg maintains cheerfully that patriarchy is not only universal, but inevitable (Goldberg, 1979).

The thesis of universal male dominance, whether upheld by feminists or by anti-feminists, is supported by a substantial body of scholarship. Much of this is anthropological. Rosaldo and Lamphere, for instance, summarise the findings of a range of contemporary anthropological studies. They conclude that 'all contemporary societies are to some extent male-dominated, and, although the degree and expression of female subordination vary greatly, sexual asymmetry is presetly a universal fact of human life' (Rosaldo and Lamphere, 1974, p. 3). Historical evidence, in the form of the surviving records of earlier societies, tends also to indicate the universality of some form of male dominance. For example, Dobash and Dobash summarise the history of women's status in Britain. It is sometimes implied that before the onset of industrial

15

capitalism, a 'golden age' of sex equality prevailed, but this was in fact the era when the emerging state sought to reinforce patriarchal authority within the immediate family. In the authors' words, 'the position of married women was at its lowest ebb during the sixteenth and seventeenth centuries' (Dobash and Dobash, 1980, p. 52). The position of most women was only a little better in feudal England, when society mainly consisted of large fortified households ruled by their feudal lord. Though women's status may have been somewhat higher in Saxon times, this was preceded by the rule of the Romans for whom the family 'was the cornerstone of society and . . . one of the strongest patriarchies known' (ibid., p. 34).

The 'evidence' for the virtual universality of male dominance is at first sight overwhelming, but should not be accepted too uncritically. Counter arguments have been of two main kinds: the citation of apparent exceptions to the rule and a more telling critique of the way male dominance has been conceptualised and investigated.

Some writers have argued that in prehistoric times societies existed in which women were not only free of male domination but were themselves the rulers. These were the so-called 'matriarchies'. The earliest systematic exponent of this view was Bachofen, writing in the mid-nineteenth century. Basing his analysis on surviving mythology, he suggested that matriarchy developed out of 'mother right', the mother's right in her own children (see Bamberger, 1974). Much more recently, this theme has attracted several feminist writers. Davis, for instance, drawing again on mythological evidence, elaborates an account of matriarchal civilisation in ancient Sumer, Crete and Egypt (Davis, 1971).

We may agree with Webster that just to entertain the possibility of ancient matriarchies is intellectually liberating (Webster, 1975). But though the possibility cannot be dismissed, data to support it are unsatisfactory, consisting primarily of accounts of matriarchy in myth and archaeological evidence of goddess worship. It is widely accepted by now that myths do not necessarily have a basis in history. Bamberger draws on her research into the primitive peoples of the Amazon basin and Tierra del Fuego to suggest that myths about a former matriarchal system, which women somehow abused, may help to legitimise existing systems of male dominance (Bamberger, 1974). Similarly, Merck argues that in Greek mythology the Amazons appeared not 'as an independent force, but as the vanquished opponents of heroes credited with the establishment and protection of the Athenian State' and may have been used 'as a justification of that culture's radical subordination of women' (Merck, 1978, p. 96). Though there is considerable archaeological evidence of goddess-based religions in prehistoric societies, this cannot be taken as proof of matriarchy.

Alternatively, it is suggested that in some primitive societies, past and even present, women have been the social equals of men. Oakley, for instance, tells us that amongst the Mbuti pygmies 'the role of biological sex as a determinant of social role and status seems to be negligible' (Oakley, 1972, p. 149). Draper describes the 'relaxed and egalitarian relationship between men and women' in the bush-living !Kung (Draper, 1975). According to Brown, 'Iroquois matrons enjoyed unusual authority in their society, perhaps more than women have enjoyed anywhere at any time' (Brown, 1975, p. 243). Proponents of this view often go on to attribute male dominance in other societies to specific causes such as the emergence of private property or new farming methods. It is obviously difficult to prove or disprove such an interpretation. Some of the more recent examples offered, however, have been challenged. For instance, it has been pointed out that although women of the Iroquois enjoyed real economic and political power, only men could be their chiefs. This raises the more fundamental problem with the thesis of universal male dominance: how male dominance is defined and identified.

These epistemological problems have not only been cited to refute feminists' insistence that women are oppressed. They are also raised by many feminists themselves who recognise that the thesis of universal male dominance can become self-confirming, creating expectations that then modify perceptions and, at worst, lending fuel to those who argue that male dominance is inevitable and right.

Firstly, doubts have been shed on the 'objectivity' of cross-cultural and historical evidence. For instance, the majority of anthropological studies, including those contributing to Murdock's much-cited Human Relations Area Files, have been undertaken by men. These male anthropologists brought with them assumptions about women's role and status derived from their experience of modern Western society. Their assumptions shaped and were often reinforced by the way they went about their research, most of all the fact that they talked mainly to other men. In reaction, several feminist anthropologists who describe themselves as revisionists have consciously resisted assumptions of male dominance and have focused their research on women's attitudes and experience. As a result, they argue that women's power in pre-industrial societies has been underestimated: in particular, women's power within the domestic domain is often considerable and important not only intrinsically but for the indirect influence it gives them over public affairs (see, for instance, Friedl, 1967).

This leads on to the second criticism, that male dominance has been conceptualised too crudely. There are any number of ways in which individuals or groups can exercise power over one another, ranging from the most tangible use of force or control over material resources to intangible psychological and even 'magical' influence. There is little doubt that some of these, and perhaps the most important, are the special prerogative of men. Rosaldo points out that in contemporary societies 'culturally legitimated authority' is attributed to men rather than women (Rosaldo, 1974, p. 21). Similarly it is difficult to argue with Goldberg's assertion that patriarchy is universal when patriarchy is defined as 'any system of organisation (political, economic, industrial, financial, religious or social) in which the overwhelming number of upper positions in the hierarchy are occupied by males' (Goldberg, 1979, p. 25). Partly as a consequence of male authority, 'prestige value always attaches to the activities of men' (Mead, 1935, p. 302). Whether this means that women have internalised this evaluation of themselves or that authoritative males discount women's higher self-evaluation is not so easy to say. Radical feminists are probably right also to argue that men largely monopolise both the legitimate and the illicit use of physical force in society, including the family.

For all that, women are not powerless. They have their own means of exercising power, for instance their sexuality, their essential role in reproduction, their influence over their children and their various domestic skills, sometimes including magic. In many contexts they can also use their kinship ties, mutual solidarity or economic contribution. Likewise there are many different aspects of women's status, such as their control over their economic product, their say in household decisions, the extent of their property rights, sexual autonomy, public esteem and public authority. As Whyte reminds us, these do not necessarily all vary together, His own crosscultural analysis indicates that, in a given society, women can be dominant in some respects at the same time as they are subordinate in others (Whyte, 1978, pp. 168-9). The third important qualification which feminists are now more ready to acknowledge is that some women apparently oppress other women and indeed men because of their superior social position as members of a particular class, race, caste or other élite group.

All these reservations do not in my view invalidate the thesis of male dominance but they do imply it should be used with care. We must avoid too ahistorical or transhistorical a concept of male dominance and seek instead to specify the form it takes in each society.

Male dominance or patriarchy?

It is this concern with precision that has led some to question the use of the term 'patriarchy' as if it were exchangeable with 'male dominance'. This is not entirely a matter of semantics. Given patriarchy's centrality to contemporary feminist analysis, it is worth looking briefly at its origins and the meaning it has been given.

The word patriarchy is derived from the Greek 'patriarches' meaning 'head of the tribe'. The original patriarchs were the tribal heads referred to in the Old Testament. Later the term described certain of the most eminent bishops within the Christian Church, including the Pope. In seventeenth-century England, Robert Filmer, the conservative political theorist, advocated patriarchalism, meaning by this the system of rule in which the king's supreme authority was mirrored and reinforced by the father's authority within his household. McDonagh and Harrison suggest that Marx similarly took patriarchy to connote 'a specific relation of domestic production, in which the head of the household owned or controlled the means of production and organised the labour of its members' (McDonagh and Harrison, 1978, pp. 28-9). Weber also took up the term 'to describe a particular form of household organisation in which the father dominated other members of an extended kinship network, and controlled the economic production of the household' (Barrett, 1980, p. 10).

While these usages are not identical, they have in common a focus on the authority of the male head of the family, whether in its extended or in its nuclear form. Feminists, particularly radical feminists, in the late 1960s picked up the term, making it central to their analysis and greatly expanding its coverage. It has come to mean something like 'rule by men', although the precise definitions vary with differing theoretical approaches. One of the earliest exponents of this new usage, Millett, writes 'the principles of patriarchy appear to be two-fold: male shall dominate female, elder male shall dominate younger' (Millett, 1972, p. 25). Firestone, though she does not define patriarchy, implies that it is a system of social organisation in which men's control of women is based on their power over wives and children within the family. Eisenstein, writing later, places even less emphasis on the authority of fathers, largely equating patriarchy with male supremacy in all its forms (Eisenstein, 1979). Lack of agreement on the precise definition of the term is hardly grounds for abandoning it. On the contrary it shows, as Beechey argues in her review of theories of patriarchy, that the concept has been used 'in an attempt to think through real political and theoretical problems' (Beechey, 1979, p. 68).

What has been questioned is the necessity of using the term in this generic sense, when 'male dominance' or 'male supremacy' would do instead. As Rubin suggests, if we define patriarchy more narrowly, and in keeping with its traditional meaning of one form of male dominance based on the authority of the head of the household, it helps to distinguish between the different forms that male dominance can take (Rubin, 1975). Accordingly, in this book, 'male dominance' refers to male power over women, as a whole and 'patriarchy' is reserved for forms of male power stemming from the authority of the father or male household head.

Whatever term we use – male dominance, male supremacy or patriarchy – it stands for a far-reaching social subordination of women. How has this come about? As Rubin writes, 'The question is not a trivial one, since the answer given it determines our vision of the future, and our evaluation of whether it is realistic to hope for a sexually egalitarian society' (ibid., p. 157). Upon the answer also depends the strategy that feminists adopt to achieve such a society.

The subordination of women has been explained in an enormous variety of ways, both by feminists and by their opponents. Explanations are often multi-stranded, pointing to the concurrence of different levels of causation. Some veer more towards a materialist account of women's oppression, emphasising its basis in human biology or the organisation of economic production; others prefer to stress the role of social or cultural imperatives. But these factors cannot be neatly compartmentalised. Only the most dogmatic economic determinist would, for instance, argue that the boundary between culture and economy is clear-cut. Not only, as Marxists know, does economic organisation powerfully affect society but economic behaviour inevitably reflects its cultural context. Still less amenable to pigeon-holing is the human unconscious as 'discovered' and construed by Freud, which is neither a direct product of biology nor a simple extension of social reality into the individual psyche but a domain with its own complex life (see Rose, 1983). Therefore, although I have divided the following discussion of explanations of male dominance into those emphasising biology, culture and the economic system respectively, this is for reasons of intelligibility and is not intended to imply that these elements are either easily defined or independent of each other.

Anatomy as destiny

The oldest, and most obvious, explanation for women's oppression is the biological differences between men and women. Nonfeminists who take this line tend to argue that male dominance is natural and inevitable, a conclusion recently challenged by a number of feminist social scientists. At the same time other feminists, in particular many radical feminists stress the physical dimension of male dominance even while they seek to overcome it. Sayers' useful book, *Biological Politics* (1982), summarises much of this debate. One point she is anxious to establish is that biological arguments have never been produced in isolation from a specific social or indeed political context. For instance, the 'science' of craniometry or brain measurement was initially developed in the early nineteenth century in connection with colonial policy; not until the late 1860s, when feminists were beginning to press for changes, most significantly for changes in educational provision for women, was it invoked to explain and justify inequality between the sexes.

Sayers also demonstrates the palpable absurdity of many of these biological arguments, primarily but not always as employed by antifeminists. Thus the principle of the conservation of energy could lead Dr Stanley Hall, the 'acknowledged founder of academic psychology in America' to assert that 'over-activity of the brain during the critical period of the middle and late teens will interfere with the full development of mammary power and of the functions essential for the full transmission of life generally' (cited by Sayers, p. 10). Beliefs, or more properly myths, about menstruation have been truly extraordinary, going back to Pliny's description of menstrual blood 'depriving seeds of their fecundity, destroying insects, blasting garden flowers and grasses, causing fruits to fall from branches, dulling razors' (cited Sayers, p. 111). Menstruation has been used to justify women's exclusion from a series of professions and on the other hand some radical feminists have celebrated menstruation as a link with the rhythms of nature and with each other, one group even holding a symbolic 'Bleed-in'. What this all indicates is that one should be extremely wary of the claim that biological arguments about the status of women are objectively and scientifically based.

Notwithstanding, the natural physical differences between the sexes have been used to explain and legitimise women's inferior social position since before Aristotle. Until very recently such arguments emphasised woman's distinctive reproductive role, but also her physical vulnerability, seen as a consequence both of this reproductive role and of men's greater strength, and, less frequently, the smaller size of woman's brain. These physical features were supposed, even by some nineteenth-century feminists, to limit women's personality and potential, rendering them inevitably socially inferior.

From the late 1930s new data have emerged calling into question either the existence of significant physiological differences between the sexes or the conclusions drawn from them. Anthropological evidence has been enlisted to show that childbirth does not necessarily disrupt a woman's working life and that childrearing is not always assumed to be the woman's responsibility. Sex differences in physical strength have been found to be culturally variable. 'In Bali, where males do little heavy work, males and females resemble each other in body size and shape. But Balinese men who work as deck coolies under European supervision develop the heavy musculature we think of as a male characteristic' (Oakley, 1972, p. 143). It has in any case long been contended that technological advance should render such differences in physical strength increasdingly irrelevant.

Research also indicated that it was not so much absolute brain size as its relationship to body size that could be associated with intelligence, in which respect women were slightly superior to men. In the 1970s, however, the argument linking sex inequality with the brain has resurfaced in the context of research into the way the brain is organised. It has been suggested that whereas in men the left hemisphere of the brain specialises in language and the right in spatial information, in women the left must cope with them both. Some of the reasoning behind this thesis appears to me questionable and the conclusions drawn have been challenged by feminists pointing out that such a difference may reflect rather than cause contrasting educational experiences, but it remains the most recent and academically respectable variant of the simple biological reductionist case (see Sayers, pp. 97–103).

Otherwise in latter years biological explanations of male dominance have tended to come in the guise either of psychoanalytic interpretations or of socio-biology. Freud himself was no crude biological reductionist: for him it was not the actual differences between the sexes but the psychological constructions these gave rise to that were most determining. He maintained that in infancy boys and girls shared masculine and feminine traits and were both primarily attached to the mother. The differentiation began as they became more aware of their genitalia as a source of pleasure and as distinguishing males from females. The boy's phallus-centred desire for his mother produced the Oedipus complex which could only be resolved by repressing this desire and identifying with the otherwise castrating father. The girl on the other hand concluded that she *had* been castrated and suffered from 'penis envy'. Her subsequent psychological development depended on how this was resolved. To acquire a 'normal' female outlook she must transfer her attachment from mother to father and substitute for penis envy desire for a child of her own. But there were other possibilities; persistent penis envy and refusal to accept her maternal role could result, for instance, in a 'masculinity complex'.

If Freud was reluctant to espouse biological determinism, many of his followers, especially in the United States, have been less so. As we shall see feminists have responded in two rather different ways. Some dispute the importance of penis envy and drawing on the work of certain of Freud's disciples, argue instead that men envy women's child-bearing capacities. Others hold that Freud read the female subconscious aright but failed sufficiently to recognise that rather than the cause it was the consequence and perpetuating mechanism of an external social system of male dominance.

Increasingly popular and influential in the 1970s have been socio-biological explanations for male dominance which assume that social behaviour ultimately derives from the process of biological evolution. This line of reasoning has been employed to show why it has been necessary, in evolutionary terms, for females to take primary responsibility for children and for males to pursue a strategy of 'philandry' to maximise the numbers of their offspring. Most pertinently, male dominance has been attributed to innate male characteristics in turn needed for species survival. Tiger, for instance, argues that in primitive societies, dependent for survival on hunting, the process of natural selection reinforced the innate genetically transmitted tendency for men to form hierarchically bonded groups. Though such male-bonding may now be less socially necessary, it continues to give communities their 'spinal column . . . their interdependence, their structure, their social coherence and in good part their continuity', while excluding most women from positions of authority (Tiger, 1969, p. 60). Rather than male-bonding, other writers have focused on man's innate aggression. Goldberg provides a particularly uncompromising rendering of this theme. Although accepting that male dominance reflects the interaction of sex-related hormonal differences and environmental cues, he maintains that men are predisposed, through their endocrinological endowment, not simply to a particular kind of aggressive or dominant behaviour, which achieves dyadic or social dominance in specific societies, but to *whatever* behaviour is required for dominance. Since all societies are hierarchical in one way or another, man's hormonal endowment means that 'the environment that is necessary for patriarchy is inherent in society itself' and patriarchy is inevitable (Goldberg, 1979, p. 85).

As Sayers points out, while such socio-biological justifications for male dominance claim to be new they are directly descended from similar rationalisations offered by social Darwinists in the nineteenth century. Their scientific status has also been called into question by effective feminist criticisms of their assumptions about the importance of hunting in primitive societies, their frequent unwarranted inferences from the observed behaviour of primates, their subjective use of archaeological evidence and their often circular reasoning (see Leibowitz, 1975; Slocum, 1975; Sayers, 1982). Oakley does not rule out the possibility that men are innately more aggressive than women, but points out that in humans the relationship between hormones and behaviour is extremely complicated. Even if differences were verified not only in hormonal levels but in the 'hormonal sensitivity of the central nervous system in men and women . . . it would not create two distinct types – male and female – but a whole range from very male to very female over which individuals would be distributed as they are for other variables'. And the effect of such differences upon behaviour would still be debatable given 'the enormous dependence of the human species on learning processes' (Oakley, 1972, p. 191).

The feminists cited so far in this debate have vigorously denied that women's oppression is rooted in biology. Their objection is understandable since, given the widespread tendency to associate what is natural with what is good, acceptance of the natural origins of male dominance can easily seem an acceptance of male dominance itself. The early radical feminist, Millett, rejects biological explanations on such grounds. Although her discussion of the role of biology tacitly acknowledges the issue to be more complex than she allows, she argues that there is insufficient evidence that women's oppression originated in biology, that biological differences between the sexes are probably irrelevant to male dominance today and that to emphasise them plays into men's hands (Millett, 1972).

But other feminists, particularly radical feminists, accord biology much more weight. A pioneering analysis that locates male dominance in the biological differences between men and women is provided by Shulamith Firestone in the *Dialectic of Sex*. She claims that she is applying the analytical method, dialectical materialism, which was prescribed by Marx, but whose profound implications, as a man, he was incapable of seeing. She elaborates a materialistic theory of history based on relations not of production but of reproduction. In fact, she goes as far as agreeing with the ideologues of male dominance that the unequal division of the sexes is natural. For though sex differences do not of themselves imply inequality, reproduction of the species has inevitably required, given prevailing levels of technology, the 'biological family' or basic reproductive unit of male-female-infant, which is inherently unequal. First, women have been made dependent upon their menfolk through their biological vulnerability associated with menstruation, the menopause and other 'female ills', constant painful childbirth, wet-nursing and the care of infants. Then, since human infants take so long to grow up, their dependence upon adults is prolonged. In particular there develops an intense mother-child interdependency, which in turn helps to shape female psychology. Finally, these reproductive differences have underlain the sexual division of labour and power. Now, although 'man is increasingly capable of freeing himself from the biological conditions that created his tyranny over women and children', as its beneficiary 'he has little reason to want to give this tyranny up' (Firestone, 1970, p. 18).

Firestone emphasises the biological determinants of male dominance. Even though such psychological factors as motherly feelings or men's enjoyment of power enter into her account, they are firmly rooted in biological differences between the sexes and would not exist without them. She does not conclude either that men are superior or that male dominance is inevitable or right. On the contrary, she approvingly quotes de Beauvoir as saying 'Human society is an antiphysis – in a sense it is against nature; it does not passively submit to the presence of nature but rather takes over the control of nature on its own behalf' (ibid., p. 18). But male dominance will not easily be ended. Given its basis in the relations of reproduction it can only be overthrown by revolution. In a conscious echo of Marx, Firestone argues that women must seize control of the means of reproduction with the object of destroying not only male dominance but 'the sex distinction itself'.

Other radical feminists have explored the role of physical violence in women's oppression. Susan Brownmiller in *Against Our Will* sees sexual rape as playing an essential part. Rather than the act of an abnormal individual, she argues that rape, the threat and indeed the ideology of rape, have been 'nothing more or less than a conscious process of intimidation by which all men keep *all* women in a state of fear' (Brownmiller, 1975, p. 15). Mary Daly in *Gyn/Ecology* (1978) provides a further devastating litany of the different ways in which men have physically assaulted women: through 'suttee' or widow-burning, in India; foot-binding in China; mutilation of female genitals by excision of the clitoria or sewing or locking up of the vagina in Africa; and even, under the veneer of modern science, contemporary gynaecology and 'therapy'.

Brownmiller explains rape and male dominance primarily in

terms of the anatomy of human copulation; males are more constantly aroused and given the structure of human genitalia are physically able to overcome female resistance. Daly indicates, however, that men have been driven by envy and the urge to exploit women's power to create life and the psychic creativity that goes with it. Here she is representative of the recent trend towards a more positive evaluation of female biology and the distinctive woman's nature to which, to varying degrees it is believed, this gives rise.

An important source of such 'pro-woman' ideas has been those post-Freudian analysts, notably Karen Horney, who took issue with the 'phallo-centric' supposition that penis envy significantly determined female psychology and suggested instead that from the start little girls' different physiological make-up led to a distinctive feminine psychological development. In France where this possibility has been pursued in the context of an intellectual tradition centred on discourse and the symbolic as levels of determination, which does not therefore generally permit of biological reductionism in any simple form, writers such as Irigaray and Cixous have none the less sought to derive a concept of femininity from the nature of female sexuality. They have contrasted the multicentredness of female sexual sensation – 'Women don't have one sex organ. They have at least two, which can't be identified singly. Actually they have many more than that. Their sexuality, always at least double, is *plural*/multiple' (Irigaray, cited by Duchen, 1986, p. 90) – and the plural. changing responsive female nature that is its counterpart with the unitary, controlling, foreclosed male sex urge (see the helpful discussion by Duchen, 1986, pp. 90–2).

In America more attention has been devoted to women's childbearing role, as for instance in Adrienne Rich's *Of Woman Born* (1977). Here she takes issue with Firestone's negative account of motherhood, the pain of childbirth, the mother's vulnerability. Instead she proposes a distinction between the institution of motherhood, through which men dominate women, and the experience of motherhood which brings a woman into powerful and unique touch with her own body, creativity and emotion. Men have sought to dominate women because they fear their immense power as mothers and envy their ability to give birth. Through the institution of motherhood they have been able to suppress and control women, even to appropriate their creative powers.

Radical feminists like Firestone, Brownmiller and Rich, while not denying the psychological dimension of women's oppression, still ultimately locate its origins in biological differences between the sexes. One longstanding feminist criticism of such an approach has been that it is precisely these differences which have been cited to justify male dominance. This certainly is a dangerous possibility with arguments for an 'essential', biologically-rooted feminine nature. The claim 'different but equal' has always been difficult to mount in the face of one group's entrenched power. But to say that relations of reproduction, while technology was primitive, gave men power over women is neither to justify male dominance in the past nor to condone it now. As Richards points out, even if men were found to be naturally dominant because of their hormone endowment, feminists would not need to deny it, for it would still not entitle men to rule. 'Ought cannot be derived from is' (Richards, 1980, p. 44). If male dominance has been a feature of virtually every known society, how can we explain it, except ultimately by reference to what distinguishes men from women? It does not in any way follow that what distinguishes the sexes constitutes the basis of separate 'essential' natures. What it seems to me must be acknowledged, and despite caveats regarding the subjectivity of 'objective' biological data, is that women's reproductive role originally made them both vulnerable and necessary to men. Any adequate explanation of women's oppression, any proper understanding, as we shall see, of the birth of feminism and especially of women's liberation and any effective feminist strategy must take this into account.

Explanations emphasising culture or ideology

A second form of explanation for male dominance, while recognising 'material' factors whether biological or economic, tends to give greatest weight to culture in the broad sense of both social practices and beliefs. Again it has been used by feminists and non-feminists alike.

A first and eminently reasonable step is to distinguish between biological sex and gender. To quote Oakley, '"sex" is a word that refers to the biological differences between male and female: the visible differences in genitalia, the related difference in procreative function. "Gender" however is a matter of culture: it refers to the social classification into "masculine" and "feminine" (Oakley, 1972, p. 16). Though a person's sex usually determines their gender, exceptionally in our society and more frequently in some others the two are unrelated. Moreover what is understood by 'masculine' and 'feminine' is subject to considerable cross-cultural variation. A woman's social identity is based on her gender, not directly on her sex.

But explanations of the culture type go much further than this. First, they have been used to account for the sexual division of labour, seen to underlie male dominance. Almost everyone seems agreed on the universality of a sex-based or, strictly speaking, a gender-based division of labour, except possibility in the case of the Mbuti pygmies, as we have seen. There is considerable variation in the actual content of men's and women's social roles. In some societies, women engage in activities such as hunting and fighting which elsewhere are identified with men. Margaret Mead's research has been cited to show that in the Arapesh and Trobriand Islands men share in the care of small children. Drawing on such findings, Oakley is most insistent on the variability of women's role:

> The chief importance of biological sex in determining social roles is in providing a universal and obvious division around which other distinctions can be organised. In deciding which activities are to fall on each side of the boundary, the important factor is culture . . . other cultures have developed sex roles quite different from our own (Oakley, 1972, p. 156).

But this relativism can be overdone. A number of feminist anthropologists maintain that, despite cross-cultural variations in their content, sex roles show significant continuities. Specifically, in most contemporary societies women have primary responsibility for child-rearing. The context of this responsibility is the institution of the family.

Once more we must acknowledge the tremendous variety of forms this institution can take, as Edholm (1982) demonstrates, marshalling anthropological evidence of differing understandings of the nature of parenthood, incest taboos, the widespread practice of adoption, definitions of marriage and patterns of mobility between households. Yet if we take Gough's definition of the family simply as 'a married couple or other group of adult kinfolk who cooperate economically and in the upbringing of children, and all, or most of whom share a common dwelling' (Gough, 1975, p. 52), it must be nearly universal. Women have more responsibility for children, their activities are more family-centred than men's and this shapes other aspects of their social role.

How can this element of continuity be explained? One explanation would be biological, either that women are naturally suited for child-rearing or that physical dependence on men for a long time gave women little choice. But it has also been attributed to cultural factors.

On the one hand, non-feminists have suggested that the sex-based division of labour is functional in some sense to the proper and stable ordering of society. Okin traces this theme from the writings of Aristotle through to the functionalist sociology of Talcott Parsons. Though Parsons maintains that the biological differences between the sexes provide a logical basis for the sexual division of labour, he explains and justifies it primarily as the prerequisite of the modern nuclear family whose contribution to society is indispensable. The family promotes social stability and continuity, in particular through its socialisation functions, and the stability of the family in turn requires that wives specialise in child-rearing, housework and the articulation of 'expressive', as opposed to instrumental, masculine values. Parsons does recognise the psychological strain such role-differentiation imposes on both sexes, and especially women, but sees it as a necessary price for the maintenance of the family (see Okin, 1980, pp. 241–6).

Such arguments are of course unacceptable to feminists. But none the less many invoke culture to explain the sexual division of labour. They rightly point out that just because women *bear* children, there is no logical reason why they should be mainly responsible for rearing them. Culture is brought in to bridge this logical gulf, though it is never quite made clear what it is about culture, or cultures, that otherwise vary so tremendously, that brings nearly all of them to assign child-rearing to women.

Another kind of cultural explanation emphasises the consequences for women of the differentiation between private and public spheres. Rosaldo provides a good example of this approach. She attributes this differentiation to the 'fact that in most traditional societies, a good part of a woman's adult life is spent giving birth to and raising children' (Rosaldo, 1974, p. 23). In this context, she defines the domestic sphere as 'those minimal institutions and modes of activity that are organised immediately around one or more mothers and their children', while the public sphere comprises 'activities, institutions and forms of association that link, rank organise or subsume particular mother–child groups' (ibid., p. 23). Women's mothering role, which Rosaldo insists reflects organisational as much as biological constraints, limits their political and economic activities and focuses their concern on the domestic sphere. Men, on the other hand, having 'no single commitment as enduring, time-consuming and emotionally compelling – as close to seeming necessary and natural – as the relation of a woman to her infant child' are left 'free to form those broader associations that we call society' (ibid., p. 24). Rosaldo suggests that such subjective compartmentalisation, which does not of course preclude objective interdependence, fosters male dominance. The implication is that first, by distancing man from his family, the separation of public and private spheres lends him more authority within it. But the man also has more time and opportunity to shape the public culture which then evaluates women's role.

Ortner offers an interesting development of this argument. She suggests that a major reason why women's role is universally deemed secondary is that it is associated, because of its domestic setting as well as because of women's reproductive functions, with nature as opposed to culture. In so far as culture has an imperative to maintain itself, it devalues the nature it seeks to transcend. This perceived opposition of culture to nature then readily translates itself into the opposition of male to female. So culture requires the subordination of women because they are identified with nature (Ortner, 1974).

Many feminists criticise an analysis of women's subordination based on the distinction between a private and public sphere, for the same reasons they reject a concept of politics that locates it within a specific public arena. Friedl also argues that this approach may exaggerate the importance of the male-dominated 'public' sphere in many societies. In the Greek village she cites, 'the private and not the public sector is the sphere in which the relative attribution of power to males and females is of the greatest real importance'. Furthermore, within this private sphere, women informally have considerable power over decisions about the household's economy and their children's futures (Friedl, 1967, p. 97).

On the other hand, while this approach perhaps underestimates the role of biological differences, it does point to an actual, if regrettable, aspect of women's lives. Indeed, the notional separation of domestic and public spheres is often buttressed by a differentiated use of space. In one Provençal village, Reiter discovers a 'sexual geography', dictating not only that women spend more time than men in the village itself, but that they spend a minimum of time in 'public' places, except the church and three backstreet village shops (Reiter, 1975). This approach also helps to explain variations in women's status. Rosaldo suggests that 'women's status will be lowest in those societies where there is a firm differentiation between domestic and public spheres of activity and where women are isolated from one another and placed under a single man's authority, in the home' (Rosaldo, 1974, p. 36).

If the cultural interpretations cited so far tend to be favoured by 'liberal' feminists, then a third approach which links psychoanalytical insights with theories of language and anthropology has been explored by writers who would generally see themselves as anti-reformist. They would not necessarily recognise themselves as sharing a common approach however; their arguments in addition are often hard to follow drawing on a peculiarly dense body of theory and not always expressed for maximum clarity. Lumping them together in this way still makes them more manageable for present purposes.

Marxist feminists who found the 'traditional' Marxist approach, in which material relations of production largely determine the 'superstructural' realm of culture and ideology, inadequate for explaining women's experience, have sought new ways to theorise the relative autonomy of ideology and thence the ideological construction of women's role. Through the work of the highly influential French neo-Marxist, Louis Althusser, who devoted considerable attention to the question of ideology, they were drawn to the psychoanalytic theorist, Jacques Lacan, who understood the processes of psychological development in children, described by Freud, as the means by which a patriarchal social order reproduced itself. Lacan himself was influenced by the concept of the anthropologist, Claude Lévi-Strauss, of a Symbolic Order, the system of signs expressed as language through which social relationships acquired meaning and which had to be internalised by society's members. For Lacan the central principle of the Symbolic Order was the Law of the Father, which he saw as being internalised by the individual through the resolution of the Oedipus complex.

Lacan himself said little directly about women. One of the first attempts to apply his analysis to the question of male dominance was Juliet Mitchell's ambitious study, *Psychoanalysis and Feminism* (1974). Mitchell tends to accept the assumption of both Freud and Lacan that female psychological development reflect the centrality of the phallus either literally embodying or symbolising male power. She implies that the immediate cause and mechanism of male dominance is this process of internalisation. Though doubtful of the possibility of identifying the origins of the system of male dominance, she takes up Lacan's suggestion that syndromes within the subconscious represent the residual imprint of the way in which individuals were first incorporated into the kinship system. Kinship is of course of critical importance in primitive societies, constituting the 'idiom of social interaction, organising economic, political and ceremonial, as well as sexual activity' (Rubin, 1975, p. 169). Mitchell invokes Lévi-Strauss's argument that the fundamental principle underlying all kinship systems which explains their otherwise mystifying variety of rules and institutions, is the exchange, through marriage, of women between men. In this way the biological family is transcended to create a broader society linking different biological families together. She speculates that the Oedipus complex, with its incest taboo and assertion of male superiority or more precisely the authority of the (dead) father was necessary for the exchange of women.

Mitchell goes on to point out that in modern capitalist society the role of kinship and therefore of the exchange of women has been largely superseded by more directly economic forms of exchange. However, the 'biological' nuclear family, still crucial to the repro- duction of capitalism, has inherited and given a new twist to the Oedipal syndrome, simultaneously driving it deeper and fuelling it: 'the mother and sister or father and brother you sensually cannot have are also the only people you are supposed to love' (Mitchell, 1974, p. 378).

Rubin's argument is similar, but as an anthropologist she warns against too literal an interpretation of the concept of the exchange of women. In many primitive societies such a transaction is either only implicit or scarcely discernible. Instead she suggests we use the concept as 'a shorthand for expressing that the social relations of a kinship system specify that men have certain rights in their female kin and that women do not have the same rights either to themselves or to their male kin'. These rights are based on the ultimate control of female sexuality but extend far beyond (Rubin, 1975, p. 177).

Mitchell and Rubin then both accept and elaborate on a phallocentric account of women's psychological development, while speculating on the ultimate origins of such a system. In France interest has centred rather on the way in which 'phallogocentric' discourse has construed a false idea of woman and perhaps repressed a true feminine. As Duchen (1986) relates, French feminists pursuing this inquiry are heir to a formidable intellectual tradition concerned with demonstrating the connections between power, language and 'knowledge', and most directly to Jacques Derrida's discussion of how language creates meaning and to Lacan. For writers such as Kristeva, Irigaray and Cixous, a primary way in which patriarchy oppresses women is through language, its phallo-centredness, its limited binary logic and hierarchies of meaning, and feminists must attack this discourse through deconstructing its texts to expose their repressed meanings and by themselves defying the seemingly neutral rules of language.

The argument that male dominance is to a large extent culturally determined finds perhaps its most explicit and elaborate formulation in the writings so far cited. But of course a great number – probably the majority – of feminist writers imply that male dominance is primarily a cultural phenomenon. They emphasise the role of 'socialisation' and especially the way that children assimilate sex roles through a process of imitation, identification and internalisation (Oakley, 1972, pp. 179–80).

The family is seen as the crucial site of socialisation. Indeed, since children spend more time with their mothers than their fathers, the ironic fact may be that mothers are the single most powerful agents of their daughters' acquisition of gender. In modern societies, a second important socialising agent is school education. Numerous studies document the sexism inherent in educational policy, the range of subjects open to girls, the content of textbooks, the male-dominated staff hierarchy and the assumptions of teachers in Britain and the United States (see, for instance, Byrne, 1978; Lobban, 1978). What is empirically less well established, though probable, is that these features of the official and 'hidden' curricula independently affect pupils' gender identity. Increasingly feminists also stress the role of language in perpetuating assumptions about sex-roles and differences (see for instance Spender, 1980).

It would be foolish to deny the role of socialisation in the continuation of male dominance. But is it the main explanation? Women appear to acquiesce, even collude, in their own oppression. If, in the short term, this is entirely due to socialisation, we can still ask why socialisation takes this form. It cannot explain itself. Secondly, is women's seeming collaboration a mere result of conditioning or false consciousness, or does it reflect a kind of rationality? Women are oppressed and, as Sapiro points out, oppression implies not simply men's direct material power over women but their indirect ability to make women feel inferior and unaware of alternative ways of living. Even so, Sapiro argues, within those constraints women are not necessarily irrational. Drawing on games theory, she suggests that women pursue a strategy of minimising the risk of loss (Sapiro, 1979). It is at least possible that many women staunchly champion the family and their traditional role within it, because these form the context of their painstakingly acquired skills, power and self-esteem. To enter the 'masculine' world is to risk losing these hard earned benefits with no guarantee of compensating status or success in the other world's terms.

There is then a danger in placing too great an emphasis on socialisation, and the autonomy of culture and ideology. They are much better at explaining how structures and values of male-dominance persist than how they come into being or how they change.

Male dominance and the economy

We come now to the third type of explanation, which emphasises economic factors determining male dominance. Though the economy cannot be simply reduced to material relations of production, such an approach is clearly, like that which centres on biological differences between the sexes, more 'materialist' than our second type of explanation and its exponents have generally been Marxists.

No one with feminist pretensions will deny that Marx's own contribution to this subject is entirely inadequate. McDonagh and

Harrison summarise this contribution as follows. Marx identifies three fundamental aspects of social activity: the production of means to satisfy needs, the creation of new needs and the reproduction of the species. The third of these he sees as natural and unproblematic. Accordingly, in *The German Ideology*, he and Engels view the sexual division of labour prior to the emergence of an economic surplus as natural and egalitarian. Even in the context of early capitalism, Marx does not consider reproduction to require specific analysis. Instead he understands patriarchy, as we have seen, as a system of father-dominated household production. Since he identifies patriarchy solely in terms of production, not (biological) reproduction, he can quite logically argue that it emerged together with the institution of private property. He can predict its erosion, at least among the property-less proletariat, with the fuller development of capitalism:

> However terrible and disgusting the dissolution under the capitalist system of the old familial ties may appear, nevertheless modern industry, by assigning as it does an important part in the process of production, outside the domestic sphere, to women, to young persons, and to children of both sexes, creates a new economic foundation for a higher form of the family and of relations between the sexes (McDonagh and Harrison, 1978).

Marx has been criticised for neglecting the political economy of reproduction. But the main shortcoming of his contribution is that it is so sparse. In his writings he never turns his full attention to the question of women, though Engels suggests that he planned to. This also means that different writers have been able to put rather different interpretations on what Marx did say.

Those seeking a more satisfactory Marxist account of male dominance have in the first instance turned to Engels's *Origin of the Family, Private Property and the State*, which is centrally concerned with this question. Strongly influenced by the anthropologist Morgan, Engels posits successive stages in the evolution of the family broadly related to changes in technology and relations of production. In the era of 'primitive communism' he suggests that a form of group marriage prevailed. This was not, as those with 'brothel eyes' might suppose, the institutionalisation of sexual depravity, but it did allow women considerable sexual freedom.

Within this system children belonged to their biological mother, not their father. In the next stage, for reasons of clan survival but also because women wanted it, there was a gradual transition to the 'pairing family'. This was not accompanied by any decline in women's status. Even though the natural division of labour centred women's activities in the home while men procured food outside it, women had as much sexual freedom as men, they retained their 'mother right' and may even have presided over some form of matriarchy. The origins of patriarchy lie instead in the subsequent emergence, through 'the introduction of cattle breeding, of the working up of metals, of weaving and finally field cultivation' (Engels, 1972, p. 66) of an economic surplus. Men, because of the sexual division of labour prevailing, just happened to be best placed to appropriate this surplus. They now wanted to pass it on to sons they knew to be their own, and their new economic power gave them the means to do so. Through 'the World historic defeat of the female sex', mother right was replaced by father right and the patriarchal household was installed.

If Engels is open to criticism for his assumption that the sexual division of labour was originally natural and egalitarian, as well as for his many factual inaccuracies, his is still one of the first sympathetic analyses of male dominance and usefully made the link between reproduction and relations of production. Some Marxist feminists have sought to build directly upon his analysis. Probably the most elaborate and ambitious attempt is Evelyn Reed's *Woman's Evolution*. She reinterprets a wealth of anthropological evidence to argue that the first era of human existence was 'matriarchal'. By this she means not that women were dominant – in fact, sexual egalitarianism prevailed – but that the basic social unit, or clan, revolved around the 'motherhood' or set of woman kin collectively. In fact, it was woman who had 'humanised the species' by introducing the taboo on sexual relations between kin. Anthropologists have mistaken this for an incest taboo but it was really a taboo against cannibalism, preventing conflict amongst kinsmen over women. This taboo in turn maintained the matriarchy, so long as it obliged men to seek mates amongst the members of a different clan but remain in their own clan. Men had few rights as husbands or fathers, especially since their role in reproduction was only imperfectly understood (Reed, 1975).

While Reed's reconstruction of this matriarchal society is at least plausible, she does not take it much further than Engels himself in explaining exactly why and how the transition to a patriarchal society occurred. One consequence of the emergence of an economic surplus, she suggests, was the institution of the bride-price which may have helped society and the husband to regard both his wife and her children as property he had paid for. But she does not explain why men bought women rather than the other way round.

Other Marxist feminists concerned with the origins of male dominance have turned not to Engels directly but to the debate amongst, principally French, Althusserians about precapitalist social formations. It is suggested that in such societies an economic surplus may already exist which, while not yet the basis for private property or class formation, is associated with increased control by the male elders of the means not only of production but also of reproduction. Marxist feminists have seen in this approach a chance to move away from traditional Marxism's emphasis on production and to explore relations of reproduction which could be of more direct relevance for women's oppression. Unfortunately as Edholm *et al.* have pointed out, analysis has been impeded by using reproduction to mean, in this context, three rather different things: social reproduction or reproduction of the total conditions of production, reproduction of the labour force, and biological reproduction (Edholm *et al.*, 1977).

O'Laughlin applies this approach in her study of the Mbu Kpau people of Chad. A detailed examination of their organisation of production and reproduction leads her to conclude that the unmistakeable and ritualised pattern of male dominance does not result from simple biological differences. Nor does it reflect a technologically determined sexual division of labour, since 'within production as a whole there are few sexually assigned roles outside the domestic sphere and the contribution of both sexes are equitable'. Male dominance instead appears to arise from the relations of production and reproduction associated with the existence of an economic surplus. Male elders in practice, if not juridically, control the material means of reproducing production, such as seeds and implements, and also control women's reproductive functions, both child-bearing and child-rearing (O'Laughlin, 1974, p. 306). If this kind of inequality exists prior to the emergence of private property, the question remains why this should be so.

One possible answer is the increased importance of controlling population rates, as labour-intensive production and the possibility of a surplus make labour power more valuable. However, as Edholm *et al.* demonstrate, there are a number of logical problems with this explanation (Edholm *et al.*, 1977).

These speculations focus on the economic origins of women's oppression. At the same time, Marxist feminists have asked how far and in what ways male dominance is necessary to different modes of production, most particularly to advanced capitalism. As we have seen, Marx and Engels believed that the development of capitalism, by expanding the property-less proletariat and drawing women back into the public workforce, would begin to undermine sex inequality. It was only socialism, by finally eliminating private property and making possible the collectivisation of child care and other formerly domestic functions, that could eliminate it. But Marxist feminists have tended to emphasise and seek to account for the limits to women's emancipation under contemporary capitalism.

They have considered first women's role in public production. While the proportion of adult women in public employment steadily increased until by 1980 they constituted 39.4 per cent of the workforce (though two-fifths of these were in part-time jobs) in the United Kingdom, their occupational and pay levels remain consistently and markedly inferior to men's. One initial explanation was that women, fettered by domestic obligations and the ideological constraints that go with them, helped capitalism by swelling the 'reserve army of labour' and thus depressing labour costs (see Beechey, 1977). Subsequently it was recognised that women workers tend to be concentrated and segregated in particular jobs where they are not in direct competition with men, but it could still be argued that they provide capital with a cheap and flexible source of labour (Breugel, 1979).

Secondly, and again largely within the confines of a traditional Marxist framework, writers have emphasised women's contribution to capitalism as consumers. Weinbaum and Bridges even argue that such consumption amounts to work, since housewives in making their purchases must 'reconcile production for profit with socially-determined needs' (Weinbaum and Bridges, 1979, p. 199).

The most extensive and original debate has been about the relationship between advanced capitalism and women's domestic labour. Molyneux, writing in 1979, reckoned that this debate had generated over fifty articles (Molyneux, 1979a). Specifically, it is about how far and in which ways women's domestic labour is necessary to contemporary capitalism.

One aspect of this question concerns women's contribution as housewives to production. Marx and Engels depict domestic labour under capitalism as unproductive, in the strict sense that it does not produce commodities for exchange and so does not generate surplus value for the capitalist. With the advent of second-wave feminism this formulation appeared unsatisfactory. Benston helped to launch the domestic labour debate, when she argued that the cause of women's oppression under capitalism was precisely the economic necessity of their domestic labour. Even so, she followed Marx in distinguishing between the use-values created by house-work, which she argued were necessary to maintain the economic system, and other productive labour. In fact, she suggested that there was a separate, if subsidiary and dependent domestic mode of production, which was precapitalist in form (Benston, 1969).

Seccombe followed Benston in pointing out the social necessity of women's domestic labour. He rejected the argument that it constituted a distinct mode of production, and went further in emphasising the inefficiency of domestic labour. Sheltered from the direct impact of the capitalist market-place, housework was not subject to its law of value or to capitalism's relentless drive for profit-making innovation. It was indeed 'the least efficient organ-isation of a labour process existent within capitalism' (Seccombe, 1974, p. 17). A number of feminists took issue with this conclusion. In particular Costa and James argued that women's domestic labour did, ultimately, contribute to surplus value, by freeing men from the need to do housework and thereby making them available for wage labour. This kind of analysis, incidentally, largely underpinned the demand for 'Wages for Housework', which enjoyed a brief but intense vogue in the mid-1970s (Costa and James, 1972). Yet the mileage to be got from arguing that women's domestic labour creates surplus value appears limited, both theoretically and, from a feminist stance, tactically. As Gardiner *et al.* point out, over the last one and a half centuries many types of domestic labour have been replaced by goods and services provided by the market or the state, such as 'laundries and prepared foods, education and health care', indicating that they are not necessarily purveyed more cheaply and efficiently within the family than outside it (Gardiner *et al.*, 1980, p. 248). And a political demand that women's domestic labour be waged can appear to condone the prevailing sexual division of labour.

More promising is the examination of domestic labour's role in capitalist reproduction. Seccombe, for instance, finds it integral both to the reproduction of labour power and to the reproduction of relations of production. He suggests that domestic labour reproduces labour power simultaneously on a daily and on a generational basis: 'The former gets the wage worker to the plant gates every morning, the latter reproduces the next generation of both wage and domestic labour power' (p. 14). Reproduction of the labour force requires not only physical maintenance but psychological inputs – soothing feelings, promoting family harmony and sexual services. In the reproduction of the relations of production, the role of women's domestic labour is principally ideological. Most important of all is the mother's part in the early socialisation of her children into attitudes and perceptions appropriate to their role in bourgeois society. Barrett adds that the housewife 'plays the role of normative lynch-pin in the family, providing an incentive for the man's motivation to work as a breadwinner and cushioning him against the alienation of his labour power' (Barrett, 1980, p. 174).

The argument that women's domestic labour is essential to the social reproduction of capitalism has more immediate plausibility than the parallel claim for its contribution to production. Certainly in the context of contemporary capitalist society it would be difficult to deny that it contributed to social reproduction of the economic system. But Marxist feminists such as Barrett and Molyneux have themselves recently pointed out the limits of this line of reasoning. Given that it posits the separation, under industrial capitalism, of wage and domestic labour, it does not explain why men should have been associated with one and women with the other. How did women come to be the domestic labourers? Even if this problem is by-passed, it is not clear, as Barrett points out, that the reproduction of labour is best served, from the capitalist's viewpoint, by the way that labour is currently organised. 'If we compare it to a system where migrant workers live virtually in barracks with their costs of reproduction largely borne in the hinterland we can see that the overall costs incurred in reproducing the working class through the present system are not as low as they might possibly be' (ibid.,

p. 221). Finally, Barrett suggests that the concrete reality of women's domestic labour within the typical nuclear family plays less part in reproducing the relations of production than what, following McIntosh, she terms the 'family–household' system. This is the combination of an ideology of 'familism', based essentially on the bourgeois nuclear family, and the reality of a great diversity of household forms. It is the family–household system that socialises its members into compliance with capitalism and simultaneously maintains women's social subordination. This does of course raise the question of whether this family–household system plays such a role only in advanced capitalism or whether, as seems to be the case in existing industrialised state socialist societies, it contributes to social stability in industrial societies as a whole.

In sum, and as a number of Marxist feminists have conceded, women's oppression cannot be simply explained by its functionality for capitalism. On the other hand, capitalism has built upon and reshaped pre-existing differentiation in gender roles and, in some respects, though not necessarily narrowly economic ones, may by now be dependent upon such a differentiation.

Brief mention should be made here of French feminist Christine Delphy's rather different attempt to explain male dominance in economic terms (Delphy, 1977). She describes her method as Marxist but in insisting that women constitute a separate class is really a radical feminist. Following Benston, she sees the family as the site of a distinctive mode of production, based on patriarchal exploitation, but she refuses to see it as in any way dependent on the capitalist industrial mode of production it coexists with. Though in some ways attractive, obvious problems arise with this approach. Delphy, for instance, argues that all wives are exploited 'even if they have one or two servants', a difficult proposition to accept. More fundamental is her failure to analyse the relationship between the family economy and capitalism (Barrett and McIntosh, 1979).

It appears that economic imperatives are no more capable of explaining on their own either the origins or the continuation of male dominance than are biology or culture, although they have probably been a major determinant of the degree and forms of oppression as well as of the possibilities of women's liberation. Quite evidently an adequate explanation must draw on all three causal strands.

It has also become apparent in the course of this discussion that the question of male dominance can be posed in different ways. Are we concerned with its origins, its present causes, its preconditions or its perpetuating mechanisms? As Mitchell writes, 'more or less, every type of explanation contains some truth'; the problem is that 'the answers are somehow more accurate that the question' (Mitchell, 1974, p. 364). It seems probable to me that biological differences did give rise to male dominance, in the sense that men were motivated to control women because of their reproductive powers and were able to do so because they were physically stronger and perhaps innately more aggressive. Even now it is above all women's reproductive role that enables men to keep them subordinate. Yet these sex differences do not necessitate or justify the sex-based division of labour or unequal evaluation of sex roles. The institution of the family, women's mothering role within it, these are cultural phenomena which reflect and reinforce, especially through processes of psychological internalisation and the separation of domestic and public spheres, the system of male dominance. Culture in turn is importantly determined by economic forces. Emergence of an economic surplus may well have facilitated man's more systematic domination over women as well as over other men. Industrialisation and the imperatives of advanced capitalism have further strengthed aspects of male dominance, while in other ways tending to undermine it.

Women's place: change and diversity

Beyond such speculation it is probably not fruitful to go. For in our very discussion of these questions it has become apparent that whatever common elements may exist in women's oppression, its lived experience has been enormously varied. There are real dangers in over-generalising. Women's position has not only varied from one historical era to another but differs between and within contemporary societies.

New feminist research from the 1960s has itself been a catalyst in the systematic collection of information about women and perhaps ironically, has thereby sharpened our awareness of the differences between women. The wealth of new 'data' is indeed almost overwhelming, requiring ever greater specialisation and defying attempts at any overarching synthesis. At the same time it should be remembered that data are not only incomplete but often presented in suspect conceptual 'containers'. Even in the UK official statistics defining for instance women's rates of economic activity, occupations or class affiliation are shot through with anachronistic assumptions about women's role within the family (Allin and Hunt, 1982). Such assumptions are, however, most pernicious as incorporated into calculations of women's economic contribution and income in Third World countries.

First and obvious, women's position has changed over time. Thus in Britain, women's paid employment increased steadily from the 1950s until by 1985 they constituted 41.5 per cent of the paid workforce. At the same time much of the increase was accounted for by married women taking part-time jobs, with lower rates of pay and less job and union protection, and did not in any significant way erode the sex-segregated occupational structure. It was against this background of increased female employment that second-wave feminism took off.

Now, from the mid-1970s and especially under Conservative governments from 1979, recession, rationalisation and related government policies have affected women's paid employment and domestic responsibilities in ways that are still not entirely clear. Women appear to be losing jobs more rapidly than men, particularly in manufacturing, though there are problems in gauging the real level of women's unemployment. Government statistics include only those who register, in 1985 nearly one million women, but it is estimated that at least 300,000 women, including many married women ineligible for unemployment benefit, should be added. Women are however also, for the moment, entering new jobs at a faster rate than men, though these tend to be part-time, low skilled jobs in the service sector. Whether this pattern can continue, given cutbacks in public sector employment and the impact of new technology, is in doubt.

At the same time, women are increasingly likely to be the family breadwinner, or at least contributing to essential family income. By 1983 only around 11.3 per cent of all households consisted of a working husband, economically inactive wife and dependent children. There are now nearly a million single-parent families, of which the vast majority, nearly 90 per cent in 1983, are headed by women. In this context the impact on women of reductions in already meagre state nursery school provision, school meals, institutional care for the elderly or sick can only be guessed. The serious implications of such changes for the feminist movement and policies towards women are pursued in later chapters.

But, secondly, at any given time there is also tremendous diversity in the lived experience of women. This is currently true even between countries of the EEC. Thus if by the beginning of the present decade, 38 per cent of the total adult female population was in paid employment, the rate for individual countries ranged from 58 per cent in Denmark and 50 per cent in the United Kingdom to 28, 25 and 15 per cent respectively in the Irish Republic, Italy and Greece. Amongst the factors accounting for these differences were not only the level of economic development but 'cultural' characteristics, including notably the place of organised religion. All the great world religions, at least since prehistoric times and in the past, have tended to embody and reinforce traditional understandings of male and female nature and the corresponding division of labour, whatever scriptural and schismatic exceptions may be found. This is still largely true for instance of Roman Catholicism. Its influence has been especially marked in Ireland, where for historical reasons in which opposition to British dominion played an important part, it has retained an unparalleled moral ascendancy in the affairs of the nation, even if this is now under challenge. Over 90 per cent of the adult population of the Republic describes itself as Catholic and according to one survey in 1981, 86 per cent of these go to church at least once a week. Traditional Catholic values have been a significant contributory factor in a national birth-rate which, though beginning to decline, remains the highest in Europe. Recent legislation has made contraception more widely available but abortion on any grounds is still illegal (see the further discussion in Chapter 6) and following a referendum in July 1986 there is still no right to civil divorce.

Within societies, too, women are divided in all kinds of ways. In Britain, as in most Western democracies, a basic division is that of social class. Empirically there are of course difficulties in ascribing women to a particular social class, given the tendency to define class in terms of occupation. In official surveys, women's jobs tend to be less finely differentiated than men's and married women have been assigned to the social class of their husbands. The experience of working-class women offers many contrasts with that of middle-class women, for instance as regards paid employment. Given they have had less access to formal education or specialised training, that in competition with men they are still more hampered by domestic and mobility constraints and that they are dealing with a labour market in which assumptions about women's abilities and proper place are probably more tenacious, they generally face a very restricted, if any, choice of jobs. Reading for example accounts of women's work on the assembly line of a car components factory or as unskilled operatives in a tobacco factory (as reviewed by Beechey, 1983), it is difficult to see in what sense this could offer 'liberation'. (The relationship between women's paid employment, political awareness and participation is discussed more fully in the next chapter.)

It should also be noted, though this is not the same point, that studies in a number of Western societies indicate that poverty is disproportionately concentrated amongst women. In the United States, there has been considerable recent discussion of the 'feminisation of poverty', that not only are more women poorer than men but that their share of poverty is increasing (see Nelson, 1984). Even in Scandinavia as Hernes writes 'if there exists poverty . . . it is concentrated among women, especially as heads of household' (1984, p. 27).

Besides differences of social class and income, women are divided on the basis of ethnicity or race. In Britain, women from ethnic minorities, especially those of Afro-Caribbean or Asian origin, face particular problems of discrimination and racism. Up against racist immigration policies and physical attacks, they have increasingly questioned the assumptions and priorities of white feminists. For instance, they have argued that marches to 'reclaim the night', through deprived inner-city areas can appear to condone the stereotype of black men as potential racists. At a more theoretical level, they have suggested that feminist critiques of the family as a central site of women's oppression fail to recognise that the family can sometimes offer their only source of solidarity and security (Bhavnani and Coulson, 1986).

Beyond these distinctions within and between Western industrial societies (and state socialist societies discussed in Chapter 4), is the ever more apparent contrast between women's experience in these societies and in the 'Third World', in so far again as it is legitimate to generalise about so vast a region. First, in pre-colonial societies there appears to have been considerable variation in women's position from one community to another. In a pioneering work, Boserup (1970) linked these to women's agricultural role. Where shifting cultivation prevails, in more thinly populated areas, as still can be found in parts of Africa, women do much of the farming and sex roles are correspondingly relatively egalitarian. As population increase demands more intensive agriculture, using the plough, women's involvement in farming may decline and with it their status. With still greater population pressure, however, farming may require more labour-intensive methods, as in Egypt, China and parts of India, and women will be drawn back into the agricultural workforce. Whatever the determinants of women's standing in pre-colonial societies (and for a more detailed analysis see Tinker, 1976; Etienne and Leacock, 1980), there is wide agreement that colonial policies, though not always to women's detriment, generally were associated with a decline in their status. These policies are more fully discussed in Chapter 4.

Subsequent development policies have all too often echoed colonial assumptions about male and female roles. In 1973 for instance, the US Department of Labour reported that in Africa only 5 per cent of women worked (cited by Tinker, 1976, p. 23). Yet it is now widely recognised that women carry the heaviest burden of agricultural labour, currently constituting 60–80 per cent of agricultural workers in Africa and Asia and over 40 per cent in Latin America (Bandarage, 1984, p. 497). Where industry has developed, women, as in nineteenth-century Europe, have found it difficult both to obtain factory work and to combine it with family responsibilities, though a recent development has been precisely the employment of young, single women in the 'runaway' shops of multinationals. Nash (1977) attributes the special vulnerability of Third World women (excepting of course a privileged urban middle-class) to these countries' 'dependence' on Western metropolitan economies, and while such an analysis may be oversimplified, in a sense it is true that such women are the last link in the chain of exploitation.

The status of Third World women, even more than in the West, is also shaped by traditional religious values. Chapter 4 will consider some of the consequences for women of the reassertion of Islam and the pivotal place within it of the traditional family. Yet Third World women, including those who are themselves in opposition to such practices as female circumcision or enforced resumption of the veil, deeply resent their Western sisters' failure both to appreciate the context within which such practices occur and to acknowledge the contribution the West itself has made to the present character of Third World societies. Once more it is evident that as the circle of dialogue between women widens, they become more conscious of differences and conflicts. Later chapters consider the implications for feminism as a movement.

This does more immediately bring us back to theoretical constructions of male dominance. No feminist would deny that differences exist in society, besides those between men and women. What is in question is the relative importance of these differences for women. Marxist feminists for over a decade have been attempting to 'marry' class analysis with one based on sex–gender divisions. Now in response to the higher political profile of black women both inside and outside feminist groupings, some have also begun to consider ways of integrating ethnic or racial divisions into this analysis. Given their previous recognition that male dominance occurs within a class context and the fact that radical divisions often coincide, up to a point, with class divisions, they may be better placed to do so than radical feminists. On the other hand, as Barrett and McIntosh frankly acknowledge, there is the danger for Marxist theory that 'the introduction of a third system must necessarily fragment the analysis that was already creaking at the seams over feminism' (Barrett and McIntosh, 1985, p. 41).

The fundamental question is still whether beyond these differences women do meaningfully share a common oppression. Lees argues that women's oppression as women is not necessarily more 'real' or 'basic' than other forms, nor should it automatically have priority as a political concern. But it is the most *ubiquitous* form and it is embedded in the social division of labour in the most fundamentally integral fashion. 'Oppressions based on class, race, religion have in common their ability to rely upon, and indeed . . . strengthen family and community as forms of solidarity and resistance on the part of the oppressed. Sexual oppression, however, is located within these very institutions' (1986, p. 95). This is why women's oppression is difficult to see, why women can so easily be divided. It means, as Lees says, that women have no pre-existing social institutions on which to base their struggle and on the other hand that eliminating sexual inequality would require the most far-reaching social upheaval of them all.

The inevitability of male dominance?

To argue that male dominance is virtually universal is emphatically not to say that it is inevitable. This book itself is but one symptom of the far-reaching influence of feminist ideas. Feminism in turn has arisen not in a social vacuum but as a response to the changing circumstances and opportunities associated with industrialism. Forces are at work in society helping to undermine the system of male dominance. But feminists need to accelerate and consolidate their impact by bringing the issue into the public political arena. A later chapter will show how public policy and the state have themselves played a real, if secondary, part in maintaining women's oppression. On the other hand, women can use public politics in their own interests. It is to women's political participation that we turn in Chapters 3 and 4. Chapter 3 concentrates on participation in politics as voters and at 'grass-roots' level in political parties, movements and groupings, while Chapter 4 looks at women's involvement in political élites and the behaviour of women leaders.

2
Women's political behaviour

Of all aspects of the relationship between women and politics, it is women's political participation that has received most sustained attention from political science. There is a substantial literature on the subject, some more, some less sympathetic to the feminist perspective. Quantitative evidence, though uneven in its coverage, is relatively abundant and expanding.

Yet despite its volume, the literature is in some ways disappointing. First is the problem of bias, not simply in the evaluation, but also in the perception of 'facts', as far as these can be distinguished. Such bias occurs not only in the sexist accounts of the 1950s and 1960s but, more disarmingly, in some feminist critiques. Bias is no doubt unavoidable in social science, even at its most rigorously behaviourist. How much more so in a field so emotive, so concerned with questions of 'prejudice' and 'consciousness' as this.

The other main problem is that the forms of participation studied have been largely confined to politics, narrowly and conventionally defined. At the level of grass-roots political behaviour, interest has centred upon participation within formal, constitutional, government-oriented institutions or procedures. This leaves largely uncharted a whole range of political behaviour which influences decision-making in society, and provides a quite misleading view of women's political involvement.

The extent of women's participation in grass-roots politics

Voting

Within this narrowly conceived range of political behaviour, studies of women have concentrated on voting patterns. The political

50

importance of voting is in dispute. An elector provided with a choice of candidates clearly has more impact than if faced with a single slate. Yet even in a competitive party system, the value of the individual vote is questionable. Given the infrequency of elections, the at best limited choice of candidates, the profusion of safe seats, the inadequacy of the information supplied to the electorate and the independence of candidates once elected, political scientists tend to stress the psychological satisfaction voting gives the voter and its role in legitimising the political authorities and systems, functions no so different to those diagnosed in totalitarian states. Such cynicism can be overdone. The policy changes following the 1979 British General Election have at the least reminded us that, cumulatively, votes can sometimes matter very much.

The relationship of the vote to other forms of political participation is also unclear. Voting is sometimes understood as the first step in a succession of increasingly demanding political acts, but it may be more realistic to view it as logically distinct, as:

> A unique form of political behaviour in the sense that it occurs only rarely, is highly biased by strong mechanisms of social control and social desirability enhanced by the rain-dance ritual of campaigning, and does not involve the voter in major informational or other costs (Marsh and Kaase, 1979, p. 86).

Although voting may have its limitations as a criterion of political participation, women's exercise of the vote has especial meaning against the background of suffragist struggles. The suffragettes, however mistakenly, perceived the vote not simply as a symbol of political emancipation but as a means to effective political participation. In Britain and the United States they endured severe privations to gain it. Women still do not everywhere possess the same formal voting rights as men, though since women finally gained the vote in Liechtenstein in 1986, the only exception at national level is Saudi Arabia. In certain countries they have only very recently been enfranchised, the most well-known example being Switzerland, where women were unable to vote in national elections until 1972. How fully have women exercised their hard-won franchise?

In some countries, including incidentally not only socialist states but also Australia, voting is in effect compulsory; our interest is therefore primarily in how far women have used their vote when given a real choice between voting and abstention. Further, official voting records rarely differentiate by sex, so that figures cited tend to be based on surveys conducted immediately before or after an election. As a result, their reliability depends not only upon the accuracy of the sample surveyed but upon the respondents' truthfulness.

It has been widely observed that women do not vote with the same frequency as men. This has been the conventional wisdom concerning British national and local elections in the past (see, for instance, Blondel, 1965, p. 55), although the few relevant studies do not unanimously support such a conclusion. Data from Butler and Stokes's analysis of the 1964 and 1970 Parliamentary elections (see Butler and Stokes, 1974) have been reworked to show that women's turnout fell marginally short of men's; in 1964, 90 per cent of eligible women and 92.5 per cent of eligible men voted, while in 1970 the corresponding figures were 83.3 per cent and 87.1 per cent (Baxter and Lansing, 1980, p. 150). Again, the apparently well-founded consensus in the United States was that women were less inclined than men to use their vote (see, for instance, Campbell *et al.*, 1960, p. 483; Gruberg, 1968, pp. 9–16). Data from the Centre of Political Studies at Michigan University (a major source for statistics relating to women's political behaviour) showed a continuing excess of the percentage of men over women voting in the Presidential elections from 1948 to 1972. From 13 per cent in 1948, the differential dropped to 3 per cent in 1964 and 1968, rising again to 6 per cent in 1972. A similar gap was recorded for other Western democracies in the 1950s and 1960s, not only France and West Germany but also the progressive Scandinavian polities of Norway, Sweden and Denmark. The at first glance surprising deviation from this pattern is Italy where, since enfranchisement in 1945, women have voted at a consistently higher rate than men (see Currell, 1974).

The data indicate an even more pronounced tendency for male voting turnout to exceed female in the 'developing' countries. For Latin America, this has been reported in Colombia and Brazil, although the gap has closed quite rapidly in Argentina and Chile. A consistent differential in voting turnout between the sexes is also recorded in India.

This generalisation now requires major qualification. In the first place, as the figures cited illustrate, the differential typically has not been large. In the second, over time, in Western democracies it has frequently diminished to negligible proportions or disappeared outright. This is apparent in the voting rates for American Presidential elections already cited. By the 1980 Presidential elections women had caught up with men at a 59 per cent turnout (*Time*, 17 October 1983). In Britain by the 1979 General Election, 49 per cent of voters were women and 51 per cent men (Butler and Kavanagh, 1980, p. 343) and Husbands writes that the post-election survey of the 1983 General Election conducted by himself and Dunleavy showed that if anything a slightly higher proportion of women than of men voted (Husbands, 1986, p. 309). For parliamentary elections in the Nordic countries – Denmark, Finland, Iceland, Norway and Sweden – Skard and Haavio-Mannila report 'Since the 1930s, the electoral turnout has risen for both women and men until there is now no longer any difference to speak of' (1985a, p. 40). In West Germany by 1976 the difference was only 0.8 per cent. Moreover any residual differences usually vanish when voting rates are controlled for such intervening characteristics as age or education. In the third place, in developing countries, studies indicate a tendency for the differential to narrow the longer women have had the vote and with increasing urbanisation. The implications of these variations are discussed further below, but they do suggest that women's tendency to vote less than men is not inherent but contingent and transient.

Other conventional forms of participation

I have argued that the political significance of voting, both its impact and the individual commitment it requires, is usually slight. We need to examine more demanding forms of political participation. Although we can draw upon several systematic studies, information remains inadequate, patchy and still dependent on an unnecessarily limited view of what such participation includes. This is not to say that the kinds of participation studied are unimportant, however. Besides, they constitute the usual pre-requisite for more élite political participation; if women's participation in this conventional sense is less than men's, we have at least part of the explanation for their under-representation in political élites.

Again, the general finding has been that women do participate less than men. This is alleged in Britain, though evidence is thin. Dowse and Hughes told us firmly, 'One of the best researched findings in British politics is that women participate less and declare lower levels of interest in politics than do men'. However, as indices of participation they relied on office-holding and voting behaviour and cited no British evidence at all (Dowse and Hughes, 1972, p. 192). Baxter and Lansing use the Butler–Stokes data to show a modest sex differential in political activity related to the 1964 and 1970 British General Election campaigns.

In America, data from the Centre for Political Studies covering the national elections of 1952, 1964 and 1972 show male activism to exceed female, when activism consists of campaigning for political parties or their candidates, membership of a political club or organisation or attendance at a political meeting, the latter two activities in the context of a party political campaign (Welch, 1977). This definition of activism is of course extremely narrow. Using a similar concept of activism, Black and McGlen in Canada find a small but significant sex differential in 1964 which had diminished but not vanished by 1974 (Black and McGlen, 1979). Nielson and Sauerberg report the findings of a pre-election survey in Denmark in 1977, which showed 11 per cent of men and 10 per cent of women to be party members and 39 per cent of men but only 31 per cent of women to have been involved in 'legal' political activities. They conclude, however, that sex is not an important predictor of political involvement (Nielson and Sauerberg, 1980). On the other hand, relying on survey data from three regions of Southern Norway in 1974, Lafferty argues confidently that, 'In sum, sex is the most important "structural" determinant of political participation in Norway' (Lafferty, 1978, p. 25). Overall for the Nordic countries and citing a long list of sources, Skard and Haavio-Mannila can still conclude that 'a consistent feature throughout the Nordic countries is that women are less active than men . . . in party membership, attendance at political meetings, involvement in elections campaigns' (1985a, p. 48).

That differentiation by sex in the rate of political participation is a cross-cultural phenomenon is further underlined by a study, published in 1978 but based on data collected between 1966 and 1971, of political participation in seven countries: Austria, India, Japan, the Netherlands, Nigeria, the United States and Yugoslavia. The authors calculate rates of participation by combining measurements for a number of indicators: voting, activity in electoral campaigns, 'communal activity' meaning citizen contact with government officials on matters of general interest, and 'particularised contacts' or citizen contacts with government officials on matters of concern to a specific individual or group. This is clearly a broader conception of political participation than some of those cited above. They find that, in this sense, men participate more than women in all seven countries, though the differential is least in the United States and the Netherlands (Verba *et al.*, 1978).

Data for women's membership of political parties and interest organisations, where available, tend to confirm this picture. Even in Western democracies, parties are often remarkably vague about the precise figures. In Britain, women are substantially represented in the membership of the two main parties. Hills, drawing on official Labour Party figures and studies of local Conservative Associations, estimates that they constitute approximately 40 per cent and 51 per cent of these parties' membership respectively (Hills, 1981a). Lovenduski (1986a) quotes an estimate that 15 per cent of the membership of the Social Democratic Party are women and suggests that female membership of the Liberal and Scottish National Party are probably higher. There are no comparable statistics for the United States where party membership is often barely distinguishable from electoral support. Rates in the Nordic countries have risen steadily over the last decade, now averaging 30–40 per cent and in Christian parties and the Finnish Liberal People's Party 50 per cent and over (Skard and Haavio-Mannila, 1985a). In other West European countries they are lower, though by 1983 in France they ranged from 27 per cent in the Socialist Party (PS) and 36 per cent in the Communist Party (PCF) to 40 per cent in the Giscardien UDF and 43 per cent in the Gaullist RPR. By 1983, in West Germany women were still only 25 per cent of the membership of the Social Democrat Party (SPD) and 23 per cent of the Christian Democrat Party (CDU). They were, however, 50 per cent of Green Party membership (Lovenduski, 1986a). As might be expected, women fare least well in what might be called the 'new' European democracies, Spain and Portugal, but had reached 40 per cent in the Portuguese Socialist Party by 1983 and were 30 per cent of the Spanish Centre Democrats.

Party membership is especially necessary for political advancement in communist states. By 1982 women constituted 27 per cent of the Soviet Communist Party and in most other East European countries are around 25 per cent, except in East Germany where they have reached 31 per cent. Similarly, in Cuba, just under 19 per cent of party members are women (*The Guardian*, 28 May 1980). As Chaney notes, 'General membership parties are a fairly recent phenomenon in Latin America' but she estimates that in the late 1960s women formed 15–20 per cent and 20 per cent of the various parties' membership in Peru and Chile respectively (Chaney, 1979, pp. 91–2). A study conducted in Mexico around 1970 found 23 per cent of men but only 8 per cent of women with experience of party membership, while before military rule was imposed in Uruguay, 17.8 per cent of men and 7.2 per cent of women belonged to the equivalent political clubs (Aviel, 1981).

Verba and Nie provide data on participation in a range of organisations, not all of them directly political, in the United States. They find that 8 per cent more men than women belong to at least one organisation although only 2 per cent more are active in at least two. The difference, they conclude, is small (Verba and Nie, 1972). In their seven-country survey, Verba *et al.* find that, with the exception of the United States where men's lead is 'negligible', their rates of affiliation to institutions in general, and to political institutions in particular, are consistently higher than women's (Verba *et al.*, 1978). This pattern is particularly clear in Latin America, where Aviel cites a study in Uruguay indicating the predominance of men in unions, political clubs, economic organisations and social and agricultural clubs, and a survey of a Columbian town, where 84 per cent of the members of non-religious organisations were men (Aviel, 1981). But before leaving this question we should also consider whether the assumption that women are less likely to join political organisations does not partly reflect a view of what such organisations are together with a concentration on national rather than local organisations (Hernes, 1984b; Lovenduski, 1986a). Hernes and Hänninen-Salmelin (1985, p. 126) provide an impressive breakdown for the four Scandinavian countries of women's participation in different kinds of organisation which indicates that in consumer organisations, and those characterised as 'humanitarian and social' as well as in religious and temperance organisations, women are frequently more numerous than men.

Quantitative data on women's participation in (non-feminist) interest organisations are otherwise extremely hard to find with the important exception of trade union membership. Here again women are generally under-represented in the sense both that they form a lower proportion of total membership than men and that women employees are less likely to join unions. None the less their membership rates have increased quite dramatically over the last decade or so in Western industrialised countries. This partly reflects the drive in the 1970s to recruit the newly employed and low paid, who in both cases tended to be women, into the unions, though as Lovenduski points out there have been significant variations between countries. In 1983 women were 31 per cent of union members and just over 30 per cent of the paid work-force in the UK. Women's trade union membership rates are higher in the Nordic countries at over 40 per cent in the main federations, except in Norway where in 1982 they formed 33 per cent of members in the Federation of Trade Unions, and rising to well over 50 per cent in more specialised professional and civil service union federations (Hernes and Hänninen-Salmelin, 1985, p. 123). Thirty per cent of trade union members in France in 1982 were women. In 1981 in West Germany 21 per cent of the membership of trade unions affiliated to the main federation, the DGB, were women and in Italy women were an estimated 30 per cent of trade union members.

Outside Western Europe, in 1982 women were 25 per cent of trade union members in the US and more than a third in Australia. Rates are particularly high in some East European countries, exceeding 59 per cent in the Soviet Union by 1982 (Lovenduski, 1986a) but, with only the temporary exception of Poland, these states accord their unions little political independence. Given their generally still very low rates of participation in the paid work-force, Third World women, especially in Muslim countries and in Latin America, tend to form only a tiny minority of union members (Aviel, 1981).

Overall, the evidence suggests that women's political participation, conventionally defined, is everywhere less than men's. Even so, a number of caveats are in order. The first is that political activism tends in any case to be a minority attribute. Second, these sex differences are not constant but vary noticeably over time and across cultures. Of the seven countries in their study, Verba *et al.* find that America and the Netherlands exhibit the least and India, followed by Nigeria, the most (1978). Indeed Lynn shows that if data for the Presidential elections of 1968, 1972 and 1976 are analysed together there is no significant difference in the sexes' rate of political participation in the United States, except that men donate more funds to the election campaign (Lynn, 1979). Black and McGlen also observe a narrowing differential over time in Canada (1979). Though women's share of party membership has risen steadily but slowly over the last two decades in most of the countries for which we have information, both women's rate of unionisation and their share of union membership have often increased dramatically. Again, the implications of these variations must be discussed further below, but they suggest that, as for voting, sex differences in political participation, conventionally defined and at grass-roots level, are not fundamental but could eventually fade away.

Less conventional politics

In any case a satisfactory account of politics, as well as a comprehensive picture of women as participants, requires us to broaden the definition of political participation. There are other kinds of activity that intentionally influence the making of public policy. We need in particular to consider what can be called *ad hoc* politics, not fully integrated into the formal political process or institutionalised, *protest* activity directed against the existing regime and a range of political activities falling somewhere between these.

Ad hoc participation means participation in political campaigns that are relatively short-lived, throwing up makeshift organisations and tending to rely on direct tactics such as pickets, squats and self-help projects. Typically, too, they focus on issues of local or community concern. Women's involvement in such activities is not new, though information about the past is limited. In Britain, for instance, women were prominent in the eighteenth- and early nineteenth-century food riots, as well as the 1837 demonstrations against the Poor Law (Stacey and Price, 1981, p. 41). In eighteenth-century France, women 'were often central figures in food riots and market disturbances', revealing 'political awareness and a certain modicum of political skill' (Levy and Applewhite, 1980, p. 10). But it is the scale of this involvement from the 1960s, together with changing academic perspectives, that has drawn it to our attention.

In Britain women have been conspicuous in the community action movement. This really got under way in the 1970s, though its leadership and ethos owed much to the New Left student politics of the 1960s. It is essentially urban, focuses on local issues and combines elements of self-help with pressure on the authorities. A collection of essays edited by Majorie Mayo and written revealingly not by political scientists but by sociologists, social workers, feminists and other activists, describes rather impressionistically women's often preponderant role in housing campaigns, child-care projects and the local claimants' union (Mayo, 1977).

Several studies have provided a similar picture in the United States. In the late 1960s community politics was encouraged by the student and civil rights movement on the one hand and the federal government's new urban aid programmes on the other. As in Britain, women, both middle-class and working-class, were subsequently keen participants. Gittell and Shtob, who usefully summarise a number of relevant sources, tell us 'Neighbourhood associations and community-action councils have a high female involvement, according to all observers of the government-sponsored organisations . . . and to War on Poverty research studies' (Gittell and Shtob, 1980, p. 574). McCourt provides a pioneering study of white working-class women's participation in eight politically active community organisations on the south side of Chicago. She finds that a majority of the most active women are over 40 years old, not in paid employment and far from consciously sympathetic with the values of women's liberation. The trigger to their political involvement is the threat posed to their neighbourhood by racial tension, declining school standards or industrial pollution (McCourt, 1977). Schoenberg also describes how, in several inner cities, the older women members of longstanding ethnic communities were mobilised by the perceived deterioration of their neighbourhood (Schoenberg, 1980). Other women have campaigned for greater popular control of local health services and for welfare rights.

Further evidence for women's *ad hoc* participation comes from Norway. Hernes and Voje cite an opinion poll which showed that 49 per cent of male and 47 per cent of female respondents had recently taken part in one or more *ad hoc* political actions. The figures for both sexes seem surprisingly high but the authors are chiefly interested in the implications for women who, they suggest, 'come into their own in this type of activity'. They incidentally note that many such political activities arise in neighbourhoods where women not in paid employment predominate (Hernes and Voje, 1980, p. 177).

From women's participation in *ad hoc* politics, we turn to protest politics, directed against the political authorities and often taking an illegal or violent form. If hard data remain elusive, the body of relevant qualitative materials has grown appreciably over the last five or so years, confirming that this is an important aspect of women's political behaviour.

A relevant starting point is the Barnes and Kaase study. They designed a questionnaire to measure 'protest potential', that is, the readiness to resort to direct, even illegal and violent, political action. Their data from Austria, Britain, West Germany, the Netherlands and the United States indicate that in Europe, less so in America, protest potential is positively though not strongly associated with being male. However, except in Austria, women are slightly more likely than men to belong to the sub-category of protesters, those whose repertoire of political action is confined to direct action and precludes conventional politics. Although these findings relate only to intentions, they are remarkable and 'may well mean that women report low participation rates in conventional politics not merely because of their traditional inactivity, conditioned by lower educational levels, but from a sex-based lack of identification with conventional politics' (Barnes and Kaase, 1979, p. 184).

Women have often played an active role in revolutionary movements. This was as true of Britain's own seventeenth-century Revolution (see Rowbotham, 1974, p. 10) as of each of the French Revolutions of 1789, 1830, 1848, 1870 and 1968. Levy and Applewhite, in their study of *femmes sans-culottes* in France's first Revolution, trace the 'evolution in their political sophistication and influence that ultimately led to repression at the hands of Thermidorian officials fully cognizant of the implications of feminine political activities' (Levy and Applewhite, 1980, p. 10). In Russia, 'women were prominent in all the socialist movements . . . beginning with agrarian reformers and ending with the Bolsheviks'. Although they rarely attained leadership, in the October Revolution women fought in the streets: 'the poor women of Petrograd . . . stormed out to defend the Red Revolution, alongside boys of ten and men armed only with shovels' (Salaff and Merkle, 1970, pp. 171–3).

In South America too women are reported as participating significantly in peasant revolts and urban guerrilla movements in Argentina and Brazil (Jaquette, 1973). By 1977 they were around 25 per cent of the membership of the Tupamaros in Uruguay. In Pinochet's Chile, women have been 'present on the three battle-fronts which the Resistance has set: underground, prison and exile' (Diaz, 1985, p. 33). Most recently they were active in the Sandinista National Liberation Front in Nicaragua, where by the time of the final offensive in 1979 they were an estimated 30 per cent of its membership. In El Salvador, the FMLN is a coalition including four 'political–military' organisations. In one of these, the FPL, female participation has been reckoned as high as 40 per cent (Reif, 1986). In another Third World region, women were prominent in the uprising against the Shah of Iran, where, as Tabari writes, their 'well-organised . . . contingents became one of the distinguishing features of the street demonstrations' (Tabari, 1980, p. 19).

In so far as nationalist movements are distinguishable from revolutionary activity, they too reveal a long tradition of female participation. Women's contribution to the protracted struggle for India's independence from British rule is well known. In Africa, Algerian women played a prominent part in the FLN's (*Front de Libération Nationale*) war of terror against the French and the *colons*, smuggling arms, even planting bombs, and joined in full force the insurrections of December 1960 and July 1962 (Ainad-Tabet, 1980). Women actively supported the wars of independence against the British in Yemen (Molyneux, 1979b). Likimani (1985) provides a vivid account of women's part in the Kenyan Mau Mau. Little describes the role of women's brigades in the nationalist movement in Zambia, women's involvement in the Kenyan Mau Mau and in resistance to the French in the Ivory Coast (Little, 1973). In Zimbabwe, women joined the freedom fighters in large numbers. Typical is the experience of Sarudzai Chichirunya who:

> was 19 when she learned to handle a sub-machine-gun and went to fight the liberation war in Robert Mugabe's guerrilla army. In her platoon of 35 people, who slipped through the bush to wipe out a Rhodesian security base one May morning, three-quarters were women, carrying AK-47s, mortars and bazookas.

The number of women eventually involved in such activities is estimated at over 10,000 (*The Guardian*, 21 October 1980). Again most recently women are reported as active participants in movements of national resistance in Namibia and Eritrea. Many decades earlier women took part in successive independence movements in Latin America. In Gran Colombia, from around the end of the eighteenth century:

> women contributed to the independence movement in numerous ways. First, and perhaps most dramatic, was their personal participation in combat, accessory actions and espionage. Second, women lent their support in their traditional helping roles as hostesses of political *tertulias* and as nurses. Third, they made significant economic contributions by donating moneys and supplies to the insurgents (Cherpak, 1978, p. 220).

Generally in these movements women have been expected to play a primarily auxiliary role, in keeping with traditional sex-role assumptions, or if women have been used as messengers or even, as in the FLN in Algeria, as assassins, it is because they were less likely to attract attention or suspicion. Increasingly though, women are also described in combat roles, as in the freedom struggles in Zimbabwe, Namibia and Nicaragua. It is furthermore clear that women have not been absent from the more violent or, as they are sometimes called, 'terrorist' wings of such movements. The media have highlighted their role in such organisations as Baader–Meinhof, the Irish Republican Army (IRA), the Symbionese Liberation Front and the Palestinian Liberation Organisation (PLO). Indeed by 1978, 60 per cent of the terrorists sought by the police in the Federal German Republic were women (Jacobs, 1978, p. 166).

In their opposition to existing regimes, women have often faced severe personal danger and privation. In Tsarist Russia from 1850–90, 21 out of 42 people sentenced to hard labour for life (the customary punishment for terrorists) were women (Evans, 1977, p. 181). In the present century, just after Franco's death in 1976, one-third of Spanish political prisoners were female (Thiercelin, 1980). In Turkey, hundreds of women were arrested and many were tortured under the martial law established in 1971 (Sertel, 1980). Perhaps most terrible is the record of treatment of female political prisoners under the military regimes of Argentina, Chile and

Uruguay. Not only is rape almost a commonplace, but the women have been subjected to innumerable further forms of sexual torture and degradation (Bunster-Burotto, 1986).

Women's participation in these oppositional movements, even more perhaps than their *ad hoc* politics, contrasts vividly with the picture of their conventional political activity presented earlier. But we need also to consider a range of activities that do not fall neatly into either the *ad hoc* or protest category. One of these is industrial militancy. Siltanen and Stanworth suggest that in the general literature on what they call 'work-based politics', women tend to be portrayed as 'less likely to take part in routine forms of worker resistance at the point of production, and less likely to initiate militant action to support their demands' (1984, p. 11). One of the contributors to their book, Watt, finds in his sample of women workers in a Glasgow tobacco factory relatively high levels of support for collective and strike action where there was a majority decision in its favour (Watt, 1984). But instances of female industrial militancy are in any case legion. In nineteenth-century Britain perhaps the best known is the matchgirls' strike but it was by no means isolated (see Rowbotham, 1974, pp. 61–2). Nor are examples confined to the Western world. Much earlier this century it was the refusal of women port workers to load rice that triggered the 1918 Japanese Rice Riots and in China in 1922 thousands of women workers in Shanghai silk factories went on strike for higher wages and a shorter working day (Jayawardena, 1986, p. 23). Two recent examples are the strike of women workers in the Dong-11 Textile Company in South Korea in 1977 and the similar industrial action of women in the Lucy textile factory in Peru in 1979 (both reported in Davies, 1985).

The stereotype of workers' wives opposed to industrial militancy also has to be questioned. Thus in Siglo XX, a large Bolivian mining complex, when in 1961 a number of male union leaders were arrested, their wives set up a Housewives Committee to orchestrate protest which then went on to support the miners' struggle and to demand better medical supplies, paraffin, food provisions and so forth (de la Chungara, 1985). In Britain the obvious very recent example has been the organisation of Women Against Pit Closures in support of the miners' strike of 1984–5. According to *The Guardian* (13 May 1984) more than 10,000 people took part in the demonstration it called at Barnsley.

All these instances in no way prove that women are more capable or even as capable of industrial militancy as men but they do challenge any presumption that they are innately or always less so. In a second area of political involvement not easily slotted into traditional political science categories, the peace movement, women on the other hand do appear to have been particularly active. Byrne and Lovenduski (1983) suggest that the peace movement in Britain falls into their category of 'protest group'; as such its membership is less sectional and its organisation looser than in the typical 'protectional' interest group while its aims are more far-reaching and radical than those of a 'promotional group'. It is revealing of social science attitudes prevalent at the time that Parkin's study (1968) of British Campaign for Nuclear Disarmament (CND) supporters in the 1960s discussed mothers' influence on young members' attitudes but nowhere women's membership as such. One can infer from his data, however, that 40.7 per cent of his sample of 358 members were female. Wilson also tells us that:

> from the beginning women were centrally involved in the campaign against the bomb and one of the early demonstrations consisted of 2,000 women with black sashes and flags walking on a pouring wet Sunday from Hyde Park to Trafalgar Square. Once under way, CND always attracted large numbers of women (Wilson, 1980, pp. 177–8).

My personal impression is that women have played a prominent role in the revival of CND since the end of the 1970s. But the clearest case of women's involvement has been the women's peace camp set up at Greenham in 1982 to protest against the installation of Cruise missiles, and the activities it generated. 30,000 women took part in the first big demonstration 'embracing' the base in December 1982 and at least eleven further camps were established. Admittedly Greenham has drawn significantly on the energies and inspiration of the women's liberation movement but it is doubtful whether the two can simply be equated.

We have been looking so far at women's participation in public politics in ways that are less conventional but still direct. A complete account of women's political behaviour should not ignore its more indirect forms. That women should so often have been confined to these indicates the limits to their political participation.

At the same time, by indirect means, in the past and even today, women have not only exercised considerable political influence but made clear their interest in political questions.

Women participate in politics, informally and indirectly, through their menfolk, particularly in societies where politics is relatively uninstitutionalised. A spate of recent anthropological studies – once more, political science is silent – illustrate how women manipulate the public sphere of decision-making, apparently dominated by men. Through carefully staged histrionics they force domestic disputes into the public domain, or they simply threaten to shame their menfolk in this way. Often women play on men's fears of their supposed supernatural powers, as amongst Berber groups in North Africa (Nelson, 1975). Perhaps women's greatest source of political leverage is their role as 'structural links between kinship groups in societies where family and kinship are the fundamental institutions of everyday life' (ibid., p. 559). It enables them to mediate in marriages which often form part of important political alliances, and gives them access to an invaluable information network. Kinship may also provide the basis for a further source of influence, the extensive women's solidary groups or networks, through which they can reduce their practical dependence upon men and also help to shape 'public opinion' in ways that the male decision-makers cannot afford to ignore. Wolf recalls:

> In the Taiwanese village I knew best, some women were very skilled at forming and directing village opinion toward matters as apparently disparate as domestic conflicts and temple organisation. The women who had most influence on village affairs were those who worked through the women's community (Wolf, 1974, p. 162).

As societies 'modernise', the evidence suggests that these sources of indirect political influence come to count for less. Even so, Jaquette argues that in Latin America the salience of 'clientelism' in politics may provide some women with new opportunities. Clientelism is the process by which central political institutions of the modernising state are linked to the traditional periphery by a hierarchical chain of personal dependency relationships. Women's key position in informal kinship networks may enable them to influence the operation of these relationships (Jaquette, 1976).

From the thoroughly privatised base of the modern nuclear family, women's scope for such indirect political influence must normally be minimal, but even here mothers are important agents of their children's political socialisation, as we shall see.

A second form of indirect political participation is taking part in women's associations. While these are relatively organised and permanent, they are usually depicted as apolitical. Women's associations assume a variety of guises, and can be found in both preindustrial and industrial urban societies. They proliferate for example in West Africa, where many in the past enjoyed and a few still enjoy today a direct say in community politics. Even the less directly powerful associations have political significance. Leis describes such an association in a south Nigerian village. It holds regular meetings, elects its own officers, settles disputes between members, regulates aspects of the local market, lends money and imposes effective sanctions on transgressors of its rulings, whether men or women (Leis, 1974).

In more urban and industrialised contexts, women's associations are legion (I am excluding here feminist groups, as well as those political and professional women's organisations whose pressure group character is overt and widely recognised, such as America's League of Women Voters). Political scientists have generally ignored their political potential – partly, one suspects, because their membership is female. Feminist social scientists also often depict such associations, particularly in those countries where women have formal political rights, as reactionary. Obviously such associations are a very mixed bag, in terms of membership, formal arrangements and activities. While feminist criticisms may frequently be well founded, however, this is not a reason to underestimate their role as a vehicle for women's political influence.

Towards the end of the nineteenth century, and while women were still denied the vote in Britain and the United States, associations of, mainly middle-class, women proliferated; many took up charitable and social service functions, which in turn often led into campaigns for social reform. In the United States such organisations included the Charity Organisation Society, which 'aimed to reconstitute the able-bodied poor by putting them in contact with a "friendly visitor", a middle-class female volunteer who tried to bring middle-class values into the immoral environment'; the General Federation of Women's Clubs, which in the

1890s was revising its original emphasis on literary and cultural activities in favour of social service and reform; and the famous Women's Christian Temperance Union, founded in 1873 to promote temperance but later extending its concerns to issues such as prison reform, child-labour laws and even women's suffrage (see Gittell and Shtob, 1980, pp. 68–9). Although these associations and their British counterparts could often rightly be accused of helping to maintain the existing social system, they played an undeniable political role in helping to bring many such issues to the attention of politicians and the public.

Turning to the twentieth century, as Delamont – again, significantly, a sociologist – notes, in Britain 'No good social science research has been done on the large organisations for women, such as the Women's Institutes, Townswomen's Guilds, Women's Royal Voluntary Service, Citizens' Advice Bureaux and Mothers' Union' (Delamont, 1980, p. 192). Yet in 1978 it was estimated that around three million women were in all-female organisations. Most of these organisations are careful to present themselves as apolitical. Even so I suggest that they play a political role in at least two ways. First, individual branches and, occasionally, national organisations take up particular issues. The successful joint campaign of several such organisations to remove turnstiles from public lavatories may not seem exactly world-shattering, but they also supported the demand for child benefits to be paid to mothers. Second, 'it is in the women's organisations that those with a capacity or a taste for leadership can most easily achieve it' (Encel *et al.*, 1975, p. 278). Some women may for that very reason prefer to remain in this relative cul-de-sac rather than venture out into male-dominated politics. But it is also relevant that many local Conservative women councillors are recruited from this background. The same is true of women in the United States in local, and even sometimes state-level, politics. In the rather different world of Latin American politics too it has been suggested that women's charitable organisations and activities in Colombia, Chile and the Dominican Republic have been readily mobilised to provide support for centre and right-wing parties and movements (Aviel, 1981, p. 161).

To sum up, women's participation in conventional political activities, of a grass-roots or rank and file kind, is less than men's but the difference is often small or at least diminishing. Women also participate politically in other ways, directly through *ad hoc*

campaigns, protest action and related forms of activity and indirectly through informal, personal influence and through women's
associations.

Women's political attitudes

What has been the impact of women's political participation?
Although women took part in public politics long before winning
the vote, it was this prospect that led both sympathisers and critics
to ask what distinctive contribution women would make. The
debate, which was replicated in many countries, ranged between
two extreme positions. On the one hand, many suffragists, accepting the Victorian, idealised view of women as private and untainted,
argued that their participation could only be beneficial, imbuing
politics with a new sense of morality. The American feminist,
Elizabeth Cady Stanton, maintained that the effect of female
suffrage would be 'to exalt purity, virtue, morality, true religion, to
lift man up into the higher realms of thought' (cited by Elshtain,
1974, p. 464). Similarly, Julia Ward Howe insisted that 'The very
intensity of our feeling for home, husband and children gives us a
power of loving and working outside of our hmes, to redeem the
world as love and work only can' (cited by Bernard, 1979, p. 280).
Opponents of women's suffrage, on the other hand, emphasised
that women's sheltered background and limited moral intellectual
faculties ill suited them for politics, and that their politicisation
would have disastrous consequences for family life and, ultimately,
social harmony. So Dicey warned 'a revolution of such boundless
significance cannot be attempted without the greatest peril to
England'(cited by Currell, 1974, p. 2).

In the event there seems little basis for either of these apocalyptic
prophecies. Female suffrage has not transformed society or politics.
Yet both non-feminists and feminists regularly suggest that
women's political attitudes and impact differ subtly but significantly
from men's. As before, the evidence cited to support such claims is
patchy and often ambiguous. None the less the generalisations
made about alleged differences provide a useful framework around
which to present the discussion.

Female political activity is male-dominated

Many studies conclude, and some simply assume, that women's political behaviour is dominated by the men in their lives (see, for instance, Campbell *et al.*, 1960; Charzat, 1972). In the first place, wives are presumed to adopt the political views of their husbands. Thus, observing the similarity in political outlook between spouses, Lazarsfeld *et al.* deduce 'The almost perfect agreement between husband and wife comes about as a result of male dominance in political situations' (Lazarsfeld *et al.*, 1968, p. 141).

The feminist critique of this assumption questions not so much the finding that the reported political preferences of husbands and wives converge as the construction put upon it. Goot and Reid argue that evidence to support such a construction is less than convincing. Sometimes it is second-hand, as when respondents were asked about influences on their mother's party allegiance (Butler and Stokes, 1974). Or it is based on too few instances, as when Milne and Mackenzie drew their conclusions from the replies of 24 out of 240 women (Milne and Mackenzie, 1958).

Two more careful studies do tend to lend more support to this generalisation. Beck and Jennings, using data gathered in the US in 1965, show that wives' political attitudes are further from their own parents and nearer their in-laws' than are husbands' (Beck and Jennings, 1975). Weiner, to prove that this does not result from selective mating, goes on to demonstrate that a couple's political views become both more homogeneous and close to the husband's original views over time (Weiner, 1978). Still, even if these studies do establish that wives adjust to their husbands' political attitudes, more than vice versa, this may be because 'It is still the case that within marriage male careers and status tend to predominate, and it may therefore be that the women who change are reacting to extra-familial influence, or adapting to an entire milieu rather than, as it were, yielding politically to a man' (Evans, 1980, p. 214). There is also a curious contradiction between this finding and women's reported tendency both to vote less than men – they evidently do not follow their husbands into the polling booths – and to be more conservative than men.

It has similarly been supposed that children, including daughters, adopt their fathers' political views (see, for instance, Lazarsfeld *et al.*, 1968). Goot and Reid again question the reasoning behind this supposition, and show that sometimes parental influence is simply equated with paternal influence. For instance, Butler and Stokes assume fathers' influence on partisanship to be greater, because it is most visible, but simultaneously observe that 'when the mother was partisan and agreed with the father, she strongly reinforced his influence on the child . . . when she was partisan and disagreed with the father, she was if anything a little more likely to carry the child with her' (Butler and Stokes, 1974, p. 53). Moreover, a study in the United States of the impact on children's partisanship of parents whose party identifications differ finds that mothers have only slightly less influence than fathers on their daughters (Jennings and Langton, 1969). If, then, the generalisation that husbands dominate their wives' political behaviour has received some empirical confirmation, there is little evidence that fathers dominate the political attitudes of their children, or at least of their daughters.

Women are conservative

A generalisation that is by now almost a cliché and which appears more securely founded, at least in terms of the recent past, is that women are politically more conservative than men. Thus a standard comment of British electoral studies has been that women are more likely than men to vote for the Conservative Party (see, for instance, Blondel, 1965, p. 60). Indeed, they were blamed for the Conservatives' victory in 1970. By 1979 this gap had narrowed considerably to around three percentage points. And in the 1983 General Election according to the BBC/Gallup 1983 Election Survey, the pattern was actually reversed with around 45 per cent of men but 42 per cent of women voting for the Conservative Party (Norris, 1986a). It should be noted, however, that according to the survey used by Dunleavy and Husbands women, were still more likely to vote Conservative than men, which if nothing else indicates that these sex differences are becoming too marginal to be reliably identified by current survey methods (Husbands, 1986, p. 309).

Even in the past, observers may have exaggerated and misunderstood female Conservative voting in Britain. Not only did Rose estimate the gap between male and female Conservative voting in 1974 at only 2.5 per cent (Rose, 1974) but, as early as the 1951 and 1955 General Elections, it was pointed out that:

the associations between age and voting, and to a more limited extent, sex and voting, were attributable partly to the basic relationship between social class and voting, through the effects of differential death rates on the class structure of different age and sex groups . . . because until recently higher death rates occurred in the lower social groups and among males, so that the longer-lived tended to be women of the higher social strata (Milne and Mackenzie, 1958, pp. 59–60).

More recent studies confirm a strong relationship between female Conservatism and longevity; for instance, Baxter and Lansing, reworking the Butler and Stokes 1964 General Election data, find that generational differences amongst women were pronounced: while older women voted Conservative at about the same rate as men of their age, and while middle-aged (30 to 59) women were 8 percentage points ahead of men in their rate of Conservative voting, young women voted Labour at a rate (57 per cent) 11 points higher than young men. They conclude that women's conservatism in Britain is a 'generational artefact' (Baxter and Lansing, 1980, p. 157). However, as Evans points out, this leaves unresolved the question of whether older women's conservatism is a function simply of the life cycle or also a result of their assimiliation of partisan values at a time when the Labour Party was not yet perceived as a viable contender for national power (Evans, 1980). We should also note Francis and Peele's finding that in Britain, young women are no less conservative than older women on certain issues, such as the choice between tax cuts and maintaining levels of social expenditure (Francis and Peele, 1978).

Female conservatism has also been, and in many cases continues to be, a feature of voting behaviour in other West European nations. It is strongly associated with the presence of an influential Roman Catholic church; one author in fact suggests that women's vote prevented the communists coming to power in France, West Germany and Italy (Devaud, 1968). But, up to the 1970s, women were apparently more inclined than men to vote for conservative parties in every country for which information is available including not only Greece, Belgium, Switzerland and the Netherlands but also Sweden and Finland. This difference, the evidence suggests, is declining. Though in the 1978 French legislative elections, 48 per cent of women's vote but only 43 per cent of men's went to the conservative coalition parties, the UDF and RPR, this margin was smaller than the 10–12 per cent differential in the earlier years of the Fifth Republic. In West Germany's 1976 Bundestag elections, 47.6 per cent of men but 43.1 per cent of women voted for the socialist SPD, while 47.2 per cent of men but 48.8 per cent of women voted for the two conservative parties, the CDU and CSU – not an astounding difference. In Sweden, in respect of conservatism, 'surveys conducted during the 1970s found no discernible difference between men and women's voting behaviour' (Eduards, 1981, p. 223).

Already in 1974, Jaquette observed, in the context of United States politics, where in any case a conservative orientation is less easily equated (easier in the 1980s perhaps?) with support for Republicans or Democrats, from the existing evidence 'it is not clear that women are as conservative as their European counterparts' (Jaquette, 1974, p. xxii). More recently considerable interest has been focused on the emergence of a 'gender gap', with men more likely than women to vote Republican. At the 1980 Presidential election, polls indicated that 45 per cent of women supported Carter and 47 per cent Reagan while for men the percentages were 36 and 55. Exit polls for the 1984 election showed Reagan leading Mondale by 25 per cent among men but only 10 per cent among women. As Norris points out, this has stimulated politicians to find new ways of appealing to women voters, particularly since women make up over half the population and turn out to vote at equal rates with men. But it has also prompted debate as to why women should be less ready than men to vote for Reagan – is it because of his opposition to women's rights, his aggressive foreign policy or welfare cutbacks? Norris herself concludes that none of these explanations suffices on its own: 'Women are more liberal and men are more conservative across a wide range of issues (Norris, 1985a, p. 196).

Norderval (1985) suggests that there may also be a gender gap emerging in Scandinavian countries. In Canada, Vickers and Brodie (1981) argue that the Liberal and Conservative parties have again been difficult to distinguish in terms of a left–right spectrum, although at the time of the 1984 General Election, as under Reagan in the United States, differences were becoming clearer. By 1980 women were marginally more likely to vote Liberal and men Conservative while in 1984 the Conservative lead among men was

22 per cent but among women only 13 per cent (Norris, 1985a). Australian women are reported as giving greater electoral support than men to the conservative Liberal Party, however, though during the 1970s this tendency diminished.

In addition to electoral behaviour, women's patterns of party membership have also suggested political conservatism, as evident in figures for West European countries cited earlier. In Australia women form approximately one-half of the membership of the Liberal Party but one-quarter of Labour Party membership. The impression of female conservatism has recently been reinforced by the prominence of women's organisations in America's Moral Majority and by women's role in such bodies as SPUC (Society for the Protection of the Unborn Child).

Corresponding information for the developing world is somewhat scant, but data from Latin America lend support to the thesis of women's conservatism. Unusually, in Chile's 1970 and 1971 General Elections and in Argentina's 1965 General Election, women voted in separate booths and their votes were separately tallied. On each occasion women inclined rather more than men to the conservative parties, which were also the parties identified with the Roman Catholic church. Lewis does, however, point out that Argentinian women did not support parties of the far right (Lewis, 1971). In Chile and Brazil women figured prominently in demonstrations against Allende and the 'liberal' Goulart respectively. In Brazil the women were generally Catholic and middle-class, mobilised by appeals to their morality and warnings of the danger posed to family life by the imminent threat of 'communism'.

Despite the weight of evidence and inference I have cited, the generalisation of female conservatism requires careful qualification. In the first place, the differences between the sexes should not be exaggerated. Rarely does the differential between male and female support for conservative parties, as far as it has been recorded, exceed 10 per cent, and there is a widespread tendency for it to narrow and indeed as we have seen even to reverse in certain countries. Second it is commonly found that people's political attitudes become more conservative as they grow older, so that in countries such as France, West Germany, Australia or Britain, female conservatism has been shown as in part a function of women's greater longevity. In Argentina, Lewis finds that women in urban districts tend to vote on class lines while in the countryside they vote more conservatively than their class or status would dictate. This suggests that female conservatism will decline as the isolation of rural women breaks down (Lewis, 1971).

Not only does this evidence indicate that female conservatism is marginal and perhaps declining, but other findings actually run counter to the generalisation that women are politically conservative. Even when conservatism is simply taken to mean support for conservative political parties, particular studies can be cited of localities in Australia and in Belgium where women were found to give more support to the Socialist or Labour Parties than men (Goot and Reid, 1975). But counter-evidence can also be produced when conservatism is defined more broadly.

This raises the more fundamental objection to this generalisation: the concept of conservatism is too broad to be discriminating. If it is taken to connote right-wing political attitudes, it is demonstrably no more characteristic of women than of men. In Argentina, for instance, we noted that the female vote leant more than the male towards parties representing the status quo, but not towards the radical right. As Goot and Reid point out, poll data indicate that electoral supporters of the Poujadists in France, the Neo-Fascists in Italy, the National Socialists in Germany and the Ultras in Northern Ireland were disproportionately male. Perhaps it is more accurate to equate female conservatism with adherence to the established political order. In that case of course the established order could be a 'socialist' one; in so far as the concentration of Soviet women party workers in 'indoctrination' positions reflects their preference rather than more practical constraints, which is debatable, it would support such an interpretation (Moses, 1976). Even so, can this easily be squared with the observations cited earlier of women's protest potential, their participation in *ad hoc* and revolutionary politics? Possibly one could argue that, in some of these activities, women are protecting their own or their loved ones' interests, bound up in a traditional order. For instance, women engage in community action campaigns often to protest against deteriorating housing and neighbourhood conditions, At other times, this would be extremely difficult to maintain, and the very methods that women employ in *ad hoc* and protest politics do not indicate undue respect for established political institutions.

Even if we set aside such unconventional politics, the thesis of female conservatism may exaggerate the extent of women's positive commitment to conservative values. As we shall see, women have consistently been found to be less politically knowledgeable or involved than men and, most relevant to the present discussion, they have been reported as thinking less ideologically than men. In a reworking of the data collected for the Barnes and Kaase project, Jennings and Farah find that in all five of the nations under consideration (Austria, Britain, the Netherlands, the United States and West Germany), women are less likely than men to recognise, employ or understand concepts associated with the political left and right (Jennings and Farah, 1980).

Finally, as Evans reminds us, it is now widely recognised that individuals' political attitudes are difficult to identify and not necessarily internally consistent (Evans, 1980). Conservatism, it follows, does not exist subjectively as an integrated system of values and beliefs. Not surprisingly, women's attitudes to various political questions may not be consistent either with one another or with a standard conservative line. There is, as we shall see, considerable evidence in the Western democracies that women are more pacifist than men, an attitude not entirely consonant with orthodox conservatism. Evans further cites findings in Britain that women are 3 per cent more likely than men to believe that the police should be armed at public demonstrations but 4 per cent less likely to favour restoration of capital punishment, an indication of the complexity of women's political preferences (ibid., p. 219). Similarly Francis and Peele, using data collected by Butler and Stokes during the 1970 General Election, chart attitudinal differences between the sexes and between generations on a series of contemporary political issues. A complicated pattern emerges; they discover that while differences in the partisanship of the sexes decline steadily with successive generations, a parallel convergence is apparent in only three out of the six selected issues, those concerning the Labour Government's ability to control price increases, immigration and the seriousness of strikes. On the other hand, between younger men and women there is only modest convergence on attitudes to joining the European Community. Women at all ages are more likely than men to be critical of the influence of big business and younger women are, if anything, more inclined than older women to prefer tax cuts to social expenditure. The authors use these findings to argue that convergence of political attitudes between the sexes increases with the political immediacy of the issue, but they also demonstrate the absence of an internally logical relationship between the attitudes themselves (Francis and Peele, 1978).

The assertion that women are politically more conservative than men is acceptable only if these differences are recognised to be marginal and perhaps transitory. In any case we need to be clear what is meant by 'conservatism' in this context and to remember that a 'conservative' disposition can embrace a range of contradictory attitudes on specific issues.

Women personalise politics

Another frequent contention is that women are more candidate-oriented, as opposed to issue-oriented, than men; that is, they tend to personalise politics. The most famous cited example is female support for Eisenhower as American Presidential candidate in 1952 which, it is said, transformed his slim majority into a landslide victory. Again, however, the evidence to support this is inadequate. Indeed Shabad and Andersen (1979), after a careful examination of citations, conclude that it is drawn from a single source: Campbell *et al.*'s study of American voting behaviour, which in any case reported that sex differences in this regard were minimal (Campbell *et al.*, 1960). There is counter-evidence: Goot and Reid (1975) refer to a survey conducted in Canada specifically to discover whether Trudeau was especially attractive to women voters which indicated that he was not. Jones also cites an opinion poll taken in Japan in 1972 which found that women were actually less candidate-oriented than men (Jones, 1975).

Shabad and Andersen use data on the US Presidential elections from 1952 to 1976, some of which formed the basis of the Campbell *et al.* study, to pursue the question further. They reveal a small and diminishing difference in the sexes' tendency to appraise a candidate in terms of personality rather than issue or party consideration. Observing that the majority of both sexes stress personality considerations, they examine the responses that have been lumped together under this heading. They find that relatively few respondents, though slightly more women than men, are concerned with purely personal characteristics that have little political content, such as the candidates looks or family life. Instead, they are principally influenced by their perception of candidates' competence, followed closely by their capacity for leadership and trustworthiness (Shabad and Andersen, 1979).

Women are moralistic

Women's political participation has also been labelled moralistic. We saw that female suffrage was widely expected, either approvingly or disapprovingly, to introduce a new moralism into politics. Moreover, female conservatism has been associated, especially in Roman Catholic countries, with the influence of the Church. On *a priori* grounds female moralism in politics could be anticipated.

There is some evidence to support this. First, women have frequently been found to hold more pacifist views than men on the issues of war and nuclear arms. In America this has been documented by successive studies. Baxter and Lansing summarise research findings based on Presidential election surveys from 1952 to 1976 showing that 'women differ from men most strongly on issues that pertain to war and peace'. For example in 1952, 48 per cent of men but only 32 per cent of women approved of America's military involvement in Korea. In 1968, over half the men respondents but more than two-thirds of the women disapproved of intervention in Vietnam. Both the size of the sex differential and its constancy over time are remarkable. Baxter and Lansing find it is younger, better educated women who are most 'dovish', suggesting this tendency could increase (Baxter and Lansing, 1980, pp. 57–9). We have already noted women's prominent role in the British peace movement. In the summer of 1981 also thousands of European women marched to Brussels in a protest against the nuclear arms race organised by five Norwegian women's peace groups (*The Guardian*, 25 July 1981).

Tangentially related to the issue of nuclear weapons is that of nuclear power, though it is an ecological as much as a moral question. In the United States a Gallup poll found that, following the incident at Three Mile Island, 71 per cent of men but only 59 per cent of women were opposed to closing of all nuclear plants (Baxter and Lansing, 1980, p. 59). Nuclear power has become a central theme of Swedish electoral politics; in the referendum of March 1980, 46 per cent of women as against 31 per cent of men opposed it, though women's party preferences seem not to be affected by the issue (Eduards, 1981).

Women have also been depicted as more puritanical than men. This is in part the legacy of women's campaigns in the United States and Britain against prostitution and alcohol. Indeed the bootleggers of America's prohibition days were ironically much indebted to the exertions of the Women's Christian Temperance Union. In Sweden a referendum held in 1922 showed 59.1 per cent of men but only 41.5 per cent of women to be against prohibition. Rather more recently Gruberg cites surveys conducted during the 1950s in the American West and Midwest which 'showed a real divergence between the sexes on such issues as prohibition, legalised gambling and prostitution' (Gruberg, 1968, p. 13).

As an extension of this puritanism, and against the background of American women's involvement in the urban reform movement of the Progressive era, women have also been associated with 'reformism', in the sense of efforts to 'clean up' government and fight corruption. Lane in particular asserts this characteristic only to dismiss it, in a memorable phrase, as 'a bloodless love of the good' (Lane, 1959, p. 212).

One objection to the charge of women's political moralism is that, with the exception of their pacifism, this trait is insufficiently documented. But a second major objection must be to the assumptions that underlie it. How realistic is it to read disinterested moralism into these attitudes, in so far as they exist? For instance, 'many women voted for prohibition because drunken husbands were poor providers and physically abused women and children in the home. Thus it was not "moralism" but self-interest that determined their decision in some cases and social awareness in others' (Epstein, 1981, p. 134). Male critics often imply that women's pacifism is a function of ignorance and fear but it could reflect a greater realism about the human costs of war. Thirdly there is again the question of definitions. What is 'moralism'? By implication it contrasts unfavourably with a more profound and robust sense of 'morality'. But in so far as it does partake of the moral, would we really want a public politics entirely unencumbered by moral considerations?

Women are apolitical

This brings us to a more fundamental characterisation of female participation as essentially apolitical. In discussing generalisations about women's political behaviour so far, I have frequently pointed to inadequate or contradictory evidence. Nor is it unfair to suggest that some commentators have too readily leaped to conclusions congruent witn stereotypes of female personality and sex roles. They have exaggerated sex differences thus helping to perpetuate the folklore they defer to.

Of all the charges brought against women's political behaviour, apparently the most solidly founded is that they know less about politics, are less interested and less psychologically involved in it than men. Evidence can be cited from the United States, Britain, Australia, Canada, France, West Germany, Italy and Denmark amongst Western democracies. Thus Inglehart (1981), using data for eight countries from EEC surveys in the 1970s, found that women were consistently less interested in politics than men; almost half the female respondents said they never discussed politics at all. Even so she noted that these sex differences were less significant than variations between nationalities and people with different levels of education. More recently a Euro-Barometer survey conducted at the time of the 1984 elections to the European Parliament showed that women were both less knowledgeable about the Parliament and less inclined to express an opinion about it than men. Neither sex, however, evinced great interest and there has also been some narrowing of the gap between the sexes since 1977 (*Women of Europe*, 1984, Supplement No 21). For Eastern Europe, information is extremely thin and confined to Yugoslavia, Czechoslovakia and the Soviet Union; it suggests that, even in these countries, mass mobilisation has not eradicated a similar sex difference in levels of political interest (Wolchik, 1981). Less surprisingly, perhaps, such a difference is reported in India, and in a discussion of women's role in Ghana (Smock, 1977). To reinforce this conclusion we can refer again to the Verba *et al.* seven-nation survey of political participation; women were found to score consistently lower than men on political interest and psychological involvement, in Austria, India, Japan, the Netherlands, Nigeria, the United States (though here the differential was very small) and Yugoslavia (Verba *et al.*, 1978).

Yet even this generalisation requires qualification. A first point to stress is that most people are pretty apolitical, on a conventional understanding of what 'political' means. Second, in the United States and Britain the reported differences in the politicisation of the sexes are slight. Nor are differences elsewhere unchanging; on the contrary, surveys in Australia, Canada and France have shown the gap to be narrowing steadily. Sex differences in political interest are further reduced when intervening variables, in particular level of education, are accounted for.

Beyond these factual qualifications, there are questions about the underlying assumptions. It is not so much that the assumptions are sexist, at least not directly so. Rather politics has been conceptualised in a narrowly conventional fashion. Consequently measures designed to score political knowledge or involvement are excessively oriented towards this kind of politics. As Evans asks, 'Do the items of factual information about office holders etc., which are commonly used, in fact comprise the most salient basis for political understanding?' (Evans, 1980, p. 221). Women, I have shown, are not inevitably apolitical; they can get involved in politics when its concerns and mechanisms are accessible to them. It is probably true that women are less 'political', in a conventional sense, than men, but that is quite different from saying that they do not appreciate the political dimension in social life.

Women are politically superior

Although many commentators, including on occasion feminists (see, for instance, Iglitzin, 1974), conclude from the kind of information presented so far that women participate politically like inadequate men, suffering from 'insufficient masculinisation' (Jaquette, 1974, p. xviii), other feminists suggest or at least hint at an alternative interpretation according to which women's participation stems from a distinctive and superior motivation. This is part of a more general feminist argument that women are superior to men, either innately or because of the way they live, which I considered in the Introduction. This view is not to my knowledge systematically expounded anywhere in relation to women's political participation. It is useful to piece together the outline of such a position, drawing upon fragmented sources, and it runs as follows.

Women are firstly more percipient than men, seeing through the façade of conventional politics. Their own experience has shown them that politics, as presently practised, is about power. Moreover real political power is concentrated and little affected by apparently democratic processes of popular participation. Consequently women see less point than men in conventional political participation. Thus Amundsen suggests that one reason they vote less than men may be their rejection of the present political system (Amundsen, 1971, p. 142). Bourque and Grossholtz also speculate that women's tendency to rate their political efficacy, that is their ability to effect change through politics, lower than men's, and their evaluation of candidates on the basis of personality, in so far as it is proven, is evidence not of political immaturity but of a shrewd appraisal of the political system (Bourque and Grossholtz, 1974).

Secondly, women are more democratic than men; they eschew power as an end in itself. Their experience of male dominance has alerted them to the ways in which power can be abused. An emphasis on democracy is a particular feature of the women's liberation movement, but it has also been suggested that women, because of their own oppression are more sympathetic with the plight of the 'underdog' of whatever category.

A third observation, stemming from the previous two, is that women are more radical than men. They are more willing and more able to challenge existing political practices and concepts. Again this is primarily asserted in the context of women's liberation which has radicalised legitimate politics by bringing issues formerly considered non-political into the political arena and challenging prevailing definitions of the political. Cockburn also suggests that, in community politics, 'Women . . . in action tend to be intractable and uncompromising . . . to be unexpected, to think up new ways of doing things . . . Women are often total in their demands' (Cockburn, 1977, pp. 63–4). Bernard considers that women may have a special role to play in 'the task of restructuring the future' (Bernard, 1979, p. 283). She cites Boulding, another feminist, who describes women as living until now on the 'underside' of history. This experience, Boulding contends, provides women with 'a special resource. It is society's free fantasy space, its visioning pace, its bonding space. It is a space in which minds can learn to grapple with complexities that are destroying the overside' (Boulding, 1976, p. 789). The view that women are potentially more radical than men would find further support from the evidence of their participation in protest and revolutionary politics cited earlier.

Finally, women are more ethical and humane than men. In so far as they participate in conventional politics, they bring to it concern for ordinary human beings and for ethical standards of conduct. This was of course an argument used repeatedly by nineteenth-century suffragists, but today's feminists produce it too. Stoper and Johnson for instance quote Gloria Steinem's belief that women in politics can contribute 'by tempering the idea of manhood into something less aggressive and better suited to this crowded, post-atomic planet' (Stoper and Johnson, 1977, p. 195). Bernard holds that 'the contribution of women to general policy has actually tended to be altruistic, on the humane side and their contribution to political life benign' (Bernard, 1979, p. 282). Bourque and Gross-holtz suggest that if women evince little interest or expertise in specific policy areas it is because these areas do not really matter; on issues like peace and capital punishment, women do have definite and more humane opinions than men (Bourque and Grossholtz, 1974). As we have seen there are some grounds for this supposition, particularly for saying women are more pacifist than men. However it is not necessary to resort to biological explanations – women's role as the bearers of new life – as some feminists would advocate, to account for these sex differences. Not only rules of scholarship but political expediency warn against their exaggeration; as Stoper and Johnson point out, it could play into the hands of male politicians happy to confine women to traditionally 'feminine' political roles.

I must re-emphasise that such a case for women's political superiority has yet to be systematically advanced. Nor, in this form, would it appear much more tenable than the 'sexist' interpretations that it rejects. At the least, however, it is useful simply in pointing up the arbitrariness of many traditional readings of women's political behaviour and in providing an alternative paradigm.

The preceding paragraphs do not exhaust the catalogue of perceived characteristics. For instance, it has been suggested that women are more fickle in their political loyalties than men, but, as Goot and Reid point out, supporting evidence is thin. Of more interest and plausibility is the frequent assertion that women are more oriented towards local than national politics, a possibility whose implications are further considered in the following chapter.

The overall conclusion of this survey of evidence and argument must be that few dramatic differences exist between the two sexes' political attitudes at grass-roots level. Women do appear more conservative in certain respects, less knowledgeable about and interested in politics, at least conventional politics, and perhaps more moralistic. But these differences should not be exaggerated and in many contexts they dwindle to vanishing point.

Determinants of women's political behaviour

We must now ask how such distinctive features as have been uncovered in the scope and content of women's political participation can best be explained. It is interesting to note that even feminist explanations in political science emphasise characteristics of women themselves rather than relevant features of the political system. Moreover, these explanations differ not so much on the range of factors conditioning women's orientation to politics as on which is the most important. In the following discussion I shall distinguish broadly between relevant characteristics of women, on the one hand, and of politics on the other, although of course they are interdependent.

The effects of childhood socialisation

Beginning with women, which of their attributes most shape their political behaviour? Early studies tended to refer simultaneously to women's 'mentality of minors' (Duverger, 1955, p. 129), their immediate situation and their position within the structure of society, without attempting to unravel these strands. Later studies have sought to distinguish explicitly the effects of socialisation or sex-role stereotyping from those of factors variously labelled situational or structural. Since the theoretical frameworks of these studies do not entirely coincide, the terms 'situational' and 'structural' are not always used the same way and their usages overlap. All the same, they offer a useful framework for analysis.

Political socialisation has been defined as the 'interaction between the social system and an individual, whereby both predisposition for and skills relating to participation in the political sphere are internalised' (Flora and Lynn, 1974, p. 51). Those writers who emphasise the role of socialisation in forming women's political attitudes and aptitudes generally make two further assumptions. They assume that this political orientation arises within the context of already established sex roles and, secondly, that these more basic sex roles are principally instilled in childhood.

A classical exponent of this thesis is Greenstein. While he accepts that situational or structural factors may contribute to adult political attitudes, he finds the origins of these attitudes in childhood experience. In a much quoted passage, he writes:

The political differences between boys and girls do not seem to flow mainly from a rationalistic developmental sequence in which the girl learns 'politics is not for girls' hence 'I am not interested in politics'. Rather there is a much more subtle and complex process in which – through differential opportunities, rewards and punishments which vary by sex, and by identification with one or other parent – a sex identity is acquired. Among other things this learning process associates girls with the immediate environment and boys with the wider environment. Political responses, developing as they do relatively late in childhood, fall into the framework of already present nonpolitical orientations (Greenstein, 1965, p. 125).

To support his argument, he cites several earlier studies and his own research with New Haven schoolchildren, although in fact his own data indicate only small differences in political interest and knowledge between boys and girls. Two feminist political scientists have separately endorsed this view (though on other occasions they both appear to reject it). Iglitzin stresses the role of socialisation in creating apolitical women; she refers to her own survey, conducted in 1971–2, of a group of American 11-year-olds who, she found, were already instilled both with broad sex-role stereotypes and with sex-stereotypical orientations to specifically political issues (Iglitzin, 1974; Amundsen, 1971).

Other feminists object to this interpretation as faintly insulting but also inaccurate. It portrays women as passive subjects of a male-dominated culture and as retaining, long after they have ceased physically to be children, their childlike psychological dependence upon men. It thus implies that women lack the attributes of rationality, adulthood or aggression which, as we shall see, have been identified as prerequisites of successful political participation.

In so far as sex differences in political orientations *can* be demonstrated amongst schoolchildren, these could reflect the children's realistic anticipation of their future options. But, in any case, studies both in Britain and in the United States have failed to discover significant sex differences in schoolchildren's political attitudes. Dowse and Hughes found that, although such differences existed within their sample of Exeter pupils, they were marginal and rarely statistically significant (Dowse and Hughes, 1971). Similarly a study of schoolchildren in Illinois led its authors to conclude 'the political differences between boys and girls, uncovered in this study, are, in general, minor' (Orum *et al.*, 1974). Two further studies, as we shall see, have demonstrated the decisive influence upon adult political attitudes of factors other than childhood socialisation, while Welch concludes from her analysis of women's political participation that, when situational and structural factors are taken into account, the independent contribution of socialisation disappears altogether (Welch, 1977).

Rather than claiming the primacy of such early socialisation, we might therefore prefer to argue that it is decisive only under specific circumstances. For instance, Campbell *et al.* found that distinctive traditionally female political attitudes were most prevalent amongst the old and least educated women. This led them to suggest that childhood socialisation instilled more differentiated sex identities in the past than nowadays, so that women brought up in those times and unexposed through education to alternative values retained these stereotypical attitudes as they grew older (Campbell *et al.*, 1960). Similarly, in both Canada and Argentina, studies have shown that it is the women most sheltered by tradition – older, less educated, religious, rural – who show the greatest divergence in social and specifically political attitudes from their menfolk (Black and McGlen, 1979; Lewis, 1971). Even those who argue for the importance of situational factors paradoxically imply that, in the absence of such situational stimuli as employment outside the home or higher education, childhood socialisation has a more lasting effect upon political attitudes. Feminists could still question these modest claims for socialisation, explaining traditional female political behaviour as a rational response to women's adult situation. If women are apparently apolitical, it is because they lack a stake in politics, as conventionally understood, and if women are conservative it is because patriarchy has obliged them to acquire a stake in the traditional order. This raises the whole difficult question of the relationship between rationality and oppression that we first encountered in examining the causes of male dominance.

Immediate constraints of women's situation

An alternative interpretation of women's political behaviour emphasises the immediate situation that constrains and prompts them. According to this view, domestic and mothering responsibilities, that keep a woman housebound and out of the paid workforce, limit her interest and actual involvement in politics. She has less occasion to learn of and discuss political affairs and less time and freedom to undertake political work. Political scientists have long acknowledged these constraints even while preferring to stress the impact of socialisation. 'The sheer demands on a housewife and mother mean that she has little opportunity or need to gain politically relevant experience' (Lipset, 1963, p. 206). Campbell *et al.* also noted the negative associations between the presence of small children at home and women's voting turnout.

Further empirical support for this interpretation comes from several more recent studies, primarily in the United States. Pomper, in his survey of electoral behaviour in the United States, confirms the dampening impact on women's political participation of small children in the home (Pomper, 1975). Three other studies are centrally concerned with the effects of situational constraints on women's political behaviour. Andersen shows that the main increase in female political participation in the United States over the years 1952 to 1972 was amongst women employed outside the home (Andersen, 1975). Tedin *et al.* use sibling pairs to test for the influence of socialisation and situational factors on sex differences in political participation. They conclude that situational factors, such as college education, can over-ride the impact of childhood socialisation (Tedin *et al.*, 1977). Welch, using the same data as Andersen, provided by the Centre of Political Studies, tests for the role of socialisation, situational and structural factors. She controls for three kinds of situational factor: whether the respondent is employed outside the home, whether she is married and whether she has children at home. Employment outside the home, she confirms, is associated with a dramatic increase in political partici-pation, but she finds that the other two indicators have little independent impact (Welch, 1977). Mossuz-Lavau and Sineau's careful analysis of French 1978 survey data also lends some support for this view. Constructing their sample around four categories of respondent, women in paid employment, formerly employed women, housewives and men, they find little significant differences between them in reported electoral participations rates. Once it comes to more demanding forms of participation such as party membership or campaigning, women now or formerly in paid employment are more active than housewives. However, they also find that at every rung of the occupational ladder women are less politicised than their male counterparts, except within the most highly qualified cadres and that, other things being equal, younger women are more politicised than older (Mossuz-Lavau and Sineau, 1983). Lovenduski (1986a, p. 131) cites the finding of an unpublished paper by Carol Christy, using participation data for several European countries, that outside the United States the association between women's paid employment and poitical participation is weak and significantly affected by such intervening variables as education level and age.

If there remains some uncertainty as to the impact of paid employment on women's participation in conventional politics, its relationship with other forms of political participation is still less clear. Indeed, as we have seen, such studies as exist suggest that the women who take part in community action are predominantly housewives. It is argued that community politics addresses the kinds of issues with which women as housewives and mothers are most immediately concerned. In particular it is about consumption, and housewives are the front-line consumers, as shoppers and as recipients of state-provided services. As Wilson writes, in Britain 'The division of labour within the family usually means that it is women who go to the rent office, women who attempt to grapple with the schools, women who are interviewed by the social workers' (Wilson, 1977, p. 4). Similarly, in the United States, Weinbaum and Bridges argue that 'It is housewives' responsibility for nurturance on the one hand and the impossibilities of helping other human beings be healthy and creative within the constraints of the practice of the present system on the other, that create the incredible tensions of the practice of consumption work' and impel women into community politics (Weinbaum and Bridges, 1979, p. 199). At the same time the less institutionalised character of such politics makes it easier for housewives to participate.

To return however, to conventional political participation, Welch has reservations about the importance even of situational factors. Since her data show the effect of family responsibilities to be negligible and since she believes that women will increasingly take up outside employment, she concludes that, in the United States at least, situational factors are becoming increasingly less relevant. Possibly confirming this thesis, Flora and Lynn find that becoming a mother does not necessarily reduce a woman's rate of political participation, unless her consort refuses to share parental duties. The focus of her participation may however change to iussues relevant to her child and to local rather than national politics (Flora and Lynn, 1974).

Structural explanations

Welch argues that by now the most significant causes of the lingering differences between male and female rates of participation in the United States are structural. She understands this term quite narrowly. Some 'structuralists' refer to social structure as a set of power relations which largely determine individual behaviour. Heiskanen, for instance, maintains that the social structure, incorporating both class relations and patriarchy, positively discourages female political participation (Heiskanen, 1971). In a broad sense she is obviously right, but her analysis does not facilitate a more precise identification of the mechanisms through which structure, in this sense, operates. Welch, on the other hand, simply inquires how far women are over-represented in those sections of the population at large whose rates of political participation are particularly low, and for present purposes this approach seems most useful.

Nearly all studies seeking to explain sex differences in political participation stress the role of education. They find not only that women's participation increases with the level of their educational achievement, but that often amongst the most highly educated sex differences narrow to insignificance. By now, in the United States, sex differences amongst those with college education in rates of overall political participation are marginal, and in voting turnout entirely disappear. Though Baxter and Lansing report that in Britain education has less bearing on women's participation rates, in the Netherlands Verba *et al.* find that at higher educational levels sex differences in political activism diminish and women even outstrip men in voting rates (Verba *et al.*, 1978). An inverse relationship between such differences and women's educational achievement has also been found in Canada, in several Latin American countries and in India, where female voting turnout is highest in those states with the highest literacy rates. On the other hand, Bentzon finds that education makes no significant difference in Denmark (Bentzon, 1977). Verba *et al.* discover that while, in the countries studied, higher educational levels erode the sex differential in degrees of political concern, in Japan, Nigeria, Austria and India this does not spill over into rates of political activism.

Duverger, back in 1955, had raised the question of the relative impact of education and employment. He was convinced that education was the most decisive influence on women's political participation, arguing that 'economic independence has no more succeeded in banishing a general mentality born of a tradition dating back thousands of years than has the conquest of political rights' (Duverger, 1955, p. 152). The evidence, however, is contradictory. The finding that in the United States and Canada the first and most politicised employed women were the professionals, that is, presumably, the most highly educated, seems to confirm Duverger's thesis. Welch also shows that sex differences in political activism are minimal amongst college and even high school graduates who are unemployed but rather more significant amongst the less educated unemployed. But other studies indicate the relevance of both education and employment. It is tempting to conclude, therefore, with Jennings and Niemi, that the impact is cumulative (Jennings and Niemi, 1971).

The other major structural variable which appears to determine women's political participation is age. In the United States, sex differences in voting turnout are greatest among the elderly. Baxter and Lansing's analysis of the 1964 and 1970 General Election data in Britain reveals a more complicated relationship. The differential is greatest between men and women aged 65 and over, narrows between the ages of 50 and 65 is even marginally reversed in the age band 30 to 50, but opens up again below the age of 30 (Baxter and Lansing, 1980, p. 150). We may be able to explain this discrepancy first by attributing young women's low voting rate to their responsibility for infants and second by noting that, although the sex differential is minimal, for this age group in the United States this is primarily due to the low voting turnout of young men. Against this explanation, though, we have the finding of both Welch, and Flora and Lynn that motherhood does not depress political participation. Age, as we have seen, is also associated with variations in women's conservatism. The correlation, is revealed not only in voting behaviour and the results of opinion polls, but by the finding that young women are especially ready to contemplate protest politics (Barnes and Kaase, 1979).

The list of pertinent structural variables is still not exhausted.

Class, not surprisingly, has a bearing upon conservatism. For instance, we saw that Milne and Mackenzie explained British women voters' conservatism in the past in terms of the greater longevity of middle- and upper-class women. In Argentina, Lewis finds that upper-class women are more conservative than either upper-class men or lowe-class women (Lewis, 1971). Class, or caste, has also been shown to affect women's political participation rates in India, though in complex fashion. Survey data suggest that it is women from the middle tiers of the caste hierarchy who participate most. This may be because upper caste women are more confined to their homes, while the poorest low caste and outcaste women lack the resources, including free time and energy, required for political participation (Muni, 1979). Urbanisation, finally is found to vary negatively with women's conservatism in Chile, and positively with their political participation in Canada, the northern States of America and Yugoslavia.

There are, in sum, considerable grounds for arguing that the pattern of women's political participation increasingly reflects their overrepresentation in certain disadvantaged social categories that cut across sexual divisions. This does not, of course, explain why women should be disadvantaged in this way and whether their relative socio-economic position will automatically improve in the future, as Welch for instance appears to assume. But in any case this structural coincidence is for the moment not the whole story and we still need to refer to socialisation and situational factors as well.

Even so, if we conclude our analysis at this point, we present a one-sided and conservative picture. The brunt of the responsibility for these sex differences (as far as they exist) falls upon women. Moreover, as Hernes and Voje suggest, such an explanation creates future expectations which in turn prolong these differences (Hernes and Voje, 1980). For we ignore the positive deterrents implied by political systems and institutions themselves. The more specific and crucial impact of these deterrents on women's penetration of political élites is the subject of the following chapter. But the present chapter remains incomplete without some indication of political constraints upon women's grass-roots participation.

The first point to be made is a general one, but still important. Politics, in the sense we have used it in this chapter, is a public activity. In communities where there is no real distinction between private and public, between the life of the family and a transcending community, politics as a distinctively conscious activity of decision-making on behalf of the community is likely to be at a minimum. As politics has emerged as an aspect of social organisation, so has some kind of demarcation between the private, nonpolitical sphere and the public. I have already discussed the patriarchal assignation of women to the private or domestic sphere. The most systematic attempt to tie this in with women's political participation in contemporary Britain is provided by Stacey and Price.

They describe how, in the feudal era, the distinction between personal and public power was negligible; feudal ladies like their lords, Queens like Kings, ruled households coterminous with their fiefdoms or kingdoms. Though from the twelfth century a distinct public sphere, with an impersonal machinery of government, was developing, contraction and insulation of the private sphere was gradual. Stacey and Price follow Weber in ascribing to the growth of nineteenth-century capitalism the crystallisation of an emerging public domain of bureaucracy, industry and commerce. The political counterpart of this process was assertion of new liberal-democratic norms of freely elected government directing an impartial bureaucracy, while this ideal was never fully realised, its partial implementation greatly impeded the exercise of private power in public politics; political office was increasingly a function of merit.

Initially, therefore, women's exclusion from politics was accentuated, since they were restricted to a narrow and powerless private sphere. However, the logical corollary of a politics based on public merit rather than on ascription was eventually perceived to be the admission of women, on a basis of formal equality with men, into the political arena. And so it might be supposed that in the longer run the process of political institutionalisation has benefited women. But Stacey and Price argue that such formal rights are of little use to women without corresponding changes in family structure and the ideology that legitimates it. Women in practice remain tethered by their domestic responsibilities and the attitudes associated with them, unable to compete on equal terms with men in the public political world (Stacey and Price, 1981).

What, following Stacey and Price, I am suggesting is that, leaving aside questions of the character of specific political institutions, their very location within a non-domestic sphere makes participation more difficult for women than for men. This obstacle, paradoxically, increases, assuming that family roles remain largely unchanged, in societies with highly differentiated processes for public participation. Consequently, women have many ways of exercising informal political influence when politics is less institutionalised and may prefer, in more institutionalised political systems, to participate in *ad hoc* or even protest politics.

There are further specific aspects of contemporary politics that positively deter women. Most blatant but, at grass-roots level, increasingly unusual are actual legal barriers. Rarely are women now denied the vote, as women. But other voting qualifications can especially disadvantage them, as for instance the literacy requirement in Brazil and Peru.

More significant is the role of political institutions themselves in discouraging, or indeed encouraging, women's political participation. Discouragement may be direct as in Egypt where in the mid-1970s it was reported to be almost impossible for women to join the ruling party in rural areas (Smock and Yousseff, 1977). Or it may be indirect as in West Germany where Christy (1985) suggests that one reason why sex differences in party membership rates actually *increased* in the 1970s was that the Social Democratic Party was recruiting growing numbers of men through the labour unions. At the same time political parties have sometimes gone out of their way to recruit women, as for instance France's Socialist Party from the late 1970s (Bashvekin, 1985). In Guinea, according to Little, Sekou Touré encouraged women to join the PDG (Parti Démocratique de Guinée) because at the outset his party needed the active support of underprivileged groups, who had most to gain from the policy changes he was promising. He may also have felt it wise to appeal to social categories, like women, which cut across divisive ethnic loyalties (Little, 1973). In many other instances, such as Nkrumah's Convention People's Party in Ghana, and in Malaya's United Malays National Organisation, women have been vigorously recruited, at least into the women's sections, primarily as a means of mobilising women's vote at election time (Manderson, 1977). A party, too, may devote particular energy to the recruitment of women members at specific times, as for instance in the recruitment drives of the Soviet Communist Party in the 1920s, during the Second World War and from the mid-1960s onwards (Lapidus, 1978).

Beyond such deliberate policies, political institutions can be uninviting to women. Simply because they have been until recently exclusively male, because men still dominate their leadership positions, women are discouraged. Then also male dominance tends to generate a 'masculine' style and atmosphere. Political scientists often specify the behaviour traits, not commonly associated with women, that effective political participation in contemporary democratic politics requires. Sometimes the activist is depicted as rational in the sense of being able logically to relate ends and means. The stereotypical woman of course is not rational, in this sense, but emotional, at best intuitive. Alternatively the activist is expected to be adult and responsible, in contrast to women's alleged dependence and immaturity. Finally a less idealistic version of democratic politics requires the participant to be competitive and aggressive, again the opposite of women's supposed passivity. Of these three attributes – rationality, responsibility and aggressiveness – it is the third which feminists (including myself) may be most prepared to accept as a prerequisite for effective participation in contemporary politics and to agree is a trait currently exhibited less by women than by men. Moreover, within male-dominated political institutions, women may be facing not only a competitive style, but also male hostility directed specifically, if half-consciously, at them as intruders.

Then again, such institutions will function in ways practically convenient to the men who established and run them. Considerations such as where, when and how often meetings are held will be more serious deterrents to élite political participation but may also constrain participation at grass-roots level.

Finally, it is frequently suggested that politics, as presently practised, focuses on issues that are peripheral to women's interests; women lack a 'stake' in the subject matter of conventional politics (see, for instance, Lane, 1959). This argument can only be accepted with reservations. Issues such as defence, foreign policy and economic policy clearly are of urgent relevance to men and women alike. What is more true is that conventional politics tends to neglect or to label as 'administrative', 'social' or 'cultural', issues that are of most immediate concern to many women, such as nursery school provision, or standards of housing or education. This is one reason, we have seen, for women's participation in community action.

The pattern of women's political participation cannot, in conclusion, simply be explained by reference to their personality, practical situation or even distribution within the social system. Features of conventional politics themselves act as deterrents. It is in this context that the appeal of women's associations, of 'unconventional' political participation and, as we shall see, in Chapter 5, of women's liberation, becomes so easy to understand.

This discussion has been primarily concerned with explaining the differences in male and female political participation and so I have said little about the impact of second-wave feminism itself. The extent to which feminist values have been absorbed and their interaction with other forces for change are not easily gauged, but undoubtedly feminism has contributed from the late 1960s to the erosion of sex differences at the levels of political participation considered in this chapter. Surveys in European countries and the United States indicate growing social acceptance of women's political participation. Feminists have helped to bring issues of particular salience on to the political agenda while male politicians have more consistently and assiduously courted the women's vote in taking up at least some of these issues and appearing more welcoming to female activism. The impact of feminism varies from country to country and cannot be assumed to be irreversible but it has helped to modify women's political attitudes and the institutional context of public politics. How far it has thereby enhanced women's political power or changed policy are questions to be taken up by later chapters.

3
Women in political élites

If women's political behaviour increasingly resembles men's at the grassroots, differences remain stark further up the ladder. Women are still grossly under-represented within those élites, where by definition political power is concentrated. Why should this be so and, from a feminist viewpoint, does it matter?

One problem in attempting to answer these questions is again bias in the literature (see, for instance, Carroll's critique, 1979). But two further difficulties arise. One is conceptual: how is political power distributed between different élite institutions and positions? Without knowing this, it is difficult to evaluate and compare women's political achievements. It is often suggested that women's importance declines the nearer to the real locus of political power one goes.

This is allied with a further problem, that of the data. Until the 1970s, information about women in political élites was hard to come by. As Bourque and Grossholtz note, the 'classical "élite studies" assume that those élites will be men and seem little concerned to investigate the few women who do appear' (1974, p. 252). Since then extensive data have been gathered on the numbers, backgrounds and roles of women legislators, primarily in Britain and the United States, but coverage of other aspects of women's participation in élite politics still remains fragmentary. Yet in terms of political power, legislatures may be no more, or even less, important than, say, political bureaucracies.

A minority presence

There have always been individual women who have wielded vast political power. They have included Cleopatra, Queen Elizabeth

95

the First, Catherine the Great of Russia, the warrior–saint Joan of Arc and Louis XV's mistress, Madame de Pompadour. In more recent times a succession of women have emerged at the political helm of their countries: Eva Perón, Golda Meir, Sirimavo Bandaranaike, Indira Gandhi, Margaret Thatcher, Cory Aquino and Norway's Grö Harlem Bruntland. Nor can their achievement be explained simply by their family connections; in this respect the record of Mrs Meir and Mrs Thatcher is especially remarkable. But the brilliance of these few stars should not blind us to the near absence of other women from the political firmament.

It is generally recognised that women form a tiny minority within political élites. So obvious is this that a detailed enumeration would be superfluous, the more so since the statistics date so rapidly. A brief survey is necessary, however, just to emphasise the scale of women's under-representation. It also shows the range of variation, and possible direction of future change.

We can usefully distinguish between different institutional arenas of political participation. First are the institutions that form a channel of 'numerical representation' – that is, representation on the basis of 'one person, one vote' – parties and representative legislatures. Second are the agencies of interest representation and third the institutions of political administration: these two are in many parts of the world increasingly fused together in what could be called a 'corporate' system of participation. A fourth institutional arena for political participation, especially important in the United States, is the judiciary. Less formally integrated into the political system are the communications media. Finally, political influence is wielded outside these through informal and direct means.

National legislatures

Studies of women in political élites have hitherto centred excessively on their participation in the institutions of numerical representation, and particularly their role in legislatures. Women's under-representation in national legislatures is extensively documented and a summary of the latest information available is presented in Table 3.1. The British General Election of June 1983 produced 23 women Members of Parliament or 3.6 per cent. This was only slightly more than the 19 women or 3 per cent elected in 1979. And indeed the high point of female representation – 29

Table 3.1 Women's representation in national legislatures or equivalent bodies

Country	Institution	Total members	Women members	Women as percentage of total	Year	Source
Albania	Central Committee	—	—	15.4	1971	Wolchik, 1981
Algeria	National Popular Assembly	260	10	2.6	1979	Ainad-Tabet, 1980
Argentina	—	—	—	2.0	1975	Katzenstein, 1978
Australia	House of Representatives	148	8	5.4	1986 (foll. 1983 election)	Australian High Commission
Austria	Lower House			10.0	1981	Castles, 1981
Belgium	Lower House	212	16	7.5	1986 (foll. 1985 election)	Belgian Embassy
Brazil	Lower House	479		0.1	1986	Brazilian Embassy
Bulgaria	Central Committee			10.2	1976	Jancar, 1978
Canada	House of Commons	282	27	9.6	1986 (foll. 1984 election)	Canadian High Commission
China	Central Committee			10.0	1977	Katzenstein, 1978
Colombia	—			3.0	1975	Katzenstein, 1978
Costa Rica	—	57	3	5.3	1979	Aviel, 1981
Cyprus				2.8	1981	Mossus-Lavau and Sineau, 1984

Country	Institution	Total members	Women members	Women as percentage of total	Year	Source
Czechoslovakia	Central Committee			15.0	1979	Wolchik, 1981
Denmark				24.0	1985 (foll. 1981 election)	Skard and Haavio-Mannila 1985b
Egypt	—			2.0	1975	Katzenstein, 1978
El Salvador	—			3.0	1975	Katzenstein, 1978
Finland	Parliament			31.0	1985 (foll. 1983 elections)	Skard and Haavio-Mannila, 1985b
France	National Assembly	577	32	5.5	1986 (foll. March elections)	French Embassy
German, E.	Central Committee			13.0	1981	Lovenduski, 1986a
Germany, W.	Bundestag			10.0	1984	Vallance and Davies, 1986
Greece	Parliament			4.0	1984	Vallance and Davies, 1986
Guatemala				2.0	1975	Katzenstein, 1978
Guinea				27.0	1975	Katzenstein, 1978
Hungary	Central Committee			12.0	1976	Wolchik, 1981
Iceland				15.0	1985 (foll. 1983 election)	Skard and Haavio-Mannila, 1985b

Country	Chamber	Seats	Women	%	Date	Source
India	Lok Sabha	542	36	6.6	1986 (foll. 1984 election)	India Today January 1985
Iran	Majlis	270	2	0.7	1980	The Guardian 7 July 1980
Ireland	Dail	166	14	8.0	1987 (foll. Feb election)	
Israel	Knesset	120	10	8.3	1986 (foll. 1984 election)	Israeli Embassy
Italy				8.0	1984	Vallance and Davies, 1986
Japan	House of Representatives	512	7	1.4	1986	Japanese Embassy
Lebanon				0	1973	Katzenstein, 1978
Liechtenstein	Landtag	15	1	6.7	1986	Swiss Embassy
Luxemburg				14.0	1984	Vallance and Davies, 1986
Mexico				8.0	1975	Katzenstein, 1978
Netherlands				19.0	1984	Vallance and Davies, 1986
New Zealand		95	12	12.6	1986 (foll. 1984 election)	New Zealand High Commission
Norway	Storting			35.0	1986 (foll. 1985 election)	Norwegian Embassy

Country	Institution	Total members	Women members	Women as percentage of total	Year	Source
Panama		505	0	0	1979	Aviel, 1981
Paraguay				7.0	1975	Katzenstein, 1978
Peru		100	2	2.0	1978	Aviel, 1981
Poland	Central Committee			8.0	1976	Wolchik, 1981
Portugal				8.0	1986 (foll. 1983 election)	Lovenduski, 1986a
Romania	Central Committee			9.1	1976	Wolchik, 1981
Soviet Union	Central Committee			3.8	1981	
Spain	Cortes			5.0	1982	
Sri Lanka	State Assembly		4	2.4	1977	Kearney, 1981
Sudan				5.0	1973	Katzenstein, 1978
Sweden				28.0	1986 (foll. 1985 election)	Swedish Embassy
Switzerland				11.0	1984 (foll. 1983 election)	Mossuz-Lavau and Sineau, 1984
Syria				4.0	1973	Katzenstein, 1978
Tunisia				4.0	1973	Katzenstein, 1978
Turkey				3.0	1984 (foll. 1983 election)	Mossuz-Lavau and Sineau, 1984

Country	Chamber	Total	Women	%	Year
UK	House of Commons	635	28	4.3	1987
US	House of Representatives	435	23	5.0	1986 (foll. mid-term election)
Venezuela	—	205	11	5.4	1979

Aviel, 1981

women MPs – was achieved in 1964 following Labour's victory in the October General Election. Since the 1983 elections, five more women have joined the House through by-elections, bringing the total by March 1987 to 28. In the House of Lords, in 1979, there were 39 women out of a total 303 life peers (13 per cent) and seventeen peeresses in their own right, that is less than 2 per cent of hereditary peers (Stacey and Price, 1981, p. 149).

Following the mid-term Congressional elections of November 1986, there are now 23 women in the US House of Representatives (5.3 per cent). This marks no increase at all on the number elected in 1984, which was in turn only slightly up on the preceding, ninety-eighth, session, with 21 women. Before that, in the ninety-seventh session there were 19 and in the previous two sessions 18. Nor had there been a steady increase from the early 1960s. In the eighty-seventh session, 1961–2, 17 women were elected to the House but thereafter their numbers fell precipitately, and only began to pick up again in the 1970s. Moreover in the Senate, America's powerful upper chamber, the number of women after the 1984 and 1986 elections remained at two, and the Senate has only ever admitted a total of 14 women members. All in all the scale of female representation in the national legislatures of Britain and US, where second-wave feminism has been so vigorous and in contrast to the steady increase elsewhere, is quite remarkable.

Women's legislative presence in the old Commonwealth countries was similarly sparse until recently. In 1980 they formed less than 5 per cent of Canada's lower house, 4.3 per cent of New Zealand's legislature and in Australia there was not one woman in the House of Representatives. However, following the federal elections of 1984 there were 27 women members (9.6 per cent) in Canada's House of Commons, while Australia's last federal elections in 1983 brought eight women (5.4 per cent) to the House of Representatives. In addition women make up nearly one-fifth of the Australian Senate. Following the snap General Election in New Zealand in 1984, the numbers of women in the national legislature went up to 12 (or 12.6 per cent).

Britain aside, in Western Europe women do least well, as might be expected, in those countries that only recently adopted more democratic forms of government. In 1984 they were 4 per cent of national legislators in Greece, 5 per cent in Spain though more impressively 8 per cent in Portugal. Given what has been said of the strength of traditional Catholic values in the Republic of Ireland it may also seem somewhat surprising that after the November 1982 General Election, women were over 8 per cent of Dail (lower house) members, though this represented a jump from previous lower levels. In France and Italy women's parliamentary representation has been erratic. From just over 4 per cent in 1978, women rose to 6 per cent of French deputies in 1982 but following the last General Election in 1986 are back at 5.5 per cent (32 deputies). In Italy female membership of the House of Representatives soared to 16 per cent in 1980 but fell back to 8 per cent in 1984. In West Germany, where women's representation has grown steadily but slowly, by 1984 they formed 10 per cent of Bundestag members. The increase has been more dramatic in the Netherlands, 19 per cent by 1984. But of course the most sensational increases have been in Scandinavia, with women's share of legislative seats reaching 24 per cent in Denmark after the 1981 General Election, 28 per cent in Sweden after elections in 1982 (it remained at 28 following the 1985 General Election), 31 per cent in Finland following the 1983 General Election, and 35 per cent after the 1985 elections in Norway's Storting.

In communist countries, women's representation in the national, or federal, assembly is, comparatively speaking quite respectable: for instance, 31 per cent of the Russian Supreme Soviet, before the 1979 elections, were women. Few Western political scientists dispute, however, that the independent legislative influence of the Supreme Soviet is marginal. Revealingly, Jancar reports that, while the powers of Yugoslavia's federal assembly were enhanced from 1953 to 1970, 'the participation of women showed no significant increase' (Jancar, 1978, p. 91). In the Central Committee of the Communist Party the proportion of women members is predictably low. In 1980 it was only 3.3 per cent in the Soviet Union, though Wolchik's data for 1976 indicate that in other East European states it was somewhat higher, rising to 12 per cent in Hungary, 15 per cent in Czechoslovakia and, though precise figures are not available, still higher in Albania and East Germany (Wolchik, 1981). The corresponding percentages for Cuba and China were 8.9 per cent and 10 per cent respectively.

It is not surprising to find that the numbers of female legislators are very small in Third World countries, though it is also more difficult to get relevant information. India is something of an exception. Following the 1980 General Election, women members constituted 5 per cent of the Lok Sabha (lower house) and after the last General Election in December 1984 there were 36 women MPs or 6.6 per cent. On the other hand, in Sri Lanka, the high point of women's representation in the State Assembly was in 1970, when there were six women MPs, constituting 3.2 per cent (Kearney, 1981).

Women's legislative presence is still lower in many Latin American and Middle Eastern countries where, in any case, most legislatures lead a precarious and constrained existence. Chaney notes that in the early 1970s 'Before the recent flurry of coups, 55 women served in the lower houses and eight in senates of the 21 American republics. This is about 2 per cent of the total' (Chaney, 1979, p. 99). After the 1985 federal elections in Brazil, less than 1 per cent of the new Representatives were women, suggesting that the present trend towards redemocratisation in Latin America will not necessarily bring any rapid changes in the recruitment of women legislators. Two countries where women have fared better are Costa Rica (5.3 per cent in 1979) and Venezuela (5.4 per cent in the same year), which Aviel attributes in part to their more genuinely competitive party systems.

Even these figures do not fully reveal the quantitative limits of women's legislative role. Most available evidence shows the rate of *turnover* of women legislators to be proportionately higher than for their male counterparts. As we shall see, this may reflect, as in Britain, a preference for male candidates in safe seats or, as in the Soviet Union, the frequently symbolic reasons for including token women on the official slate of candidates. In either case women legislators appear more dispensable.

It might be tempting to suggest that women do better in upper than lower chambers. Figures provided by Mossuz-Lavau and Sineau (1984) indicate this is so for instance in the Netherlands, Austria and Belgium. In Ireland, too women have had a consistently higher share of seats in the Seanad than in the Dail – 10 per cent in 1986 – and Australia provides an even more striking instance. However, this does not hold for France, Italy, West Germany or Spain, amongst others, and most notably in the United States. Nor does there appear to be a simple inverse relationship between the relative power of the upper house and the proportion of women members.

There is, on the other hand, some tendency, at least at local if not at regional level, for the rate of female representation to increase in lower-tier assemblies. For instance, by 1986 14.8 per cent of state legislators in the United States were women (and this represented a threefold increase over the previous 15 years). It has also been easier for women to enter provincial than federal assemblies in the past in Australia and Canada. Wolchik suggests a similar pattern in Central Committee membership in Czechoslovakia (Wolchik, 1981) and it is marked in the composition of popularly elected councils in Eastern Europe (Jancar, 1978). As against this, in 1979 female representation in the West German *Länder* was 8.5 per cent, roughly the same as in the Bundestag, and in the provincial assemblies of the Netherlands at 16 per cent was slightly less than in the National Parliament. In India, too, women's representation in both the Lok Sabha and the State Assemblies has hovered around 5 per cent (Katzenstein, 1978).

At local level, the tendency for greater female representation is somewhat clearer. By 1983 women were 14.4 per cent of county councillors in England and Wales, 11.1 per cent of regional councillors in Scotland and 7.9 per cent of Northern Ireland district councillors (Lovenduski, 1986a). In the United States by 1984 women were 8 per cent of county board commissioners (a considerable jump from 3 per cent in 1977) and by 1985 were 14 per cent of members of municipal and township governing boards (note: figures not available for six states). There were women mayors in four of the 100 largest cities. Without giving specific figures, Vickers and Brodie note the relatively high percentage of women elected to municipal councils in Canada; this is partly, they suggest, because municipal politics is non-partisan and therefore not seen as a stepping stone to higher political office (Vickers and Brodie, 1981). Similarly in 1974, women held 13.3 per cent of local council seats in New Zealand (Halligan and Harris, 1977). Following local elections in 1983, women were 14 per cent of the membership of the French Conseils Municipaux, though this represented a recent increase and stood in contrast to the 3.8 per cent of female membership of the Departments' Conseils Généraux. In West Germany by 1983 women were 13 per cent of all local government councillors (Lovenduski, 1986a). Since levels of female representation in the Nordic parliaments are already so high there is perhaps less scope for local councils to exceed them. In Sweden women were 31 per cent of county councillors and 29 per cent of local councillors in 1982, while in Norway by 1984 they were one-third of county councillors though only 24 per cent of local councillors.

The rate of female representation is also higher in local than in national assemblies in most East European countries, excepting Yugoslavia; by the early 1980s it was running at over 40 per cent in East Germany. Chaney reports that in 1967 women were 4.7 per cent of municipal councillors in Peru and 7.8 per cent in Chile (Chaney, 1979, p. 104). Even in Brazil where in 1975 there was only one woman in the national legislature, 60 women mayors were elected between 1972 and 1976, though these were in the economically most backward regions and at a time when the powers of local government had been heavily circumscribed (Blay, 1979).

In the Republic of Ireland, however, despite high feminist hopes before the last local elections in June 1985, the results were only a marginal increase of women county councillors to 7.7 per cent and an actual drop in woman county borough councillors from 13 to 11.3 per cent (Randall and Smyth, forthcoming). In Finland, Italy as well at least on data for the 1970s, Sri Lanka and Japan, women do rather worse as local than as national representatives. The concentration of female representation at local level cannot therefore be regarded as an iron law, more a rule of thumb.

It is hardly necessary to add that women councillors tend not to be recruited in proportion to their numbers to leading council roles. By 1983 in Britain, they held 12.2 per cent of Committee chairs in the Shire counties, 5.7 per cent in Metropolitan Counties and one chair in the GLC. In France after the 1983 local elections women were still less than 4 per cent of maires (Lovenduski, 1986a). Even in the Nordic countries, 'women are almost totally excluded from the most senior positions in the local government system . . . – including the office of mayor, municipal director and chairpersons of councils, boards and committees. At the end of the 1970s and the beginning of the 1980s, the number of women in these posts ranged from 0 to 6 per cent' (Sinkonnen, 1985, p. 86). Furthermore, in a pattern we shall repeatedly observe, women even in Nordic countries have been disproportionately channelled into those committees dealing with education, housing, social services, childcare, health, that is fields that could be depicted as an extension of women's traditional concerns and as opposed to finance, employment, transport, planning and building.

Women in the European Parliament

Some mention should be made here of women's role in the EEC Parliament, now embracing 12 nations. As Vallance and Davies (1986) note, since direct elections were introduced in 1979, it has included proportionately more women than the constituent national parliaments. In 1979 they formed 16 per cent and in 1984 17.3 per cent of European Parliamentarians. They tended moreover to be promoted in proportion to their numbers, though to less prestigious senior posts or typically feminine areas of concern. One reason for this 'surprise' as Mossuz-Lavau and Sineau (1984) describe it, must be that the European Parliament as yet lacks legislative powers. None the less a relatively strong female presence at Strasbourg has been helpful to the feminist cause as we shall see.

Political parties

Women's penetration of national and local assemblies is in turn largely determined by their position within the main political parties. As we have seen they are under-represented in parties' general membership, but this alone cannot account for the small numbers of women in high party office. In Britain according to available information they have not exceeded 11 per cent of Labour Party Annual Conference delegates and in 1985, and again in 1986, accounted for only 8 of the 29 members of the National Executive. Although 38 per cent of delegates to the Conservative Party Annual Conference in 1980 were women, this body lacks the policy-making powers of its Labour Party counterpart and during the 1970s female representation in the National Union's Executive Committee remaine around 20 per cent (Hills, 1981a). There are reportedly 13 women in the 21 strong Executive Committee of the Green (formerly Ecological) Party (*The Guardian*, 18 November 1985) but this is hardly a route to the top. In the United States though equal representation of the sexes is mandatory in the National Committee and most state committees of the two main parties, often the women selected have lacked an independent power base in the party and their role has been symbolic. Following the introduction of the 'McGovern' rules, and the pressure from organisations such as the National Women's Political Caucus, representation of women at the Democratic Party Convention leaped to nearly 40 per cent in 1972. By 1976 it had fallen back to 33.7 per cent, however, while the corresponding rate for the Republican Party was 31.5 per cent (Lynn, 1979, p. 414). However, one consequence of the 'gender gap' alarm was that in 1984 nearly half of all Democratic Convention delegates and 44 per cent of the Republican equivalent were women.

A proportionate decrease in female representation as one ascends the party hierarchy is evident in all other Western democracies, though not every party, for which information is available. In 1981 Lovenduski and Hills (1981a, p. 527) commented 'Ironically women's higher proportionate memberships of right-wing parties are not normally reflected at the level of party office holding' and it remains true that conservative parties do not promote women at the same rate as men. Parties on the left and, in Scandinavia also parties of the centre, are much more willing to advance women. Nowadays several such parties recruit women to leading positions in proportion to and even exceptionally in proportions greater than their share of party membership. Thus by 1982 in France, women were only 8 per cent of the membership of the Executive Board of the Gaullist RPR though 43 per cent of its membership, while they formed 15 per cent of Executive Bureau members but only 21 per cent of the general membership of the Socialist Party. In 1983 there was only one woman in the Executive Board of Italy's Christian Democratic Party and none in the powerful party secretariat although women constituted 40 per cent of the party membership at large. Similarly in Spain, by 1982, women were approximately 35 per cent of the membership of the conservative party (AP) but 13 per cent of its National Executive; on the other hand they were 9 per cent of Socialist Party (PSOE) membership but one eighth, actually a higher proportion, of its Federal Executive Commission (Threlfall, cited by Mossuz-Lavau and Sineau, 1984). Once more it is the Scandinavian countries, and notably Norway and Sweden, which lead the field. By 1982 the proportion of women in the Executive Committee of the Norwegian Labour Party (40 per cent) equalled their party membership rates while in the Centre and Liberal Parties they were over-represented in the leadership, with 33 per cent of membership and 45 per cent of Executive Board places in the Centre Party and 42 per cent of membership, 56 per cent of Executive places in the Liberal Party.

likewise in Sweden, women's share of executive positions matched their share of membership in the Social Democratic Party (30 per cent) and the Liberal Party (44–45 per cent). But even in these countries, though the 'contagion effect' of rising levels of female leadership has spilled over from parties of the left to those in the centre, women remain at a disadvantage in conservative parties. In 1982 they were 40–45 per cent of Norwegian Conservative Party membership but 19 per cent of its Executive Board, and the corresponding figures for Sweden were 41 per cent and 30 per cent (Norderval, 1985).

If women remain proportionately under-represented in the party leaderships of more 'developed' countries, there has none the less been a steady tendency for their share to grow over the last two decades. That under-representation is probably much greater in Third World countries, though as already noted relevant information is scarce. Aviel points out that in Latin America most parties segregate women into separate sections and though women may, as in Mexico, be present on the national executive committee, they are generally there in virtue of their responsibility for the women's sections and women's programmes (Aviel, 1981). During the struggle for national independence in Vietnam, large numbers of women joined the Vietnamese Communist Party and some achieved leadership positions, but with demobilisation in 1975, party cards were called in and in the subsequent redesignation of cadres, men were given preference. All of this is not to deny that a number of women have recently emerged as party leaders: in Bangladesh Sheikh Hasina Wajed of the Awami League and Begum Khaled Zia, leading a seven-party opposition alliance, in Pakistan Benazir Bhutto of the Pakistan People's Party, in Turkey the wife of the former Prime Minister Ecevit leading the Social Democratic Party are examples. The reasons for their pre-eminence will be considered later but they rarely signify a general increase in women's leadership roles.

National governments

At the apex of the representational hierarchy, within national governments, women often virtually disappear. Britain has never had more than two female Cabinet ministers at one time and under

Mrs Thatcher, since 1979, there has been no woman member of the Cabinet with the important exception of herself. In the United States women have fared rather better. Carter appointed Juanita Krebs as Secretary of Commerce and Patricia Roberts as Secretary of Housing and Urban Development in 1977, a total of two out of eleven Cabinet appointments. Following his resounding electoral victory in November 1980, Reagan's first Cabinet contained no women at all but by 1983 he had appointed Elisabeth Dole as Secretary of Transport and Margaret Heckler as Secretary of Health and Human Resources.

In other Western democracies there have been few women Cabinet ministers, though their numbers have grown in recent years. For example, by 1980 Canada had seen a total of six, four of whom were appointed after 1972 (Vickers and Brodie, 1981). Two of the 20-strong Cabinet formed in New Zealand after Labour's electoral victory in July 1984 were women. In 1983, in both West Germany and Italy there was only one woman minister. A significant exception to this pattern was in France under President Mitterand and so long as he could also call on a left-wing majority in the National Assembly. The three Mauroy governments included six women, one, Edith Cresson, serving as Minister of Agriculture. In the government that followed in 1984, formed by Fabius, there were three women ministers, Edith Cresson, now responsible for industry and trade, Georgina Dufoix for social affairs and Huguette Bouchardeau for the environment, as well as three women below full ministerial status, making women's total share of government posts just over 14 per cent (see Lovenduski 1986a; Duchen, 1986; Northcutt and Flaitz, 1985). However, the 14-strong Cabinet announced by Chirac, leader of the Gaullist RPR, in the wake of the 1986 National Assembly elections, included no women. Otherwise women have done best in the Netherlands and Scandinavia. In the Dutch government formed after the 1984 General Election, women were two out of 16 Ministers and three of seven Secretaries of State (Lovenduski, 1986a). From the early 1970s, the countries of Scandinavia have all tended to include at least two women in the governments. In Olof Palme's Social Democratic government formed in Sweden in 1982, five out of 19 members or 26 per cent were women, though they held only two ministries. By 1984 there were five women all ministers, out of a total 27 government members in Denmark, that is 19 per cent. Women by 1983 held three out of 17, or 19 per cent of government posts, all of them

ministries, in Finland. But the prize goes to Grö Harlem Brundt-
land, who on becoming Prime Minister of Norway for the second
time in May 1986, selected for her minority Labour government
seven women, not counting herself, out of a total of 17 (over 40
per cent).

Women are better represented within the governments of
Western democracies than in either Soviet bloc or Third World
governments. In the case of communist countries it is appropriate to
consider women's numbers both within the formal governments
and within the party politburos. For 1976, Jancar identifies 494
strictly government positions (including national ministerial posts,
membership in state councils and chairmanships of national
assemblies) in the Soviet Union and Eastern Europe taken as a
whole, of which women held twenty. At the same time out of a
corresponding total of 172 politburo places, women filled nine
(Jancar, 1978, p. 89). In May 1982, Yugoslavia was the first East
European state to appoint a woman Prime Minister: Milka Planinc
(*The Guardian*, 16 January 1982). In the Soviet Union itself,
following the 1986 Communist Party Congress, the appointment of
Alexandra Biryukova as a Central Committee secretary was
presented as a sign of changing times but significantly her responsibilities were to be for social development and the family, and for
two decades now there has been no woman in either the Council of
Ministers or the Politburo. Available data indicates still less
participation by women in Third World governments. In 1969, in all
the Latin American states taken together, there were only four
women in Cabinet-level posts (Chaney, 1979). In certain countries
women have recently had more success; by 1979 three of the 12
government members in Costa Rica were women. On the other
hand the new government announced by Garcia in Peru in July
1986, and Cabinets formed by Neves in March 1985 and Sarnay in
February 1986 respectively in Brazil were exclusively male. Turning
to Asia, between 1952 and 1975 India boasted only one woman
of Cabinet rank, beside Indira Gandhi, though eleven other women
were ministers in the union government and two were chief
ministers of state governments (Katzenstein, 1978). None of the 14
Cabinet members appointed by Mrs Gandhi in January 1980 were
women. Her son, Rajiv, included one woman, Mrs Moshina
Kidwai, in his Cabinet of 14 members, on taking office in January
1985, and a further two women were recruited to the government.
As against this in Sri Lanka by 1981 only four women, amongst

them Mrs Bandaranaike, had ever served in the Cabinet (Kearney, 1981).

Even these statistics do not fully reveal the extent of women's marginalisation in national governments. For once more we find the tendency to relegate them to those fields considered to be the logical extension of traditional feminine concerns – health, welfare, education, culture, the family, consumer affairs. Most frequent of all perhaps is women's appointment to education posts. In 1983 for instance, in West Germany, Italy and the Republic of Ireland the only woman Minister was responsible for education. There was also a female Education Minister in Chile. Most recently in the government formed in Colombia in 1986, the only woman was again made Minister for Education. This kind of specialisation can be found throughout the world. Even in Scandinavia women tend to be assigned to these feminine areas and there has never been a woman Minister of Defence.

It is relatively well-established, therefore, that the proportion of posts held by women within political parties, representative assemblies and national governments, throughout the world, is small and increases in roughly inverse proportion to the power they bestow. There *has* been a significant increase over the last ten to fifteen years; in the course of revising the first edition of this book I have been impressed by exactly how much steady growth there has been. Even so, women continue to be seriously under-represented and thus handicapped in the policy-making process. The full extent of their handicap only becomes clear when one also examines their participation within the other political arenas I have identified.

Unions and other interest organisations

In Western democracies at least, interest groups, particularly the 'peak' economic interest organisations, constitute an important second channel of political influence. Information available suggests that women are if anything more marginal in these than in the 'numerical' channel. Given that there are so few women in business managements it is not surprising that they are nearly invisible in its senior ranks. Not surprising, but of the greatest consequence for women's political influence, given the direct and indirect power exercised by business. In Britain by 1986 there were only seven women on the boards of directors of the 100 leading companies (*The Times*, 17 October 1986). In 1983 only two of the 400 members of the General Council of the Confederation of British Industry were women, and only 65 of the total 3025 members of its various committees. Finkelstein suggests that in the early 1970s men outnumbered women in top corporation posts in the United States by about 600 to one, although there was evidence that increasing numbers of women were moving into occupations that fed into these posts (Finkelstein, 1981).

There were no women in the top executive bodies of Italy's largest employers' organisation – Confindustria – in 1983 and only two out of its 600 board, council and commission members were women. In the same year women formed less than 1 per cent of the general assembly of the CNPF (Conseil National du Patronat Français) in France and there was one woman (1.8 per cent) on its management team (Lovenduski, 1986a). Of the 20 leading companies in the Republic of Ireland in 1985, not one had a woman as chair, managing director or chief executive and amongst the entire combined membership of the Boards of Directors there featured only one woman. None of the principal officers of either the Confederation of Irish Industry or the Federated Union of Employers was female (Randall and Smyth, forthcoming). Here for once and significantly women have not made great progress even in Scandinavia. For instance, by 1982 there was not one woman among the 460 directors of associations in the Confederation of Swedish Employers.

Women's membership of trade unions, we have seen, though proportionately less than men's is often substantial. They form even so a very small minority of office-holders. In 1980 70 per cent of the membership of Britain's National Union of Teachers was female, yet women accounted for less than 10 per cent of its National Executive. In the powerful Transport and General Workers' Union, women made up 15.9 per cent of the membership but in the 41-strong National Executive were without a single representative. By 1984 only two national unions had women General Secretaries. In the Trades Union Council itself, the number of places reserved for women was increased in 1981 from two to five out of 42; subsequently it was raised to six. By the 1986 Annual Conference women formed less than 15 per cent of the 1000 delegates (*The Guardian*, 5 September 1986) and on the Council there was a total of eight women members out of 48, including two who had been elected to non-reserved places, Brenda Dean (SOGAT) and Joyce Winsett (NUPE). In the United States, women accounted for only 7 per cent of trade union office-holders in 1978. By 1983 there were two women out of a total membership of 37 on the ruling council of the AFL-CIO (Goodin, 1983). Similarly women held twelve out of 489 official trade union positions in Australia in 1978. Figures for Western Europe in 1981 show that everywhere, except in France's CGT (Confederation Générale du Travail) 'Women are under-represented on the highest union decision-making bodies by a factor of two or more and in most countries the factor is nearer to three' (Lovenduski, 1986a, p. 172). This includes Scandinavia; indeed, as Lovenduski points out, it is 'something of a curiosity' that Swedish trade unions, so ready to take up women's cause in employment policy, have so few women leaders. In 1983 women were only 7 per cent of executive committee and 13 per cent of council members in the largest, blue-collar, federation, the LO and even in the white-collar TCO, for which women form more than half the membership at large, were only 20 per cent of executive committee members (Statistics Sweden, 1985).

Union leadership in East European countries and the Soviet Union includes a higher percentage of women – for instance 34.6 per cent of the All-Union Central Council of Trade Unions in the Soviet Union by 1982 – but we have already observed that these unions lack political weight. A recent exception was Poland but women appeared to make few inroads into Solidarity's male-dominated hierarchy (*The Guardian*, 5 November 1981). In Third World countries, women's absence from trade union leadership is most marked of all. Thus by 1977 there were no women in the executive bodies of Venezuela's four labour confederations (Aviel, 1981).

Employers organisations and trade unions are generally seen as the two major kinds of economic or producer interest group but do not of course exhaust the list. Especially in countries where agriculture still contributes a significant share of GNP, farmers' organisations may have considerable political influence, but women are unlikely to play much part within their leadership. Thus in the Republic of Ireland, the Irish Farmers' Association was for some time reckoned 'the country's most effective lobby' but in 1986 all sixteen of its leading officers were men (Randall and Smyth, forthcoming).

All in all these figures suggest that women's presence within the leadership of interest organisations falls short even of their role in the 'numerical' channel, an impression reinforced by the finding of a survey in Norway that only 7 per cent of full-time employees and 9 per cent of elected officials of interest organisations are female (Hernes and Voje, 1980). If women seek political power, they should be concerned, not only because these organisations feed into and supplement the numerical channel but because in many Western democracies they come together with government and bureaucracy to form a corporate policy-making channel.

Bureaucracies

Before exploring the implications of corporatism further, let us turn to women's position within government bureaucracies. Again information is incomplete and comparison is further hampered by differences in the structure of national bureaucracies. In 1983, though women accounted for 47 per cent of non-industrial civil servants as a whole in Britain, they were only 4.5 per cent of senior civil servants, that is under-secretaries and above and there was no female permanent secretary. When in June 1985 Anne Mueller was promoted to that position in the Management and Personnel Office she was only the fourth woman ever to hold it (*The Guardian*, 12 June 1985). Likewise, within the top echelons of the United States administration, even after an increase, women formed a tiny 2.3 per cent (Lepper, 1974). Although in 1975 women comprised 30 per cent of New Zealand's public servants, only 0.4 per cent of these were in senior executive positions as compared with 13.3 per cent of the men (Place, 1979). Silver reminds us that, at the apex of the French bureaucracy, 'the Grand Corps de l'Etat – Conseil d'Etat, Cours des Comptes, Inspecteurs des Finances – are the most prestigious non-elective institutions of the French government'. But in 1974 they included a grand total of nineteen women, or 3 per cent of their membership (Silver, 1981, p. 230). By 1983 this had increased to 5.4 per cent. That same year women held 5.8 per cent of the top executive positions in Italy and 5 per cent in West Germany though none in the senior-most 'beamtete staatssekretaere' (Lovenduski, 1986a). In the Republic of Ireland by 1986 there were still no women among the 18 secretaries and a total of three among 82 deputy and assistant secretaries. Rates in Sweden and Norway, at 4.5 per cent of comparable top bureaucratic positions, do not appear to diverge from this general pattern (Mossuz-Lavau and Sineau, 1984, p. 39), though the rate in Finland may be rather higher.

Though in many developing countries it is socially acceptable for educated, middle-class women to work in the government bureaucracy, they rarely rise to senior positions. Katzenstein did, however, note a striking increase by 1972 in the rate at which women were being recruited for the prestigious Indian Administrative Service, Indian Foreign Service and Indian Police Service (Katzenstein, 1978, p. 476). Chaney also notes that in Chile women have made remarkable inroads into these sections of the bureaucracy dealing with finance and personnel, because of their supposed honesty (Chaney, 1979, p. 101). The record of international development agencies is little better. Rogers suggests that the UN establishment in New York has only been spared prosecution for sex discrimination in its recruitment policy because of its immunity from American law. In 1980 there were virtually no women experts working for the Technical Assistance Recruitment Services (TARS) which services all the different UN agencies (Rogers, 1983).

Little has been written about the role of women in local and regional administration. In 1976 in English local government, out of over 500 chief executives, two were women. Even though women staff predominate in education and social services, there were only two women chief education officers out of 116 and eleven women directors of social services out of 127 (Hills, 1981a, p. 27). In local administration in the United States in 1978, women held an average of 10.5 per cent of 'management positions' (Sigelman, 1976). These findings suggest that women may be better represented, though only marginally so, in local than in national bureaucracies.

The near invisibility of women in bureaucratic leadership is the more remarkable because, throughout the world, the state itself is one of their principal employers. As an additional handicap, the few women who get there are disproportionately concentrated in those sectors of administration with traditional 'feminine' concerns. Even in Finland, in 1981, of women employed at the level of advisory officer and above, 38 were based in the Ministry of Education and 37 in the Ministry of Health and Social Affairs but at the other extreme four in the Ministry of Defence (Hernes and Hänninen-

Salmelin, 1985, p. 117) though this appears to be a considerable advance on figures for 1974. Studies in New Zealand, France and other Nordic countries have reported a more skewed distribution.

'Corporatist' institutions

The dearth of women in bureaucratic élites, and their virtual absence from those sections dealing with defence, foreign affairs, finance and the economy, is again at least as important in determining women's political influence as their under-representation in the 'representative' arena. From nation to nation the precise relationship between the bureaucracy and political institutions which are, however loosely, 'representative' is varied and elusive, but few doubt the real and expanding power of state bureaucracies almost throughout the world. One manifestation of this power is the growth of corporate channels and mechanisms of policy-making in which the process of consultation between government and, above all economic, interests has been increasingly institutionalised outside the parliamentary arena. Elements of corporatism have been noted in many Western democracies though it is perhaps most openly acknowledged in Scandinavia. One of its central features is the proliferation of committees, councils, boards and commissions, under the aegis of the different ministries or simply directly accountable to government or parliament, within which representatives of group interests and bureaucrats confer in the making and implementation of government policy. We need, therefore, to know how well women are represented on these consultative and managerial bodies, though relevant data are still hard to come by outside the Nordic countries.

Of Britain, Stacey and Price write:

> Of the 425 members of 41 public boards of a commercial character in 1978, we find just 28 women (6.6 per cent). The Post Office had two women out of a total membership of 18; British Airways had one woman out of 15 members and the National Enterprise Board, one out of 11. Many boards had no women at all, including the Electricity Board, the British Gas Corporation, British Rail and the Scottish and Welsh Development Agencies.

In addition there was one woman out of ten members of the Manpower Services Commission, and, in 1979, one woman councillor out of nine in the Advisory, Conciliation and Arbitration Service (Stacey and Price, 1981, p. 148). By 1982 women's share of the various ministerial consultative committees ranged from 2 per cent of those associated with the Department of Industry to 30 per cent in those attached to the Home Office. In 1983 there were 14 women among the 200 members of France's Economic and Social Council and two out of 80 members of Italy's National Council for Economy and Labour (Lovenduski, 1986a). In the Republic of Ireland in 1985 only two of the 23 members of the National Economic and Social Council were women. Women were also severely under-represented on the boards of a number of important 'state-sponsored bodies' and were entirely absent from several of the most powerful, including the Central Bank and the Industrial Development Authority. The issue of women's representation in corporate bodies has been discussed most extensively in the Nordic countries where it is recognised that this channel is at least as influential in policy-making as the 'numerical'. Numbers of women on ministerial consultative committees have been low though there has been a perceptible increase from the early 1970s and especially in Norway following the Royal Resolution of 1973, as strengthened in 1976, which obliged nominating agencies to propose female as well as male representatives. The proportion of women on public boards, councils and committees in Norway climbed from 10 per cent in 1970 to 27 per cent in 1981 (Hernes and Hänninen-Salmelin, 1985).

The judiciary

Outside the United States, political scientists do not generally emphasise the political role of the judiciary. In a very broad sense, however, the judiciary is political everywhere, and in the more conventional sense it often contributes to policy-making in Western democracies, and not only when they have a federal system of government. In Britain by 1983 women were 4.1 per cent of High Court judges, which marked a small increase over the previous five years, but no woman has ever sat on the Judicial Committee of the House of Lords or as a judge in the Court of Appeal. Similarly in 1985 in the Republic of Ireland there was no woman in the six-member Supreme Court and only one of the fifteen High Court judges was female. In the United States judiciary, the numbers of women have grown, particularly under the sponsorship of President Carter, but by 1979 women were still less than 4 per cent of federal trial judges and 8.3 per cent of Court of Appeals judges (Cook, 1979). In 1981 President Reagan appointed the first woman, Sandra O'Connor, to the Supreme Court (*The Guardian*, 8 July 1981). Lovenduski suggests that by 1983 women were at most 5 per cent of the senior judiciary in West Germany. The one real exception is France; by 1983 women there had still made little headway in the administrative legal system but within the ordinary system accounted for 30 per cent of judges, reflecting in part increased recruitment of women into the Ecole Nationale de Magistrature over the previous ten years. As Lovenduski comments, this 'feminisation of the French judiciary . . . represents a remarkable achievement' (1986a, p. 223).

The media

While the political arenas discussed so far are the most influential, mention must also be made of the communication media. Although their independence from government and economic interests is always precarious, particularly outside the Western democracies, the media remain the public's primary source of information about public matters.

It is particularly hard to find details of women's participation in the media but once more it seems clear that they rarely achieve leading positions. By 1982 women were reported to be 22.2 per cent of newspaper journalists, though with a rather higher rate of NUJ membership than male journalists, but only 8.8 per cent of senior editorial staff in Britain (Smith, 1982). Employment figures collected by the Association of Cinematographic Television and Allied Technicians (ACCT) for Independent Television in 1986 showed women as 20 per cent of employees, 16 per cent of the second schedule, including directors and producers, though only 2.7 per cent of the Producer/Director category. This reflected a considerable increase in the percentage of women directors from 1974. In the United States by 1982 men still held 90.4 per cent of the top newspaper and magazine editorial positions (Tinker, 1983, p. 45). In 1985 editors of the Irish Republic's four national dailies, three evening newspapers and five Sunday newspapers, as well as of 49 provincial newspapers were men. There were two women amongst the nine members of the national broadcasting authority, RTE, but only one woman amongst its 30 senior managers.

Leadership outside institutionalised politics

Moving beyond these institutionalised arenas, one might expect women to assume leadership more frequently in direct or revolutionary political activities. This may be true within community action groups, though the evidence is contradictory. In Britain Mayo *et al.* found women's representation within the leadership much lower than their high participation rates warranted (Mayo *et al.*, 1977). Gallagher in particular suggested that in London women were likely to take the initiative only in the most deprived neighbourhoods. She described how in South-East London, women on a council housing estate organised a campaign against a council decision that threatened to worsen their already grim housing conditions, led a homeless families action committee and figured conspicuously in the campaign of a local claimants' union. However, on a new estate nearby, their role within the tenants' association was strictly limited. She concluded that women assumed leadership roles only when their menfolk were too demoralised to pre-empt them (Gallagher, 1977).

In revolutionary or 'anti-system' politics women, though active, are rarely the leaders, the high-profile exceptions of such women as Bernadette Devlin (in her pre-Parliamentary days), Angela Davis and Ulrike Meinhof notwithstanding. In both the Russian and the Chinese Revolutions, though women were deliberately mobilised into revolutionary activity, 'even during the most democratic period of rapid change women played limited roles'. They were not allowed to develop any power base of their own, and few women won permanent positions of influence (Salaff and Merkle, 1970, p. 167).

Women may achieve significant political influence indirectly, through their private relationship with male politicians. In the twentieth century, the woman who most successfully travelled this route to public power is Eva Perón. In a revealing discussion of her career, Navarro writes, that 'by the time she died, on 26 July 1952 she was undoubtedly the second most powerful figure in Argentina', but she observes that 'she held neither an elected post nor an official position in Peron's government', and that her authority was always a reflection of Perón's (Navarro, 1977, p. 229).

It was at one point suggested that Rosalynn Carter, wife of the recent American President, exerted considerable informal influence (Holden, 1980, p. 14), but those two examples are remarkable precisely because they are so unusual. It must be emphasised that both women had been single-mindedly devoted to the furtherance of their husbands' power and policies, and their own influence was entirely dependent upon their husbands' position. Probably more numerous are those women whose political influence derives simultaneously from their private relationship with a politician and from a formal political position, for instance the wives of Presidents Tito and Ceausescu of Yugoslavia and Romania respectively, or Imelda Marcos in the Philippines. The fate of Mao's widow, Jiang Quing, and indeed more recently of Imelda Marcos, illustrates the perils of presuming too far on that authority.

The preceding survey has shown, first, how very few women achieve political office or leadership. Second, it has illustrated the tendency for their representation to vary inversely with the distribution of political power. Even the striking increase in female parliamentarians in Sweden, Norway and Finland needs to be set alongside the growing influence of the corporate channel of decision-making, in which women's role is still marginal. Third, we have seen the variations between different countries, ranging from women's near invisibility in many developing countries to their substantial presence in the numerically representative institutions of Scandinavian politics. These variations indicate that levels of social and economic development may influence but by no means determine women's access to political élites. Amongst developed countries compare, for instance, women's participation in Sweden and Australia. Amongst Third World countries contrast India with Iran. Two political factors that seem particularly associated with higher rates of participation are left-wing parties and explicit central sponsorship, and we shall come back to these issues. The fourth finding has been the gradual but often cumulatively significant increase over the last two decades in women's share of leadership roles, to the point where this cannot simply be dismissed as tokenism. And yet there are still obvious qualifications to this generalisation, amongst them most strikingly the failure of women's position in the national legislatures of Britain and the United States to improve since the early 1960s.

Why so few?

How can we explain these findings? Chapters 1 and 2 have already supplied part of the answer: women's generally subordinate roles in *all* areas of modern public life, together with their rather lower rates of grass-roots political participation. But an adequate analysis must identify the constraints more precisely. Here we can draw on a considerable literature, though focused primarily on women in Britain and the United States in legislatures and governments.

First, we must concede that it is not always or entirely a disadvantage to be a woman in politics. A woman's relationship to a particular man may give her access to considerable indirect political power. In electoral competition with men, women candidates have the advantage of greater conspicuousness. Joan Lestor, the British Labour Party MP, has even been quoted as saying: 'Any young woman in politics is at a distinct advantage; there are lots of young men around, but if you are a woman and you are reasonably articulate and can state your case, you are noticed and remembered much longer' (Phillips, 1980, p. 74). Some women are currently benefiting from the growing recognition that genuinely representative institutions must include at least a few women; for instance, Vallance suggests that it is easier for women than men to get on a parliamentary constituency's short-list of candidates (Vallance, 1979).

Such potential advantages still fail to offset the cumulative constraints on women's participation in élite politics. These constraints can best be discussed without, it is hoped, doing too much damage to the subtlety of individual authors' arguments, by continuing and developing the distinction made in Chapter 2 between characteristics of women themselves and characteristics of politics and political institutions. It is helpful, following Lapidus, to view these as the supply side and the demand side of women's political participation (Lapidus, 1978). On the supply side are the principal factors determining the availability of women politicians. We are interested not only in the women who do come forward but also in those who don't. On the demand side are the political and institutional factors governing the recruitment and role assignment of political élites in general, and female politicians in particular. Of course supply and demand are not mutually independent: women may, for instance, anticipate either practical difficulties in combining domestic roles with political office or outright discrimination. Such points of interdependence will be indicated as we proceed.

The supply of women: socialisation

At face value, the main reason for the scarcity of women in public office is simply that so few women actively seek it. In Chapter 2 I distinguished between the implications of socialisation and of situational or structural factors for women's political behaviour. The distinction is also helpful in identifying the reasons for this restricted supply of aspiring female politicians.

Many discussions of this question in the United States emphasise the effects of socialisation; for instance, Githens and Prestage began by observing that 'The problems confronting women in politics have been attributed chiefly to the tensions between ascribed and achieved status created by female socialisation. This explanation often tends to be diffuse and vague' (Githens and Prestage, 1977, p. 5). But they do not offer an alternative perspective, choosing rather to elaborate the 'dynamic of interaction' through which these tensions are experienced. In particular they incorporate the concept of social 'marginality', defining the marginal actor as 'a person who seeks to change his identification from one stratum to another but who is unable to resolve the related choices between value systems and between organised group ties'. Women will be especially vulnerable to such tensions, say Githens and Prestage, because they rely more than men upon the esteem of others. The psychological costs of marginality will deter most women from seeking political office but will also condition the behaviour of the women who attain it.

Kelley and Boutilier likewise define the crucial prerequisite for adult political activism as an activist modern sex-role ideology and a sense of personal control over one's 'life-space'. Although they accept that motherhood can impede more demanding forms of political participation, this is, they believe, principally due to a mother's fear of social disapproval if she appears to neglect her children; the practical constraints of motherhood are only marginal. In a startling passage, they assert that:

An activist woman for whom politics has become salient will not find that lack of a baby sitter, uncooperative husband, or young children are sufficient to keep her from voting or possibly even from running for an office. The cost of not engaging in the behaviour may be too high (Kelley and Boutilier, 1978, p. 11).

They underline the need for the right kind of childhood socialisation if women are to achieve political prominence.

The authors cited also stress the influence of socialisation upon the way women behave after they have acquired office, which obviously has consequences for their subsequent political career. Similarly Constantini and Craik, from their survey of men and women in leading party positions in California, concluded that women devoted more time and energy to routine party work than men and that women's ambitions were confined to party office, while men were much more likely to seek public office. They swiftly detected a 'marked resemblance to often noted sex-role differences in the family. The male party leader, like the husband, is more likely to specialise in the instrumental function of the system involved. The female party leader, like the wife tends to specialise in expressive functions' (Constantini and Craik, 1977, p. 238). The eagerness with which they espoused this sex-role reductionism is the more striking since, as Carroll rightly points out in her criticism of this piece, their own data only indicate very marginal differences in motivation between the sexes (Carroll, 1979).

It has further been suggested that women politicians adopt 'amateur' rather than 'professional' political styles. Thus Lynn and Flora deduce from their survey of delegates to the 1972 United States National Party Conventions that, because of their fear of social disapproval, women delegates are apparently less personally ambitious than men, and are also more likely to perceive and engage in politics in terms of ideas and principles rather than competitive strategies. They characterise this approach as amateur, though this evaluation seems highly questionable, reflecting a very American and 'masculine' concept of politics. It is also contradicted by the finding of a succession of studies that women in politics tend to be especially earnest and conscientious, a trait barely compatible with amateurism (Lynn and Flora, 1977).

Situational constraints

Other writers prefer to stress the impact of situational constraints, most especially of motherhood. One influential argument has been advanced by Lee, whose survey of leading local politicians in four New York suburbs persuaded her that women are not deterred from such participation because they find it either boring or corrupt. Though they often believe that politics is an unsuitable activity for women, or at least expect men to think so, and though they anticipate discrimination, none the less both sex-role stereotyping and discrimination are, she argues, noticeably diminishing. The most serious and enduring obstacle is responsibility for children at home which, while it need not deter women from routine forms of political participation, such as voting, does impede their access to political office. The crucial factor is time, and not so much the amount of time available as women's inability to control *when* they will be available for political work (Lee, 1976). (Incidentally, Hernes and Voje suggest that the unpredictability of women's daily schedule, when they are responsible for small children, may be one reason for their preference for non-institutional forms of political participation (Hernes and Voje, 1980).)

Lee's thesis has been explicitly echoed in a number of studies. More important, there is a wealth of evidence that she is right. For instance, of the 27 women British MPs elected in October 1974, only two had children under ten years of age. Nine years later, in 1983, this was still true. The same tendency for women participants to be either single, or married or divorced without young children, was noted in the United States Congress and state legislatures and in the Norwegian Storting in the mid-1970s. More recently Lovenduski (1986a) suggests that European data continue to confirm this pattern. Wolchik cites findings in Czechoslovakia that women are less politically active after marriage and the birth of children and that they give domestic responsibility as the main reason for not accepting public office (Wolchik, 1981, p. 271). The only contrary evidence comes from the Irish Republic where in 1985 at least four of the 14 women TDs (MPs) had young children. Responsibility for small children may be less of an obstacle to participation in local than in national politics. Bevs found that in American Boards of Education there was actually no significant difference between men and women members as regards the number and age of their children (Bevs, 1978). This may be because such political work is less demanding and closer to home, a conclusion supported by the British women MPs who told Phillips that while their children were young they had confined their political activities to local government (Phillips, 1980).

Not only does motherhood inhibit women from seeking political office, it also means that by the time their children are old enough to require less constant care, such women are themselves relatively old for embarking upon a political career. This is reflected in the frequent finding that women politicians are somewhat older, on average, than their male counterparts. The female state legislators interviewed by Githens complained they were handicapped by gaining political office only in middle life, too late for the competition for leading roles within the legislature or a bid for a seat in Congress. They also, incidentally, felt themselves disadvantaged in this competition because they lacked the required occupational backgrounds (Githens, 1977). As we shall see, the appropriate job experience is a vital ingredient of 'eligibility' for élite politics, and it is women's maternal responsibilities (under, of course, the prevalent sexual division of labour) which in large part prevent them from gaining such experience.

These conclusions are, it seems, in contradiction to Kelley and Boutilier's claim that once women are politically enthused, no such practical obstacle will hold them back. But their own data also contradict their argument. Amongst the thirty-six active political women for whom they provide biographical details, twelve had no children at home at the time of their political involvement (a further three probably didn't either but the book does not make this clear). Eight of those with children were themselves wealthy enough to have servants or had rich relatives who could arrange for their children to be looked after. Of the remaining three, Ellen Grasso found support in her extended family; the other two, Golda Meir and Eva Broido, did have to struggle to combine their roles as mother and politician. Indeed Meir wrote in her autobiography, 'to this day I am sure that I didn't harm the children or neglect them, despite the efforts I made not to be away from them even an hour more than was strictly necessary'. Her decision to combine motherhood with a demanding public role was evidently a painful one (Kelley and Boutilier, 1978, p. 131).

More recently Vallance and Davies have also produced rather persuasive theoretical arguments against the assumption that responsibility for small children is a political handicap. They rightly point out that this has not prevented women doing many other kinds of jobs, for instance around one-quarter of all doctors in Western Europe are women. When it comes to their own data on women

MEPs, however, they seem to acknowledge that small children do pose problems. They find that most women, as well as men, MEPs are over 45, so that their children are likely to be grown up but that those with younger children admit they have difficulties in coping, while others have postponed a political career until their children were old enough (Vallance and Davies, 1986, p. 41).

Women's availability for élite political roles is also related to their employment outside the home, but the relationship is complicated and not entirely clear. In Chapter 2 evidence was cited to show that women's paid employment was positively related with grass-roots political activity, but this was explained in terms *both* of socialisation and of situation; childhood socialisation was counteracted by influence and opportunities associated with a specific new situation. Employment outside the home is also presumed to correlate positively with more élite forms of political participation. For instance, Lovenduski and Hills, summarising their findings for twenty different countries, note a broad association between political activism, at grass-roots and élite level, and women's participation in the workforce, except in Japan and Italy. Yet, as Currell points out, employment outside the home imposes on women who are still expected to be housewives, and especially if they have young children, a dual burden of work which can scarcely leave them time or energy for more demanding forms of political participation (Currell, 1978, p. 8). A number of studies indicate the predominance of 'unemployed' housewives amongst women in what could be called the intermediate range of political activities, for instance local party activities, local government and even in US state legislatures. Alternatively the women are often part-time workers. Schoenberg cites one study, of American working-class women whose participation in community politics increased when they took on part-time jobs, but decreased again if they worked full-time (Schoenberg, 1980). A sample survey of local councillors in England in the mid-1970s suggested that 91 per cent of women councillors were housewives, retired or employed part-time (Hills, 1981b). However, this pattern is reversed at the level of national politics. A tentative explanation for these apparent inconsistencies can be offered. Participation in the paid workforce *does* change women's political awareness and aspirations. This is reflected in the impact of paid employment both on women's political participation in the long term and, more immediately, on their grass-roots activism. On the other hand, employment outside the home *does* contribute to women's dual work burden and that is why, at the intermediate level of political participation, housewives without outside work commitments predominate, often together with women in part-time work. However, the kinds of attitude, skills and experience compatible with holding office at the summit of the contemporary political system presuppose paid employment, and indeed employment of a specific kind, and this is part of the explanation for the small numbers and only very gradual increase of women in this political arena. Again then, while a combination of childhood socialisation and more direct situational influences are at work, the further up the political hierarchy one goes, the more salient the situational constraints.

There remains one further and important aspect of women's situation – it could also be explained in terms of their location within the *structure* of educational and occupational opportunity – which potentially limits their availability for the political élite. Seligman *et al.*, in analysing the process of political recruitment, distinguish between three stages: certification, selection and role assignment. The certification stage entails the informal delimitation of an eligible pool of contenders (Seligman *et al.*, 1974, p. 14). Eligibility criteria are, of course, a function of the political institutions themselves and thus a feature of the demand for women politicians but, given these criteria, it is significant that fewer women than men can usually satisfy them. One customary aspect of eligibility is educational attainment. It is therefore relevant to note that in Britain there are still 4 men for every 3 women studying at degree level and although, in the United States, only slightly fewer women than men complete the first three years of college, significantly fewer complete a fourth year. Chaney suggests that women at university do not typically study in the more politicised faculties and therefore miss out on the student politics that has proved an important training-ground for the future politicians (Chaney, 1979, p. 91). Though referring to Latin America, this point is more widely applicable.

Secondly, there are certain professions peculiarly compatible with a political career. In Britain, Currell finds, MPs frequently combine their political work with a private law practice, a director-ship, a consultancy, journalism or even a doctor's general practice, where they can work flexible hours. These professions may also benefit from the MP's status and provide insurance against possible electoral defeat. In addition, certain occupations such as teaching, law, public relations, journalism, trade union organisation, and even acting, develop communication skills that are vital to the successful politician. Of all the MPs elected in 1970 and 1974, 31 per cent of the Conservatives and 43 per cent of the Labour members were drawn from the professions (mainly lawyers in the former and teachers in the latter). Women do not play a prominent role in most of these professions. Moreover their extensive employment in clerical grades of the civil service and in local government may be a further disadvantage, since civil servants are restricted in the range of political activities they can undertake while the employees of a local authority may not serve as its councillors (Currell, 1978). In the United States since 1900, nearly one-quarter of state legislators have been lawyers, and Gertzog (1984) reports that as the role of family connections in women's recruitment to Congress diminishes, Congresswomen are increasingly likely to be legally trained. Yet in 1979 only 3 per cent of American lawyers were women, though 25.3 per cent of law students (Lynn, 1979); by 1982 women accounted for 14.1 per cent of lawyers, certainly an improvement. Githens (1977) found that in the Maryland legislature 33.8 per cent of delegates were lawyers and 38.7 per cent were businessmen, with these two groups also dominating the standing committees. In Iowa's legislature farmers featured even more prominently than lawyers and businessmen but this was little comfort for women aspirants (King, 1977). In the Irish Republic, although lawyers, farmers and others are also numerous, the single largest occupational category in the Dail is 'commercial' meaning primarily small businesses like shopkeepers and publicans. It is thought that they have had particular opportunities to cultivate the kind of network of local contacts so essential in Irish party politics. Again few women are likely to have such a background (Randall and Smyth, forthcoming). Nor is the picture very different in Eastern Europe; for instance in the Soviet Union women are greatly under-represented in those industrial, technical and agricultural professional specialisations which are most convergent with political leadership roles (Lapidus, 1978).

Stiehm has taken the question of eligibility one step further, arguing that women cannot be taken seriously as candidates for executive positions so long as they are not recruited on a similar basis to men for military and police duties. Building upon Max Weber's argument that the definitive function of the state is the control of force, Stiehm maintains 'If women will not, cannot, or if it is thought that they will not or cannot exercise force, they are poor candidates for office with coercive responsibility' (Stiehm, 1979, pp. 1–3). Here we may note that while women's military role in the United States remain slight, it has significantly grown through the 1970s. From 1971–6 the percentage of military personnel who were women grew from 1.6 to 5.2 per cent. As Parr writes, 'The number of women serving in the armed forces greatly increased; military women were assigned to a much wider range of jobs and began to serve on ships other than hospital vessels; military service academies opened enrollments to women; coeducational basic training camps were established' (Parr, 1983, p. 238). Whether or not Stiehm's thesis applies to the United States and other Western democracies, obviously women will be enormously disadvantaged in those countries, particularly numerous in the Third World, where governments are drawn entirely or in large part from military personnel. Aviel finds that in Latin America as might be expected, women are least well represented in military regimes, though there is a tendency, as such regimes consolidate their hold, for women to be increasingly co-opted, however symbolically. He quotes the Peruvian saying 'If you want to go into government, enter the military' and points out that this option is not generally open to women, except in Peru since 1976 and Cuba, where women are trained as officers (Aviel, 1981, p. 169).

Relatively few women actively aspire to political office because they lack motivation, but more importantly because there are specific constraints on their freedom to do so and they are less able than men to satisfy the requirements of certification. Their reticence is not, however, independent of the political system itself; the ethos and male chauvinism of politics is a deterrent, the practical operation of political institutions is difficult to reconcile with the demands of young children unless husbands are unusually co-operative, and it is the political system which determines the necessary attributes of its recruits. Women in not putting themselves forward may then be rationally anticipating the obstacles to a political career.

The demand side: political institutions

Turning to the 'demand' side of this interaction we begin with an obvious but essential observation. Whereas in grass-roots political activities, such as voting, campaigning for a local election and lobbying a local politician, there are no logical constraints on the numbers of participants, there is inevitably competition between the would-be participants in élite political activities. It is not simply that the sort of people who go in for them happen to be aggressive, and that aggression is a quality traditionally associated with men rather than women. Much more fundamentally, every political office won by a woman must be at the expense of male contenders. Moreover, the more powerful a political position is perceived to be, the greater will be the competition for it. Nor is this observation confined to institutionalised politics. Even within a revolutionary movement or an *ad hoc* political organisation without regularised procedures for selecting the leadership, only a limited number can be the leaders. Given men's competitive edge in any current leadership contest and their dominance of the existing selection processes, women who seek political power are operating within an entirely different political context than when they simply join in grass-roots political activity.

But the institutionalisation of politics poses further obstacles. The role of major 'institutional barriers', to use Hills's term (Hills, 1978), is illustrated by the effect of their relative absence on the careers of Mrs Gandhi and Mrs Bandaranaike. Both achieved political prominence through their personal association with leading male politicians, in political systems whose central institutions were still relatively permeable. Katzenstein suggests that this low level of political institutionalisation accounts for the contrast, in India, between the visibility of a number of influential women politicians and the low overall rates of women holding political office (Katzenstein, 1978). There are many other examples in Third World countries – Cory Aquino in the Philippines, Mrs Eugenia Charles in Dominica, Benazir Bhutto in Pakistan and Sheikh Hasina Wajed and Begum Khaled Zia in Bangladesh already referred to. But this pattern is by no means confined to the Third World. In Britain during the first decade of (limited) female suffrage, five out of the eleven women MPs owed their position to this 'male equivalence', in Currell's phrase (Currell, 1978).

Moreover in the US Congress between 1917 and 1976, 73 per cent of women Senators and 50 per cent of women Representatives were the widows of Congressmen (though Kincaid, in particular, is anxious to dispel any impression that their advent to Congress was either automatic or involuntary, pointing out for instance that less than 3 per cent of Senators and 9 per cent of Representatives who died in office were succeeded by their widows (Kincaid, 1978).

Even today, nearly one quarter of all TDs in the Irish Dail are close relatives of former or incumbent TDs, which is, as Gallagher notes 'exceptionally high for a modern legislature' (Gallagher, 1984, p. 259). Family connections have been the single most important route for women TDs; of the 26 women TDs from 1922 to 1981, 13 were widows of men TDs or nationalist leaders and only five could be described as 'self-starting'.

The institutional barriers to political recruitment and promotion are less and less likely to be legal ones. This was not always so. Thus, in Britain, women were not allowed until 1918 to stand for Parliament, and until 1946 married women could not work in the civil service. The removal of these legal barriers has still left women facing a labyrinthine edifice of vested male interests and conventions. Three particular obstacles can be identified. Listing these in order of their reliance upon male chauvinism, the first, and by no means the least important although it has nothing to do with men's attitudes to women, is the way that, at each level, political advancement requires 'appropriate' political or occupational experience. To get to the top you have, typically, to have climbed the lower rungs, which also means that you have to begin climbing early enough to leave yourself time. More clearly related to male chauvinist assumptions are the ethos and organisation of political activity at each level, which reflect the styles and convenience of men, as was pointed out in Chapter 2. Finally, the direct expression of male prejudice and power is outright discrimination.

Institutional barriers to becoming a legislator

To assess and illustrate the extent to which these obstacles reinforce one another and deter women, let us examine in more detail the routes to the political pinnacle for women in Britain and the United States, confining ourselves largely to the 'numerical representation' channel because it is on this that political scientists have so far concentrated. Our starting point will be eligibility for the national legislature. In the informal process of 'certification' for these bodies, I suggested, certain occupations in which women are usually only a small minority, carry special weight. Consequently women rely on having had the right kind of previous political experience instead. In Britain, this means that the main reservoirs from which women have been recruited for Parliament are political parties, local government and trade unions.

We have seen, however, that women, though constituting nearly half the membership of the Labour and Conservative parties, do not achieve high party office in anything like this proportion. Hills asks how far this is simply the result of the parties' formal rules. At constituency level, the rules for the composition of the Labour General Committee (GC) do not oblige branches to send women delegates but may give women members overall a slight edge in voting for delegates, through the separate representation of Women's Sections, while Conservative branches are required to send two representatives, one of each sex, to the Constituency Executive Council. The limited evidence available suggests that even at this level women are under-represented in both parties: one recent survey of eighteen Labour GCs found women were only 30 per cent of their membership though 40 per cent of party membership at large. There is no specific requirement for women delegates to the Labour Party Annual Conference, while the Conservative constituency associations are obliged to send at least one woman out of up to seven delegates to their Annual Conference. Women's numbers are correspondingly higher in the Conservative Annual Conference, though it should be remembered that this body has much less say in party policy than does its Labour counterpart. Of the twenty-nine members of the Labour Party's National Executive Committee (NEC), only five, who in practice are nominated by the trade unions, must be women. Of the 200 members of the Conservative Executive Committee, a much less powerful body than the Labour NEC, only chairpersons of the Women's National Advisory Committees, at national and area level, are automatically women. In sum, the internal rules of the two parties do not assist women, particularly in the higher reaches of party organisation, but neither can they account for women's disappointing record. To explain this we must refer to the situational constraints discussed earlier in this chapter but also to the strong possibility of discrimination. Hills cites one Labour Party survey of women activists, in 1972, 45 per cent of whom felt that male contenders for party office were always or often given preference over equally qualified women and a further 33 per cent of whom thought this was sometimes the case (Hills, 1978).

The second source of women in Parliament is local government. Vallance points out that of the twenty-seven women MPs elected in October 1974, seventeen had local government experience (Vallance, 1979). Once more, though, we have seen that women are under-represented amongst local councillors. Yet, 'to become a candidate for local government in either party is not a complicated process' (Hills, 1978, p. 9). Labour Party candidates, nominated by party branches, trade unions and other affiliated organisations and then, frequently, screened by a constituency party committee, are vetted by the party Local Government Committee and ultimately selected by the branch they wish to represent. In the Conservative Party, wards find their own candidate, subject to the Constituency Association's approval, and they need not even be a party member. These procedures do not at face value disadvantage women or explain their small numbers in local government.

Bristow looks for a relationship between the extent of female representation in a local authority and its socio-economic environment. Women are best represented in London councils and worst in Welsh councils, but paradoxically, outside London, they do better in rural than in urban areas. Most striking is the correlation between the extent of women's representation and the affluence and, to a lesser extent, the conservatism of the authority, again excepting London. Bristow leans towards an explanation that emphasises the availability of middle-class housewives (Bristow, 1980). Hills rightly criticises Bristow both for making assumptions about women's class from data based on men, and for ignoring the attitudes of the recruiting parties themselves. She points to evidence of bias against women candidates, when selecting for safe seats, in both parties. However, this does not succeed in accounting for the variations in women's rates of council membership (Hills, 1981b).

We should in passing note that success in local government is valuable for would-be parliamentary candidates in a number of other European countries, where, as Mossuz-Lavau and Sineau point out, local councils 'are the breeding ground for parliamentary candidates' (1984, p. 20). It is especially crucial in the Irish

Republic, because of the role of 'localism' in constituency party politics and the fact that local parties largely dominate the process of selecting parliamentary contestants. Of TDs in the Dail elected in November 1982 66.3 per cent previously served on a local authority. In these circumstances it is particularly disappointing that women's representation in local councils failed to make the anticipated upward leap following the June 1985 local elections.

If women's penetration of party and local government élites is limited, it far exceeds their office-holding in trade unions, as I have shown. This despite the Women's Conference held annually since 1926 and the local and national Women's Advisory Committees established in the mid-1930s. As a result of pressure by the Women's Conference over the last three years, the TUC finally agreed to increase the statutory quota of women delegates to the TUC from two to six out of 42 as we saw. Overall we must agree with Vallance that so long as these three areas of political activity remain the main 'feeders' of women into Parliament, there is little prospect of a dramatic surge in the numbers of would-be women candidates (Vallance, 1979).

Turning now to the United States, among those Congresswomen who do not owe their seat at least partially to their dead husband, that is amongst the younger or more junior women members, the commonest prior political activity has been membership of a state legislature. We need therefore to begin by examining the recruitment of women to these legislatures. We have already noted that women's representation at this level has been steadily increasing though it still constitutes less than 15 per cent. Although by 1986 no state had less than three women legislators, female membership tends to be concentrated in particular states. The highest rate, 33 per cent, was in New Hampshire, followed by Vermont and Wyoming; the lowest, 2.3 per cent, was in Mississippi. But with few exceptions, it was not the states with the largest share of women legislators which returned women to Congress.

Since women are much less likely than men to 'step sideways' into the state legislature, on the strength of their professional eligibility, they are more dependent on alternative recruitment channels. Chief amongst these are political parties and voluntary associations. Women are by now probably as likely as men to be involved in party activity, but there is ample evidence that they are much less likely to assume leadership roles. The expectation that 'Women do the lickin' and stickin', while men plan the strategy' still prevails (Boneparth, 1977, p. 289). Alternatively or, often, additionally would-be women legislators have been active in community work. Through such activity a woman can develop organisational and social skills, she will become acquainted with political processes and officials and may perceive a political dimension to community issues. A further stepping-stone, frequently mentioned, is membership of a local authority, either through election or appointment. Diamond reports that in 1971 approximately two-thirds of both male and female members of the combined state legislatures of Connecticut, Vermont, New Hampshire and Maine had held some other public office prior to election (Diamond, 1977).

Women remain under-represented in local government, though we have noted the increase in their numbers since the mid-1970s; furthermore Constantini and Craik suggest they may be most numerous in those local authorities which are not partisan and are therefore not perceived as stepping-stones to higher political office – though perhaps we should be wary of the inferences these authors make from their data (Constantini and Craik, 1977).

Women with a background of party activity, community work or local public office may be invited by the local party to run for state office, they may contest the party primary or they may run as independents. Although about 28 per cent of the women candidates for state and national office interviewed by Hightower lacked this background (they had instead become involved in politics through the New Left and particularly the women's liberation movement, in the late 1960s), her study was based in the New York area, so that this high percentage is probably atypical (Hightower, 1977). More importantly, such women would not be recruited by the parties, but would have to recruit themselves.

There are, therefore, different ways to be selected as a candidate. Women who choose to contest party primaries are obviously less certain of selection than those whom the party recruits, particularly because they often encounter more difficulty in raising the campaign funds than do male contestants. Campaigning in the United States, as is well known, is a very expensive activity. 'Women do not ordinarily have access to large sums for campaigning, even if they are from wealthy families . . . nor do they have the contacts to tap outside financial resources, lacking access to the "oldboy" networks that donate a great deal of primary campaign money' (Epstein,

1981, p. 139). On the other hand, it is regularly observed that parties tend to select women candidates, without a primary contest, for seats that they are unlikely to win. Primaries are more likely to be held in constituencies which are considered 'safe', so that if a woman succeeds in the primary, she stands a better chance of also winning the seat.

At this point we must ask why women do so much better in some states than in others. Many factors are at work and, as Diamond shows, once a legislature has established a precedent of having a relatively large number of women members, this is itself the single best predictor of women's future numbers. None the less, the fundamental determinant appears to be the extent to which membership in a state's legislature is prized and contested. Women do best in those legislatures in which the ratio of seats to population is highest, whose constituencies are predominantly rural and which operate as 'citizen' rather than 'professional' bodies, that is as gatherings of public-spirited citizens rather than of full-time, aspiring politicians. In the Southern states, this explanation must be supplemented by reference to the impact of that region's tradi-tional, patriarchal culture. Again, we can explain the minimal numbers of women in the upper chambers of state legislatures – in 1985 they held 9.9 per cent of all state senate seats – in terms of the greater competition for the limited number of seats within them, together with the knock-on effect of the scale of female representa-tion in the lower house (Diamond, 1977).

I have considered so far the institutional process by which the pool of women eligible for national legislative office is constituted. Next we must examine the process of recruitment itself. In Britain, as in the United States, many women who would be eligible in terms of the criteria already discussed do not seek legislative office. Commentators like Kelley and Boutilier might like to put this down to childhood socialisation. An explanation at least as plausible is women's rational anticipation of further institutional barriers. If they have responsibility for young children they may be deterred by the time needed for travelling to and from the constituency they are contesting. If elected, they will face potentially difficult decisions about where they and their family should live. They will also face the prolonged and 'unsocial' hours of parliamentary sittings, together with the lack of creche facilities in an institution estab-lished for and by men. Less tangibly, they may fear the prejudice of the public and of male MPs. This is both reflected in, and perhaps encouraged by, the treatment of women politicians by the press. As Phillips notes 'the press expects that women candidates' moral standards must be absolutely beyond reproach, an expectation that is not made of their male colleagues' (Phillips, 1980, p. 106). For instance, when the *Daily Mirror* learned that Labour candidate Tessa Jowell was a divorcee, living with a married man, it ran a story entitled 'Love Confessions of Labour's Tessa'. As is better known, the press reacted viciously to two women MPs who deliberately drew attention to themselves as victims of male prejudice: Maureen Colquhoun, who declared publicly that she was a lesbian, and Helene Hayman, who breastfed her baby in the House of Commons. The physical appearance of women politicians holds a particular fascination for the media, and this inevitably trivialises women's political contribution.

The women whom such prospects cannot deter encounter further obstacles in the selection process, as Hills recounts. The Labour Party maintains two lists, the 'A' list of candidates nominated by trade unions and the 'B' list of candidates nominated by constituency parties, from which constituency parties select their shortlist of potential candidates. (There is an increasing tendency for would-be candidates to bypass these lists and approach the constituency directly). Conservative Central Office as well as the central organisation of the Liberal and Social Democratic Parties keep similar lists of approved candidates. Before the 1983 General Election all four main parties were anxious to be seen to promote women candidates. Within the Labour Party, women in the Campaign for Labour Party Democracy's Women's Action Committee and in Fightback for Women's Rights campaigned for higher rates of women's representation in the party and as parliamentary candidates. Between 1979 and 1983 the percentage of women on the Labour Party's lists rose from 10 to 15. On the trade union-sponsored 'A' list however, women were still only 4.5 per cent. The percentage of women in the Conservative and Liberal party lists also rose to 10 and 11 respectively and the Social Democrats came in with a record 17 per cent.

Party lists notwithstanding, the decisive agent of selection remains the constituency party, or at least its governing bodies. In fact, women seem to stand a good chance of being selected on to constituency shortlists. The Social Democrats have actually made it mandatory for two women to be included on any such shortlist and elsewhere a token woman seems almost *de rigueur* to give a list democratic credibility. It is in the next stage that the bias appears. Hills (1981b) found that in the Conservative Party women were less likely than men to be selected as candidates at all, while in the Labour Party they had a better than even chance. The percentage of women candidates has been rising in all parties. By 1983 it was 6 per cent in the Conservative Party and 12 per cent in Labour. In the smallest parties it was much higher, nearly 23 per cent in the Ecology Party. The real problem has been that women are considerably less likely than men to be nominated for safe seats. Thus in October 1974, 27 out of 161 women candidates were elected as against 608 out of 2,282 men, making the odds for men 3.7:1 but for women 6:1. In the 1979 General Election, 19 out of 138 women candidates were elected, increasing the odds against women to 7.3:1. This reflected the victory of the Conservatives who ran a total of only 31 women candidates. In the 1983 General Election there were a record number of women candidates, 276 or 10.7 per cent, but the eventual number of women elected was no higher than in 1979.

Vallance (1984) points out that this indicates it is not enough to press for more women to be selected as candidates. They have to be selected for seats they stand a good chance of winning. Constituencies in the south-east of England show greater readiness to select women than those further north. For women seeking Labour Party nomination this means that 'the areas most predisposed to accept a Labour woman are those where the party has least electoral power' (Vallance, 1984, p. 307). It is reported that the Labour Party has selected more women for traditional Labour seats, including the first black woman candidate – Diane Abott – this time round. If Labour wins no more seats than in 1983 the number of Labour women MPs is still likely to rise from 10 to 16, and if Labour does as well as the Conservative Party, the total could be 29 (*The Guardian*, 13 December 1985).

To pursue further the question of why so few women are selected for safe seats, it was suggested in the past that women were an electoral liability, because voters of both sexes preferred to vote for men. Possibly this was true in the early years when women stood for Parliament. It is always difficult to disentangle the effects of a candidate's sex from all the other variables that could influence electoral behaviour. In so far as it is possible, however, Vallance concludes that in recent General Elections the impact of a candidate's sex on voting results has been negligible (Vallance, 1979). Hills concedes, on the basis of an analysis of the General Elections of 1966, 1970 and October 1974, that the gender of the candidate may have a very marginal impact on electoral outcome. She does also point out that in these elections women's candidature did not in practice affect the outcome in any constituency (Hills, 1981b, p. 227). Darcy and Schramm reach a similar conclusion in their study of the elections for the US House of Representatives in 1970, 1972 and 1974, finding that when voting differentials are controlled for a candidate's party and incumbency status, their sex has little independent explanatory power (Darcy and Schramm, 1977). On the basis of an impressionistic survey of five general elections in Australia prior to 1977, Mackerras (1977) concluded that women did not lose votes, though it must be said that a later, more rigorous analysis which includes the 1980 General Election, finds that, taking other factors into account, women candidates do lose votes though the margins involved are very slight (Kelley and McAllister, 1983). The irrelevance of the candidate's sex has also been demonstrated in studies of local government elections in Britain, the United States and New Zealand. The only other Western democracy where sex has been reported as making a difference is Greece (De Giry, 1980). Yet, with the exception of Finland, in all these countries the available evidence suggests that women candidates are less likely than men to be chosen for safe seats. It is not the electorate that does not want women, so much as the 'selectorate', even if this partly reflects a mistaken anticipation of electoral attitudes.

A further obstacle to women's recruitment to Parliament may be the single-member first past the post electoral system. A good deal of interest has recently focused on the implications of electoral systems for women's representation. Several writers suggest that the party list version of proportional representation (PR) particularly favours women, because it encourages national parties to devise slates of candidates which are representative of the main groups in society, including the two sexes, so as to maximise their electoral appeal. As Vallance says, in a system such as ours 'where only one candidate is selected, all the pressures are to choose the standard product, largely middle-class, middle-aged and overwhelmingly male'. She cites Bogdanor's argument that 'whereas under a single-member system it is the *presence* of a candidate who deviates from the norm that is noticed, in any list system it is the *absence* of a woman, the failure to present a balanced ticket, which will be obvious' (Vallance, 1984, p. 308). A second, related, reason why such lists are more likely to include women may be that the choice at this level is not of the either/or kind as it is for instance in a single-member constituency, so that women are less directly in competition with men. Certainly advocates of PR can make a formidable case. For instance, in France, women's numbers in the National Assembly declined after 1958, when the PR system was replaced by a version of plurality voting, and on the other hand, when PR was reintroduced for European elections in 1979, women's share of French seats in the European Parliament rose to 21 per cent while they remained only 4.3 per cent of the national legislature. Proportional representation party list systems coincide with comparatively high rates of female membership in national legislatures in the Scandinavian countries and the Netherlands. Though lower in Belgium, Italy and Israel for example, women still do better in these countries than in Britain, France or the USA (though it must be acknowledged that in both New Zealand and Canada, with single-member plurality voting systems, rates of women's representation have risen considerably over the last few years). Norris (1985b), using a stepwise multiple regression analysis on data for 24 liberal democracies concludes that the type of electoral system is the single most significant variable in explaining variations in women's legislative participation rates but that cultural attitudes, as measured by an index of 'egalitarianism' are also relevant.

If the electoral system does make a real difference, however, I would suggest that this is in part because it allows the central party leadership more say in the selection of candidates, and central leadership, these days, is more inclined than local to promote women. (This may incidentally be one reason why women in Britain have recently done so well in by-elections; the national party leaders take a more direct part in the proceedings, including the selection of candidates.) The Irish Republic is a case in point. Ireland has a single transferable vote (STV) version of PR which means that there are multi-member districts but these are relatively small, sending 3–5 members to the Dail, and selection of candidates has tended to be dominated by local party organisations and traditional clientelist orientations. However, party leaders can, exceptionally, impose additional candidates on constituency lists and recently their greater interest in sponsoring women candidates has contributed to the increased number of women TDs. In sum, PR can make a difference but only in conjunction with other favourable circumstances. Since such circumstances do prevail in Britain, its introduction here would almost certainly boost women's representation. Its introduction in the USA would entail such changes in the party system that there is little point in guessing what the eventual consequences for women's political participation would be.

Staying with the US, we find a still greater reluctance among political party leaders, or influentials, to sponsor women candidates. In 1970, 1972 and 1974, out of 1099 contested elections for Congressional office, only 87 featured women candidates. By 1980 women were 6.3 per cent of candidates for elections to the House of Representatives. It must be relevant that Congress is the most powerful legislature in the world, both because of the wealth and international power of the United States and because of its degree of constitutional and political independence from the executive branch of government. But it has also been argued that women candidates or potential candidates have particular difficulties in raising the funds necessary to fight electoral campaigns. Analysing campaign receipts for the 1980 congressional campaigns, Uhlaner and Schlozman conclude that women candidates do not face any specific disadvantages as women, as opposed to substantial disadvantages as non-incumbents (1986).

Barriers inside the legislature

We must finally consider the institutional constraints facing women who do become legislators. Since there are few women candidates for safe seats, the rate of turnover of women members is high, compounding the disadvantage of being on average somewhat older than their male colleagues at the outset of their legislative career. Furthermore, some women MPs feel like intruders in the 'gentlemen's club' atmosphere of the House of Commons, while Congresswomen reported 'generalised resistance in informal relations' and exclusion from such important informal organisations as the 'club' (Gehlen, 1969, p. 37). However, when Vallance matches men and women MPs according to their length of service and other relevant qualifications, she finds that their chances of reaching Front Bench positions are roughly equal. Both Gehlen (1969) and Gertzog (1984) finds no obvious evidence of recent discrimination against women in promotion to committee chairs and other leadership positions, in the House of Representatives, particularly when account is taken of the importance attached to length of service as a criterion for promotion. Gertzog, however, points to women's exclusion from the most powerful informal House caucuses, suggesting that this may handicap them in seeking leadership positions and getting women's issues onto the agenda. What has been much more noticeable is women's specialisation in the traditional 'feminine' fields as far as government appointments go in Britain and in committee assignments in Congress, though Gertzog finds by the ninety-eighth Congressional session, from 1982, that this pattern is breaking down. Incidentally a similar over-concentration of women in parliamentary committees dealing with 'feminine' issues has been noted in a number of West European countries. In the French National Assembly in 1981, ten women served on the Committee on Cultural, Family and Social Affairs, three on the Committees on Foreign Affairs and Defence respectively and none on the Finance Committee. This pattern still holds in the Scandinavian legislatures (see Norderval, 1985, p. 84). In 1985 there were nine women serving on the Swedish parliamentary committee on cultural affairs, three on the foreign policy committee, two on the defence committee and none on the 15-member finance committee (Statistics Sweden, 1985, p. 58). It is often not clear how far such specialisation stems from the actual preferences of women politicians. But when we learn that Sir Harold Wilson, who is often singled out as the British Prime Minister who did most to encourage women in Parliament, admits that he would never have dared appoint a woman overlord of those strongholds of male chauvinism, the Home Office, the Treasury and the Foreign Office, we cannot doubt that institutional barriers are still sometimes decisive (Phillips, 1980).

This analysis suggests that any satisfactory explanation of the dearth of women politicians must stress not simply women's availability but the way this is shaped by the character of modern politics. Not only can parallels be traced in the experience of women in other Western democracies, it is clear that such institutional barriers also exist in communist systems. To begin with, women are less likely than men to be party members, the prerequisite both for higher party office and for professional advancement, which in turn can lead to higher political position. Though women's incidence in district and regional party bodies is higher than in Central Committees, they 'appear to be excluded from those positions of regional party leadership, such as district first secretary, which serve as recruiting channels into the central party élite' (Wolchik, 1981, p. 261). The women who do reach the Central Committee moreover tend to have occupied lower party and government positions prior to this promotion than their male colleagues. A disproportionately large number of them have been involved in mass organisational and propaganda work, whose status within the party, Moses suggests, is relatively low (Moses, 1976). Accordingly, women within the Central Committee have less authority, a more rapid turnover rate and less likelihood of top party office. This pattern prevails throughout Eastern Europe, though Wolchik finds sex differences in political careers and recruitment channels greatest in Poland and Hungary.

Given these cumulative institutional hurdles, discrimination is simply the last straw. There are of course real difficulties with the concept of discrimination. It is almost impossible to prove the intention to discriminate. Even with full information, it is often difficult to know whether a person apparently discriminated against on grounds of their sex, possessed all other legitimately relevant qualifications for the position concerned. But if we simply infer discrimination from the discrepancy between the proportion of the eligible contestants who are female and the proportion of those selected who are female, then it would appear that such discrimination, though declining, is by no means extinct. Tolchin, for instance, finds it rampant in the process of recruitment for the American judiciary, whether its basis is selection on merit, partisan election or non-partisan election (Tolchin, 1977). UN agencies, such as UNICEF and the FAO, will refuse to appoint women to posts in countries where they argue the indigenous government will not accept them, although this may not in fact be so (Rogers, 1983, pp. 50–1).

Strategies for women?

Let us assume for the moment that feminists should want to increase women's participation in political élites. Chapters 5 and 6 are centrally concerned with feminist strategy. Here I shall briefly suggest which factors emerge from the preceding analysis as most conducive to a leading political role for women.

If the question was posed at the level of the individual aspiring woman politician, an initial, frivolous answer would be 'Take out Norwegian, Swedish or Finnish citizenship'. Women's chances also seem to be somewhat better, other things being equal, in the more industrialised nations, though within these paradoxically their representation is sometimes greater in rural than in urban areas. Examples are state legislatures in the United States and local councils in Britain, France and Yugoslavia. This may be because there is less competition for government or party office in rural areas. On the other hand there are more women in urban than in rural local authorities in Sweden, Finland and the Irish Republic.

What this does all indicate is of course that particular strategies need to be tailored to the political system in question. Thus in the Republic of Ireland, experience in local government seems to be especially helpful for aspiring politicians. In the United States being wealthy or in a position to tap other wealthy people's resources is indispensable.

It is also evident that tactics will vary according to which channel of political participation one is broaching. Within the judicial channel the first step must be increasing the numbers of women who qualify as lawyers (this will of course also increase the pool of women 'eligible' for parliamentary careers). The proportion of women amongst law students is reported to be growing in the United States, Britain, France and Ireland. Promotion within the judiciary is very much on a step-ladder model. As Lovenduski points out, judges in the British High Court and above are selected from amongst the group of barristers qualifying as Queen's Counsels. By 1983 women were 11 per cent of barristers in England but only 3 per cent of QCs (Lovenduski, 1986a, p. 217). Careers in government bureaucracy are similarly graduated. In France a critical initial stage is getting into one of the Grandes Ecoles or higher professional training colleges, notably the Ecole Nationale d'Administration (ENA). Though the ENA was from its creation in 1945 coeducational in principle, during the 1970s 90 per cent and still by 1983 75 per cent of its students were male. It is from the ENA that members of the Grands Corps are primarily drawn. With the coming to power of the socialist Government in 1981, efforts were made to reduce the rigidity of the system and to promote women, with what long-term results remains to be seen. Women civil servants have also been recently appointed in increasing numbers to the politically important private offices of ministers and in 1984 held seven of 44 posts in the President's Office (Lovenduski, 1986a, pp. 223–3; Mossuz-Lavau and Sineau, 1984, pp. 40–44). In Britain the Civil Service authorities now monitor ethnic minority and female employment and have designated eqality officers.

It is apparent, however, that for the moment and within the context of conventional politics, women generally have more hope of penetrating the 'numerically' representative institutions than other political arenas. Prerequisites for entry are easier to satisfy, and the process of recruitment and promotion is more susceptible to pressure from below. In regards to this numerical channel a number of points can be made.

First, women do best where competition is least, for instance in local rather than central government or in some state legislatures more than in others, indicating perhaps the most promising starting point for women's assault on the political citadel. In some countries standing for the upper chamber of the national assembly may serve this function; such for instance appears to be the experience of a number of Irish women TDs who formerly served in the Seanad. Possibly contesting elections for the European Parliament can also play this role. Apart from the intrinsic importance of being an MEP, a woman will enhance her eligibility for national parliamentary office through gaining relevant experience. Even if she loses the election campaign she will have had useful publicity. There is always, though, the danger that by approaching national politics via less powerful or prestigious bodies one ends up in a powerless cul-de-sac.

Second we have seen that women's chances of selection and election are greatest under the party list system of proportional representation. Perhaps, then, women in Britain should be campaigning for adoption of PR. There is a further debate about exactly which form of party list system most assists women. Rank-ordering arrangements, prevalent in Norway, Sweden and Iceland, mean that the party leadership itself ranks candidates, so that those further down the list have less chance of getting a seat. Preferential voting arrangements allow the voters to reorder the list of candidates as they choose. It is argued that this format, used in Denmark and Finland, has been more advantageous for women (Norderval, 1985). Obviously the implications of rank-ordering depend on the priorities of the party leaderships concerned.

Mossuz-Lavau and Sineau consider whether it makes a difference if elections are direct or indirect. They note, as we have done, that in some countries women are better represented in the upper than the lower chamber of the national assembly. Where, however, these upper chambers are indirectly elected, there has been, they suggest, a tendency to over-represent rural areas, leading as in France and for a long time in the Netherlands, to 'anti-feminist' attitudes and low levels of female representation. On the other hand, where members are appointed, this can help women, as in Ireland and Britain (Mossuz-Lavau and Sineau, 1984).

This brings us back to the importance of sponsorship. So often we find that the critical factor is not the willingness of women to come forward, the attitude of the electorate or even, in itself, the mechanism of the electoral system but the readiness of the political leadership (which must generally be assumed to be male) in parties, unions, government, to take steps that will *ensure* increased female representation. Sponsorship can take any number of forms. It ranges from the personal encouragement of a political leader, such as Mahatma Gandhi or Sir Harold Wilson, to some system of quotas or other form of positive discrimination in recruitment. In 1972 Sweden's Liberal, Social Democratic and Communist Parties virtually simultaneously adopted quota systems to increase women's access to leading party positions, an example followed since by a number of parties elsewhere; these include the French Socialist Party which adopted a 10 per cent quota of women for its steering committee, politburo and secretariat in 1973, extended to 20 per cent in 1979, Norway's Liberal and Socialist Parties and the Dutch Labour Party which called for a 25 per cent female presence at all levels. Some further parties reserve places for women, as in the British Labour Party's NEC, but Mossuz-Lavau and Sineau argue that this disadvantageously affects women's status. It implies that women are there to represent other women in the party and deal with women-related issues, and it tends to restrict women's representation to this limited form (Mossuz-Lavau and Sineau, 1984, p. 116). Parties can similarly set quotas for women candidates in local and national elections. Again it has been the Swedish Communist and Liberal Parties, the Dutch Labour Party and the French Socialist Party who have led the way. Even then it must be said that actual rates of women candidates do not necessarily achieve quota targets. Saddest of all, in 1986 the French Socialist Party facing the prospect of mortal combat with the right, and despite its official policy of a 20 per cent quota of women candidates, in practice kept down their number to around 8 per cent (*The Guardian*, 7 January 1986). While instances of positive discrimination are relatively rare, chiefly confined to a few countries and parties in the developed world, it is noteworthy that the Congress Party in India has long required that 15 per cent of its candidates in state elections whould be women. Though this quota is rarely achieved, the concentration of women candidates in the Congress Party is striking.

It is tempting to argue further that such sponsorship, and political opportunities for women in general, tend to occur within parties, and other political institutions on the left. But this can only be maintained with considerable qualification. In Britain women are more likely to be selected as parliamentary candidates by the Labour than the Conservative Party, though hitherto their chances have been highest of all with the Liberals. Labour women MPs are also more likely than Conservative to achieve government office. In local elections, however, outside London, women do best in rural Conservative authorities. In a succession of other European countries, figures cited by Mossuz-Lavau and Sineau show that women were a higher percentage of parliamentarians of left-wing than other main political parties: in Norway (1982), Denmark (1979), Holland (1977), Portugal (1982), Switzerland (1983), Austria (1979), Italy (1983), Belgium (1979) and France (1983) (Mossuz-Lavau and Sineau, 1984, pp. 82–4). The recent increase of parliamentary representation in Australia and New Zealand reflects the advent of Labour governments. On the other hand in Sweden and Norway, Liberal and Centre Parties nowadays show at least as great a will to promote women as the left-wing parties. And of course outside Western democracies, 'socialism' is no guarantee of an increased political role for women. Even the great Allende is reported as saying 'When I say woman, I always think of the woman-mother. When I talk of the woman, I refer to her in her function in the nuclear family . . . the child is the prolongation of the woman who in essence is born to be a mother' (cited by Aviel, 1981, p. 168); not surprisingly he included no women in his government. The extent to which the left is a friend to woman is a thorny question (see my further discussion: Randall, 1986a) but in so far as left-wing parties have taken the lead in bringing women into public politics, what motivates them? Mossuz-Lavau and Sineau argue that ideology must be given some credit. 'It was unthinkable that political movements holding egalitarian principles which have always given pride of place to defending oppressed minorities should help to perpetuate a situation where half the electorate was excluded from political decision-making centres' (1984, p. 90). But self-interest has also been at work. Left-wing parties look for their electoral support and political activists to less privileged social sectors.

What about the contribution of women's organisations? There was for some time a lively debate about the merits of the women's sections within the British Labour and Conservative parties. These exist at branch level, electing delegates to higher level women's organisations and ultimately to the Women's Annual Conference and National Women's Advisory Committee. Their principal function is to provide an exclusive forum for women and, in the past at least, they have espoused a very traditional view of women's political role. More recently, particularly in the Labour Party, many have been influenced by feminist ideas and begun to press more strenuously for women's representation within the main body of the party. Even so, opinions differ as to how far they promote women's influence in the parties. On the one hand they could provide 'useful preliminary training and experience for a subsequent career' but on the other the danger is that 'able women may satisfy their aspirations within these associations where there is less competition for prestige party positions, and thereby be diverted from contemplating a career as an elected representative' (Currell, 1978, p. 12). Women's sections may also encourage men in the party to persist in viewing women as politically different, and in some sense marginal. In Norway and in Canada, feminist party members have been less reservedly critical of the women's auxiliaries, but in the Australian Labour Party and under the influence of women's liberation, these have helped to liberalise policy on women. We have seen how in many Third World countries, and even up to a point in communist states, the women's sections have been used both to mobilise and to contain women's political activism. On balance, it appears that women's sections are not the best focus for women's political energies, but that, when imbued with feminist ideals, they can still be valuable in pressing for greater female representation.

This brings us to the role of more explicitly feminist organisations. Rather than constituting a section of a pre-existing party, women have at certain times attempted to launch their own, for instance in France and Canada. The most successful attempt has been in Iceland, where the Women's Party formed in 1983 won 5 per cent of the vote. But while it may encourage other parties to run women candidates, this strategy does not seem likely directly to bring large numbers of women to power. Other feminist organisations have concentrated on increasing women's presence within existing political institutions. There is no doubt that this strategy has been pursued furthest in the United States, where in 1971 a National Woman's Political Caucus was formed, with branch caucuses in all the fifty states. From the first, and following a deliberate policy, it was bipartisan, and it has put pressure on both parties not only to select women candidates for state and congressional elections but to appoint them to the whole range of public political offices. Growing out of the NWPC were two further bodies, the National Women's Education Fund set up in 1973 with the object of providing women with more information and training to prepare them for political participation, and the Women's Campaign Fund, formed in 1974 to raise funds for feminist Congressional candidates. While it is difficult to distinguish between the broader influence of the women's movement and the specific work of these organisations, they must take some of the credit for women's increased participation in Congress and especially in the states legislatures (Fraser, 1983). A Women's Electoral Lobby was formed in Australia in 1972 with the same objective, and similarly the British 300 Group, founded in 1980, has sought to transcend party divisions and promote women's political participation, though with only modest results to date. Additionally feminist-inclined women have formed informal or more formal groups *within* political parties and trade unions in order to press for a greater role for women in the political leadership. An example is the Women's Action Committee in the British Labour Party. In the United States a Coalition of Labour Union Women (CLUW) was set up in 1974 to promote women within the overwhelmingly male union hierarchy, though its membership by 1983 was only 16,000 (Gelb, 1985).

There are lessons that feminists can learn about narrowly political strategies to increase women's political role, but this analysis has also underlined the constraints upon that role imposed by women's present domestic obligations and occupational patterns. How feminists can hope to change these is a subject for later chapters.

A distinctive contribution?

It may be argued that we need to know more about the behaviour of women politicians, before deciding whether, as feminists, we want to increase their numbers. Do such women make a distinctive contribution to policy and politics, and is that contribution compatible with feminist objectives?

Several writers have argued that we need to differentiate between types of women politician in terms of their personal and political backgrounds. Though each author offers a rather different classification, we can make a very basic distinction between three sorts of women in politics. First are the 'male equivalents', the women who acquired political office through their relationship to politically prominent men and who, with notable exceptions like Margaret Chase Smith, the first woman to run for the United States Presidency, could be expected to have traditional assumptions about women's political role. Second are the great majority of women politicians in modern societies, women who came into politics relatively late, after bringing up their children and without a background of employment in one of the professions that 'converge' with political office. Such women will have a range of political styles and orientations. These can perhaps be summarised in Diamond's distinction between the Traditional Civic Worker and the Women's Rights Advocate. They are probably unlikely to be politically very ambitious (Diamond, 1977). Finally, we may be witnessing the emergence of a new breed of woman politician, who enters politics relatively young and with a background of professional employment, notably in law, and who though not necessarily single or without children will have found ways, through the co-operation of an enlightened husband or the ability to pay for professional child care, to prevent domestic responsibilities impeding her career (Stoper, 1977). Such women will share feminist values, if only to the extent that these are instrumental to their own success. They will be more ambitious, more ready to put themselves forward uninvited and more prepared to face political contest.

Despite the difficulties of generalising, it is still instructive to examine these women for political style, policy orientation and attitude to women's rights. Crudely, we could ask whether traditional sex-related differences in behaviour, as far as these exist, carry over into the élite political arena or whether women politicians, through the processes of selective recruitment and secondary political socialisation within political institutions, come to behave just like the men.

Existing studies show that women in politics vary both in the extent to which they perceive style to be a problem and in their preference for a 'feminine', 'masculine' or somehow androgynous style. Diamond finds that those women who opt for a feminine style are also those least likely to be aware of the problem. Nearly always, however, women politicians avoid behaviour adversely associated with the feminine stereotype, such as emotionalism and flirtatiousness. They nearly always compensate for women's supposed silliness by doing their 'homework' with extreme conscientiousness. At the same time, some women who are by no means 'feminine' in their political ambitions are not averse to exploiting the popular idea of womanhood in their public image. In Latin America, the role of the 'supermadre' has been almost indispensable for aspiring women politicians and' as Lynn and Flora suggest, may have been the means by which those women reconciled themselves to their own ambitions (Lynn and Flora, 1977). Mrs Thatcher has been happy to present herself as an ordinary housewife, trying to balance her housekeeping budget and, more recently as the nurse ministering a sick national economy who must be cruel to be kind.

Women legislators have been described as a little less active than men, less willing to speak up and less inclined to initiate. Vallance writes of 'a certain sense of anti-climax' when reviewing the achievements of British women MPs, mainly because of their ineptitude for self-advertisement (Vallance, 1979, p. 111). Women in India's state assemblies are particularly timid, but this must be partly due to their male colleagues' unrestrained chauvinism (Mazumdar, 1979). Women legislators have also been reproached for their lack of ambition and amateurism. Kirkpatrick finds them to be rather more moralistic than men, preferring to see politics as problem-solving rather than as a power-struggle (Kirkpatrick, 1974), while Diamond's women are averse to bargaining and resistant to lobbyists. The question is whether such behaviour does reflect a genuinely different orientation to politics, or whether it is a rationalisation of women's weaker political position. After all, Diamond points out that lobbyists are less likely to approach women politicians in the first place, because they are perceived as less powerful. Again, Diamond notes the salience of women legislators' relationship with their constituents, suggesting that the constituents find them approachable and sympathetic. Githens argues that many women legislators would like to play a specialist role in policy-making, but are forced, because of their lack of appropriate political or occupational experience, into playing the delegate role, representing the views and interests of their constituents (Githens, 1977).

Are women politicians more 'liberal' or 'radical' than men? Hills points out that in Britain's Parliamentary Labour Party during the Parliament that ran from October 1974 to 1979, 12 per cent of women but only 6 per cent of men were in the left-wing Tribune Group (Hills, 1981b). We are dealing, of course, with tiny figures. In the United States, Diamond has shown women state legislators to be slightly more liberal than men, for instance in their views on how best to discourage riots and civil disorder. Gehlen also found Congresswomen over the years 1968 to 1974 marginally more liberal than Congressmen in the same political party, as indicated by interest-group ratings and voting patterns (Gehlen, 1977). Norris, most recently, has compared the voting records of the 41 Congresswomen in the House of Representatives between 1969 and 1983 with those of a matched sample of Congressmen. Constructing a liberal-conservative index by which to evaluate votes, she finds that party is the single best predictor of index ratings but when this is controlled for, there is a consistent tendency for women to be more liberal than men (Norris, 1986b). All authors emphasise, however, that the differences are minor.

The difficulty of distinguishing between what women would like to do and what they are obliged to do arises again when we turn to the policy areas they specialise in. Their concentration on 'women's subjects' – health, welfare, education, and more recently women themselves, and consumer affairs – is universal. Only exceptionally does a ministerial appointment deviate from this rule, for instance Barbara Castle's designation as Transport Minister and then Secretary of State for Employment and Productivity. How far is this a matter of choice? In Congress and the state legislatures, those committees, as far as they are identifiable, that deal with traditional feminine concerns have in the past included a disproportionately high number of women, though such specialisation shows signs of erosion. Congresswomen have also tended to concentrate on these subjects, when introducing bills (Gehlen, 1969 and 1977).

Similarly, in the British House of Commons, Private Members' Bills submitted by women have generally been of this kind. However Vallance has compiled an 'index of specialisation', based on the proportion of interventions in debates by women MPs, excluding ministers, concerned with health, welfare, education or consumerism. In 1950 the index was 42 per cent, in 1964 29.3 per cent, and in 1974 39 per cent. Overall she concludes that these women 'are not exclusively, even mainly, concerned with women's affairs' (Vallance, 1979, p. 197). Women's affairs still dominate the contributions of women speakers in the assemblies of such different countries as Australia, the Soviet Union and India. Even so, this may in part reflect, or anticipate the pattern of committee appointments over which women legislators have little say.

The remaining question is arguably the most important. Do women politicians promote women's rights? Once more, the evidence is contradictory. Although individual British women MPs have always campaigned valiantly on behalf of their sex, Vallance and Currell describe the typical woman MP as seeing herself as an MP first and a woman second. Currell however, found amongst women parliamentary candidates a growing tendency to explain their own experience in social rather than personal terms, that is a greater feminist consciousness (Currell, 1978). Vallance too points to the emergence of a new solidarity amongst Labour women MPs, largely stimulated by attempts to revise the 1967 Abortion Act. As Chapter 6 will describe, this has played no small part in the major legislative gains made for women during the 1970s. In the United States, Kirkpatrick found that only three of the forty-six women state legislators she interviewed did not support the Equal Rights Amendment, but generally they were reluctant to campaign for women's rights partly because they risked losing the political credit with their male colleagues they had so painstakingly acquired (Kirkpatrick, 1974). According to Gehlen, Congresswomen in the 1960s were more sympathetic to women's rights than Congressmen. Carroll (1984) found in her 1976 survey of American women candidates for state or national office that they scored high on feminist attitudes but no so well on feminist behaviour, as indicated by organisational affiliation or initiating discussion on women's questions during campaigns. She suggests, therefore, that they are best described as 'closet feminists'.

In 1977 a Women's Caucus was formed in Congress, including 15 women, all but three Congresswomen at the time. It was led initially by the redoubtable Bela Abzug and worked on legislative priorities and interrogation of administration officials. In order to get round funding problems, in 1978 it set up the formally independent Women's Research and Education Institute which by the beginning of the 1980s had six full-time staff. From the start its rule that decisions must be unanimous created difficulties. After the 1978 Congressional elections when it lost several of its most stalwart members, and especially following the change of caucus rules which obliged it to include men, it declined in significance. Gertzog (1984) suggests that its finest hour was in extending the deadline for ratification of the Equal Rights Amendment (see Chapter 6) but that otherwise its impact on legislation has been slight.

Vallance and Davies, on the other hand, argue that women's increased representation *has* made a difference in the European Parliament since 1979. Though these women cannot take all the credit, they heightened awareness of issues related to sex equality is striking. From 12 written questions placed before the chamber that dealt with such issues in 1978, by 1979 the number had risen to 45. And it is unlikely that the equality directives of the late 1970s (discussed more fully in Chapter 6) would have been followed through in the 1980s with an Action Programme and further directives without the concerted pressure of the women's committee (Vallance and Davies, 1986). In Norway, Hernes and Voje find that women in 'corporate' political institutions have a fairly high degree of feminist consciousness, with 18 per cent of their sample in self-styled feminist groups (Hernes and Voje, 1980). In Sweden, too, by 1980 women MPs were discussing ways of uniting across party lines on women's issues (Eduards, 1981). Elsewhere there is less evidence that women politicians are strongly committed to liberating their sisters. Whether it is Canada, India or the Lebanon, on this question they toe the party line.

This raises the question of whether a certain 'critical mass' in numbers of women delegates is required before the effect on policies will be felt. It has been suggested for instance that senior women administrators are particularly valuable because they are more likely than their male colleagues to be responsive to women's problems and perspectives, especially in the context of national and international development agencies. But their impact will be greater if they remain 'clustered' in specific departments or agencies rather than being scattered, with a 'token' woman in each sector. The token woman appointee will be under pressure to side with the majority group in that organisation against their own and to adopt acceptable, stereotyped roles, as well as being subject to extra stress (Rogers, 1983).

It seems, in conclusion, that women politicians do not behave very differently from men. Their differences in political style are at least partially attributable to their lack of power. Similarly their apparent specialisation in feminine areas of policy-making largely reflects the roles assigned to them by male-dominated political institutions. Finally, while under the influence of women's liberation, women politicians in Western democracies may be growing more sympathetic with feminist values, they will not usually risk their careers for them, and this is as likely to be true of the new breed of women in politics as of the earlier incarnations.

4

How politics affects women

It only really makes sense to emphasise women's participation in public politics if it can be shown that policy outcomes do affect women. This chapter looks at the impact of public policy on women. The growing literature that examines such policy in different national and historical contexts makes clear that women, as a distinct group, *have* been importantly affected. A comparative approach also suggests a possible explanation for the form that policies towards women have taken.

The primary concern here is with the impact of 'male-dominated' politics, and so analysis will be confined to developments prior to the second wave of feminism in the late 1960s. The focus will be on the impact of politics on women's status. Social scientists employ the term 'status' in a number of different ways. Here, following Giele, it will be equated with 'life options' (Giele, 1977a, p. 4). This chapter examines women's options in the following spheres: powers within marriage, control of sexuality and fertility, rights and duties as mothers, control of wealth and income, employment and education.

Non-Marxist and Marxist political scientists are increasingly agreed that the political sphere is not simply instrumental to social forces, to groups or classes; it has practices, resources and interests of its own and acts back upon society. By what means has public policy impinged upon women's status? Laws have often been passed which, while reflecting prevailing or least socially dominant attitudes, reinforced these attitudes by articulating them, imparting definition and authority, and thus helped to prolong them beyond what would otherwise have been their 'natural' lifespan. For

157

instance, France's Napoleonic Code included a clause attributing all powers within marriage to the husband, which was not revoked until 1938. At other times, however, such laws reflected not so much dominant values embodied in practice as prevalent myths that were contradicted by reality, so that in fact the laws changed women's status. The law could also anticipate changing values, as for example Britain's 1967 Abortion Reform Law.

Usually the law or policy would be backed up by sanctions or the positive distribution of resources. Thus in many countries in the past and still in some today, procuring an abortion is a crime punishable by law. The law regulates, through the use of sanctions, what women can do. It also intervenes in women's access to resources; it can deny women rights to property and income, or, as more recently, it can actually direct public resources in ways that influence women's status, as in subsidies for nursery provision.

Laws and policies have not only affected women's status directly. In the past, indeed, it has often seemed that the law had little to say specifically about women. Part of the reason was the importance attached to the 'privacy' of the family, within which women were largely confined. Nowadays in Britain such privacy is increasingly absent as the Welfare State authorises the intervention of social workers, magistrates and the police; Wilson goes so far as to say that 'social welfare policies amount to no less than the state organisation of domestic life' (Wilson, 1977, p. 9). Even so McIntosh argues that the state still 'intervenes' less conspicuously in the lives of women than of men (McIntosh, 1978, p. 256). As she rightly concludes, this requires us to examine not only the direct effects of policies upon women, but also the part played by the state 'in establishing and sustaining systems in which women are oppressed and subordinated by men' (ibid., p. 259). Such an approach reveals that apparent respect for privacy has often in fact been 'coercive', as when the public authorities refused to intervene in wife-battering. It also points us to the indirect implications of present policies: for instance, the way in which social security is administered in Britain tens to reinforce the wife's economic dependence on her husband.

Politics and women's status in Britain

If these are the means by which policy has helped to shape women's status, what has been the cumulative impact of politics and policies upon women? The example of Britain over the last one and a half centuries, which is relatively well documented, is a useful starting point.

Despite their different specialism and approaches, writers on this subject are in startling agreement. They show that, with only minor exceptions, the cumulative effect of a vast battery of laws and policies was, directly and indirectly, to reinforce women's dependence upon men and responsibility for home-making and child-rearing. During the eighteenth and much of the nineteenth centuries women lost all legal identity – including property rights – on marriage, had little control over their own fertility and virtually no redress against rape, were severely discriminated against in employment and pay, were denied access to higher education and were deprived of all rights to participate politically and as jurors. In the twentieth century the picture has of course become more complex: a growing number of policies have promoted women's independence, legal, political and financial. At the same time, policies associated with the development of the Welfare State have seemed to undermine that independence and certainly to be predicated upon women's 'traditional' domestic role. By the end of the 1960s therefore, and before the full impact of the women's liberation movement, the implications of public policies for women's independence were somewhat contradictory. What was clear was that they still had not challenged women's primary responsibility for the care of children and the home. These points will be considered further, as we examine policies affecting the six aspects of women's status distinguished earlier.

Women's status in Britain has firstly been influenced by the way that *marriage* is defined and regulated, through statute, judicial decision and for administrative purposes. Marriage has historically been the lot of the majority of women; even nowadays, most women marry. For example, in 1973 approximately 90 per cent of women aged 25 to 44 were or had been married.

Under eighteenth-century common law, a woman upon marriage lost her separate legal identity. Blackstone wrote, 'the very being or legal existence of the woman is suspended during the marriage, or at least is incorporated and consolidated into that of the husband under whose wing, protection and cover, she performs everything' (O'Donovan, 1979, p. 136). Her husband decided the education and religion of their children. Most seriously, perhaps, the woman lost all rights to ownership or control of any property, or income, she brought into the marriage.

Despite these incapacitating restrictions, the conventional view was that the law did not interfere with the essentially private realm of marriage and the family. Though the husband, as head of the household, was supposed to provide for his family, this was not legally enforceable. The most oppressive consequence of this compulsory privacy was that the wife had no legal recourse against physical assault by her husband.

Marriage law has become steadily less harsh. Beginning with the Matrimonial Causes Act of 1857, the legitimate grounds for divorce have widened. The 1882 Married Women's Property Act gave women legal authority over the property they brought into the marriage. In 1886 women became eligible for custody over their children following divorce, though the subsequent judicial assumption that mothers should normally have custody, given inadequate financial assistance, has proved burdensome in a different way. Not until the 1970s were wives allowed a share of property acquired during the marriage. Not until the 1976 Domestic Violence and Matrimonial Proceedings Act were wives provided with some, albeit limited, protection against violent husbands. Perhaps most important, as we shall see, the administration of income tax, national insurance and supplementary benefits has reflected, and still partly reflects, the assumption of female dependence, which is increasingly belied by the facts. In 1974, for instance, in over half a million couples the wife was the main earner, while in a further seven million couples, where the husband was under 65, the wife contributed around a quarter of the family budget (O'Donovan, 1979, pp. 135–6).

The second major aspect of women's lives to be considered concerns their *control over their own bodies*, or more specifically their sexuality and fertility. Clearly this is importantly affected by the policies towards marriage already discussed. We must also examine availability of birth control, of contraception and abortion, as well as public policy on rape.

In the nineteenth century, birth control depended upon sexual abstinence, primitive forms of contraception, backstreet abortions and a high natural rate of infant mortality. Abortion was illegal; under Section 58 of the 1861 Offences Against the Person Act, its procurers were liable to imprisonment. Though the sheath and diaphragm were in production by the 1880s, the government would not permit public health authorities to provide birth control information.

Birth control policy changed dramatically, before the 1970s, as a result of political factors at least as much as technological innovations. Although from the early nineteenth century neo-Malthusians, as well as socialists such as Owen, had advocated contraception, it was Marie Stopes who, in the 1920s, began to make family planning respectable. As Lewis points out, one of her most effective arguments was that it would contribute to the improvement of the race by making mothers and babies healthier and by controlling the fertility of women who were 'unfit' to have children (Lewis, 1979). Although in 1930 the Government accepted that birth control information should be provided to married women on specific medical grounds, it was not until 1949 that this was extended to all married women, perhaps because of fears in the mid-1930s of a population decline. The contraceptive pill, developed in the United States, became commercially available by the early 1960s. Initially it was provided by family planning clinics and family doctors, but the 1967 National Health Services (Family Planning) Act authorised local authorities to give family planning advice and appliances to anyone in need, and if necessary free of charge. As Greenwood and King make clear, the present situation is far from ideal, yet it represents an enormous improvement (Greenwood and King, 1981).

By the end of the nineteenth century doctors regularly performed abortions when a woman's life was in danger. Legislation in 1929 recognised this, and in 1938 legal abortions were also permitted to safeguard a woman's physical or mental health. In 1936 a small but committed group of feminists formed the Abortion Law Reform Association, whose pressures underlay a series of attempts, beginning in 1952, to reform the law by means of a Private Member's Bill. When, assisted by the thalidomide scandal and a sympathetic Labour government, David Steel's 1967 Act was passed, it was still ahead of public and medical opinion. In the 1970s, therefore, second wave feminism had to defend, not to win, abortion law reform.

As writers like Brownmiller have emphasised, public policy towards rape matters not only to the actual rape victims but to all women as potential victims. It also matters because of the attitudes to women's sexuality and indeed their independence, that it implies and condones (Brownmiller, 1975). Although British law has long recognised it as a serious offence, in practice it has proved extremely difficult to get a rape conviction. Even the 1976 Sexual Offences (Amendment) Act did not make it that much easier.

Until the 1976 Act, rape was not a statutory offence but was governed by the common law. In the early nineteenth century it was punishable by death. This may however have been one reason for the very low rate of convictions. In 1810, of twenty-four committed to trial on rape charges, sixteen were not proceeded against, six were acquitted, two convicted and one executed (Toner, 1977, p. 98). Although the death penalty was lifted in 1840, convictions remain rare. Rape victims were deterred by the difficulty of persuading the police they had a case, by the requirement in practice though not in law of corroborative evidence, by the defence's right to cite the previous sexual conduct of the prosecutrix and by their own lack of anonymity. Despite changing attitudes of women, police, jurors and lawyers, in 1975 there were still 1040 rapes recorded as crimes by the police, though many more were reported and doubtless still more committed; 544 men charged with rape came before Magistrates' Courts, 321 were found guilty and 241 imprisoned. In this respect then, policy towards women's sexual self-determination had not greatly improved by the 1970s.

The third area of policy to be examined centres on women's role as *mothers* and in the home. Here we find steadfast adherence to the assumption of women's primary responsibility for housekeeping and childrearing. In the nineteenth century there was no direct intervention in this private sphere; rather policies, such as those we have examined on marriage and divorce, served indirectly to reinforce such a role. During the twentieth century policies have more directly confirmed it. From the 1930s, and especially with the consolidation of the Welfare State, state supervision of women as mothers and homemakers has increased through the agency of health authorities, social workers, even school teachers. McIntosh even suggests that the vogue for 'community care' in the late 1960s was really premised on the voluntary extension of women's nurturant role (McIntosh, 1979, p. 170). On the other hand public policies have provided little assistance to women seeking to combine these domestic responsibilities with outside employment, through for instance day-care provision for children or adequate maternity leave.

During the Second World War, public nursery care increased tenfold, first to cope with evacuees and later to offset women's conscription into industry. These 'war nurseries' however 'were all along intended to be temporary devices and not to be taken as any foundation for post war practice' (Riley, 1979, p. 105). Responsibility for their maintenance was subsequently transferred to the discretion of local authorities, so that by 1969 only 21,000 children had state day-nursery places, priority being given to children of single mothers or 'problem homes'. By the 1960s provisions for maternity leave within the public sector were widespread, and particularly generous amongst white-collar workers, yet it was not until the 1975 Employment Protection Act, and under pressure to conform to European Community guidelines, that improved maternity leave facilities were extended to most full-time women workers. The possibility of paternal leave, or shared parental leave, not surprisingly was never seriously mooted.

Public policy has also influenced women's *income*, both its extent and whether women receive it directly. At least until the 1970s, that policy clearly reflected and reinforced women's economic dependence on men, as an examination of its impact upon women's earnings, taxation and income maintenance will show. Firstly, during the nineteenth century, women's earnings typically fell far short of what men received for comparable work. In 1888 the TUC did call for equal pay, but this was mainly because of fears of women's wages undercutting those of male workers. For the most part, the male-dominated unions did not press the issue, particularly since, in their negotiations with employers, they were demanding a 'family wage': a wage for the male breadwinner sufficient to support his wife and children. Whether or not they 'merely couched their arguments in terms which would appeal to social reformers and some sections of the capitalist class in order to further their own ends', this demand implied a highly dependent role for married women, at a time when most women were expected to marry, and was incompatible with the principle of equal pay (Land, 1980, p. 57).

During the two world wars, as women were temporarily drafted into traditionally male occupations, Government paid lip-service to the principle of equal pay, but no steps were taken to enforce it. In 1954, following the report of a Royal Commission on Equal Pay and a campaign mounted by feminist groups and women MPs, equal pay was legislated for women in the civil service and teaching. During the 1960s, support for the principle of equal pay for *all* women workers grew steadily in the unions, reflecting both continuing fears that female wages could undercut male rates of pay and the fact that women were the main source of new members. The Equal Pay Act was not passed until 1970.

Secondly, from the introduction of income tax in 1799 until 1972, the income of husband and wife was aggregated for tax purposes, and treated as the husband's responsibility. Women, thirdly, have been affected by the web of social security provision elaborated during the twentieth century. In fact they were largely ignored by the 1911 National Insurance Act, while between the wars 'throughout the social security system there was discrimination against women and especially against married women' (Wilson, 1977, p. 120). Eleanor Rathbone's campaign, waged for more than twenty years, for a family allowance to be paid directly to the mother was resisted by Conservatives and the labour movement alike. The Beveridge Report of 1942, which set out the guidelines for the first 'universal' system of national insurance, enshrined the economic dependence of married women. It argued that, since 'during marriage most women will not be gainfully employed, the small minority of women who undertake paid employment or other gainful occupations after marriage require special treatment differing from that of a single woman'. These women would not normally be expected to contract into the system of benefits at all, but if they did they would only be eligible for benefits 'at a reduced rate' (cited by London Women's Liberation Campaign for Legal and Financial Independence and Rights of Women, 1979, p. 20). The social security system also penalised households diverging from the 'norm' of male breadwinner and immediate dependants, such as the approximately half a million fatherless families reported in 1971. In the 1970s, married women's rights to pensions and to sickness and unemployment benefits were substantially enhanced, but supplementary benefit still went to the husband and, under the infamous 'cohabitation' rule, this principle was even extended to unmarried couples.

The possibility of women's *employment* outside the home has been indirectly affected by many of the policies already described. Public policies, or their absence, have had a more direct effect on the types and levels of employment open to women. Though their impact in the nineteenth century was purely restrictive, they have more recently contributed to a limited expansion of women's employment opportunities.

Beginning with the 1842 Mines Regulations Act, a succession of laws during the nineteenth century limited the hours and occupations that could legally be undertaken by women and children. As Humphries shows, they were supported by a strange combination of interests, and for a complex set of reasons, but one concern that was uppermost was to preserve working-class 'family life' (Humphries, 1981). Alexander has also shown how protective legislation was introduced into areas of competition with men, rather than all employment (Alexander, 1976). The provisions of accumulated protective legislation, which have been codified in the 1961 Factory Act, together with the 1920 Employment of Women, Young Persons and Children Act and the 1936 Hours of Employment (Conventions) Act, apply only to industrial occupations and do not cover such areas of growing female employment as offices and hospitals. As a consequence, feminists have always been divided on the desirability of protective legislation (Banks, 1981).

Protective legislation was often defended in terms of the need for married women to devote themselves to their families. After the First World War, in 1919, the Women's Employment Committee of the Ministry of Recovery hoped that 'every inducement, direct or indirect, will be given to keep mothers at home' (cited by Lewis, 1983b, p. 24). However, Lewis suggests that there was always some ambivalence in applying this principle to working-class mothers, because of the fear that if their husbands could not provide for them they would become dependent on the state. In practice the system of national insurance between the wars was used to ensure that such women did seek paid work, and in particular to channel them into 'suitable' employment as domestic servants.

In the nineteenth century women were also excluded from most of the emerging professions. Since access to them required specialised education and training, from which women, as we shall see, were debarred, this *de facto* male monopoly went largely unchallenged for many decades. Around the turn of the century a number of court cases were brought by women who *had* achieved the requisite qualifications. These are discussed by Sachs and Wilson, and typically pivoted on the curious question of whether even single women counted as 'persons'. In case after case, the 'impartial' male judiciary ruled they did not, a finding only overturned by the

Judicial Committee of the Privy Council in 1929 (Sachs and Wilson, 1978).

Government and the law further contributed to women's employment opportunities by their own policies of recruitment and promotion. Until 1946 married women were excluded from the pensionable establishment of the civil service. The legal profession was for long united in its resistance to female invasion, and women are still singularly under-represented in its higher reaches.

Finally, public policy-makers have only very recently been prepared to consider intervention in cases where sex discrimination is suspected in private sector employment. The first proposal for legislation against it was introduced in 1967 and then only as a Private Member's Bill.

We come lastly to women's opportunities in *education*. Though government has contributed to a steady expansion in women's formal education, feminists rightly remain critical of the conventional sex-role assumptions that pervade policy-making in this field.

In the early nineteenth century, school education was provided chiefly by the Church, charitable foundations and private fee-paying establishments; secondary education was available primarily for middle-class boys. The four English universities admitted no women students. During the 1860s, feminists like Emily Davies waged a vigorous campaign for the expansion of girls' secondary education, for women's teacher training – Queen's College and Bedford College in London were founded for this purpose – and for women's access to university education. As a result of their influence, changing labour force requirements but also its interest in producing 'good mothers', the Government, as it increasingly supervised and eventually supplied primary and secondary education, assumed this should be for girls as well as boys. In the meantime, by the turn of the century, several universities were beginning to admit women students though Cambridge refused to award women university degrees until 1948. Though women by the early twentieth century appeared, formally speaking, to enjoy equal opportunity in primary and secondary education, Byrne argues that in tertiary education (and only approximately 9 per cent of girls go on to higher education from school) they continue to be discriminated against by local authorities who provide grants and by employers who authorise day-release (Byrne, 1978).

The main feminist criticism is now of the informal assumptions of educational policy-makers which contribute to women's continuing underachievement. In Wolpe's phrase, the 'official ideology' of education, from the regulatory Codes of the nineteenth century down as far as the 1959 Crowther Report and the 1963 Newsom Report, maintained that women's education must prepare them for motherhood and domesticity (Wolpe, 1978). For instance the Crowther Report urged that girls' education anticipate 'the prospect of courtship and marriage' and that girls' 'direct interest in dress, personal appearance, in problems of human relationships should be given a central place in their education' (cited by Wilson, 1977, p. 83). Such an ideology condoned, if it was not the sole cause of, the differentiation of subjects for boys and girls, the hidden sex-role assumptions in the language and content of the syllabus, the concentration of women teachers in 'maternal' roles in infant schools or subordinate roles in secondary schools and the sex-stereotyped careers advice offered to schoolgirls. Any serious attempt to eradicate these more subtle educational inequalities has been prompted only by the revival of feminism in the 1970s.

This brief survey of policies towards women in Britain has shown their assumption and reinforcement of women's traditional role as mothers and housewives. At the same time such policies assisted some widening of women's life options in the twentieth century. Indeed, they may have played some small part in the emergence of the women's liberation movement.

Explaining policy towards women: a comparative approach

To what extent have policies towards women in other parts of the world resembled those in Britain? Under the influence of second wave feminism, studies have proliferated, both of policies towards women in different countries and of particular policy areas, although few are explicitly comparative. It is therefore possible to compare the British experience with findings elsewhere.

Such a comparison helps to identify the main factors shaping policies towards women. One hypothesis has been that they are functional to, or principally determined by, the particular *type* of economic system, in Britain's case advanced capitalism. To begin with, then we can look at what has happened in another advanced capitalist society, the United States.

The American experience

Nineteenth-century laws regulating marriage closely paralleled those in Britain except that, because of the federal system of government, their precise content varied from state to state. By the end of the nineteenth century each state had passed a Married Women's Property Act, giving the wife the legal right to own and control her separate property and earnings. Otherwise, up until the 1970s, the law continued to assume the wife's economic dependence upon her husband.

Turning to policies with implications for women's control of their own fertility and sexuality, mistrust of state intervention, and decentralisation, have helped to make birth control policy rather more oppressive than in Britain. The federal Comstock Law of 1873, which prohibited the importation, inter-state transportation or spread of information about contraceptive devices, prompted similar laws in about half the states, many of which still restricted their distribution and display as late as 1968. Against a background of pressure from Planned Parenthood, led by Margaret Sanger, from changing public attitudes and from the availability of the pill, which was first approved by the Food and Drugs Administration in 1960, the Supreme Court ruled in 1965 that the Constitution's 'due process' clause included a married couple's right to privacy and therefore its right to choose whether or not to use contraceptive devices. This right was not extended to unmarried couples until 1972. In addition the Federal Government has been unwilling to provide family planning as a public service except, from the mid-1960s, for the poorest social groups; others must rely upon the private sector. Abortion was banned by most state legislatures by 1900, partly as a result of the growing influence of the medical profession and its drive to discredit 'unqualified' medical practitioners. Not until the late 1960s did several states liberalise their abortion laws and this was only condoned by the Supreme Court in 1973 (Gordon, 1977). The political system of the United States has also provided severe obstacles to the implementation of abortion law reform. Policies towards rape appear, however, to have broadly paralleled those in Britain, though again with minor variations between the fifty states.

As in Britain, women's primary responsibility for child care and housekeeping was in the nineteenth century presumed rather than assisted by public policy. Though this presumption has continued to inform policy, women have received even less support in their domestic role than in Britain. Adams and Winston suggest that this is because, even more than in Britain, 'American policy . . . continues to presume certain fundamental incompatibilities between women's marriage, motherhood and work roles' (Adams and Winston, 1980, p. 8). In the first place, 'the US has the distinction of being the only major industrialised country in the world that lacks a national insurance plan covering medical expenses for childbirth and is one of few governments in industrialised nations that does not provide any cash benefits to working women to compensate for lost benefits' (ibid., p. 33). Secondly, public nursery provision has only been available during the Depression and the Second World War, as well as, since 1962, for the poorest families. Local authorities, too, provide a minimal home-help service.

Reviewing policies that affect women's income, we find that the administration of income tax, social security, pensions and welfare has closely resembled the British pattern in reinforcing women's economic dependence. Several writers have shown how the welfare programme, originating in 1935, encourages single mothers not to find work but to look for a male supporter, while in the meantime the Welfare Department acts like a 'traditional husband' (see, for instance, Iglitzin, 1977; Kinsley, 1977). However, the Equal Pay Act was passed as early as 1963, as a result of pressure by unions and by moderate feminist organisations. Despite its limited scope, it has been sympathetically interpreted by the courts. Indeed Murphy attributed to it 'by far the best track record of any of the programmes for women' (Murphy, 1973, p. 25).

As in Britain, in the late nineteenth century American women were restricted in their employment opportunities by protective legislation and by general judicial support for a male monopoly in most professions. By 1890, however, 13 medical colleges had been opened for women students and in 1880 the first woman was admitted to practise at the bar of the Supreme Court. By the 1960s public policy may have been rather more helpful than it was in Britain. The first legislation to prevent sex discrimination was passed in 1964 when the criterion of 'sex' was added to Title 7 of the Civil Rights Act. This clearly predated the emergence of women's liberation, though one feminist Congresswoman, Martha Griffiths, helped to secure it and though it was only under pressure from the women's movement that steps were taken to make its implementation more effective.

Education policies, finally, have probably been less discriminatory in the United States than in Britain. 'Girls benefitted from the development of public education that began around 1830. By 1890 there were actually more girls enrolled in high schools than boys' (Giele, 1977b, pp. 308–9). Moreover, 'by 1882 the higher education of American women was an established fact . . . in striking contrast to England' (O'Neill, 1969, pp. 43–4). By 1880 there were 40,000 women students (a third of the total), even if the education they received was not always of a very high standard (Evans, 1977, p. 118). Even in the 1960s, while in Britain about one-third of university students were women, in the United States they were approximately one-half. None the less feminists have been swift to point out exactly the same insidious forms of sex discrimination in the curriculum and organisation of education.

This comparison of policies towards women in Britain and the United States reveals, then, many similarities. However, American women have perhaps been more fortunate in those policy areas affected by the ideological commitment to equality of opportunity, education and, recently, pay and employment. They have certainly been less fortunate when policy is influenced by the widespread American mistrust of direct intervention in family life and of social expenditure by government, for instance in the areas of birth control, nursery and home-help provision, maternity leave and welfare.

Policies in Sweden

Amongst contemporary advanced capitalist societies, the most striking contrast in policies towards women must be between the United States and the countries of Scandinavia, perhaps most of all Sweden. Sweden is clearly capitalist, in that the state does not significantly intervene in relations of production in the private sector or maintain an extensive industrial sector. Yet public policies towards women are more enlightened than anywhere else in the world (if still, from a feminist viewpoint, only a beginning).

The evolution of Swedish marriage law has in many respects adhered to the American pattern, though as early as 1921 the

Marriage Law provided for the equal division of property between husband and wife, upon divorce. But the principle of family privacy has never been so strong, partly because bringing up children has been seen as a public responsibility. From 1924 the Child Welfare Board, through its local agencies, has possessed extensive powers of intervention in family relationships.

Birth control policies have diverged much more radically from the American model. From the 1950s, county maternity clinics have been obliged to provide information, advice and contraceptives virtually free to all women over 15, regardless of their marital status. Abortion law reform, which began in 1938 following a Royal Commission, progressed steadily up to the 1975 Act which gave women almost entire 'freedom to choose' until after the eighteenth week of pregnancy. The theoretical freedom of choice is backed up by adequate public provision of abortion facilities. In addition, Sweden is one of the two countries (the other is Denmark) outside Eastern Europe which include rape within marriage in their criminal codes (Brownmiller, 1975).

The greatest contrast is, however, in policies affecting women's role as mothers and housekeepers. In 1931 the Government undertook to pay a lump sum to each woman on the birth of her child, to cover extra expenses. Over the years this provision was amplified, so as to enable a working woman to stay at home for the first six months after the birth, with between 20 and 80 per cent of her normal rate of pay, depending upon how high it was. We can also note, though strictly outside the period covered in this chapter, Sweden's Parental Leave scheme, introduced in 1974. This entitles the mother or father if he has custody, to a nine-month allowance, beginning with the birth of the child. If both parents were working, the maximum allowance is increased to compensate for one of them staying at home and is up to 90 per cent of their pay. The parents can also split the leave between them. Further, though some day-care facilities for children were available earlier, the report of the Day Care Commission appointed by the Government in 1965 resulted in the increase of day-care places by over 500 per cent. Starting with the 1943 Social Home Help Act, the Government also subsidised both local government and voluntary home-help services, so that by 1980 approximately 10 per cent of young couples made use of them.

Turning to policies affecting income, Sweden has not yet legislated for equal pay but this is partly because by 1962 the peak business and labour organisations, the SAF and LO respectively, had themselves negotiated an equal pay policy. Indeed by 1965 the wage gap between the sexes was much narrower than in the United States. Taxation and income maintenance schemes have disadvantaged married women as in the United States. Even so it is significant that the various sources of income maintenance for single parents (usually women) are so generous that very few need to go on welfare.

There was no legislation against sex discrimination in employment until the 1970s, because the Government again preferred to leave such matters to the representatives of business and labour. The reason, however, that the Social Democrats, Sweden's dominant political party until the mid-1970s, are still reluctant to ban sex discrimination is that they fear it would preclude positive discrimination which they recognise as necessary.

Finally, since the 1960s the Government has seriously considered ways of reducing sex-role stereotyping in schools, so that by the 1970s it was being reported that 'Sewing and woodwork, as well as home economics and child care are obligatory for both sexes', textbooks were being vetted for sexist content and, in a pioneering scheme, the Government was selectively training staff from each school and sending them back to initiate programmes to broaden sex-role attitudes (Baude, 1979, p. 153).

While then policies in Sweden appear to come closest to what feminists might prescribe, it must be stressed that many Swedish feminists themselves point out their deficiencies. Hernes (1984a) for instance argues that their effect has been to reduce women's dependence on individual men but to increase their dependence on a still relatively male-dominated state, as citizen, employee and client. Even so, one is bound to wonder why policies have progressed so far in Sweden. The immediate reason appears to be the predominance in Sweden of a particular brand of social democracy which, while committed to private enterprise, simultaneously believes that the state should extensively intervene in the *distribution* of the economic product, so as to minimise social inequalities. To this end, it collects the fullest possible information; in fact it has been suggested that the Swedish Government makes greater use of research findings than any other (Adams and Winston, 1980, p. 40). Social democracy in Sweden has also been influenced by feminist thinking, from the end of the last century, as we shall see.

But it is less clear why Sweden should have acquired this political orientation. Historically Sweden's small, relatively homogeneous population and the absence both of a fully fledged feudal era and, from an early period, of a powerful Roman Catholic church may be presumed to have encouraged egalitarian values and practices. Eduards (1986) also stresses the early spread of literacy and the fact that there was virtual freedom of political association from 1864, so that with industrialisation new democratic rights could be pursued without intense conflict. Sweden's neutrality during the Second World War protected her economy and contributed to subsequent prosperity and growth. Eduards also suggests that in the post-war era, the unusually central role of sectoral interest associations – representing business and labour – in economic policy-making, that we have already remarked upon, has left political parties more scope, and I should add perhaps more necessity, to define themselves ideologically in reference to other kinds of issues, such as sex equality.

It seems clear that while policies in the three advanced capitalist societies examined here share certain basic trends – the liberalisation of marriage laws, greater legal and material support for contraception and abortion, measures to remove direct sex discrimination in employment and pay, and expanding educational opportunities for women – they none the less differ strikingly both in their commitment to these objectives and in their response to women's burdens as mothers and in the home. An interesting footnote to this discussion is women's experience in Nazi Germany. Of course, the German economy then may not quite qualify as 'advanced' and it was, moreover, initially in crisis. It is still difficult to explain Nazi policies towards women simply in terms of the functional requirements or consequences of the economic system. Admittedly, Nazi ideologies were not entirely consistent in their view of women and their apparent objectives diverged considerably from their actions. Even so, their policies represented a remarkable drive to put the clock back, as embodied in their famous slogan of 'Kinder, Kueche, Kirche'.

While Hitler and Goebbels might argue that 'women's proper sphere is the family' on grounds of ideology, other Nazis stressed women's traditional role for more pragmatic reasons. Above all they wanted to increase the output of healthy Aryan babies. Measures to achieve these ends were enacted primarily in the mid-1930s, before re-armament and then war created new priorities.

Women were encouraged to stay at home and have children by the marriage loan scheme, eligibility for which at first depended on the wife giving up her job, and by increased maternity benefits. At the same time, birth control of any kind, at least for Aryans, was prohibited. Employment of women in the civil service and several of the élite professions was cut back. The Nazis did not fully realise their objective of segregated education, with a more 'feminine', less academic curriculum for girls, but they managed to reduce the proportion of women students from 18.9 per cent in 1932 to 12.5 per cent in 1934 (Stephenson, 1975).

The Third World: colonialism, nationalism and 'development'

At this point it may be instructive to turn to women's experience in countries of what is now referred to as the Third World. While all committed, at least rhetorically, to the goal of economic development, the new Third World nations have pursued different strategies, some overtly capitalist, others nominally socialist with a prominent state sector. With the exception of a small group of socialist states, notably China, Cuba and Vietnam, which are best discussed in the following section with the countries of the Soviet bloc, most are in fact highly permeable to indigenous and international capitalist forces, so that it is logical to consider them in conjunction with Western capitalist societies. On the other hand, they obviously differ from the latter in being less industrialised and at a severe disadvantage in terms of international economic competition. How have policies affected women from the nineteenth century, both under colonial rule and subsequently?

Pre-colonial societies were neither static nor uniform. Within them accordingly women's status, as far as we know, ranged from relatively high to low. Colonial rule itself took different forms (and not all Third World societies were directly colonised). However, in all phases of colonisation economic motives that could be broadly termed capitalist played an important part, though these were bound up with considerations of national, or imperial, power and a belief in the cultural, or indeed racial, superiority of the colonising people and its civilising mission. Whatever the specific features of colonial regimes, one further characteristic they shared was that 'colonial administrators at all levels were men'. As Rogers points out, even when women had begun to attain professional and civil service posts in their home country, they were not allowed to serve abroad. For instance, in 1921 an Order-in-Council was passed in Britain 'to reserve to men any branch of, or posts in, the Civil Service in any of His Majesty's possessions overseas or in any foreign country' (Rogers, 1983, p. 36).

The national movements that arose in opposition to colonial rule again varied according to when they emerged, how long and hard they had to struggle and, related to this, whether they were militant or based on mass support, or moderate and confined to an élite. However, one widespread feature of nationalist movements, at least outside Latin America, has been, as Jayawardena (1986) shows, a tendency to combine commitment to many aspects of modernisation with mistrust or even rejection of 'Westernism'. The precise balance of these sentiments has had significant consequence for women's status in different countries. Women, finally, have been affected by the strategies for national and economic development pursued by post-independence governments as well as by the policies of international development agencies.

In so far as colonial rulers interfered, through their policies, with women's rights in marriage firstly, they sought generally to impose the patriarchal, nuclear model with which they were familiar. The Spaniards colonising the Philippines from the sixteenth century introduced a Civil Code which severely restricted the rights of married women, who no longer had any claim on property they brought into the marriage and could not engage in any outside economic activity without their husbands' consent. Interestingly enough, when the Americans succeeded the Spaniards in 1918, though generally more sympathetic to women's rights, they did not introduce divorce until 1933 and retained husbands' veto on their wives' outside employment, on the grounds that its removal would endanger family stability (Jayawardena, 1986). On the other hand, in India, the British, supported by Indian social reformers, did seek to alleviate the plight of Hindu widows. The practice of 'suti' or widow-burning was made a criminal offence in 1829 and in 1874 the Right of Property Act gave widows, who previously had no claim on their husbands' property other than the right of maintenance, a life interest in the property though not the right to own or dispose of it. These measures, as far as they were effective, were primarily of relevance to upper caste women but there was also some attempt to reduce the practice, prevalent throughout Indian society, of child marriage.

Since independence, in many Commonwealth countries including India and much of tropical Africa, national governments have continued in their policies to enshrine the Western marriage model, though this has not necessarily always been to the advantage of individual women: for instance making polygamy illegal may not be appreciated by supernumerary wives (Tinker, 1976). In predominantly Islamic countries, however, policy remains, in varying degrees, shaped by the Sharia or Islamic law. The Sharia is not a static code and it could moreover be argued that when originally adopted it afforded many married women greater security, by entitling them to the economic support of their husband or his male kin. In theory it even allowed them to inherit property, though only half of what a man received, but it has been suggested that this was one reason why men instituted women's wearing of the veil and seclusion, practices not directly sanctioned by the Koran. To the husband, on the other hand, the Sharia gave the right to have more than one wife, to divorce his wife unilaterally and to have automatic custody of children. Though the wife is entitled to sexual intercourse, she is also obliged to bear and bring up children. Adultery by either sex is forbidden but in practice penalties for women have been more severe. The Sharia finally enjoins the wife to obey her husband as undisputed head of the household.

How far the Sharia has shaped policy has largely depended on attitudes to the West. Ataturk is famous for his determination to modernise Turkey by Westernising and for him this was symbolised in measures to emancipate women. Under the Civil Code of 1926, which replaced the Sharia, polygamy was outlawed and women were given equal rights in divorce, child custody and inheritance. Even then the family was to remain patriarchal. The husband as head of household still decided where his family lived and could prevent his wife from working outside the home. Besides, outside the urban élites, the actual impact of these changes was slight. Jayawardena cites Dr Fatima Cosar, writing in 1980 – 'in the final analysis, only a very small number of women were able to use the rights granted them by Ataturk. The vast majority of women are still tied to the land and under the social control of men' (Jayawardena, 1986, p. 42). Other Muslim countries, such as Egypt and Tunisia, followed more hesitantly Turkey's lead. But elsewhere the

Sharia and the position it accords women have been seen as essential to Islamic tradition, prized and reasserted in the face of Western values and economic exploitation. For instance in Morocco, the very day after Independence in 1957, it formed the basis of a new Family Law. Algerian women risked their lives in the struggle against French colonial rule. Frantz Fanon was moved to declare 'the place of women can never again be the same as it was before'. Following Independence both the Tripoli Programme of 1962 and the 1963 Constitution assured women equal rights but the promised new family code never emerged and laws were soon passed making the penalty for adultery twice as severe for women as for men and re-establishing men's right, removed under French law, to divorce by repudiation (Stiehm, 1976). The most dramatic instance of the reassertion of Islamic practice is of course in Iran. Under the last Shah's father, Reza Khan, in 1936 women were forbidden to wear the veil. His son instituted the Family Protection Law in 1967 which made polygamy grounds for divorce and gave women greater rights to initiate divorce proceedings. Admittedly, as Higgins (1985) emphasises, such legal changes had little time to take effect. They were moreover associated with an extremely repressive, unpopular regime. None the less, although women played a prominent, some would say essential, part in the successive demonstrations that brought down the Shah, within a month of the Revolution of February 1979, the new government under Khomeini had suspended the Family Protection Law (Tabari, 1980). Even in Indonesia, where the impact of Islam on women's status has been less pronounced, although women and reformers active in the struggle against the Dutch, after the last war, pressed for liberalisation of the marriage law, organised Muslim opposition was so effective that such a reform failed to emerge till 1975 (Jayawardena, 1986).

Women's control over their own fertility and sexuality has been affected by many of the policies regulating marriage already reviewed, for instance those concerning child marriage or Islamic injunctions surrounding adultery, divorce or wives' duty to allow their husbands sexual access and to bear children. Beyond this there is some controversy as to how far women in pre-colonial societies were able or indeed wished to limit their own fertility. Rogers cites various instances of communities in which not only infant mortality rates but birth rates were low (1983, p. 111). Colonial policies tended, however, to have the opposite effect. Rogers suggests they were pro-natalist, shaped by the exorbitant demands for servile or cheap labour. But in the nineteenth century there was also a tendency for colonial regimes to introduce prohibitions on abortion that existed in their country of origin. Thus Britain's Offences Against the Person Act was invoked in most regions of the Commonwealth. In Latin America, on the other hand, the continuing effect of former colonial policies and the firmly established Roman Catholic church was the same. The main consequence of these legal proscriptions was, however, to drive abortion underground rather than to prevent it.

With the liberalisation of British law, through the Bourne case of 1938 and then the 1967 Act, abortion policy has changed correspondingly in many Commonwealth countries, beginning with Zambia and India in 1972. One exception is Nigeria where both Catholic and Muslim opposition has defeated liberalising moves. In fact, Islamic doctrine does not forbid abortion but in practice abortion has been outlawed in most Muslim countries. This is true even of Turkey, despite Ataturk's 'advanced' policies towards women. The ban on abortion was lifted by the Shah of Iran in 1976 but its reinstatement was one of the earliest measures of the Khomeini regime. Other predominantly Muslim countries to liberalise abortion law are Morocco, Tunisia and Kuwait (Francome, 1984).

Evidence suggests that in Latin American countries illegal abortion has been rampant. In Brazil it has been estimated that one-half of all pregnancies end in abortion. Since the early 1970s several countries, including Guatemala, Costa Rica and Uruguay have widened the legal grounds for abortion. As we shall see in the following chapter, political campaigns to liberalise abortion have recently emerged, for instance in Mexico and Brazil. On the other hand the ban on abortion was tightened up in Bolivia in 1977, and in Chile, following Pinochet's coup in 1973, liberalising-measures introduced under Allende were rescinded.

Governments in several Muslim countries, including Egypt, Algeria and Tunisia, have set up networks of family planning centres. They have been particularly alarmed by the high birth rate, estimated to average 3.3 per cent a year and rising to 3.6 per cent in Iraq and Syria (Minces, 1982). Similar services are provided in Argentina and Brazil. Francome suggests they have been more effective in Argentina than in Brazil, which raises the issue of policy implementation. Resources available are typically extremely inadequate. Thus in India, although abortion has long been legalised, only an estimated 5 per cent of abortions are performed legally. A further problem has been that women seeking abortion or the means of birth control may face considerable resistance from their husbands. Both in India and Mozambique, it is reported that women may prefer to conceal from their husbands the fact that they are using contraceptives; in Mozambique husbands finding that their wives have fitted IUDs send them back to the hospital to have them removed (Savara, 1985; Rodrigues, 1985).

But it must also be recognised that measures to promote fertility control only really increase women's 'life options' if they provide greater, more informed choice. Population control programmes will rarely have this as a central objective. They seek rapid results. Often too they are in part externally funded and directed so that 'the recipient country becomes a dumping-ground for often very dangerous drugs and . . . women are used as guinea pigs' (Savara, 1985, p. 223). Despite its harmful side-effects, De-po Provera has been widely used as a contraceptive drug; IUDs have been inserted without proper supervision or follow-up. Many women have been subjected to extreme pressure to be sterilised, probably the most blatant example being the forced sterilisation campaign during India's period of Emergency Rule from 1975–7.

Third, as in advanced capitalist societies, past and present policy has assumed and idealised women's responsibility for children and the 'home', but has offered even less practical assistance. Assumptions about women's mothering role have infused education policies. By 1863, elementary education for girls in the Philippines was relatively well established but the intended product was 'devout, chaste, modest and diligent women who would become good wives and mothers' (Alzona, cited by Jayawardena, 1986, p. 159). On the other hand little has been done to ensure that women can support their children and Tinker suggests that one effect of colonial and subsequent policies discouraging polygamy and based on a Western nuclear model is that women have lost the right to assistance from husbands or male kin (Tinker, 1976).

Rogers describes how post-war development programmes incorporated a kind of Beveridge image of womanhood, even down to fears about the effects of maternal deprivation. In various women's projects, whether instigated by international development agencies or national governments, there has been an emphasis on home economics or domestic science in educational and training schemes, essentially 'using the pretensions of science . . . to impose new standards of housework'. The claim to scientific status is in fact often dubious. Nutrition counselling, for instance, is rarely based on serious research of locally available foodstuffs. Child care classes can also be amazingly inappropriate. One home economic agent in a Malawi project was observed washing a baby doll in an imported plastic bathtub filled with warm water. Neither hot water nor bathtub were available to the women. The agent also demonstrated the use of an imported disposable nappy – a luxury that village women would never buy' (Rogers, 1983, p. 94).

When discussing women's income in Third World countries we should not repeat the errors of colonial and national administrators. They have firstly tended to assume that each household will be headed by a man who will through his earnings support his wife and children. Even if married men were prepared to accept these family responsibilities, and it seems they often prefer to spend their wages on themselves, by now one-third of the world's households are *de facto* headed by women, with the proportion rising to 50 per cent in many of the poorest communities, exacerbated by patterns of labour migration. Second, especially with the adoption of internationally standardised methods for assessing national income, national planners have tended to equate income with money income, failing to recognise how crucial to the survival of rural women and their children has been access to land as a means of subsistence. These misconceptions are slowly being corrected but in the meantime have, often disastrously, permeated policies affecting women's income.

In pre-colonial societies it appears that women often had customary rights to the use of land. By the nineteenth century early colonial policies and population pressure had already reduced such access to land for women in Latin America and Asia but in much of tropical Africa where land was seen less in terms of private property than as existing for the use of the tribe or community as a whole, women retained users' rights. The new colonial rulers instigated land registration drives, converting land into the property of private individuals. Part of their object was to make it into a commodity that could be brought and sold on the open market. But in so doing they also imposed their patriarchal assumptions by discounting women's claims to land except in localities where matriliny was too firmly rooted to be entirely extirpated. Women thus deprived of their access to formerly communal land were moreover unlikely to find the cash required to buy land and engage in cash-crop cultivation.

Agricultural development policies since independence, even when designed to redistribute land and secure peasant farming rights, have all too often continued to ignore women's specific income needs, as for instance in the Malawi development scheme described by Rogers. But this observation is not confined to Africa. Deere (1986) analyses agrarian reforms designed to break up and redistribute the old estates (haciendas) and largest commercial farms in Peru under military rule from 1968 to 1978 and in Chile between 1965 and 1973. In both cases the primary beneficiaries were permanent, as opposed to seasonal, agricultural workers and heads of households, criteria which, given the way they were applied, largely excluded women.

If agricultural policies have tended to deprive women of access to land and the means of their subsistence, when they have entered the paid work-force, predictably enough it has been at lower rates of pay then men, except in quite senior professional positions. Even when, as for instance in Tunisia, Egypt and Iraq or more recently Nicaragua, equal pay legislation has been enacted, it has little effect.

Policy-makers' approach to women's employment has tended to be governed by the same assumptions as have shaped their ideas about women's income. They have greatly underestimated the amount of work that women actually do. Projecting onto Third World women expectations derived from Western middle-class models, or ideals, they have presumed such women will be largely confined to a domestic sphere which will moreover be quite limited in scope. National accounting conventions which exclude not only unpaid domestic or 'family' labour but much of the 'informal sector' of street trading, casual labour and other marginal forms of urban economic activity, have reinforced this impression. Again it is only in the last few years that the full extent of women's economic role has begun to be recognised, not only in Africa where it is perhaps most obvious but for instance in Islamic countries where 'secluded' women work in the fields and in handicrafts such as rug-weaving.

Colonial policies we saw tended to undermine women's subsistence farming activities. At the same time women were largely excluded from the expanding cash crop sector and from early agricultural training projects. This did not prevent them being employed as agricultural labourers; for example by 1911 they constituted 47 per cent of the half a million strong work-force on the tea plantations in Ceylon (Sri Lanka), earning less than the men of course.

Following independence national development programmes have continued to focus on cash crops and to be directed at male farmers. Rural extension services introducing new methods and technologies have not addressed women. Neither have they had access to the resources of agricultural co-operatives, including credit facilities, or to the particular opportunities associated with the 'Green Revolution', the programmes of intensive cultivation of wheat and rice, in India and elsewhere.

In pre-colonial societies, women have often been employed in small-scale manufacturing and as traders. By opening up transport routes and markets, colonial and later policies may in the short run have increased the scope for these activities but in the longer run by exposing them to the full blast of organised capitalist competition, they have undermined them. Now development policies are beginning to address these problems; new handicrafts projects have been sponsored in some areas though according to Rogers they are rarely sufficiently thought through (Rogers, 1983).

With these more traditional employments increasingly cut off, women have also been at a disadvantage in seeking modern industrial jobs. In fact in Latin America, during the earliest stages of industrialisation, particularly in textiles, women often were extensively recruited, for instance in Mexico, Brazil and Argentina. But with the expansion and technological advances of industry, governments have colluded with employers and male-dominated trade unions to drive women out. One extreme illustration was in Puerto Rico where the Economic Development Administration was, by the 1950s, giving grants to industries on condition that two-thirds of their work-force were men. As in Britain, protective legislation has been used to further restrict women's manufacturing opportunities. Recently, however, there has been a new twist, as multi-national companies have set up 'runaway shops' in Third World regions where they can draw on a supply of young women workers who are expected to be dexterous, docile and prepared to accept low pay (low that is compared with what the companies would have to pay elsewhere). In some cases, the government of the Third World nation in question has itself guaranteed suitable labour conditions.

While then colonial and post-colonial policy has done little to widen employment opportunities for women in general, middle-class women who have completed secondary and especially higher education have been more fortunate. Throughout the Third World they have found their way into the civil service, teaching and the medical profession. In Turkey the first woman doctor opened a clinic in 1922 and by the 1930s there were many more professional women. By the 1970s women formed 20 per cent of the teaching and 17 per cent of the medical profession (Jayawardena, 1986). The very segregation of the sexes has contributed to the demand for women teachers and doctors in many Muslim countries.

This last point underlines the importance of education for Third World women. It has been suggested that in traditional, rural societies, formal education is less necessary but with modernisation those without basic literacy skills are at an acute disadvantage. Though many criticisms can be made of the content of women's education, the chief shortcoming both of colonial and subsequent policy has been that it did not reach enough women. UNESCO figures indicate that rural Third World women are seldom literate and that the gap between male and female literacy is growing.

Colonial regimes often recognised the need to educate girls as well as boys, even if only to ensure they were 'good' wives and mothers. Missionaries shared this concern, appreciating the role of education in spreading Christian values, and provided places for girls in their own schools. Perhaps the outstanding example was in Ceylon. Coeducational primary education was first introduced by the Dutch but then expanded by the British and by Christian missionaries in the nineteenth century. In the latter decades, secondary education for girls also increased while Buddhist–Sinhalese nationalists began to open their own schools for girls as well as boys. As a result of these initiatives, continued by succeeding governments, the literacy rate for women in Sri Lanka today is around 83 per cent. In India, too, by 1882 there were 2700 educational establishments for girls and women were already graduating from the universities (Jayawardena, 1986).

Modernising national leaders have similarly promoted women's education. Minces (1982) argues that it is in those countries whose governments are most uncompromisingly Islamic that there is least formal education, even for boys. In contrast, Ataturk considered the education of women an essential element of modernisation and Turkey's first coeducational university was opened in 1921. Girls' education has expanded in Egypt, in Iran under the late Shah, in Lebanon, Syria, Iraq, Algeria and Tunisia, in which last country by 1980 50 per cent of girls were attending primary schools. None the less it is in the Arab Muslim countries and in Africa that rates of female literacy are lowest. In 1975 it was estimated that nine out of ten African women were illiterate. In Latin America, on the other hand, primary education for girls grew rapidly in the 1960s, until almost on a level with boys'.

Besides the failure of Third World governments generally to provide primary and secondary education for more than a privileged middle-class section of girls, the content of that education, not only under colonial rule and in missionary schools, but in many new nation states, particularly Muslim states, has incorporated very conservative sex-role assumptions. Indeed, where educational establishments segregate girls and women, such assumptions are institutionalised in their very structure.

To attempt to summarise the impact of all these policies, we may say that there has been a general tendency to reform marriage law in the direction of the Western model but that this has been strongly resisted in a number of Islamic states, that where it has been reformed the new law may have had little impact in practice and that its impact would not in any case be universally beneficial. Likewise there has been some trend towards liberalisation of abortion and birth control policy but with significant exceptions and new abuses. Policy-makers have almost eveywhere assumed women's responsibility for children. Yet policies affecting women's income and employment have failed to recognise both the economic value and the necessity for women and children's survival of their unpaid as well as their waged labour. Finally governments have been slower to expand educational opportunities for women than for men but the trend is generally upwards.

The emergence of these policies cannot simply be equated with the earlier experience of advanced capitalist societies, though there are parallels, nor can they be reduced to the consequences of

Western capitalist imperatives, exploiting cheaper factors of production and new markets. They have also been shaped by the
patriarchalism and cultural chauvinism of colonial rulers, the
ambivalence of new nationalist leaders towards the West and the
continuing prejudices of international development agencies and
national planners.

Policies under state socialism

If we cannot demonstrate the absence of significant variations in
policies towards women in advanced capitalist societies, nor that
such policies in the Third World can be explained as just anticipating capitalist development or the consequence of international
capitalism, can we find any consistent differences between these
and policies in state socialist countries? (By 'state socialist' I mean
here those polities in which the economy is owned and directed by
the state and where official ideology is Marxist-Leninist). Women's
experience in these countries has been the subject of a number of
recent feminist studies, most of them fairly critical.

There are several reasons why, *a priori*, state socialism might be
expected to be to women's advantage. First, it entails severe
restrictions on private property. One does not have to follow Engels
all the way to agree that in capitalist societies the emergence of
private property was associated with a marked deterioration in
women's status. Second, state socialism is premised upon full
employment. At the least, therefore, it offers to all women the
possibility of economic independence, and also the likelihood of
some kind of assistance with their domestic responsibilities.

The third reason is the character of the official ideology.
Marxism, however rhetorically, has always been committed to
women's emancipation, and no plausible Marxist government can
renege on that commitment, though it might argue the class struggle
should have priority. Perhaps more important is the theme of
egalitarianism in the ideology, even if in practice state socialism
seems to promote new kinds of inequality. Official ideology could
be helpful also in deliberately combating traditional religions,
which have prescribed a narrowly domestic role for women. A final
reason why state socialism ought to further women's emancipation
is that it is, initially at least, *revolutionary*. As such, it must
transform old attitudes and practices, including that bastion of

conservative thinking, the traditional patriarchal family and the role of women within it. Lenin remarked that 'The backwardness of women, their lack of understanding for the revolutionary ideals of the man, decrease his joy and determination in fighting. They are little worms which, unseen, slowly but surely rot and corrode' (Lapidus, 1978, p. 74). Not only will the revolutionary movement need to break down traditional family roles, it must seek positively to recruit women, together with other groups who are marginal in terms of power, to the pre-existing social order.

Given these auspicious features of state socialism, its record as the midwife of women's emancipation is distinctly disappointing. The overwhelming evidence is that public policy in state socialist societies, not only those which are industrialised, but also China, Cuba and Vietnam, has promoted women's legal and economic independence, together with access to educational and employment opportunities, but only in so far as they accord with broader national objectives. On the other hand, governments in these countries have often appeared reluctant to concede women control over their own fertility, and have made little serious attempt to free women from the 'double shift', either through 'socialising' domestic labour or through encouraging men to share domestic roles.

Women have universally benefited from the reform of marriage laws in state socialist societies. The most dramatic of such reforms, though they have yet to be fully implemented were in China. The 1950 Marriage Law, in addition to granting wives equal legal status, specifically outlawed the widespread practices of polygamy, concubinage, child brides and marriage by purchase. In Russia the legal position of most wives was also immeasurably improved. Under new marriage laws, following the October Revolution, the wife became a separate legal person, entitled to hold lands in her own right and no longer obliged to reside with her husband. Divorce became much easier; indeed for a brief period following the introduction of the 1926 Family Code, it was obtainable by postcard. The Code also recognised unregistered marriages. In their early revolutionary fervour, many Bolsheviks actually anticipated the withering away of the family, to be replaced by more communal forms of cohabitation and child-rearing. From the 1930s, official attitudes towards the family took a decidedly conservative turn, though they subsequently relaxed somewhat from the rigidity of the Stalinist era. The basic legal independence of wives has not however been questioned.

On the other hand, though women's access to publicly provided birth control has generally improved under state socialism, there remain significant, even sinister, qualifications. Socialist leaders, firstly, have been anxious to dissociate themselves from neo-Malthusianism, or advocacy of birth control by the rich to restrict the reproduction of the poor. Even in China where a massive family planning programme has been underway for some time, for a long while care was taken to justify it as a means of enhancing family life rather than simply limiting population growth (Adams and Winston, 1980, p. 41) though more recently the Chinese leadership appears to have abandoned such euphemisms.

Secondly, and more seriously, labour shortages in the industrialised state socialist economies have prompted pro-natalist policies. Abortion was legalised in the Soviet Union only because of the medical risks of illegal abortions. A mounting official campaign against abortion in the 1930s culminated in the 1936 Abortion Act which banned it outright. This was probably due not only to emerging labour shortages, but also to the regime's new concern with social stability, and possibly even to Great Russian or Slavic nationalism. Following Stalin's death, abortion was legalised again, but Heitlinger writes that 'it is still officially disapproved of' (Heitlinger, 1979, p. 128), and according to one account 'conditions in abortion clinics are extremely inhumane – staff are often unsympathetic, there is an appalling lack of privacy and anaesthetics are either not used at all, or the dose is too small to have any effect' (Peers, 1985, p. 134). East European states initially changed their policy in line with Moscow but in 1965 Romania made all abortions illegal and most of the other states have restricted their provision. Yet modern methods of contraception are neither widely publicised nor readily available except in East Germany.

The record of policies affecting women's role as mothers and housekeepers is more mixed. Women employed outside the home have received considerable financial and child-care assistance, but the assumption of their responsibility for housework has largely continued. Heitlinger states that 'compared with the Western capitalist countries, the social provisions for maternity and child care are key areas of privilege for women in the state socialist countries' (Heitlinger, 1979, p. 108). As in Sweden, these are considered legitimate objects of state intervention. In the Soviet Union, family allowances were available only to families with three or more children, but in 1981 it was officially announced that henceforth a lump sum would be payable on the birth of each child (*The Guardian*, 7 September 1981). This brings Soviet policy in line with the well-established practice of other East European states. More important, most East European governments stipulate maternity leave and allowances second only in generosity to those provided in Sweden. The women of Czechoslovakia and East Germany can claim twenty-six weeks' paid leave and take a further three years' unpaid leave without jeopardising their position at work. Lapidus does however point out that implementation of these rights rests with the trade unions, which are not always co-operative (Lapidus, 1978, p. 128).

Day-care provision for children is also, comparatively speaking, impressive. In the Soviet Union it is now available for most parents who need it, in urban areas, but the most extensive provision is in East Germany. Even so, Scott noted a disquieting tendency in a number of other East European countries, and especially in Poland, to reassess the value of nursery care for children under three years of age and to restrict its expansion (Scott, 1974). This was probably mainly a response to the declining birth rate, and also to the delayed impact of Western theories of maternal deprivation. Still, even in China, where child-care provision is far from comprehensive and fluctuates with changes in the political climate, it exceeds public provision in the United States.

It is in the area of housework that least has been achieved. Marx and Engels foresaw that such work would be socialised through the creation of communal canteens, laundries and such, though they did not consider the danger that such amenities would be largely staffed by women. In Russia in the 1920s, and in China, particularly during the Great Leap Forward, from 1958 to 1960, this was the official policy. In both countries it was clearly unsuccessful and though much of the reason lies in the inadequacy of available resources at that time, it also reflects the reluctance of the Party leadership to accord the policy priority. More recently the tendency in the industrialised socialist states has been to emphasise the 'family cell'. In fact, Lapidus suggests that economic development has given rise to a home-based 'consumerism'. Not only does public policy no longer explore more communal forms of domestic life, but this consumerism places extra demands on women's domestic energies and skills (Lapidus, 1978). Of communist countries, it is only Cuba whose 1974 Family Code specifically requires the husbands of women who go out to work to share domestic chores, and Murray suggests that this is partly because Cuba cannot yet afford to provide the most basic socialised services (Murray, 1979). In East Germany, however, schools and the media have begun to encourage some role-sharing at home. Even in the Soviet Union the possibility is being discussed in specialised journals (Peers, 1985).

Policies towards women and income in state socialist countries compare favourably with those elsewhere, though information is less abundant. In the Soviet Union, one of the earliest measures of the Bolshevik government was to decree equal pay for equal work, and successive revolutionary communist governments have followed its example. Even so, disparities continue, not only in China, where obstacles to implementation could be expected, but in Czechoslovakia where Heitlinger reports that 'Despite the equal pay legislation, income discrimination is practiced against women who perform the same type of work as men within the same qualification and tariff categories' (Heitlinger, 1979, p. 157).

The commitment of state socialist governments to full employment has undoubtedly helped to raise women's status. In the Soviet Union, such a commitment was formally declared immediately following the Revolution but only became practicable in the 1930s. Indeed the shortage of male workers, particularly during and after the Second World War, together with the emphasis in production on quantitative rather than qualitative growth, made full employment a necessity. Similarly the greater employment of women contributed to the reconstruction of post-war economies in other East European countries. Women now constitute over 45 per cent of the work-force in the Soviet Union, East Germany, Czechoslovakia and Bulgaria. They are, moreover, better distributed over the range of erstwhile 'masculine' occupations than in the West: for instance, 40 per cent of Soviet engineers are women. Women are also much more likely to work full-time than in Western industrialised states, though given their domestic burden this is not necessarily an advantage and the possibility of 'flexitime' has scarcely been broached. But they still remain heavily concentrated in the more feminine, or at least 'feminised' sectors and within these, in sex-segregated occupations. Few official steps have been taken to lessen these continuing inequalities, except in East Germany which, facing a critical shortage of skilled labour, has recently launched a scheme to increase the skills of selected women workers. At the same time, most state socialist governments maintain a list of 'protected' occupations. In Czechoslovakia, Scott finds that by the mid-1960s the 'catalogue of jobs forbidden to women (not merely to pregnant women who are protected by a much longer list) fills several pages, and effectively excludes women from any but office jobs in the building, iron and steel chemical and mining industries' (Scott, 1974, p. 19). Scott moreover suggests that protection clauses were initially disregarded, but that now they are invoked, ostensibly to protect the welfare and health of mothers and young children but also to preserve male job monopolies.

We have seen that in Third World countries women have tended to lose out in the process of agrarian development and reform. In state socialist systems there has clearly been a much greater effort to integrate women into the agricultural work-force. Deere (1986) contrasts the experience of Cuban women in this respect with those in Peru and Chile. All the same she notes that women have been less likely than men to form part of the permanent, rather than seasonal work-force and play a less prominent role in the management bodies of agricultural co-operatives.

Women, finally, have benefited enormously from the development of unified, coeducational systems of education in state socialist countries. Until the 1970s at least, women's educational achievement in the Soviet Union, as in the other industrialised socialist states, was well ahead of levels attained in most Western countries. Even so, educational policies have continued to encourage sex-role stereotyping, through for instance the role assumptions in children's textbooks, the differentiation of subjects taught to boys and girls and the male-dominated hierarchy of the teaching profession. After school, girls still opt disproportionately more for traditionally 'feminine' subjects at university, or for technical or vocational training. Although this is largely their own, albeit conditioned, choice, there is also 'substantial evidence that discriminatory admission policies persist' in certain higher education institutions (Lapidus, 1978, p. 150). In Czechoslovakia, when quotas are set for recruitment to different training schemes, some, for instance in the fields of mining and metallurgy, are exclusively reserved for boys. Scott suggests that these discriminatory policies have increased in Eastern Europe, outside East Germany, from the late 1960s.

State socialist policies, then, have provided many of the pre-requisites of women's emancipation, and yet have backed away from emancipation itself. Indeed most East European states official policies reveal a more conservative conception of women's role from the 1960s. It should be noted incidentally that this has not gone unchallenged. Newspapers and journals increasingly include articles and letters that express the discontent of women oppressed by the double shift and aware of its inconsistency with official ideology. None the less, the key question remains why the record of state socialism has not been better.

I suggest that two particular political features of state socialism, in combination, militate against women's emancipation. They are the ideology of Marxism–Leninism and the extreme scope and centralisation of political power and state authority. Although Marx and Engels acknowledged the 'woman question', their references to the sexual division of labour usually if not always suggested that it was natural, as we have seen. They believed socialism would liberate women, by bringing them into paid employment and socialising domestic production, but neither they nor Lenin explicitly contemplated domestic role-sharing between the sexes. Secondly, since Marxist–Leninists have generally assumed that socialism will bring in its train women's emancipation as they understand it, they have discouraged separate organisations or campaigning for feminist objectives, either in pre-revolutionary communist parties or in post-revolutionary socialist states. All energies must be channelled into the class struggle. Thirdly, although Marxism–Leninism is ultimately an egalitarian ideology, in the period of transition to communism it has dictated the necessity of a vanguard party and a complex array of income differentials, which have the opposite implication. White further suggests that, as the ideology of a certain kind of development, which emphasises science and heavy industry, it has tacitly elevated the status of traditionally masculine occupations and depressed the status of predominantly female spheres, such as agriculture (White, 1980).

But these ideological features are oppressive to women only because ruling Marxist–Leninists parties, or their leaderships, have largely undisputed say in policies that cover most aspects of social and economic life. This is good for women when it means full employment, equal educational opportunities or child-care provision. But when governments fail, for instance, consciously to undermine traditional sex-roles in school curricula, or to provide free and legal contraception and abortion, the political mechanism for questioning these omissions are, if not entirely absent, restricted and capricious. Women's organisations have been sponsored by Marxist–Leninist leaders, but only to act as 'transmission belts' to mobilise women into required forms of political and economic participation. Even then the life of these organisations has been hazardous; the Soviet Zhenotdel was folded in 1930, victim of Stalin's increasing paranoia, and China's National Women's Federation was suspended in 1966 during the Cultural Revolution.

Returning to the original inquiry, what does a comparison between these states and capitalist states reveal about the sources of policies towards women? We have seen that the general trend of such policies towards liberalisation of marriage, a somewhat greater sexual and reproductive autonomy for women and enlarged educational and employment opportunities has characterised both communist and capitalist societies. However, there have been real differences amongst capitalist societies. Sweden's policies, for instance, have arguably more in common with Eastern Europe, particularly East Germany, than with the United States. This suggests firstly that in all these societies policies towards women reflect certain common pressures. Secondly, these pressures do not simply derive from the economic system, narrowly understood, though this plays a part.

It is time to look more systematically at the possible explanations for the way in which politics shapes women's status. Despite the extent of the literature on policies towards women, it is generally at a low level of theorisation. No single study explicitly seeks to answer the questions posed in this chapter, though the analysis of Marxist feminists, and of Adams and Winston is particularly useful. The argument that policies pursued are functional to the economic system has been elaborated by a number of Marxist feminists, in the context of advanced capitalist societies. Its central thesis is that the state pursues policies requisite to the maintenance, in the longer term, of the economic system, though in the short term it may override particular dominant economic interests. Changes in policies towards women reflect the changing, or emerging, imperatives of the system, not excluding the demands of organised labour. The family, and women's traditional role within it, has been recognised as essential for the reproduction of the labour force, physically and ideologically, while expanding labour requirements and the utility of women's cheap labour have dictated the sometimes conflicting measures to facilitate women's employment outside the home. This argument is presented in its most reductionist form by Wilson in *Women and the Welfare State*, though it remains none the less a very useful book (Wilson, 1977). She identifies the central function of the Welfare State as the regulation and reinforcement of family life, so as to ensure the reproduction of labour. David's account of the evolution of educational policy is similar: 'the family and the educational system are used in concert to sustain and reproduce the social and economic status quo. Specifically they maintain existing relations within the family and social relations within the economy – what has sometimes been called the sexual and social division of labour' (David, 1980, p. 1). McIntosh modifies this position a little. She suggests that in capitalist society the state does sustain a specific form of household – 'the family household dependent largely upon a male wage and upon female domestic servicing' – so as to ensure the social conditions of reproduction but acknowledges that this family system has its own history and is not entirely suited for its function within capitalism. The state has to reinforce and sometimes even stand in lieu of the family household because it cannot substitute a more efficient system (McIntosh, 1978, p. 255). Other recent Marxist feminist writers qualify this further. On the one hand authors such as Barrett explicitly recognise the independent role, in the generation of policies towards women, of the 'sex-gender system' (Barrett, 1980). On the other, Riley warns against the assumption that different state institutions share common goals. For instance, in the early post-war period, British government policy toward nursery provision reflected the opposing objectives of the Ministries of Labour and Health (Riley, 1979). These authors also criticise excessively functionalist or determinist accounts of the state's impact upon women. The attacks upon the Welfare State of Mrs Thatcher's Conservative Government have shown that the state, and particularly its welfare branches, is not inevitably oppressive to women but can be the site of a sex-based as well as a class struggle, through which valuable advances are made (see Barrett, 1980, p. 246; Riley, 1981).

Some Marxist feminists seek to combine Marxist and radical feminist analyses. Though the insights of the radical feminists are often illuminating and far-reaching, as far as policy-making and the state are concerned they have tended to remain as insights with little systematic exposition. Firestone and Millett understand politics to be centrally about patriarchy, and a traditional means of subordinating women to male interests. Academic adherents to this viewpoint are rare. Hanmer argues that the modern state is based upon male violence, although this is partly mediated by ideological and economic mechanisms (Hanmer, 1978).

Barker in her analysis of the regulations of marriage and Delazay in his case-study of divorce rulings in France both imply, following Delphy, that since the results coincide with the interests of husbands, these policies – both laws and their implementation – serve to buttress the economic exploitation of women by men in the home (Barker, 1978; Delazay, 1976). The thesis that policies towards women reflect male interests is more than plausible. There are none the less difficulties with it, stated so baldly. Firstly, it is not always easy to disentangle the interests of men from those of other dominant classes or groups. For instance, Barrett points out that the state's apparent support, in twentieth-century Britain, for the family system as identified by McIntosh could be construed as being in the interests of capital, of men, or both (Barrett, 1980, p. 242). Secondly, there are some policies, such as the admission of women to university education, or the encouragement of family planning, that do not appear so directly to underpin male dominance.

The role of male interests

At this point, drawing upon both the analysis of policies towards women in capitalist and state socialist societies that has preceded, and the perceptions of Marxist and radical feminists, I should like to offer some preliminary hypotheses concerning the origin of these policies. I suggest, in the first place, that the policies reviewed over the previous pages were not all primarily concerned to ensure male dominance; they often had other immediate objectives. However, they reflected male dominance to the extent that they incorporated its assumptions and did not permit any real threat to institutionalised male supremacy in all the societies concerned.

The role of assumptions of male dominance requires little elaboration. As we saw, such preconceptions of women's proper place and functions, particularly their responsibility for the care of children and the home, which is perhaps the basis for current sex inequality, were not questioned by policy-makers until the 1970s, and then only occasionally. The protection of male dominance is also evident in the policies we have studied. Further illustrations from women's experience during wars and revolution make the point even more clearly. A number of feminist accounts show how the necessary mobilisation of women and expansion of their roles and opportunities was always kept within safe bounds. It was regarded, sometimes explicitly, as temporary, and withdrawn in the aftermath as soon as it clashed with other priorities.

We saw this, earlier, for Britain during the Second World War. Skold similarly describes how, in the shipyards of Portland Oregon, during the same war, women were encouraged by new government-sponsored training and recruitment programmes, and how by 1944 they totalled 28 per cent of the workforce. But they remained largely confined to less skilled work, in sex-segregated occupations, and were rarely promoted to supervisory grades. As the war ended, cancelled contracts led to extensive lay-offs, which included most of the women workers, although surveys indicated that the majority of them wanted to stay on. The hastily assembled crèche facilities were wound down and 'women were pushed back into "women's work", whether in the home or in traditionally female-employing industries' (Skold, 1981, p. 68).

Chapter 3 has already described how, during the Russian and the Chinese communist revolutions, though women were extensively mobilised, their access to leadership positions was limited and temporary. The post-revolutionary policy-makers gave little priority to combating the reassertion of patriarchal values, except when these contradicted their own policy objectives (Salaff and Merkle, 1970). A similar story can be told of women in the revolutions of Cuba and Vietnam and perhaps the most blatant recent example of the manipulative mobilisation of women, in the Iranian revolution.

The role of state needs

If the first element of an explanation of how policy affects women is the role of dominant male assumptions and interests, it is still insufficient on its own. For it is clear that the effect upon women of particular policies has often been incidental to their perceived objectives. This is, of course, in one sense the ultimate confirmation of the male dominance thesis that women's interests are never an end in themselves. However, it also requires us to identify those other policy constraints or targets that have most consistently shaped the political construction of women's options.

Here it may be useful, despite the obvious risk of over-simplification, to distinguish between what could be called state interests, or needs that are common from one state to another, on the one hand, and the features of particular political systems which modify them, on the other. In the remainder of this chapter I want to develop this suggestion.

Before doing so, it may be helpful briefly to indicate what is meant by the state, and its relationship to politics. If politics is understood here in its public sense, as the conscious activity through which issues perceived to be of concern to the whole community are resolved, then the state post-dates the emergence of politics and is not coterminous with it. Rather, a minimal definition of the state would be a 'centralised, hierarchical organisation which plausibly claims ultimate control over the use of force within a given territory' and which possesses some command over resources and administrative capacity (Whitehead, 1975, p. 1). Such a definition does not convey the important variations between states, in their degree of centralisation, their reliance upon force for their authority and the resources and administrative mechanisms at their disposal. It also leaves open for the moment the question of the relationship between the state and classes and interests within society. What is clear is the centrality of the state to modern politics. By now the whole world is divided into states whose boundaries are internationally recognised. Though with obvious exceptions and qualifications – for instance, civil wars or attacks on the public sector by right-wing governments – there has been a tendency for state institutions everywhere to grow in scale and the scope of their interventions and increasingly to arrogate to themselves authoritative political decision-making powers.

One must guard against reifying the state. However, Skocpol convincingly argues that every viable state must have certain interests of its own, separable from or at least not reducible to the interests of any dominant social category (Skocpol, 1979). These interests could be defined as arising from the requirements of its own survival on the one hand, and from its possession of a partially autonomous institutional and resource base on the other. This is not to say that the state exists in any Hegelian sense as a transcendental will. But those who rise to positions of authority within the state structure will find themselves caught up and constrained by these state imperatives.

I suggest further that three foremost state needs are, first, the promotion of economic prosperity or growth, which will be a source of revenue and contribute to the second, a secure international position, and the third, internal political order or stability. These three imperatives will not receive equal attention at any given time, nor are they always mutually compatible; economic development, for instance, could undermine political order. A further complication in the case of the colonial state is that it will be concerned with prosperity, security and stability in the metropolitan country as well as in the colony. Finally these different imperatives will not necessarily have convergent implications for women's status. But, in the discussion so far we have repeatedly seen how women's interests have been subordinated to one or other of them.

Some states are much stronger than others. Indeed, it is interesting that not only have writers like Whyte associated the subordination of women with increasing social complexity, including the emergence of a differentiated state structure (Whyte, 1978), but that some feminists have suggested a more direct connection between male dominance and the rise of the state. Reiter, for instance, speculates that, while in pre-state societies, kinship systems within which women often wielded great power played a central role, 'With the rise of state structures, kin-based forms of organisation were curtailed, sapped of their legitimacy and autonomy in favour of the evolving sphere of territorial and class-specific élites . . . women were subordinated along with (and in relation to) kinship' (Reiter, 1977, p. 9). Dobash and Dobash draw on English history to argue that 'In order for the State to emerge as the dominant institution of power in society, it had to displace the large feudal households as the main political and economic institutions of society'. The state needed simultaneously to deflect loyalties on to the Crown and the nuclear family. But it also needed to foster, within the family, relations of authority and deference which had earlier characterised the large feudal households and which 'were believed to be the very patterns of mind and habit necessary to achieve obedience and allegiance to the State' (Dobash and Dobash, 1980, pp. 48–9).

Whether or not the state's emergence necessarily caused or reinforced women's oppression, its growth certainly assisted it. For whereas public policies, at state level, severely restricted women's role in medieval and even later times, the machinery of the state was inadequate to ensure compliance. O'Donovan, for instance, suggests that while according to English Common Law in the early eighteenth century women upon marriage lost their separate legal identity, the local Borough courts were often willing 'to indulge in legal fictions' in order to circumvent this restriction. As the independence of local courts diminished and with the passage of Lord Hardwicke's Act in 1753, which required the public registration of marriages, such flexibility was no longer possible (O'Donovan, 1979, p. 138).

Most important, the growth of the state led to the increasing salience, or at least the more effective pursuit in public policy of the state needs I have identified. What implications have these had for women? A proper answer would require a full-length study. What follows is simply meant to indicate, drawing on the earlier analysis, how one might go about finding it.

The first object of state policy, I suggested, must be economic prosperity or, more recently, economic growth or development. The precise requirements of the economy, or at least the way these are perceived, will vary not only between different 'levels' and types of economic system but, in the short term, between similar systems. Moreover, political values, and not least assumptions about the legitimate scope of state intervention, will influence state policies in response. The consequences for women are then complicated and subject to variation. But we may find some indication by looking at specific policy areas.

One major component of a modern state's economic policy is likely to be its attitude towards employment. How does this affect women? The United States Government has, except at times of war and during the Depression, seen its role in ensuring a 'healthy' economy largely as the negative one of interfering as little as possible; at most, as Adams and Winston point out, its policies have been 'reactive', responding to rather than initiating economic development. Accordingly, even Democratic administrations have tolerated high levels of unemployment, with obvious consequences for the employment of women. On the other hand, full employment may be the 'single most important policy goal that contributes to government programmes to alleviate women's dual burden' (Adams and Winston, 1980, p. 176), as for instance in Sweden and China. Alternatively, or supplementing this commitment, official policy may seek to remedy a labour shortage, as in East Germany, by policies that enable women more easily to combine domestic responsibilities with outside work. At an extreme, as again in East Germany and, temporarily, in Cuba, labour shortages may even lead the political leadership to encourage domestic role-sharing.

A policy of full employment helps women find jobs but, in the absence of additional policies to increase the range of women's employment opportunities, its benefits are limited. Even in communist states, concern with maximising productivity in the short term has taken precedence over efforts to recruit women into the most 'productive' and high status occupations. Cost considerations have also reinforced criticisms of nursery education in several East European states, from the late 1960s, while in China Adams and Winston report a reluctance to spend more on nursery provisions than working women contribute to production. That full employment bears no necessary relationship to women's range of job opportunities is paradoxically demonstrated by the fact that it is in the United States that government and the law have shown the greatest willingness to combat discrimination in employment. This can even be seen as an extension of the *laissez-faire* approach to one of actively intervening to remove market imperfections.

Differing employment policies also have implications for education and manpower objectives. No simple relationship can be traced between women's employment and the evolution of educational policies for women in Britain or the United States. In state socialist societies, however, one part of the rationale both for the expansion of women's education and for its limitation has been their preparation for entry into the labour force. Related to this, the absence in the United States of an effective employment policy has compounded women's disadvantage in the competition for jobs. In Sweden, on the other hand, publicly funded training or retraining is available to anyone 'who is unemployed or in danger of becoming unemployed and who cannot find a job within his or her current qualifications' (Adams and Winston, 1980, p. 186).

A second important way that the state's economic objectives can affect women is through their implications for population policies, which are closely associated with employment policies in the longer term. Going back to the colonial state, we saw that pro-natalist policies resulted in part from growing demands for labour. In the 1930s, a marked decline in the birth rate in several European countries, including Britain, Sweden, Germany and France, raised fears that their long-term social and economic development would suffer. Though no major policy change resulted in Britain, these fears may have contributed to the Government's reluctance to disseminate birth control information. In the other three countries, material incentives to motherhood were increased. However, while in France and Germany measures were also introduced to discourage women from outside employment, in Sweden the Social Democratic coalition defeated a proposal to deny such employment to married women. Instead, impressed by the findings of Alva and Gunnar Myrdal that women at home were no more likely to have children than those at work, and that it was the poorest families who were having the fewest children, it chose to include married women in its commitment to a policy of full employment.

Again, we have seen that in several East European nations, the recent decline in birth rate has led policy-makers not only to increase incentives for motherhood, but to interpret protection laws more literally, to question the value of nursery care and, most seriously, to restrict if not prohibit outright access to birth control facilities. On the other hand, East Germany, in part because its immediate labour shortage is so acute, has chosen to increase nursery provision, improve women's employment opportunities and make birth control facilities freely available. Economic development may of course also be seen to require the limitation of population growth, as in India, China and Japan. While genuine control over her own fertility may increase a woman's freedom to pursue roles other than or as well as mother and housewife, when such policies mean access to abortion but not safe and reliable methods of contraception as in Japan (Pharr, 1977, p. 246), still more when they take the form of sterilisation campaigns or purveying of dangerous contraceptive devices, they can clearly be oppressive.

The second objective of state policy is national security. Its consequences for women are again complex, arising in particular from its reflection in population and defence policies. Pro-natalist policies not only reflect actual or anticipated labour shortages but simultaneously, or exclusively, more nationalist or imperialist preoccupations. This was demonstrated most blatantly in Nazi Germany, but a more recent example has been the policies of post-war France where 'It became patriotic to have large families, since the nation needed an expanding population to regain its power in Europe and to guard against attack from the enemy'. Family allowances (the larger the family, the more per child), housing policies to assist young couples, the 'salaire unique' or allowance for mothers who did not go out to work and the continuing ban on contraception and abortion, were all instrumental to this end (Silver, 1977, p. 286).

Lapidus argues that a current concern of Soviet leadership is the effect of a declining birth rate on the Soviet Union's international standing:

> Perevedentsev's view that 'a country's position in the world, all other things being equal, is determined by the size of the population', is unlikely to be confined to demographers. Frequent comparisons of Soviet population trends with those of the United States, Japan and China indicate a serious preoccupation with the strategic implications of population dynamics and prompted one recent suggestion that the Soviet leadership adopt as its goal the maintenance of a constant ratio between the size of the world population and that of the USSR (Lapidus, 1978, p. 295).

Besides attempting to regulate the size of the population, policies may be aimed at raising its quality. It was recruitment for the Boer War in 1899 that revealed to policy-makers 'the physical puniness and general ill health and debility of the British worker'. An Interdepartmental Committee on Physical Deterioration accordingly recommended that mothers should be educated in child care and daughters in cookery and dietetics (Wilson, 1977, p. 101). Nazi leaders in Germany were particularly concerned for the health of potential mothers, a concern, suggest Rupp, that helped to reconcile many women to the regime (Rupp, 1977). Even in the United States, well into the twentieth century women were not only 'protected' from certain kinds of employment, but 'exempted' from various civic duties, according to the law courts, 'in order to preserve the strength and vigour of the race' (Cook, 1977, p. 356).

Concern with national security also dramatically affects women through policies designed to provide defence, particularly in wartime. Feminist anthropologists have debated whether women's status in primitive societies rises or falls at time of war; the fact that women take on formerly masculine economic roles may be cancelled out by the heightened esteem accorded the masculine martial virtues (see, for instance, Sanday, 1974). During the two world wars the contending states were bound to mobilise women into occupations left by men and expanding armaments production. Even in Nazi Germany, to the Führer's dismay, women had to be urged back into industrial production and in 1943 compulsory recruitment was introduced, albeit with only limited success. By 1945 women constituted more than 56 per cent of the Soviet Union's industrial workforce and the 'higher educational institutions became almost entirely female' (Lapidus, 1978, p. 115). Their opportunities for taking on senior political and economic roles also expanded enormously. Supporting communal childcare and catering facilities, already much more generous than in Britain or the United States, were rapidly increased. These examples, together with the experience of women in Britain and the United States, cited earlier, suggest that mobilisation for war demands changes in women's role that must enhance their status and to that extent run counter to male interests. Still, I have already emphasised the limitations to such role changes; not only is mobilisation carefully channelled and often explicitly described as temporary but propaganda may play upon more traditional images of women. Shover relates how in Britain the image of 'womanhood' was manipulated to 'sell' the First World War. Women were portrayed simultaneously as the dependants at home in need of protection, as the slightly provocative 'girl next door' who expected men to enlist, as the sensual symbol of the nation, and even as the spirit of war and the symbol of the wicked enemy. The real victims of the propaganda were men, but it also confirmed a traditional conception of 'feminity' (Shover, 1975). In the Soviet Union during the Second World War, the state, at the same time as mobilising women, was pursuing policies that reinforced traditional sex roles, including not only an end to coeducation (fortunately later revoked) but sex segregation in concentration camps. Indeed Wilson's comment on the impact of the Second World War in Britain seems to have more general bearing: war 'has reinforced the conventions, while purporting to offer new freedoms' (Wilson, 1977, p. 127).

The third imperative of the state is political order or stability. Political stability depends partly upon coercion; in fact, one writer has argued that even a political system reliant exclusively upon terror can be stable (Walter, 1969). Usually it additionally requires some kind of persuasion, whether through socialisation or appeals to more rational self-interest. Of course, both coercive and persuasive capacity in turn depend in good measure upon the state's ability to ensure economic prosperity and a secure international position.

The state has customarily perceived the family as a bulwark of social and political stability. The family has an important socialising function, transmitting if not attitudes of positive support for the existing regime, at least a tendency to accept authority and to adhere conservatively to the way things are as normal. A family system also helps to ensure that children, and to a lesser extent the sick and the old are looked after; at the same time it engages the head(s) of the household into the existing system, so as to be able to provide for their own.

Earlier the argument was cited that the emergence of the state required the strengthening of the patriarchal nuclear family. It can plausibly be argued that in Britain the framers of the Employment Protection laws feared that women's employment in arduous work over long hours could undermine working-class family life, and hence social stability. Furthermore Wilson, amongst others, has drawn attention to the role of Britain's contemporary Welfare State in shoring up the family household system which, in so far as it assists in the ideological as well as the physical reproduction of economic relations, is clearly a force for political stability. Although this family system is no longer strictly patriarchal, it is still premised upon women's main responsibility for child care and the home.

It is also noticeable that while revolutionary movements have attacked patriarchal family systems, once in power their leaders have regularly reasserted, as the fundamental social unit, the family based upon a traditional division of labour. Though during the first French Revolution, proposed family reform was mild by later standards it was still a real advance for women. Pope describes the retrograde efforts of the framers of the Napoleonic Civil Code to buttress 'institutions that assured the stability of the State', including a severely patriarchal family (Pope, 1980, p. 221). After the experimentation in the Soviet Union of the 1920s, Stalin shored up the nuclear family, now transmogrified into the 'ideal socialist family', arguing that instead of withering away it would strengthen with the strengthening of socialism itself. Lapidus cites Trotsky's comment in 1936 that 'the most compelling motive of the present cult of the family is undoubtedly the need of bureaucracy for a stable hierarchy of relations and for the disciplining of youth by 40 million points of support for authority and power' (Lapidus, 1978, p. 112). Even during China's first Five Year Plan, from 1951 to 1956, the Party moderated its attack upon the traditional family because any ensuing political instability might jeopardise the economic programme.

As Molyneux describes, the present constitution (1980) of China as well as those of Cuba, South Yemen, North Korea, Vietnam and Mozambique, refer to the family as the 'basic cell of society'. Though marriage and land reforms have undermined some aspects of the traditional, patriarchal family, sufficient to permit the transformation of property relations and the work-force, a new 'formally egalitarian, preferably nuclear' family has taken its place as the foundation of social order. Sometimes the metaphor of the family is even extended to the state; the state or nation becomes the 'new family', the head of state, as for instance Kim il Sung in North Korea, the 'father of the people' (Molyneux, 1985). In other 'socialist' societies where revolutionary forces have been weaker, traditional or pre-capitalist forces correspondingly stronger, family relations as we have seen have been still less changed. The socialist government of Algeria was not, we saw, prepared to risk destabilising consequences of any serious attempt to reform Islamic family law.

I have suggested then some of the main ways in which policies towards women have been shaped by these three overriding state needs. On their own of course they can only reveal relatively constant variable in policy towards women; they cannot fully explain variation (though it is interesting to note that Sweden where women's status is comparatively high, has been, at least recently, neither militaristic nor excessively nationalistic, and with its small compact territory and quite homogeneous population faces few real problems of political stability). In order to explain the variations in women's experience we also need to discover how state needs are refracted through the particular characteristics of the political system.

This means taking account firstly of the configuration of dominant interests in a polity, whether they are directly represented within state institutions, are in some sense 'co-opted' into state policy-making or simply are too powerful to be gainsaid (see Goodin, 1982). As we have seen, these are very often class interests. But organised religion can also exert enormous influence, direct and indirect, on policies towards women. In Islamic countries this has been most evident where religion provides the national or cultural identity through which to resist Western economic and cultural 'imperialism'. Even in modern European states such as Spain, Italy and above all Ireland, the Roman Catholic Church until very recently has determined policy in such areas as marriage, contraception and abortion. Racial interest has also shaped policies towards women, the most stark instance being in Nazi Germany. Hecht and Yuval-Davis suggest that Talmudic law continues to regulate marriage in Israel, although most Israelis are not religious, because women are 'the bearers of the national collective'; the sole criterion of being Jewish is to be born to a Jewish mother (Hecht and Yuval-Davis, 1978). Again, despite the prevailing pronatalism in the Soviet Union, Lapidus detects efforts to reduce fertility in the Moslem regions, where the soaring birth rate threatens the hegemony of the Slavic groups (Lapidus, 1978, p. 298).

The second relevant consideration is the extent to which governmental power is centralised and political power is concentrated. In the United States many aspects of policy affecting women, such as those concerning abortion, rape and marriage, were for a long time left entirely to the discretion of state legislatures, and even now show considerable variation. As we shall see, the degree of centralisation has implications for feminist tactics. The decentralisation of governmental authority between Congress, the Presidency, the judiciary and the fifty state legislatures, together with the explicit and legitimate competition between different interests and groups for political influence, have provided feminists with a tremendous range of access points and alliance strategies, but have at the same time tended to produce extremely gradual, consensual policy changes. In Britain, where government is relatively centralised though political power is not, there is little choice about the focus of political pressure, though a number of strategic alliances are possible. On the other hand, policies that emerge need not be so 'incremental'; they may even anticipate and help to mould public opinion, as with the 1967 Abortion Act. When, as in the Soviet Union, both government and power are highly centralised, the disposition of those in authority becomes the more crucial.

Third, related both to the centralisation of power and to the character of dominant interests, is the scope of government; we have seen the contrast in this respect between Sweden and the United States. Even during economic recessions, as Adams and Winston point out, the usual response of United States governments has been to cut taxes, thus keeping down the level of social expenditure. The vast scope of government in the industrialised state socialist countries, on the other hand, means that when they do espouse policies, such as full employment, which are beneficial to women, these can actually be implemented.

These three political variables hardly exhaust the list of those that could be considered relevant, but are perhaps the most significant. Chapter 6 will further illustrate their implications for feminist strategy and tactics. But before concluding this discussion, it must be noted that I have deliberately so far largely discounted the impact of feminism itself. Well before the revival of feminism in the 1960s, the women's movement left its mark upon policies in the fields of marriage law, birth control and women's employment and education. In the following two chapters, the impact and potential of feminism will be our central concern.

5

The politics of the women's movement

Any account of the relationship between women and politics, in contemporary Western societies at least, must assign a central place to the women's movement. Earlier chapters have touched on its implications for women's political participation and for policies affecting women; now it must be examined more closely. Despite the movement's value and achievements, even because of them, this examination must be up to a point detached, pointing out weaknesses as well as strengths, the more so as we enter a time which is perhaps less hospitable to its aims.

For the purposes of this book, feminism was defined as broadly as possible. Similarly the term 'women's movement', though it may imply rather more structure and interaction, and though by definition it tends to exclude men except as outside supporters, is understood here to cover the full range of self-styled 'feminist' ideological positions. I have already suggested that in the late 1960s the new radical feminists were associated with a specific platform of 'women's liberation'. This raises the question of the relationship between women's liberation and the women's movement. Many commentators use both terms interchangeably to describe second wave feminism. Radical feminists have wanted to reserve its usage only for revolutionary feminism, since they believe that it is only through revolutionary consciousness and activity that women can be truly liberated. 'Reformists' have challenged this monopoly. For instance Jo Freeman, author of an excellent history of the first decade of second-wave feminism in the United States, *The Politics of Women's Liberation*, and a NOW (National Organisation of Women) activist, argues that in the context of the women's movement, a distinction between 'radical' or 'revolutionary' and 'reformist' is more difficult than usual to apply. She suggests that radical aloofness from the system can end up in a kind of powerless introversion, while more system-oriented and gradualistic groups may 'have a platform that would so completely change our society, it would be unrecognisable' (Freeman, 1975, p. 50). Accordingly, she proposes that 'women's liberation' should be understood to include all activities that seek radically to widen the life options open to women, in this latest phase of the women's movement. These definitional problems are significant but they can hardly be settled by academic fiat. For this reason, the present chapter will not equate women's liberation with the women's movement from the 1960s but will recognise that its boundaries, though not its core, are a subject of dispute.

The 'first wave' of feminism

We must begin by considering briefly the women's movement of the nineteenth and early twentieth centuries. Since this is the subject of a huge and growing literature, our discussion can only touch on some central developments and observations particularly relevant to feminism today.

The first concerted political demands for women's rights were made during the French Revolution and the first systematic treatise was Mary Wollstonecraft's *Vindication of the Rights of Women*, published in 1792. Almost throughout history it appears, however, that individual women have advanced feminist ideas. In England, by the seventeenth century, many middle-class or aristocratic women demanded greater equality. Mary Astell was typical in emphasising the need for women's education: 'Women are from their very infancy debarred those advantages with the want of which they are afterwards reproached and nursed in those vices which will hereafter be upbraided to them' (cited by Jayawardena, 1983, p. 10; see also Mitchell, 1976).

A substantial feminist movement, however, first began in the United States where women involved in the movement to abolish slavery, in the 1830s, drew inferences for their own situation. Three hundred women and men attended the famous convention at Seneca Falls in 1848, at which were adopted the far-reaching Declaration of Sentiments and twelve resolutions including a commitment to women's suffrage. Following the American Civil War, the political rights nominally secured for blacks (or, more precisely, black men) were not extended to women. As a result, feminists increasingly, though not to start with exclusively, focused on the suffrage issue. Two main suffrage organisations emerged: the National Woman Suffrage Association, led by Elizabeth Cady Stanton and Susan B. Anthony, which retained for some time a broad radical analysis and programme; and the American Woman's Suffrage Association, in which Lucy Stone was prominent, and whose orientation was always narrower and more conservative. At the same time 'social feminism', to use O'Neill's term for women's involvement 'in reforms or philanthropies that directly benefited women, or were of special interest to women' (O'Neill, 1969, p. 33), grew phenomenally, though they frequently took a socially conservative form, as in the activities of the Women's Christian Temperance Union. By the 1880s even the NWSA was becoming more respectable and in 1890 it merged with the AWSA to form the National American Woman's Suffrage Association, whose focus was almost exclusively women's suffrage. In the first two decades of the twentieth century, more militant and less socially conservative elements resurfaced within American feminism. Social feminists were involved in the attempt, albeit with limited success, to unionise women workers, in the settlement movement and in the campaign for birth control. Socialist feminism was making its appearance amongst the radicals of Greenwich Village and in the writings of Charlotte Perkins Gilman. The suffrage movement itself entered a more militant phase. The combination of Carrie Chapman Catt's skilful leadership of NAWSA and the more aggressive campaign, inspired by Britain's suffragettes, of Alice Paul's Woman's Party eventually secured in 1920 the passage of the Nineteenth Amendment, which entitled women to vote in national as well as state elections. But now the majority of women activists, as well as the public at large, presumed that the emancipation of women had been achieved, and those feminists who wanted to use the vote to achieve further reforms could not agree on goals or strategies. As a result, and against the background of political repression in the 1920s, feminism subsided though it did not disappear.

In Britain, also, feminist ideas spread amongst middle-class women in the 1840s. The first recognisable woman suffrage pamphlet was in 1847 by Ann Knight, a Quaker, and the first suffragist organisation, the Sheffield Association for Female Suffrage, was formed in 1851. But as an organised movement, feminism emerged in the mid-1850s, nearly a decade later than in America. To begin with it centered on a small group of women based in London, in Langham Place, which sought to improve married women's legal rights, and women's employment opportunities. The suffrage question came to the fore from the mid-1860s, and particularly following the defeat of J. S. Mill's attempt to get women included under the provisions of the 1867 Reform Act. This led to the formation of the National Society for Women's Suffrage. At the same time social feminism began to flourish, taking forms similar to those in America. Temperance was rather less of a feminist issue, however, while prostitution, through Josephine Butler's campaign against the Contagious Diseases Acts, was more prominent. The British Women's Trade Union League, originally founded by Emma Paterson in 1873, was more successful than the American initiative it inspired, particularly after 1903, when Mary MacArthur took over its Secretaryship.

The suffrage movement, now under an umbrella National Union of Women's Suffrage Societies (NUWSS) and inclined towards the Liberal Party, was making little headway, meanwhile. Emmeline Pankhurst one of its leaders, left first to join the new Independent Labour Party (ILP), and then in 1903 to found the militant Women's Social and Political Union (WSPU). When in 1904 Parliament talked out the Women's Suffrage Bill, with little resistance from either the ILP or the Labour Representation Committee, Mrs Pankhurst and her daughter Christabel withdrew from this alliance with the Left. She launched the WSPU into its famous campaign of direct action which, by 1910, and in the face of apparent Parliamentary stalemate, escalated into wholesale attacks on property, directed from an underground centre in Paris. These tactics did not have the support of the more moderate NUWSS or of Mrs Pankhurst's other daughter, Sylvia, campaigning for suffrage amongst the working-class women of London's East End. Feminists were further divided on whether or not to support involvement in the First World War. Even so feminism at the end of the war was still vigorous. As in America it was winning the vote that diffused its energies. Since this came in two stages, with suffrage granted to women aged 30 or over in 1918 but not to all adult women until

1928, Banks suggests that there was more life in British feminism in the 1920s (Banks, 1981, pp. 163–4).✗

As this brief outline indicates, there were striking similarities and significant differences between the American and British movements. The American movement gathered momentum earlier and involved many more women. O'Neill suggests that as British feminism grew more militant, American feminism became less so, apart from its brief reinvigoration in the first decades of the twentieth century (O'Neill, 1969, p. 81). Banks, moreover, argues that 'equal rights' feminism was always stronger in Britain than in the United States, while socialist feminism played little part at all in the American movement.

While perhaps feminism took off earliest and achieved greatest notoriety in these countries, it was by no means confined to them. Movements in the Nordic countries were 'probably the most successful in Europe before the First Worls War' (Evans, 1977, p. 69). Organised feminism developed relatively late, in the 1870s or 1880s, but then succeeded in mobilising a considerable section of the female population. In Sweden and Denmark women began by campaigning for economic rights – property in marriage and employment opportunities – but, caught up in the tide of constitutional reform by the end of the century were also demanding the right to vote. In Finland and Norway it was the national struggle that politicised women, and these were the only countries to grant women the vote before the First World War. In Australia and New Zealand feminist movements were smaller, dominated by temperance organisations and narrowly focused on moral reform and suffrage but could none the less in their own terms be considered successful.

Elsewhere organised feminism was less significant. In many European countries, movements were inhibited by political authoritarianism, the influence of Roman Catholicism or both. In France, feminist activities in the 1789 Revolution, which according to Evans were in any case 'really a marginal phenomenon' were firmly suppressed by 1793. The severe patriarchalism of the Code Napoleon was reinforced by a Catholic Church ready to agree that 'women belong to the family and not to public society' and which, with the 1850 Falloux Law acquired a virtual monopoly over girls' education. This had the paradoxical consequence that the feminist movement emerging from the late 1860s was closely associated with republican and anti-clerical tendencies but could not overcome republican fears that women would use their vote to support conservative and Catholic parties.

The conservatism of the women's movement in Germany, which took form from the mid-1860s under the leadership of Louise Otto-Peters was partly an adaptation but also partly sympathetic to the reassertion of political authoritarianism in that country. With the political relaxation following the end of the Bismark era in 1890, the older movement organisations became bolder in their demands, with membership rising dramatically by 1914, while a separate and more radical Suffrage Union was also beginning to make some headway. However, almost immediately war broke out, the Suffrage Union was taken over by the ultra-conservative Women's League and German feminism entered a period of deep reaction (Evans, 1977).

First wave feminism took some root in the Netherlands, where by 1913 the Association for Women's Suffrage had 14,000 members, but in Belgium, Italy and the countries of the Habsburg Empire made less impression. In Tsarist Russia, too, though by the 1890s a younger generation of feminists from a broadened social base and pressing more radical demands took advantage of the brief period of constitutional reform following the 1905 Revolution, its activities were curtailed in the ensuing phase of reaction (Evans, 1977). Jayawardena also describes how in a number of Middle Eastern and Asian countries, limited measures to improve women's marital status and education introduced by nationalist leaders stimulated more independent feminist agitation. Generally this was on an extremely modest scale but during heightened phases of nationalist struggle, suffrage campaigns sometimes assumed a more militant character as in China, in 1911, Iran in 1917, Japan in 1924 and Ceylon (Sri Lanka) in 1927. Autonomous feminist organisations were rare but in Japan two exceptions were the Seito (Blue Stockings) groups formed in 1911 and the Chinese women's association founded by Jiu Jin (Jayawardena, 1986).

A number of observations have been made about this first wave of feminism which are of relevance and interest to feminism today. First, there is widespread agreement that it arose from the conjunction of changes in women's social position, associated with the rise of industrial capitalism, with new ideologies of equality. The main catalyst for feminism was, in Goode's words, 'the gradual, logical, philosophical extension to women of originally Protestant notions about the rights and responsibilities of the individual' (Goode, 1963, p. 56). As Evans writes, liberal protestantism was founded on the 'belief that the individual, not the priest nor the Church, was responsible for his own salvation', a doctrine in principle applicable to both sexes (Evans, 1977, p. 17). Out of seventeenth-century liberal Protestantism developed the influential doctrine of the 'natural' equality of men, which however excluded women. The contradiction is exemplified in the thinking of John Locke. As Brennan and Pateman point out, the equality in nature that Locke supposed men to share was by implication abstract and moral, since he acknowledged differences in physical and mental endowment. Yet he presumed that, even in 'nature', women were unequal, because of their physical and mental differences (Brennan and Pateman, 1979). However, several of the 'philosophes' of the French Enlightenment, for instance Diderot and Condorcet, were more logically consistent and sympathetic with women's rights. Feminist thinkers were also influenced by the practical realisation of radical natural rights doctrine in the American and French Revolutions. Indeed, Mary Wollstonecraft's book was published during the French Revolution, while the Seneca Falls Declaration was directly inspired by the American Declaration of Independence (Banks, 1981, pp. 28–9). Evans sees nineteenth-century liberalism as marking the fusion of the rationalism of the Enlightenment with the moral imperatives of Protestantism. It was epitomised in J. S. Mill's essay *The Subjection of Women*, a book rapidly translated into several languages and whose effect on educated women of the time it would be 'difficult to exaggerate'. Indeed, he argues that the very appeal of Mill's essay, as of feminism as a whole, was that they 'formed part of a general intellectual movement which sought to justify the removal of formal legal discrimination against individuals on account of their birth' (Evans, 1977, p. 22).

Of course nineteenth-century liberal ideas were not only applicable to issues of constitutional reform as in Britain and the US. They also provided much of the intellectual ammunition for anti-clericalism as in France, and for nationalism, as in Austro–Hungary or the Middle East and Asia. And here too they could be pursued to feminist conclusions.

The emergence of liberalism can itself hardly be divorced from the early development of capitalist relations. For Evans, one crucial consequence was the appearance of a relatively strong, confident middle-class based in trade, administration and the professions. This middle-class would be most developed in predominantly Protestant countries and indeed, Evans maintains, an assertive Protestant middle-class was the prerequisite both of liberalism and of feminism.'Feminism, like liberalism itself . . . was above all a creed of the Protestant middle-classes'. Even in largely Catholic countries such as France, feminist leadership was overwhelmingly Protestant or anti-clerical (Evans, 1977, p. 30).

More specifically, it has been argued in the context of American and British feminism, that the readiness of some women to apply equal rights doctrines to themselves stemmed from the impact of industrial capitalism upon their role and status. Industrialisation, firstly removed many traditionally female functions from the home. Potentially this freed married middle-class women at least from many former domestic responsibilities and undermined the logic of their confinement to an increasingly narrow domestic sphere. But their husbands' conspicuous display of the new wealth entailed the idealisation of the unproductive, passive Victorian female. In the meantime, reduced production in the domestic sphere, and the resulting increased reliance on money to acquire the necessities of life, forced large numbers of single, middle-class women to seek employment in one of the narrow range of socially acceptable occupations available, often in unpleasant and humiliating conditions. Most oppressed, of course, were working-class women who despite the opposition of working-class men and the pious regrets of Victorian reformers, were incresingly obliged to labour in factories and domestic service; simply as women they suffered lowered wages and other forms of discrimination, while as housewives they endured the additional burden of the double shift.

One consequence of these social changes, emphasised by Linda Gordon, was the declining birth rate. Although some have attributed the decline to feminism itself, it was already apparent in the early nineteenth century and probably reflected both diminishing infant mortality and the fact that for non-agricultural families large numbers of children were no longer 'economic' (Gordon, 1977). The implications of this trend for feminism are much disputed, but it seems probable that it played a contributory role.

The origins of nineteenth-century feminism help to explain the character of its adherents. Above all this was a movement of upper and middle-class women; they were the women most acutely conscious of the 'gap between women's narrowed sphere and men's expanding one' (O'Neill, 1969, p. 17). They had the most time and frustrated energies to commit. This does not mean they were unconcerned about the specific problems of working-class women posed for instance by marriage law and employment conditions. It is also true, as Liddington and Norris (1978) contest, that in Britain historians may have under-represented the involvement of working-class women in feminist campaigns, especially suffrage; their study of the Lancashire area in the early 1900s brings out the contribution of 'radical suffragists', working women bringing their experience of trade union activism to the suffrage struggle. Evans tells us that in New Zealand by the 1890s working-class women's support for female suffrage was extensive despite the moderation of the leadership, but this was exceptional. One important corollary of being middle-class was access to a formal education. Jayawardena stresses the part education could play in putting Asian and Middle Easertn women in touch with progressive or feminist ideas or deeds in other countries.

It has sometimes been suggested that single, as opposed to married women were disproportionately represented in the movement. Indeed, in Britain the growing surplus of women over men by the 1850s, largely the consequence of male emigration, has been cited as a cause of first-wave feminism. Caine (1982), however, argues that both the interests of married women and married women themselves were fully evident in the movement from the start.

Though it is sometimes implied that these early feminists focused on women's rights, above all suffrage, to the exclusion of other concerns, there is increasing recognition both that nineteenth-century feminism embraced a remarkable range of activities and perspectives and that many campaigners saw woman suffrage primarily as a means to improving specific policies, for instance labour legislation or the regulation of prostitution. Banks identifies three main strands. The first, equal rights feminism, she depicts as the direct product of the Enlightenment. Strong in both countries, but expecially in England, it minimised the intrinsic differences between the sexes, and sought sexual equality in such contexts as marriage law, education, employment and the vote. The second element was evangelical feminism. She suggests that a subsidiary ideological influence on feminism, at least in the United States, was the evangelical movement of the late eighteenth and early nineteenth centuries. Great numbers of women undertook proselytising and good works. In particular the campaigns to convert prostitutes and promote temperance, as early as the 1830s and 1840s, were perceptibly acquiring feminist overtones, as they attacked the sexual double standard and male drunkenness. Evangelical feminism, which grew out of this experience, tended rather than seeking to improve the position of the feminists themselves to provide protection and moral uplift for those less fortunate than they, working-class or 'fallen' women, children, the poor. In time they came to emphasise women's moral superiority but based on their traditional role as mothers and home-makers. To this extent evangelical feminists espoused a socially conservative philosophy. Socialist feminism, the third strand, featured little in the United States and even in Britain was less influential than equal rights or evangelical feminism. However, drawing on several, though not all, of the early socialists – Saint Simon and Fourier, Thompson and Owen – as well as on Marx and Engels themselves, it was the most whole-heartedly feminist of the three traditions. It questioned current forms of marriage and the family, and advocated collectivisation of child care and housework.

Socialist feminism was hardly coterminous with the socialist movement. Even though in France and above all in Germany, by the end of the nineteenth century, socialist parties had incorporated women's rights into their programmes, these co-existed with the deepest mistrust of 'bourgeois' feminism, totally traditional ideas of womanhood persisted and women's rights were always perceived as dependent on and quite secondary to the achievement of socialism (Sowerwine, 1982; Mies, 1983). There was considerable ambivalence about giving women the vote and though the German Social Democratic Party, in particular, mobilised large numbers of women, as Evans points out these tended to be workers' wives rather than women workers.

There were two further noteworthy corollaries of this diversity. One is that these early feminists between them covered much of the theoretical ground to be traced subsequently by the women's movement of the 1960s (see, for instance, Sabrowsky, 1979). While mainstream feminism was more circumspect, individual feminists variously asserted such currently familiar claims as the equality of the sexes, the moral superiority of women, the need for separate women-only feminist organisations, the previous existence of a matriarchy, the comparability of women's sex drive with men's, and women's need both to be economically independent and to avoid the trap of marriage and children. On the other hand, it is argued that the first wave feminists did not really question the sexual division of labour within the home (even socialist feminists assumed women would undertake 'collective' child care and catering). Nor did they adequately face up to female sexuality; for instance, they advocated self-control rather than contraception, at least until the 1910s.

The movement's diversity also threatened disunity. It is frequently suggested that the cause of suffrage imposed a spurious unity on what was not one but in reality several women's movements. There were potential conflicts of interest between equal rights, evangelical and social feminists. J. S. Mill and members of the London-based suffrage organisation, while personally sympathetic to Josephine Butler's campaign against the Contagious Diseases Act, insisted that the suffrage movement dissociate itself publicly from an issue that could compromise its hard won respectability (Caine, 1982). But within these strands there were further differences of interest as well as of tactics. For instance, in the United States Elizabeth Cady Stanton wanted to restrict the vote to educated women, and by the 1890s many suffragists were even arguing that white women should be enfranchised so as to maintain white supremacy (Banks, 1981, p. 141). In Britain the suffrage movement split in 1889 on the question of 'coverture', on whether the vote should be claimed simply for single and widowed women, or also for married women who were, according to legal fiction, represented by their husbands (Morgan, 1975, p. 16). In Germany, the Suffrage Union split on the question of whether to go for a limited property-based or universal female suffrage (Evans, 1977). In fact Banks describes the apparent lull in feminism from the 1920s, with the achievement of woman suffrage, as 'a splitting into its constituent parts' (Banks, 1981, p. 150).

First wave feminism was important for the second wave, both for what it bequeathed by way of achievement and example and as a source of lessons for the future. Its achievements were considerable. Although with hindsight it is easy to see that feminists expected too much from woman suffrage, winning the vote was not a purely symbolic victory. At the least if it had not been won then it would have remained as a hurdle to be cleared in the future. But feminism achieved much more than the vote; its pressures contributed to the expansion of educational opportunities for women in Britain, to enhanced rights for married women and unmarried mothers, as well as to improved maternity and child welfare provision in both countries. Perhaps most important of all it went some way towards establishing the legitimacy of women's claim to equal treatment. Henceforth the battleground would be less that claim's validity than its implications.

The second obvious legacy was its example. Its inspiration to feminism today is clear and acknowledged in the American literature, though, as Wilson points out, English feminists have been slower to rediscover their historical roots (Wilson, 1980, pp. 197–8).

Finally, this phase of feminism provided a number of valuable lessons. It warned against the temptation to counter the centrifugal pressures of such a diverse movement by concentrating on a single concrete goal like suffrage – today's equivalent might be the Equal Rights Amendment. At the same time it showed that in the bid to broaden its appeal and maximise tactical openings, feminism could become so respectable or instrumental as to lose its radical apprehension of future possibilities. This was true, in their different ways, of each of the three traditions identified by Banks. Evangelical feminism idealised women's traditional maternal qualities, equal rights feminism pursued rights that in practice only middle-class women could enjoy, while socialist feminists relied upon the achievement of socialism to end women's oppression. Though there are always limits to what history can teach, and the context of feminism has changed almost beyond recognition, these lessons retain their relevance.

The origins of contemporary feminism

Following this first phase, feminism was never fully extinguished. Or to switch metaphors, the tide of feminism never fully receded after the first wave. The present revival has stimulated new research into the intervening years, calling into question early assumptions about a complete rupture.

It is relevant here to pursue the question of why the movement receded, for although there is much truth in the cliché that once they had the vote, women no longer shared a common goal to strive for, reality appears to have been more complicated. Admittedly some feminists may have agreed with Britain's Prime Minister, Stanley Baldwin, that 'the subjection of women, if there be such a thing, will not now depend on any creation of law . . . the grounds and justification for the old agitation is gone forever' (cited by Bouchier, 1983, p. 8), but for others the vote was just a beginning.

Evans links the waning of feminism after the First World War with the decline of liberalism in general. This was not simply because feminism suffered from increasingly repressive government not only in Germany and Italy but in the United States where during the 'red scare' in the 1920s, the extraordinary 'Spider's Web Chart' implicated individual members of businesswomen's clubs and the Women's Christian Temperance Union. Feminists themselves were inevitably drawn into the polarisation of conservative and socialist camps, which sharpened divisions among them or even submerged feminist issues in the politics of class. This was truest on the continent, where Sowerwine (1982) also argues that feminists had all along chosen, when it came to the crunch, to align themselves by class rather than gender. Jayawardena describes a somewhat analogous pattern in Middle Eastern and Asian countries with first wave feminism subsiding together with movements of national reform.

Bouchier (1983) and Banks (1980) points out that in the 1920s in America and Britain a new generation of women seemed to be enjoying increased freedom, partly of course the fruits of feminist campaigns, in education and employment opportunities, dress and above all sexual morse. This was the era of the 'flapper', defying convention, experimenting with 'androgynous' styles. Recently some radical feminist writers, while noting these changes, have put a rather different construction on their meaning. By the turn of the century, a small but vocal group of feminists were advocating celibacy rather than the degradation of heterosexual unions. These 'spinsters' were viciously attacked by some of their feminist sisters but Jeffreys (1984) argues that the 'libertarian' sexual doctrines of Havelock Ellis and his associates were a male response to this challenge to men's sexual prerogative. Ellis claimed to be asserting women's rights, but in fact his prescriptions closely accorded with the traditional male need to conquer and dominate. The new sexual freedom of the 1920s, to which Ellis contributed, succeeded in discrediting the old 'puritanical' feminism and persuading young women it no longer had relevance for them, while at the same time perpetuating assumptions of female difference and inferiority (see also Jackson, 1984).

A combination of circumstances then helped to obscure the reality of women's continuing oppression in most countries by the 1920s or 1930s and feminist organisations dwindled and fragmented, though one important exception is Scandinavia where, according to Dahlerup and Gulli (1985) women's rights groups did not disband on winning suffrage but persisted through the 1950s and contributed to discussions about sex equality predating the emergence of Women's Liberation.

In the United States, following the achievement of suffrage, it was primarily the Woman's Party, with moreover a declining membership, which pursued equal rights and specifically an Equal Rights Amendment. The larger NAWSA, which became the League of Women Voters, concentrated on women's civil education, and through the Joint Congressional Committee worked for welfare legislation, especially in the field of maternity and infant care. By the mid-1920s, the surviving movement was rent by the issue of protective legislation, which 'welfare' feminists believed to be essential to women's interests and threatened by the Equal Rights Amendment proposal. Klein notes, however, that while the mass base of the movement dissipated, women's rights organisations that survived gradually gained in political experience until by the 1950s they 'had evolved into an established lobby with greater political sophistication which succeeded in having 256 bills introduced in Congress' and could provide the continuity of skill and know-how that underpinned the resurgence of 'reformist' feminism in the 1960s (1984, p. 17).

In Britain, the WSPU rapidly disintegrated after 1919. But the NUWSS, now renamed the National Union of Societies for Equal Citizens, continued to press for equal rights. The drive to extend the vote to women under 30 was central to this activity but, with considerable Labour Party support, feminists also secured a significant extension of women's rights. For instance, women obtained equal rights to divorce and custody of children. Though feminists also pursued welfare goals, these were not initially seen to clash with equal rights. Banks suggests this was partly because Labour Party organisations, and especially the women's Cooperative Guild, provided an umbrella under which different feminist tendencies could be accommodated. The division surfaced first on the issue of family endowments; Eleanor Rathbone argued that a family allowance should be paid to mothers rather than their husbands but not on grounds of equal rights but because of women's mothering role. Equal rights feminists finally disavowed their welfarist sisters over the protective measures proposed in the 1927 Factory Bill and the movement split.

By the 1930s, in both countries, more militant and equal rights feminism was in abeyance. In its place prevailed what Banks dubs 'welfare feminism' and Wilson 'reasonable feminism'. In the tradition of evangelical feminism, this emphasised women's maternal role and the contribution this enabled them to make to social welfare. During the Depression it supported policies to alleviate poverty, as in the New Deal. Particularly in the United States, feminists were also drawn into the peace movement. Though this brand of feminism played a further limited role, in the 1920s and 1930s, in the birth control movement, birth control was itself becoming an increasingly respectable and non-feminist issue.

Following the Second World War, Wilson argues that in Britain most feminists came to believe that a new society, in which the equality of the sexes was institutionalised, had arrived. Moreover they accepted that in building this society women were naturally fitted for the primary child-rearing and homemaking responsibilities, albeit in the context of a marriage now conceived of as a 'partnership'. Women should work outside the home only before and after that part of their lives demanding full-time commitment to the needs of their young children (Wilson, 1980). In the United States too, the widespread assumption was that women already enjoyed equal rights. Strident feminism was effectively ridiculed, as a new and oppressive 'feminine mystique' held sway (Friedan, 1963). With the exception of organisations like the National Woman's Party in the United States and the 6-Point Group and the more militant Women's Freedom League in Britain, which persisted into the 1960s, less respectable forms of feminism 'led an underground or Sleeping Beauty existence in a society which claimed to have wiped out oppression' (Wilson, 1980, p. 187).

How then do we explain the resurgence of militant feminism in the 1960s? Feminist authors give this question perhaps less attention than it deserves, in view of its obvious implications for the movement's future. As far as they do discuss it, they are generally agreed which factors are most relevant, even if they differ in their emphasis. It is useful here to distinguish three levels of causality. First are those aspects of women's situation that *predisposed* them to recognise their own oppression. Second are those factors *facilitating* the revival of feminism, both ideological developments that helped to legitimise it and the existence of social and organisational networks that it could 'co-opt'. Finally are the specific events that *triggered* the revival.

Most accounts suggest that in the 1950s the contradictions in women's actual role and in normative conceptions of that role multiplied and intensified. On the one hand was the inherited belief that women had achieved equality; at the same time, in Britain, this was translated under the aegis of the Welfare State, into equality but difference, while in the United States the 'feminine mystique' told women that their self-fulfilment lay in the realisation of what made them different, their feminity. But this normative emphasis upon women's domestic role was in turn contradicted by the increased production of labour-saving domestic devices and more crucially by the availability of reliable and relatively untroublesome means of contraception, which allowed women both to limit and to space their families. It was further contradicted by the increasing numbers of women, and especially married women, drawn into outside employment by the manpower shortage, and incidentally discovering that equality did not mean equal pay or job opportunities.

Women, then, whether at home or in outside employment, experienced acute contradictions. In many respects these echoed the circumstances surrounding the emergence of feminism in the nineteenth century. They can similarly be sited in the social consequences of industrial capitalism, though its imperatives operated rather differently. The really new ingredient was the breakthrough in contraceptive technology. Indeed Firestone sees this latest wave of feminism as 'the inevitable female response to the development of a technology capable of freeing women from the tyranny of their sexual reproductive roles' (Firestone, 1970, p. 37). It certainly accounts for many of the most radical theoretical departures, including her own. But though these new forms of contraception were potentially liberating for women, they also, with the advent of permissiveness in the late 1950s, left women perilously open to male manipulation. Midge Decter is an anti-feminist writer, advocating a traditionally confined, home-centred role for women, but there is more than a little insight in her diagnosis of women's liberation as a 'new chastity' or 'a cry for the right of women to step back, retire, from a disagreeable involvement in, and responsibility for, the terms of sexual equality with men' (Decter, 1973, p. 95). She is unsympathetic, of course, because she does not recognise the extent to which women's sexual 'liberation' was into a sexuality defined and determined by the needs of men.

Though countless women experienced these role-strains, Freeman argues they were most acute for highly educated women whose sense of relative deprivation *vis-à-vis* their male peers was greatest. In the early post-war years women's academic achievement in the United States had plummeted, until in 1950 they only accounted for 24 per cent of bachelor and first professional degrees; in the 1960s it picked up again and in 1968 their share was 43.5 per cent. No such dramatic increase in the proportion of first degrees going to women occurred in Britain, where in 1970 women accounted for only 30 per cent of undergraduates, but their absolute numbers still grew with the expansion of higher education in the 1960s. The numbers of highly educated women in both countries were significantly up by the late 1960s.

Rossi further suggests that *unattached* women play a central role in a women's rights movement, because of their relative independence from men and because the supposed advantages of women's traditional role have least relevance for them. Writing in 1971, she points out that 'Since 1960, the age at marriage has moved up, the birth rate is down to what it was in the late 1930s, the divorce rate is up among couples married a long time' (Rossi, 1971, p. 66). Whether we follow Rossi or Freeman, the implication is that by the 1960s that sector of womankind most predisposed to recognise its own oppression was expanding.

But the breakthrough to militant feminist consciousness required, as in the nineteenth century, an ideological catalyst. The 1950s accent upon hedonistic consumption paved the way, by encouraging women to demand pleasure and sexual fulfilment for themselves. It was, though, the critique of this short-lived 'never had it so good society', provided by the New Left, together with specific arguments for black liberation in the American Civil Rights campaign, that gave feminism its new voice. The New Left argued that behind formal political equality and material affluence lay the concentration of political power, economic inequality and aliena- tion. Most relevantly for women, the New Left demanded the 'liberation' of the human personality, through social and political action, as expressed in the slogan 'the personal is political'. This contrasted with the belief, prevalent in the 1950s, that individual problems required individual, even psychotherapeutic, solutions. Finally, those young women actively involved in Civil Rights could hardly fail to recognise, as in the 1840s, the parallel between the plight of blacks and their own experience: 'Women are the niggers of the world'.

There remained two further conditions, the existence of social networks that feminism could co-opt and specific triggering events. These are best discussed in the context of an outline of the development of second wave feminism. Given that accounts of this development are strongly coloured by their author's experience and ideology, it is scarcely possible to present an 'objective' version. But I shall indicate the main sources consulted, and in a later section return to the question of how such 'facts' are to be interpreted.

Women's liberation in the United States

It is widely agreed that second wave feminism in the United States consisted, at its inception, not of one movement but of two, each with its own distinct origins. The first, chronologically, was the 'Older Branch', whose founders were also, typically, older than those of the later movement. Banks emphasises the continuity of this branch with the tradition of equal rights feminism, kept alive by a few gallant women's organisations and especially by the National Woman's Party. Freeman identifies two key events which both triggered the formation of this branch and provided it with a co- optable network. In 1961, on the suggestion of Esther Petersen, Director of the Women's Bureau, a governmental agency estab- lished in 1920 and imbued with 'welfare feminism', President Kennedy instituted a Commission on the Status of Women. This body produced a report, *American Women*, which, together with subsequent publications, documented the extensive remaining inequalities in women's status and opportunities, and prompted the formation of similar commissions in each of the fifty states. The work of these commissions 'brought together many knowledegable, politically active women who otherwise would not have worked together around matters of direct concern to women' and 'created a climate of expectations that something would be done' (Freeman, 1975, p. 52). Then, in 1964, the criterion of sex was added to Title 7 of the new Civil Rights Act, which prohibited discrimination in employment. (Its inclusion had been proposed by Representative Smith with the object of persuading the House to drop Title 7 altogether, but his attempt backfired). To administer the Act, an Equal Employment Opportunity Commission was established. Because its leadership appeared at first reluctant to tackle sex discrimination, feminists within the Commission privately encouraged the formation of a women's lobby outside to pressurise it.

A further stimulus was the publication, in 1963, of Betty Friedan's *The Feminine Mystique*. Together these events triggered the creation of NOW (National Organisation of Women) in 1966, which has ever since played a central role in the women's liberation movement. Under its first President, Friedan, NOW adopted a conventional pattern of organisation, with formal rules and a hierarchy of offices, and it concentrated its energies on lobbying government. Though primarily oriented towards equal rights, its platform however has always included more 'radical' elements, reflecting in particular its changing relationship with the women's movement as a whole. Thus the Bill of Rights adopted at its 1967 Conference demanded not only measures to increase equal employment opportunities but also, more contentious at the time, the legalisation of abortion. The abortion issue eventually led to the withdrawal of NOW's most conservative members, who formed, in 1968, the Women's Equality Action League, which concentrates on legal and economic aspects of equality of opportunity. At the same time a group of lawyers pulled out to found Human Rights for Women, whose rationale is the assistance of sex discrimination cases. Meanwhile, from NOW's other flank a number of 'radicals', reacting against what they perceived as its excessively centralised and élitist organisation, fed into the movement's emerging 'Younger Branch'.

Despite these secessions, both the membership and the central offices and staff of NOW continued to expand. By 1973 it had 500 local chapters and a claimed membership of 50,000, though links between the organisation's centre and the local units, even with the establishment of rudimentary regional-level structures, were and have remained poor and conflict-prone. In 1972 NOW launched its own highly influential journal, *Ms*, under the editorship of Gloria Steinem. All the while, NOW's platform grew more radical, partly in response to the pressures of the younger branch, so that for instance by 1973 it was supporting the decriminalisation of prostitution and the rights of lesbians.

The other important initiative within this older branch was the formation, in 1971, of the National Women's Political Caucus (NWPC). As we have seen, its primary objective is to promote women's participation in national and state-level political institutions, but it also lobbies for federal action on the status of women.

Before further tracing the evolution of the older branch, we must turn to its younger sister, born in rather different immediate circumstances. The trigger to its formation was young women's experience within the Civil Rights and New Left movements. As already noted, these movements provided both a legitimisation and a parallel for women's aspiration to meaningful equality. More concretely, Evans describes how the young women who joined them, often at considerable personal sacrifice, acquired a degree of influence and the 'social space' to realise new possibilities of self-development, but at the same time came up against the barriers posed by their male colleagues' chauvinism, most famously expressed in Stokely Carmichael's sneer, 'The only position for women in SNCC is prone'. In the face of this 'threatened loss of new possibility' two women in the Southern-based Civil Rights campaign issued a pamphlet in 1965, *Sex and Caste: a Kind of Memo*, in which they likened the oppression of blacks to their own, though without suggesting anything could be done about it. They helped to articulate and focus a growing awareness amongst radical women. When, at the 1967 National Conference for the New Politics in Chicago, women's issues were ruled out of the agenda, a number of outraged women decided to form their own group and circulated an address 'To Women of the Left'. By the end of the same year, such women's groups were mushrooming, based on the co-optable social network of women's contacts within the Civil Rights and New Left movements. By the end of 1968, they could be found in most major cities (Evans, 1979).

Reflecting its different origins, the younger branch was simultaneously more 'radical' and less organised than its sister. Forcefully, if unsubtly, its founding groups like New York Radical Women, and its offshoot, Redstockings, argued that sexual oppression constituted the fundamental hierarchy, which could only be overthrown by a feminist revolution. Though, to begin with, some members were reluctant to make a complete break with groups in the New Left, for which they were dubbed 'politicos', the main thrust of this analysis, reinforced by the example of black power, was to complete organisational separateness from men. It also fuelled a revulsion against male-dominated conventional politics and, within the younger branch itself, against 'masculine' organisation and hierarchy. Finally, it assumed a central role for consciousness-raising, through which women could relate their personal experiences to universal sexual oppression and, by learning together, acquire a revolutionary solidarity or sisterhood. While at the outset the impetus in terms of ideas, example and actual advice originated with groups in Chicago and New York, this branch was extremely decentralised, fragmented and fluid. Such formal co-ordination as there was came from the national conferences held periodically from 1969, and from the branch's numerous journals, newsletters and other publications.

The younger branch initially resisted the label, pinned on it by the media, of women's liberation but soon came to claim exclusive right to it. Yet almost immediately, according to the radical feminist authors of *Feminist Revolution* (Redstockings, 1978) and to Bouchier, a process of 'deradicalisation' began (Bouchier, 1979). For reasons to be discussed later, consciousness-raising had by the early 1970s lost its central place in the groups' activities. As a result, some groups simply dissolved, but increasingly others turned their energies to local and specialised feminist projects. Freeman cites, for instance, a survey in the spring of 1973 which 'found roughly: 163 publications; 18 pamphlet publishers and/or printing co-ops; 23 rape squads; 5 film co-ops; 116 women's centres; 35 health clinics or projects; 6 legal services; 6 feminist theatre groups; 12 liberation schools; 18 employment services; 12 book stores – and 3 craft stores' (Freeman, 1975, p. 119n). Its critics charged that this changed emphasis often took the form of 'cultural feminism', defined by

Brooke as 'the belief that women will be freed by an alternative women's culture'. Women's centres in particular acquired primarily a social function, encouraging friendship between women rather than outward-directed politics (Brooke, 1978).

A second change, described by Bouchier, was the increasing moderation of the branch's key publications. Thus the first two volumes of the *Annual Notes* were edited by Shulamith Firestone and were correspondingly radical, but in 1970, under her successor Anne Koedt, many of the most militant pieces were edited out. Thirdly, this branch was weakened by continuous conflicts both internal and with extraneous political tendencies. From 1970 to 1972 it resisted, in the main successfully, the attempt by the Young Socialist Alliance, offspring of the Socialist Workers' Party (no relation to its British homonym), to take over a number of women's liberation groups. It also had to contend with the vanguardist claims of the newly emergent tendency of political lesbianism. These claims probably accelerated in turn the articulation of a distinct socialist feminist position by the mid-1970s, many of whose adherents were former politicos. By 1975, the younger branch, internally weakened, milder in tone and increasingly overlapping in membership and activities with the older branch, was losing much of its distinctive character.

Writing in 1975, Freeman pointed to the increasing youthfulness of NOW's membership, the radicalisation of its programme and the growing tendency for members of younger branch groups simultaneously to join NOW for more 'pragmatic' activities, as evidence that NOW had become 'very much an umbrella group for all kinds of feminists' (Freeman, 1975, p. 93). The 1975 NOW Conference saw a 'takeover' of the leadership by a more radical 'Majority Caucus' and this was reflected in the programme of 25 demands adopted at the 1977 Conference at Houston, which included abortion and homosexual rights. It seemed to many observers that the two branches of the movement were merging. But in fact developments since have proved more complicated. Almost as soon as such suggestions were being made, there were signs of a revival of distinctively radical feminism, with the publication of a collection of papers, *Feminist Revolution*, by Redstockings, which argued that the limits of liberal feminism had been reached and that it was time to reassert a more radical and revolutionary course (Bouchier, 1983, p. 137). On the other hand while NOW under its new national leadership became more militant, its basic direction, Bouchier suggests, did not alter. The organisation was simply too large and too geographically dispersed to be transformed from above.

There was not a merger therefore and nor should one exaggerate NOW's shift towards the feminist ideological centre. The Equal Rights Amendment campaign which really got underway in 1974, and perhaps also the more responsive style of the Carter administration 1976–80, tended to confirm the older branch's orientation, both to liberalism and to working in the mainstream political process. Women's organisations and networks continued to proliferate inside Washington and out, and whether single-issue such as the National Commission on Working Women and the National Women's Health Network, both founded in 1977 and the National Women's Law Centre set up in 1981, or multi-issue like the Washington Women's Network, formed in 1976 to bring together women working in government and officers of women's organisations (see Tinker, 1983). Writing in 1983 Bouchier suggested that these liberal women's organisations 'remain firmly at the core of the women's movement, the visible public face of feminism' (Bouchier, 1983, p. 139). The ERA campaign, at least until the deadline for the amendment expired in 1982, also drew on an extremely wide spectrum of feminist groups and obliged them to present a more respectable public image. It helped to swell the ranks of NOW which by 1983 claimed 175,000 members. Bouchier estimated that the large liberal feminist organisations, such as NOW, WEAL and the NWPC, could together call on an active membership of around 300,000.

But while in the US socialist feminism has never been significant in movement terms, outside Chicago, though it has made important contributions to theory, radical feminism has not faded away but continues to provide a real, anti-system alternative to liberal feminism. Radical feminists, whether 'cultural' or revolutionary, have emphasised the limitations of liberal feminism, by focusing on the, for them, most fundamental issues of women's physical and sexual oppression. In 1976 two campaigns were launched which have gone on generating widespread support, publicity and controversy – Women Against Pornography and Women Against Violence Against Women. By 1983 around 50,000 women may have been actively involved in radical or socialist feminist groups (Bouchier, 1983, pp. 180–1).

Women's liberation in Britain

Currell's assertion that the genesis of the British women's liberation movement 'may be traced to the US' needs considerable qualification (Currell, 1974, p. 114). Feminism had deep roots in Britain, and never really died, any more than in the United States. Women in post-war Britain experienced, like American women, a malaise which surfaced, for instance in the formation in 1962 of the National Housewives Register to relieve the isolation of young housebound married women. In the 1960s, many younger women, especially students, were involved in radical politics, first the Campaign for Nuclear Disarmament, later in New Left student politics, the Vietnam Solidarity Campaign, and the revitalised Marxist parties. In all these arenas, like their American sisters, they discovered both new political aptitudes and male resistance to their exercise. It was, in fact, the Women's Peace Groups who organised the commemoration of 50 years of women's suffrage, in 1968, which Wilson identifies as 'some sort of catalyst' to the emergence of women's liberation in Britain (Wilson, 1980, p. 184.).

A second important indigenous forerunner of women's liberation, and this time without an obvious American counterpart, was the increasing militancy of working-class women. In 1968, Mrs Bilocca led a campaign in Hull for higher safety standards for trawlermen; the hostile response it met with prompted the formation of an Equal Rights Group in Hull. At the same time Rose Boland organised a strike of women machinists at the Ford works in Dagenham which triggered a spate of female industrial militancy and the creation, in 1969, of the National Joint Action Committee for Women's Equal Rights, a significant symbol, if short-lived. It drew the attention of Marxist groups, like the International Marxist Group (IMG), ever vigilant for ways of mobilising the working-class.

The decisive trigger was the example and arguments of the revived women's movement, not only in the United States but in West Germany, which reached Britain in the latter part of 1968. Rowbotham, amongst others, has described how when women's liberation 'burst' upon her, it suddenly made sense of the inchoate resentments and frustrations building up in her as an International Socialist (IS) activist. Women from IMG, IS and other socialist groups established socialist women's groups from the beginning of

1969 and produced their own newspaper, *Socialist Women*. The first women's liberation groups were formed, in the same year, in the London area, by women from a range of backgrounds including Marxist groups, the American Movement itself and the Vietnam Solidarity Campaign. These formed the basis for an overarching London Women's Liberation Workshop, co-ordinating, at its peak, some seventy local groups, and with its own journal, *Shrew*. However, the establishment of a national women's liberation movement is conventionally dated from the first national conference, held in Oxford, in February 1970. This adopted a programme of four demands: equal pay, twenty-four-hour nurseries, free contraception and abortion on demand (Rowbotham, 1972).

If second wave feminism arose rather differently in Britain, than in the United States, its subsequent development has likewise diverged considerably. Perhaps the principal differences have been the absence of any organisational equivalent to NOW and the much greater influence of Marxist feminism. As in the United States, women's liberation groups, once seeded, grew with amazing rapidity. It has been suggested that local groups placed rather less emphasis than in America on consciousness-raising and moved more immediately into specific feminist projects (ibid., p. 97). These covered a range of activities comparable to those cited for the United States. Indeed the provision of refuges for 'battered wives' was a British initiative which American women only took up in the latter part of the 1970s. But, like the younger branch of the American movement, the British groups lacked a continuous co-ordinating mechanism, other than annual conferences and publications, particularly *Spare Rib*, launched in 1972. Even the London Workshop had folded by 1973. At the 1975 Conference at Manchester, it was agreed to delegate to a committee, between conferences, responsibility for planning the next conference. This committee, known as WIRES (Women's Information, Referral and Enquiry Service), was, however, instantly suspected of 'power grabbing' intentions and its terms of reference have been severely circumscribed (*Spare Rib*, May 1978).

Although then by the mid-1970s there was still no national coordinating body for the movement as a whole, two of the most successful movement campaigns had produced their own coordinating mechanisms. In 1975 a National Women's Aid Federation was established to link and represent local groups and refuges. The

National Abortion Campaign (NAC) was set up in the same year.

Bouchier suggests that the British Women's Liberation Movement in its early years was essentially socialist, its continuity in terms of theory and membership with the late 1960s neo-Marxist and New Left resurgence readily apparent. Liberal or equal rights feminism was weaker and radical feminism slower to make itself felt than in the United States. He argues that in this respect the mid-1970s were a turning point. Legislation for equal pay and against sex discrimination which then came into effect was soon proving difficult to implement and disappointing in its results. This tended to undermine not only equal rights but socialist feminist arguments for concentrating on economic and employment issues and opened the way, as in the United States, for greater emphasis on male violence and sexuality.

Again, as in the US, conflict emerged early in the life of the Women's Liberation Movement over the question of separatism. Lesbian feminists, at the outset defensive, by 1974 were already pressing the national conference to adopt as its fifth demand an end to discrimination against lesbians. While as Bouchier says, there was some tendency for lesbians to be associated with radical rather than socialist feminism, these divisions were not clear cut. However, in 1977 militant radical feminists began calling themselves 'revolutionary feminists', following circulation of Sheila Jeffrey's paper 'The Need for Revolutionary Feminism'. They insisted on total separation of men and women's organisations, at the same time distinguishing their position from 'cultural' feminists (Coote and Campbell, 1982). They also increasingly identified revolutionary feminism with political lesbianism, not necessarily active lesbianism but the disavowal of heterosexual relations. The revolutionary feminists clashed with socialist feminists at the 1978 Conference in Birmingham. They proposed that all the six existing movement demands be scrapped and replaced by a seventh against violence to women. A bitter dispute ensued and no national movement-wide conference has been held since.

Marxist and socialist feminists had all along been involved in the full range of feminist projects, for instance they were very active in NAC. At the same time, some were primarily concerned to explore the theoretical relationship between Marxism and feminism and at a more practical level socialist feminists have been particularly anxious to reach and speak for working-class women. One vehicle for these efforts was the Working Women's Charter. Drawn up in 1974 by a sub-committee of the London Trades Council, the Charter, though moderate by radical feminist standards, incorporated many feminist demands and was designed as a minimum programme to be put to trade unions. Marxist feminists played a leading role in setting up a number of local Working Women's Charter groups to discuss the proposals and get local unions to adopt them. These groups were not entirely successful in drawing in manual worker women, though the fact that the TUC by 1978 had taken up these demands itself must be counted some kind of achievement. As Gelb (1985) notes, and in part because of the different institutional context of British politics, socialist feminists have also been much readier than most American feminists to work for change *inside* trade unions and Labour party organisations. There was a veritable influx of socialist feminists into the Labour Party from the late 1970s, resulting from problems in the women's movement, the continuing hope of building bridges with working-class women, but above all the changes in the party's ideological complexion and its greater responsiveness to feminist claims (Perrigo, 1986). The Women's Committees and similar bodies established by a succession of Labour-held coucils, beginning with the GLC in 1982 provided further scope for pursuing socialist feminist aims (see also Chapter 6).

By the end of the 1970s, then, it was the radical feminists who appeared in the ascendant and set the movement agenda. In 1980 there were 99 women's aid groups and 200 refuges; by 1983 *Spare Rib* was listing 20 rape crisis centres in England alone; from the late 1970s there were a series of marches to 'Reclaim the Night' from male attackers and most recently the issue of pornography has been to the fore, with the formation in 1983 of Pornography is Violence Against Women (PIVAW). Still the disarray of socialist feminism should not be exaggerated and, with the worsening of recession and unemployment, my sense is that the tendency in the mid-1980s is if anything the other way, towards a new appreciation of the relevance of socialist feminist analysis and priorities.

But the real challenge to radical feminism and indeed to the existing Women's Liberation Movement has undoubtedly come from 'black' women of Afro-Caribbean and Asian descent. In the American movement, this conflict broke out perhaps ten years earlier. Though it could not be described as resolved, it is possible that radical feminists at least felt less vulnerable because of their original experience of black male chauvinism in the civil rights movement. With the growth of an international feminist movement, to be discussed shortly, and of an awareness of Western complicity in the particular forms of Third World women's oppression, black women have gained confidence in Britain, establishing their own organisations, notably the Organisation of Women of African and Asian Descent (OWAAD), founded in 1978, and accusing the white movement, with some justice, of harbouring racist attitudes. One sign of their growing influence was the debate over support for Palestine. By 1983 the *Spare Rib* editorial collective declared its unanimous pro-Palestine position, though divided on whether to allow 'Zionist' responses a hearing on its pages. In a related development in 1983 NAC split, one section retaining the old name and aim of defending and extending provisions of the 1967 Act, the other calling itself the Women's Reproduction Rights Campaign, understanding women's 'right to choose' in a much broader economic and cultural context. Black feminism's impact extended to the movement's media; by 1982 half the editorial collective of *Spare Rib* were 'women of colour' while the new daily feminist newspaper, *Outwrite*, launched in 1982 has focused on women in the Third World and the position of black women in Britain.

But the other striking feature of the eighties is the diversification of the women's movement, with conferences and organisations for older women, younger women, disabled women, anarchist women and so forth. The Greenham peace campaign from 1982 attracted great numbers of British feminists, though some radical feminists regarded it as a dangerous side-tracking of the movement (Finch, 1986). By 1983, Bouchier suggests there were around 300 feminist groups of all kinds, with the total number of committed activists in the region of 10,000 and perhaps a further 20,000 sporadically active. He speculates that the active core consisted of around 2000 each of radical and socialist feminists (Bouchier, 1983, p. 177).

The movement elsewhere

Second-wave feminism has embraced a still wider range of countries than the first wave, extending beyond Western democracies to most regions of the Third World, though it has made minimal impression on the Soviet bloc nations. The movement has all the same been most vigorous in the West and Lovenduski (1986a) suggests that the prerequisite for a women's liberation movement is the full array of liberal-democratic political rights. Accordingly we find that feminism has waxed and waned with political liberalisation and repression in for instance Spain, Greece, Turkey and Brazil.

All Western democracies by now have second-wave feminist groupings of some kind, though their precise ideological emphasis, practical aims, vitality and influence vary in accordance with the particularities of their national context. Thus the feminist movement in France has been relatively small and distinguished by its tendency to intellectualism, as well as the bitternes of its internal struggles, often revolving around particular leading personalities. Following the Second World War, France enjoyed its own variant of reasonable feminism, for instance in the women's associations linked with the Communist and Socialist Parties. Though these associations remained reformist, many were radicalised by the emergence of women's liberation and came subsequently to play an important auxiliary role, as in the campaigns to legalise abortion and win women legal independence.

Second wave feminism, however, really erupted out of the 1968 student revolt, though its existence as the Movement de Libération des Femmes (MLF) was not recognised by the media until 1970. As elsewhere, the women who came to identify with this movement were from tremendously varied ideological and social backgrounds and, beyond their shared recognition of women's continuing oppression, inevitably disagreed over tactics. Amongst the hundreds of groups – the French term 'groupuscule' better evoke their fragmentation – that made up the early movement, Duchen (1986) discerns three main strands. First were the radical feminists, beginning with Femmes Revolutionnaires, formed in 1970, second was Psych et Po (Psychoanalysis and Politique) which, as its name suggests, concentrated on psycho-cultural mechanisms of women's oppression and third were socialist feminists, such as the Cercle Dmitriev, founded in 1972 and most closely linked with the new radical left. Reformist feminism, as in Britain, played little part in the MLF. One exception was Gisele Halimi, the well-known feminist lawyer, who in 1971, set up a new organisation, 'Choisir', to defend the 343 signatories of a petition against the abortion laws.

Her subsequent formulation of a 'Common Programme of Women' was mistrusted by the MLF as a bid for leadership of the movement. In October 1974, Choisir helped to launch a femininst political party, the Parti Feministe Unifiée Française (PFUF) which however failed to secure the election of any of its 43 candidates in 1978.

In the first few years feminist energies across the spectrum were concentrated and channelled into the campaign to legalise abortion. The Movement pour la Liberté de l'Avortement et pour la Contraception (MLAC) begun in 1973, spread rapidly, successfully organised illegal abortions and helped to secure the liberalisation of abortion law in 1975. But the campaign had exposed divisions in the movement which now opened up. Duchen suggests that abortion, initially a point of consensus, itself raised potentially contentious questions concerning the nature of motherhood and beyond that of femininity. Revolutionary feminists tended to see motherhood primarily as a lever of male dominance and went on to campaign against rape and domestic violence, setting up their equivalent of women's refuges – the 'SOS Femmes Alternatives'. Psych et Po had been founded in 1970 and was dominated by a wealthy psychoanalyst, Antoinette Fouque. It became increasingly absorbed in analysing female differentness, and as we have seen, influenced by the French tradition of critical philosophy, in identifying or creating an authentic feminine 'discourse'. In 1974 Psych et Po set itself up as a publishing firm, Des Femmes, acquiring for a time a virtual monopoly of feminist publishing and bookshops in France. It repudiated the rest of the MLF as excessively bound up in patriarchal ideology and largely excluded MLF writings from its publications or sales, leading eventually to a traumatic series of court cases in 1977. Finally in October 1979, the group constituted itself as a limited company with exclusive rights to the term MLF. The MLF proper fought back and may even have been reinvigorated by this attempt to usurp its place (Lewis, 1981).

During this time, the socialist feminist strand as such largely disappeared, but as in Britain, by the end of the 1970s feminists were increasingly attracted to the Socialist Party (PS). Unlike the French Communist Party (PCF), which insisted on a single, centrally determined party line and whose newspaper, *l'Humanité*, in 1978 refused to publish a statement by women activists critical of the party's treatment of women members and women's rights, the PS has been an amalgam of different ideological 'courants'.

Socialist feminists tried to form their own Courant G but failed to win the necessary share of conference votes. The forming of a socialist government in 1981 had further consequences for feminists. Committed in its electoral programme to extending women's rights, perhaps its most important step was to create a separate Ministry of Women's Rights whose budget by 1982–3 was running at over 100 million francs a year. Reminiscent of Labour women's committees in British local government, but on a much grander scale, the Ministry funded countless women's projects, including 140 National Centres for Information on the Rights of Women in different cities. The new opportunities thus opened up for feminism on the one hand encouraged greater 'realism' or willingness to work with the system. At the same time this 'virtual institutionalisation of the women's movement' (Northcutt and Flaitz 1985) threatened the automony of the MLF and went hand in hand with the marginalisation of feminist voices inside the PS, in the supposed interests of party unity.

Though by the mid-1980s some socialist feminists were discussing the need for new autonomous feminist structures to mediate between grass-roots groups and the national political arena, there was little sign of its emergence. Long before the fall of the socialist government in March 1986, women's projects were amongst the first to be cut in response to the worsening economic situation and political opposition, and the new conservative government has abolished the Ministry of Women's Rights. Although Psych et Po has largely faded out with the departure of Antoinette Fouque to the United States, all in all the movement appears to be at a low ebb (Duchen, 1986).

By contrast with France, West Germany's movement has been yet smaller, has had less impact on policy and has been strongly radical feminist in orientation. As we have seen the German feminist tradition going back into the nineteenth century was obliterated by Nazism and its sequel. The post-war generation of women in the Federal Republic was peculiarly apolitical until the 1960s. The new feminism evolved directly out of the student movement at the end of that decade, with the formation of the Action Council for Women's Liberation in West Berlin in the spring of 1968, though by convention, it is dated from the campaign to liberalise abortion launched in 1970. In 1971 the first national women's conference was held in Frankfurt. From the outset the movement was dominated by radical feminism and deeply mis-trustful of the left, consequence both of the bitter legacy of feminism's encounter with organised socialism before the First World War and of continuing male chauvinism in the German left. It was also suspicious of reformist and conventional politics, concentrating on grass-roots and cultural projects, though Schlae-ger (1978) suggests that initiatives for self-help were limited in their success by the authoritarianism of German political culture, and on the abortion issue. Given the premium on consensus and respecta-bility in German politics and the media, the movement's direct influence was modest. Even adoption of a more liberal abortion law in 1975 was subsequently hedged around by the Federal Court's addition of four conscience clauses.

Over the last decade the movement does not appear to have made any striking advances, although it has clearly contributed to a gradual but significant change in women's expectations and these by 1980 were beginning to influence the recruitment criteria and policies of the main political parties (Hall, 1981). Germany has had a particularly active wages for housework campaign. Government's severe reprisals against German terrorists also prompted intense debate amongst feminist in the late 1970s about women's relation-ship to violence and pacifism (Altbach, 1984). By the early 1980s, Schultz (1984) noted a further tendency to idealise motherhood, both its spiritual and its physical connotations, which she feared might chime all too well with the social conservatism of the new Christian Democratic administration.

In contrast again with the French and West German movements, second-wave feminism in Italy is widely adjudged to have been especially vibrant and effective. Hernes (1984b) indeed describes it as 'the largest, most vital and successful' of all the European movements. Though radical feminism has shaped both its organisa-tion and its priorities, feminist theoretical analysis has relied primarily on Marxist frameworks (Lovenduski, 1986a). And although, perhaps inevitably in a country where the Catholic Church has been so powerful, feminist campaigns have stressed women's right to physical and sexual self-determination, as in policies towards abortion and rape, they have managed to mobilise the institutions of class struggle, unions and parties of the left, in their support.

Reformist feminism enjoyed a brief post-war revival with the formation of a communist-aligned Uniona Donne Italiane (UDI). But by the 1950s, the PCI was pushed on the defensive by the cold war and saw in the conventionally-structured communist family its main 'cell of resistance'. Ergas (1982) argues that both then and afterwards the fortunes of the feminist movement were largely determined by developments in Italian party politics. Second-wave feminism once more came out of student mobilisation in 1968. Its radical feminist orientation was evident in the early emphasis on consciousness-raising and the proliferation of groups, the 'piccoli gruppi'. Lovenduski (1986a) points out that otherwise there were only two more structured feminist groups, the Movimento Liberazione Donna (MLD) which was allied to the Radical Party and prepared to use conventional political channels in leading the campaign to reform abortion law (see also Weber, 1981) and Lotta Feminista which stressed the links between women's liberation and the fight against capitalism, and led a campaign for wages for housework. None the less, and even though it was predominantly middle-class the Italian movement succeeded in mobilising such extensive support that parties on the left, including however reluctantly the PCI, could not afford to ignore it. While retaining organisational autonomy, feminists established coordinating committees with representatives of trade unions and left-wing groups and parties. As described more fully in the following chapter, the campaign by 1978 had secured reform of the abortion laws. Despite shortcomings of the reform, a consequence of this achievement was that in its aftermath feminist activism tended to subside. The movement's own clinics were in any case less necessary now and similarly the coordinating committees declined. Feminists appeared to be retreating into lifestyle concerns. Ergas associates these developments with changes in the relative positions of the left-wing parties: following the 1976 elections, the far left had been decimated while the PCI was sufficiently strengthed to have less need for feminist support.

Ergas may have exaggerated the movement's recession. Beckwith (1985) finds that by the end of the 1970s the PCI had internalised the feminist agenda to a considerable degree. From the early 1970s independent women's groups, the 'coordinamenti donne', had sprung up in trade unions, helping raise women's consciousness and solidarity and also to change male trade unionst attitudes on such questions as abortion and rape (Froggett, 1981).

By the end of the decade there was a steady feminist infiltration of professional associations, unions and parties, reflecting the more pragmatic approach of a younger cohort of women (Lovenduski, 1986a). At the same time, when Christian Democrats managed to secure restricting amendments to a law on sexual violence and harassment, about 50,000 women marched in protest through Rome (*Spare Rib*, April 1983) which hardly indicates that radical feminism is played out.

Beginning with the Dolle Minas, formed in 1970, the women's liberation movement has also been very active in the Netherlands. Even in Spain the death of Franco in 1976 and the beginnings of a return to democracy cleared the way for a feminist movement which grew and went through succeeding stages with amazing rapidity, as if to make up for lost time. Initially mainly socialist in orientation, the movement then shifted in focus to issues of female sexuality more identified with radical feminism, but by 1982 in response to new opportunities opened up under a socialist government, the socialist feminist current was regrouping and resuming the initiative (Threlfall, 1985). Women's liberation movements have also appeared in the countries of Scandinavia. Dahlerup and Gulli (1985) suggest that these have, however, been stronger in Denmark and Norway, finding their 'purest' expression in Redstockings and New Feminists respectively, than in Sweden or Finland.

Given Sweden's record in promoting equality of opportunity between the sexes, it is on the face of it surprising to learn that women's liberation groups, in the revolutionary feminist sense, have been few and far between. Chief amongst them is Group 8, founded in 1968 and reported in 1980 to include around 1000 members, mostly in the Stockholm area. Its orientation is socialist feminist.

Reformist feminism is, on the other hand, well entrenched. The liberal or 'equal rights' Frederika Bremer Association, dating back to 1894, claims over 9000 members. Even more significant, however, has been the pronounced tradition of what Banks might include as welfare feminism closely linked with the Social Democratic Party. Women's sections were established, on women's insistence and against the will of some of the Party's leaders, as far back as 1892 and ever since have strongly influenced Party policy on women. They also set the pattern for the growth of women's sections in 'virtually every party, union, professional, social and religious organisation in the nation' (Adams and Winston, 1980, p. 139). In the immediate post-war period, Swedish feminism as elsewhere was conservative in accepting that a woman could not simultaneously have children and a career. But, in 1962, earlier even than Friedan, Eva Moberg wrote *Women and Human Beings*, advocating role-sharing in the home. Though not universally accepted, her views helped to radicalise existing Swedish feminist networks. This presents us with the apparent paradox of a feminist movement which is in many respects radical in its analysis and objectives, and yet which not only relies upon a strategy of reform, but denies the need for separate women-only organisations. It may be argued that this form of feminism suits the political climate of Sweden and certainly in comparison with feminism in other countries it has been highly successful in influencing policy. Adams and Winston suggest that separate feminist organisation is inappropriate for Sweden's political system (ibid., pp. 151–2). Writers such as Safilios-Rothschild consider, however, that the absence of a powerful separate feminist movement in Sweden leaves women essentially unliberated and seriously vulnerable to reactionary moves (Safilios-Rothschild, 1974, p. 6).

Though self-styled women's liberation groups as such are still extremely rare in the Third World, reports are increasingly frequent of autonomous women's organisations campaigning for women's rights. Many of these have clearly been influenced by the Western feminist movement but a more specific stimulus appears to have been the Mexico Conference held to mark International Women's Year in 1975 and the designation of the subsequent ten years as the UN Decade for Women. There have additionally been domestic political triggers – student riots, industrial action, redemocratisation.

Women's campaigns have been most evident in Latin America. They have faced the greatest obstacles under military or extreme authoritarian regimes and in predominantly Islamic polities. Here it is encouraging to note that the first conference of the Arab Women's Solidarity Association, attended by over 2000 women and with 'strong feminist undertones', was held in September 1986 (Toubia, 1986). But many women in Islamic countries not only face severe male disapproval but are themselves torn between the desire for greater freedom and the seeming 'cultural disloyalty' of emulating Western feminism (Ahmed, 1982). At the least they will be reluctant to call themselves feminists. A similar reluctance to take on a feminist label has been observed amongst Latin American women whose male allies on the left are contemptous of such a 'bourgeois' ideology.

In Latin America where Catholicism and male machismo have together powerfully shaped the political culture, much feminist activity centres on issues related to sexual self-determination and male violence. *Spare Rib* over the last five years has reported campaigns to legalise abortion in Mexico, Brazil and Venezuela; the first rape crisis centre was opened in Mexico in 1982 and 'Reclaim the Night' marches have been held in Peru. But there have also been broader movements for women's rights. By 1980 a National Front for the Liberation and Rights of Women had been formed to coordinate such activities in Mexico. Likewise in Brazil by 1979 (Schmink, 1981) there were at least eight feminist groups and for the 1982 elections in Rio de Janeiro, women forged a 'Feminist Alert for the Elections', seeking pledges from prospective candidates on a range of issues. Equal rights groups were also emerging in Argentina by 1983.

In Asia, Pakistani women set up a Women's Action Forum in 1981 to combat moves to restore Islamic family law. Over the last two or three years Thai feminists have mobilised around the issue of prostitution. But it is in India that the women's movement has evolved furthest. Davies (1985, p. v) calls it the most 'truly anti-patriarchal and anti-capitalist' of movements anywhere in the Third World. Contact with Western feminism and the political disturb-ances of 1974 first saw a number of feminist groups form but then soon fizzle out. Vibhuti *et al.* (1985) argue that it was reports of rape incidents during the Emergency, 1975-7, that really kindled the movement, the most active organisation being the Bombay Forum Against Rape. On the other hand Butalia (1985) associates the resurgence of feminism in India with publication of the report *Towards Equality* in 1977 which showed that women's position had actually deteriorated during the preceding thirty years. In 1978 a coordinating body, Samta, was set up linking groups like the editorial collective of *Manushi*, India's internationally renowned feminist journal. Campaigns have focussed on the issues of rape, 'eve-teasing' (sexual harassment), dowry burnings and most recently pornographic cinema. The media have given them exten-sive and reasonably sympathetic coverage and they have scored a number of successes in terms of official policy though it remains to be seen if this will have any effect in practice. In 1985 the first feminist publishing house, Kali for Women, was opened. Butalia suggests that one reason for these achievements has been the involvement of older women whose previous role in the national independence struggle meant they commanded considerable respect. This does indicate the overwhelmingly middle-class, and urban, character of the movement, though in the last few years individual groups have made a particular effort to investigate and organise activities around the specific and desperate problems of women in some of India's poorest communities.

In addition to the proliferation of national movements of second-wave feminism, how far can we speak of a distinctively *international* women's movement? Writing a few years back I suggested that such a movement with its own organisational matrix had yet to emerge. This may have understated developments that had already occurred and would certainly be too sweeping a dismissal today. It remains true that the productive cooperation of women MEPs and EEC bureaucrats, whose consequences are discussed more fully in the next chapter, has not stimulated any extensive pan-European women's network. In 1980 Wickham noted that collaboration between feminist groups over ways to use EEC legislation and directives was 'noticeably lacking'. Since then there have been attempts to achieve some coordination through a Centre for Research on European Women (CREW) which held its first conference in London in May 1984 (Vallance and Davies, 1986).

Initiatives to establish dialogue on a world-wide basis paradoxically have been more successful. The organisational stimulus has been the UN's Decade for Women, 1975–85. The UN Commission for the Status of Women, set up shortly after the Second World War, eventually persuaded the UN Conference, in 1970, to adopt a resolution proclaiming 1975 International Women's Year and the following ten years the Decade for Women. An international conference to launch the decade was held in Mexico, drawing delegates from over 100 countries, and adopted a ten-year World Plan. This pinpointed the three critical areas for women as achieving equality with men, integration into national economic life and development programmes and recognition of women's contribution to world peace. A mid-term conference to review progress was mounted in Copenhagen in 1980. Alongside the official UN

Conference, met an informal Non-Governmental Organisation (NGO) Forum, bringing total participation to around 8000. The official conference consisted mainly of delegations selected on the basis of rank or personal connections rather than feminist commitment or relevant expertise. As a consequence, within the constraints of a predetermined agenda, contributions echoed the lines adopted in UN debates. The NGO Forum was more spontaneous though even here Ashworth (1982) reports that many participants were officially designated and tended to make set speeches rather than engaging in genuine dialogue.

To mark the end of the Decade a third Conference was held in Nairobi. A Preparatory Commission met in Vienna several months before the conference to draw up the 'Nairobi Forward Looking Strategies for the Adancement of Women' (FLS) which was based on the World Plan, projecting its targets on to the year 2000. This formed the basis of the intergovernmental Conference itself, whose national delegations once more included few feminists or specialists; for instance the United States' delegation was led by Maureen Reagan, the President's daughter, Imelda Marcos led the Philippines delegation and Mrs Sally Mugabe that for Zimbabwe. Many delegations were largely, some exclusively, male. 152 of 159 UN countries did, however, agree to the FLS though a number registered their reservations regarding specific clauses and though many feminists would argue that the document contained an inadequate analysis of the causes of women's problems. The real weakness of the document is of course that it is not binding.

The NGO Forum which began two days earlier attracted over 10,000 participants from 151 countries, when only 7000 had been expected, producing much initial confusion. In practice many of the delegates were again there in an official capacity. In addition there were over 2000 delegates from the United States alone, including a strong black women's contingent. Debate centred around more than 100 workshops and amongst the issues stimulating the most intense or acrimonious argument were the nature of 'black' consciousness, the liberation of South Africa (generally eliciting unanimous support), the 'liberation' of Palestine, lebianism, whether prostitution should be legalised, whether autonomous women's organisations are necessary (delegates from national liberation movements and communist parties tended to say they were not) and development policies for women (Hendessi, 1986).

It could well be maintained that these debates reveal all too clearly the differences in perspective and experience in the international women's movement. Moreover these more feminist currents had little success in directly influencing their national official delegations. But Nairobi and the previous decade have still been of tremendous importance in raising women's consciousness, in helping to generate much more extensive and systematic information about women's position and in bringing women together in a dialogue through which we are bound, however painfully, to understand one another better. Coote (1985) points out, for instance, how Israeli and Palestinian women ran a joint workshop on peace, while delegates from a number of countries cooperated in producing the Forum's daily newspaper. Around the events of the decade have moreover emerged more specialised international conferences, networks and newsletters.

A crisis in the women's movement?

In the last few years there have been recurring suggestions that the women's movement is in some kind of crisis, that it is declining or at least experiencing a lull or doldrums. According to some it has lost its sense of direction (see Barrett *et al.*, 1986), while others maintain we are now entering a 'post-feminist' stage in which old-style feminism is no longer either necessary or appropriate. It must be clear that rather different things are being said here, which I shall try to unravel and respond to.

First of all, in any assessment of second-wave feminism, we should not underestimate what has already been achieved. As Gordon and Dubois have stated (cited by Eisenstein, 1984, p. 140), 'It is vital to strategy-building to know when we are winning and when losing, and where. Failing to claim and take pride in our victories leads to the false conclusion that nothing has changed'. Just briefly to summarise some of these achievements, and concentrating on policies, though in America the movement's role in legislation was probably marginal in the 1960s, during the following decade it contributed to a succession of measures helpful to women, such as the 1974 Equal Credit Opportunity Act, the addition of Title 9 to the 1972 Education Amendments Act and the 1973

Supreme Court ruling that liberalised abortion. Likewise in Britain, though its emergence post-dated the 1967 Abortion Act and though legislation for equal pay and against sex discrimination was in large part a response to EEC requirements, second-wave feminism protected and exploited these gains. In the 1970s it either instigated or strongly influenced a number of valuable measures such as the 1970 Matrimonial Proceedings and Property Act, Part 2 of the 1975 Employment Protection Act and the 1976 Domestic Violence and Matrimonial Procedures Act. In other countries, such as France and Italy, the movement has also contributed directly and indirectly to women's increased political participation. Perhaps most significant of all, the movement has, in the United States and Britain at least, both transformed what is acceptable public opinion and behaviour and begun to undermine more private traditional attitudes towards sex-roles. One has only to see a film or documentary or read a book that is 10 or 15 years old to grasp the amazing revolution in assumptions that has intervened. In France Jenson (1985) also notes how the women's movement has changed the 'universe of political discourse', transforming the terms of the debate on issues such as abortion.

Despite all this, is the movement in some sense declining? This is not easily answered. In the United Kingdom it is not clear whether overall numbers of activists have fallen, and as Bouchier (1983) points out, this is not necessarily the key criterion; what may matter more is the degree of commitment of those who do take part. In Scotland over the last few years the movement has actually been growing. *Spare Rib* continues to list new groups, women's centres, rape crisis centres, conferences and so forth, in the main British urban centres. When women from *Marxism Today* organised a conference in July 1986, around the theme 'Women Alive and Kicking', at least 1500 women, probably a majority of them under 30 years of age, arrived and sessions were packed out. No one who took part could believe that feminism as a movement or as a set of ideas was on its last legs. Another noteworthy development has been the expansion of feminist publishing; first to be launched was Only Woman in 1974, followed by Virago in 1976, Women's Press in 1978 and Sheba in 1980. Likewise we saw how in the United States the ERA campaign helped to recharge the movement and swelled NOW's membership. In some recently democratised European countries and many Third World countries, second-wave feminism is only now really getting underway and similarly the international movement is gaining rather than losing momentum. Even so aspects of the contemporary women's movement are less reassuring. One widely observed tendency is for feminist movements as they grow older and bigger to become infinitely diverse in terms of theory, structure, tactics and activities. This can be interpreted either as fragmentation and dilution or, more positively, as a healthy 'integration' into the wider society. In Scandinavian countries, for instance, Dahlerup and Gulli (1985) find that the number of 'core' activists has diminished while feminists have increasingly found their way into the mainstream political and economic organisations. Lovenduski (1986a) also suggests that we are witnessing a second generation of second-wave feminists, who unlike the radical pacesetters of the first generation are prepared to work within already established structures. Seen in this way, diversification is an advance but there remains the danger that a weakened core of radical activists and autonomous feminist organisations will leave the movement vulnerable at times of economic decline and political reaction.

Possibly more alarming are recent developments at the level of feminist theory, and specifically the emergence of what Stacey (1983) calls 'conservative feminism', chiefly in the United States but with counterparts elsewhere. The pro-woman and liberal strands have merged into a new, revisionist position, as in Friedan's *The Second Stage* (1983) and certain of Elshtain's later writings (for instance Elshtain, 1982), which reaffirms the value of mothering and the family and seeks to transfer their caring qualities into the public domain. I shall have more to say about this argument in the Conclusion. It can be understood as a reaction to more extreme doctrines of revolutionary feminism, perhaps too as a reflection of the changed personal circumstances of individual leading feminist writers. Rossi (1971) noted a correspondence between the rise of second-wave feminism in the United States and an increase in the proportion of single childless women in the population, as we saw, and suggested that such women were particularly prominent in the movement. More recently it seems that many of these feminists have deliberately chosen to become mothers. In Britain, the US and also West Germany (see Schultz, 1984), this has contributed to a new 'mystique of motherhood', in Heron's phrase (Heron, 1980). What is disturbing is that these arguments coincide with pressures to cut back women's paid employment and a general resurgence of conservative social policy.

Which brings us to the real reason why tendencies towards movement diversification or revisionism give cause for concern, the economic and political climate. Substantial as have been the achievements of second-wave feminism, they 'have clearly only scratched the surface of women's unequal treatment' (Oakley, 1979, p. 392). They should form the foundation on which we build. But by the end of the 1970s a political back-lash was developing. This has been most vociferous in the United States, a tribute it could be said, to the strength of the American feminist movement, which paradoxically it may also have helped to revitalise. To a large extent underlying political reaction, and still more disquieting, is economic recession and its implications both for women's status and for the movement. Recession puts in jeopardy what has already been achieved, demonstrates the precariousness of changes so laboriously won. As we shall see, it has seriously undermined the implementation of women's rights policies in the fields for instance of employment, childcare, women's refuges and birth control. Recession threatens the ideological acceptability of feminist demands which can be made to seem an indulgence, a redundant luxury. At the same time, shrinking resources and class polarisation may exacerbate conflict *within* the women's movement. It has been argued that Reagan's policies are dividing American feminists; they hit low-paid women hard but professional women are now benefiting from an enlightened income tax policy that recognises childcare as a legitimate business expense. Better-off feminists accordingly have tended to concentrate on narrow professional interests or life-style issues (*Spare Rib*, 1982, August, p. 15). Even if it does not divide, recession can weaken and demoralise movements, through the steady attrition of policy gains and the increasing difficulties women face in everyday life.

It is within this context that the *internal* strengths and weaknesses of the movement assume new importance. Writers diagnosing these have inevitably different axes to grind but drawing on what they say one can piece together a number of interpretations which variously emphasise the movement's membership, ideology, organisation or strategy. In looking at these interpretations we can also examine more deeply the character of contemporary feminism.

Movement membership and heterogeneity

If all women are in some sense oppressed by men collectively, the potential membership of the feminist movement should be coterminous with the sex itself. But as has already been elaborated in Chapter 1, women are also divided. Whereas membership of a caste, minority group or class connotes a degree of self-conscious cohesion, women lack pre-existing, women only social institutions around which to identify and mobilise and instead, through the basic social unit of the family, tend to be atomised and more bound to their oppressor than to one another (Rossi, 1965; Lees, 1986). Accordingly divisions amongst women mirror those in society at large and pose severe membership problems for the movement, on the one hand excluding a majority of women, on the other creating conflict within the movement itself.

Feminism is a social movement, or a 'purposive and collective attempt of a number of people to change individuals or societal institutions and structures' (Zald and Ash, 1966, p. 327). As such it has no formal membership requirement, though many of its constituent organisations do. But even if we include supporters whose organisational involvement is minimal, it scarcely represents women as a whole.

The most frequently noted skew, now as in the nineteenth century, is in the movement's social class composition. It remains predominantly middle-class. This is not to deny that working-class women have come increasingly into contact with ideas of sex equality, through trade unions, political parties and the media, as in Italy or Britain, or that individual working-class women have been active in the movement. In defence of feminism it must also be said it operates in class-divided societies in which middle-class domination is a feature of nearly all national institutions, including left-wing parties. Earlier we also saw the specific practical obstacles in the way of women's political participation; these hit the working-class mother hardest, whether she is obliged to work a double shift or simply unable to afford labour-saving aids for housework. Cavendish (1982) found that women working with her on an assembly line harboured few illusions about their situation and exploitation by men, but caught up in the exhausting logic of the double shift, they had neither energy nor opportunity to experiment with different lifestyles or feminist politics.

Yet I have suggested that women find it easier to participate in less structured forms of politics, such as the women's movement, than in more formalised political contexts. It seems possible that working-class women are specifically deterred by their perception of feminism. This is partly because of its treatment by the media. More fundamentally, though, the movement's style and preoccupations are distinctly bourgeois. Not only do the demands of equal rights feminists often sound suspiciously like the special pleading of already privileged women, but radical feminism's emphasis on liberation and informality is hardly consonant with working-class experience. The kind of culture clash this can give rise to is amusingly evoked in the protest of the working-class feminist: 'I don't find poverty, dirt or ugliness groovy. I don't like wearing old shirts about ten sizes too big. I don't want to look like a cross between Steptoe and a Renaissance lady. I don't really like camomile tea. I don't like fighting my way through a haze of dope, incense and Indian drapes to yet another revolutionary discussion about real, true feelings' (Tension, 1981, p. 87). The intellectualism of socialist feminists can also put women off – not only working-class women be it said – but they have made more deliberate efforts to appeal to working-class women. In Britain with the winding down of the Working Women's Charter groups, there was some feeling that these links had been eroded, one reason McCrindle suggests why support for the miners' wives during the 1984–5 strike was so rewarding (Rowbotham and McCrindle, 1986; see also Barrett *et al.*, 1986). Feminists in Latin America have been particularly aware of the importance of class divisions between women. Schmink describes the continuing attempts of feminist groups in Brazil to build links with working-class women's organisations but concedes these have only been moderately successful (Schmink, 1981).

The women's liberation movements in the United States and Britain also began as almost exclusively white, though in both countries black women and women of colour have increasingly mobilised on their own behalf and challenged white hegemony within the movement. Duchen (1986) reports that in France, on the other hand, the MLF is still 'overwhelmingly a white women's movement', in which the issue of racism within the movement has yet to be addressed.

These are but two of the most obvious bases of exclusion (apart from sex itself) from participation in the women's movement. But such 'objective' differences between women have also underlain many of the most serious conflicts *within* the movement. Thus Banks (1981) traces the three strands of equal rights, evangelical and socialist feminism through to the present day reformist, radical and Marxist tendencies, suggesting that they may appeal to different types of women. Cassell, in the early 1970s, also found that members of the older branch were not only somewhat older, but 'more likely to be married, well educated, be established in their life patterns (being primarily professional women or housewives with older children), have higher incomes (whether they or their husbands earn the money)'. Members of the younger branch would have lower incomes, being often either students or low-paid clerical workers, and would be less likely to be married or have children. They would, in Cassell's phrase, be 'women in transition' (Cassell, 1977, pp. 103–4). It is my impression that radical and socialist feminism continues to appeal above all to this kind of woman. In the meantime, as has already been suggested, many older feminists as they become more established and in some cases more interested in having children, may be readier to believe that the main battles have already been won and to be seduced by the motherhood mystique and arguments of conservative feminism.

The women's liberation movement has seen a succession of confrontations, between radical and socialist feminists, between political lesbians, revolutionary feminists, black feminists, and those they criticise. All of these conflicts have revolved around real issues of the movement's development. There is still the danger that they encourage the emergence of what Ardill and O'Sullivan (1986) call a 'hierarchy of oppression', the claim that the most oppressed are the most virtuous, which can be taken to somewhat ludicrous extremes as in arguments over the permissibility of sado-masochistic practices within lesbian sexual relationships (not that this is not a genuine problem but it does not seem an adequate basis for determining who will or will not be allowed to call themselves feminist).

National women's movements in addition mirror in their own divisions outstanding cleavages of the political culture. Attitudes to the national question have for instance been a source of contention amongst feminists in the Irish Republic. But the paradigm case must be in Northern Ireland where feminist organisations have found it almost impossible to transcend the Catholic–Unionist divide and the movement, now struggling against the further burden of the impact of recession, has made little headway (Loughran, 1986). As the international movement has gathered pace and women of different cultures and economic orders have come into closer contact, yet further divisions have opened up. Many of these parallel the North–South debate; for instance we have seen that in the 1980s the question of Palestine has been a continuing source of discord. There is no point in wishing that all these divisions would go away, and to date through its protean amorphousness the women's movement has somehow managed, at least usually, to accommodate them, but they can also make it vulnerable and occasionally induce a fatal paralysis.

Deradicalisation

A second argument emphasises the ideological character and inspiration of feminism and could be termed the 'deradicalisation' thesis. It was first expounded by a group of radical feminists, writing in *Feminist Revolution* but was more systematically developed by Bouchier (1979). Bouchier's thesis was that radical or utopian theory is vital to the momentum of a social movement. 'A radical wing, constantly raising unresolved issues and generating new ones, constantly on the alert for co-operation and retreat is essential to preserve the oppositional movement from a gentle slide into the prevailing hegemony' (Bouchier, 1979, p. 397). Though his concrete application of this argument was to the American women's liberation movement, he maintained it was also relevant to Britain. Deradicalisation of the American movement, according to Bouchier, began early in the 1970s. The media played an essential part in caricaturing and ridiculing the movement's more extreme statements and tactics, then by co-opting and glamourising many of the 'safer' issues. Radical feminists did not help their cause by their refusal to use the media themselves. This made it even more necessary for them to retain control of the younger branch's internal channels of communication. Instead, as we have seen, Bouchier describes how they were increasingly edited out. He suggests that this was due to the recruitment into the movement of new women who lacked the radicalising background of the Civil Rights or New

Left movements, and who were consequently 'less committed to the long hard struggle suggested by uncompromising radical theory' (ibid., p. 393). Reinforcing this dilution of radical feminism was the institutionalisation and professionalisation within the older branch, in particular the consolidation of NOW. Undermined by these developments and facing further encroachments from the organised left, radical feminists either retreated into 'life-style' feminism or took up community projects, but in both ways were themselves deradicalised. By 1975, Bouchier suggested, this process of deradicalisation was complete.

As a description of the early development of second-wave feminism in the United states, this thesis may have been oversimplified. Freeman, for instance, preferred to emphasise the radicalisation of 'reformist' groups, particularly NOW. The emergence of a radical critique of deradicalisation could itself be seen to symptomise a turning-point. We saw that the publication of *Feminist Revolution* signalled a revival of radical feminist arguments in the late 1970s (see Brooke, 1978).

More doubtful still would be the application of this thesis to Britain. Can it firstly, be argued that radical feminism ever 'dominated' the British women's movement? The original theoretical and organisational impetus was from disillusioned Marxist feminists. The most one can say is that radical feminists successfully challenged them, and from around 1974 to 1978 were responsible for many theoretical and practical initiatives. But by the end of the decade the situation was one of deadlock. Nor can it be said that equal rights feminism has come to dominate the movement, either organisationally or programmatically. However, by the early 1980s we have observed the increasing integration of socialist feminists into the Labour Party and trade unions. Wandor noted the emergence of 'a new kind of publicly visible feminism – emancipationist feminism . . . a brand of female individualism which is not yet self-consciously political' amongst women in various mangerial positions. Such 'soft-focus' feminism, she predicted, could grow in the 1980s and was especially vulnerable to co-optation (Wandor, 1981, pp. 40–1). Talk of 'post-feminism' may reflect the same trend.

In the United States by the mid-1980s there were also trends that could lend support to a diagnosis of deradicalisation. Disheartened by the failure of the ERA campaign, the victimisation and defeat of

Geraldine Ferraro as Vice-Presidential candidate, the general conservatism of Reaganite policies and bomb attacks on abortion clinics, liberal feminism was taking fresh stock, toning down its rhetoric and preparing to concentrate its energies on promoting an 'economic equity' package of relatively specific, uncontentious legislative proposals, in the different states (Lawrence, 1985). Conservative feminism and family-centred issues were gaining ground within the movement. Likewise, in Scandinavia, France and Germany, whether on a theoretical or practical plane, radicalism seemed in retreat.

Does deradicalisation matter? Radical feminism gave the movement its uncompromising core identity as the fight of all women against all men, and in so far as this basic and to my mind essentially correct perception is weakened, the impetus of second-wave feminism will falter. On the other hand, the early formulations of radical feminism now seem crude and seriously insensitive to the different experiences of women. To attempt to make them more realistic is to invite the charge of deradicalisation, and moreover any attempt to impose, as Bouchier at one time urged, a single unifying theory, would risk further dividing this diverse movement, were it in any case possible.

The tyranny of structurelessness

A third critique of the women's movement focuses on its organisational weaknesses. Strangely enough these have been identified by feminists representing reformist, Marxist *and* radical tendencies. Usually, however, Marxists and reformists have been criticising the 'structurelessness' of radical feminism.

While in all contemporary national women's movements we could probably find some organisations with a hierarchical structure, role specialisation and formal rules, they are not typical and are often rejected by the more numerous 'radical' groups. National co-ordinating or umbrella structures have emerged, most notably in NOW, but also for instance in Britain's NWAF and NAC, but their span and effectiveness is usually limited. With the partial exception of the United States where reformist feminism has created or appropriated numerous associations with a formal membership, hierarchy of officers and high degree of professionalism, the real locus of activity in the women's liberation movement has been the small, local group, which eschewing formal rules and leadership, prefers to arrive at decisions by consensus.

Such an organisational pattern, when properly adhered to, has some undoubted advantages. It is especially suited to the important function of consciousness-raising. Also, in a small group run on these lines, ideally all members have a chance to participate and thus develop self-awareness, self-esteem, political insight and basic political skills. This experience is enormously valuable in the politicisation of women who have been, objectively, or subjectively isolated and oppressed. Moreover it is 'prefigurative' in that, as Rowbotham points out, unlike the more centralised hierarchical organisations of the Left, which are supposed to be transitional evils to a necessary end, but which, history suggests, have a nasty habit of outliving their revolutionary mission, the feminist variant of participatory democracy is supposed to embody the desired future practice and is thus intrinsically revolutionary (Rowbotham, 1979). The decentralised character of the movement also enables it to accommodate and promote all kinds of creative initiative from the grass-roots. A subsidiary advantage of including such ideologically differentiated groups within a single movement is that the perceived extremism of the radical groups makes the arguments of the reformists more acceptable. But finally the crucial advantage of this loose organisational pattern is its ability to incorporate such a diverse membership.

Yet this ideal is not always realised. Freeman reminds us that structurelessness does not necessarily prevent tyranny. Elites, based less on conspiracy than on friendship cliques, are endemic. When there are no formal procedures, they can devise and manipulate tacit rules to ensure their *de facto* control, and to exclude fringe members. De Beauvoir found the same to be true in the MLF (de Beauvoir, 1977).

When it works on its own terms, it is argued that this kind of organisation still has serious limitations. Freeman suggests it is most effective when the group in question is relatively small and homogenous in its ideological and social composition and when it focuses upon a narrow, specific task, requiring a high level of communication and a low degree of skills specialisation. Even then, because of its emphasis upon personal interaction, 'a tremendous amount of the participants' time and energy must necessarily be spent on group processes rather than group ends' (Freeman, 1975, p. 126). Otherwise, the structurelessness can be tyrannical. It inhibits individual displays of particular skills or abilities. As Hanisch, a self-styled revolutionary feminist, recognises, currently women do differ in abilities. 'It follows that if our major interest is to advance the feminist revolution, the person who does the job best should be in charge of it' (Hanisch, 1978, p. 165). This organisational pattern also encourages a new conformity. 'Sisterhood can actually produce a kind of coercive consensus which is stifling rather than liberating' (Rowbotham, 1979, p. 41). It can further inhibit group development by putting off potential new members, by preventing any record-keeping of previous discussions and decisions so that the group goes over and over the same old ground and by allowing whoever attends one meeting completely to revise projects planned by the preceding one.

Exponents of the 'tyranny of structurelessness' thesis go on to emphasise its damaging consequences for the coherence and effectiveness of the national feminist movement. It becomes more difficult to organise rapid, effective responses to new provocations and opportunities. This argument has recently resurfaced in Britain as deepening recession and government policies threaten women's jobs and increase their domestic burden. For Gardiner, it is now essential to be able to mobilise mass action at short notice: 'small scale localised action is no longer sufficient' (Gardiner, 1984, p. 203). It has also been argued that in the absence of organisation, constant conflict between groups wastes energy. Decentralisation leaves marginal groups ever prey to outside takeover, as for instance by the Young Socialist Alliance in the early years of the American Movement. Then, in the absence of formal leadership, the media can pick on individual women, the 'stars', as representing the true voice of women's liberation, leading not only to misrepresentation but to bitter recrimination within the movement itself. Contributors to *Feminist Revolution* incidentally argue that initially radical feminism *did* have leaders and that the reaction against leadership was part of the liberal takeover (see, for instance, Hanisch, 1978). Lastly critics suggest that because of its ineffective national co-ordination, the movement is taken less seriously by other political organisations and institutions than its potential membership might otherwise warrant.

Though the case for a more structured movement is in some ways persuasive, it may reflect too mechanistic an understanding of the problem. It could be argued that feminism produces the structures that it needs. In Italy, for instance, the abortion campaign generated the co-ordination committees providing effective liaison with allies in trade unions and parties. Gelb (1985) suggests that in the United States, radical feminists have become readier to introduce elements of organisation when needed, citing the example of women's refuges which have adopted a form of 'modified collective' as a compromise between external pressures and feminist principles, and have made increasing use of professionals. It must also be recognised that organisation is no panacea. Organisation can act as a brake on policy development or flexibilty, a charge many have levelled at NOW, nor will the existence of organisation prevent conflict, it may crystallise it. NOW and the NWPC have been regularly disrupted by tensions between national, state and local offices, ostensibly about membership and funding but reflecting deeper differences on campaign objectives and tactics (Costain, 1982). But as with deradicalisation, the real issue is whether more structure could be imposed without shattering the movement's fragile cohesion.

Finding the right strategy – with the Left?

Finally, and raising issues that will be taken further in Chapter 6 and the conclusion, we come to questions about the correct strategy for contemporary feminism. In particular, those concerned to diagnose the movement's current limitations have questioned the emphasis on consciousness-raising and the widespread insistence on separation and its implications for alliances, notably with the Left.

It was the radical feminists in 1968 who incorporated and developed the practice of consciousness-raising as a central activity though, as we have seen, they often subsequently moved into other projects, while the older branch took up consciousness-raising in its turn. As a technique, it was a legacy of the Civil Rights campaign, and was particularly helpful in politicising women. It went with the perception of the 'personal is political'. First, as McWilliams points out, there are aspects of a woman's oppression that only she can deal with: 'Usually either the woman is isolated or the opponent difficult to confront. It is hardly feasible to take concerted group action against a family, a lover or a boss; it is equally difficult to take on such elusive oppressors as Madison Avenue or pornographic filmsters' (McWilliams, 1974, p. 162). The consciousness-raising group ideally provides this woman with both political insight and moral support. Secondly, consciousness-raising is supposed to reveal to the women who take part, through a reappraisal of their personal experience, their common oppression by men and thus to foster a new and militant solidarity amongst them. A third extremely important function of consciousness-raising, pointed out by Eisenstein (1984), has been as a source of collective knowledge about women. It was how feminists first came to understand the significance of issues such as abortion, domestic violence and rape. The first guidelines for consciousness-raising sessions were produced in 1968 by Redstockings and included recommendations that each participant must testify in turn on whatever question was being discussed, no one else must interrupt her or pass judgement on her individual testimony, and generalisations should only be attempted once testimony was completed. The vogue for consciousness-raising was so great that, according to one estimate in 1972 there was at least one such group in every block in Manhattan (Cassell, 1977, p. 34).

Yet the drawbacks to such an exclusive focus were soon apparent. Freeman argues that many women who felt sufficiently 'conscious' wanted to do something with their new insights and released energies. But not all groups made the transition from 'rap' group to a campaign or project. Often they just fizzled out. This lends support to the argument of Adams and Winston that consciousness-raising was becoming therapy, encouraging women to find personal and 'life-style' instead of political solutions to their problems. Consciousness-raising, then, has played an invaluable part in revitalising the women's movement and continues to be important in the induction of new members but, it is argued, can lead into a political cul-de-sac.

From radical feminism, too, comes the strategy of separatism. Not only radical feminists, but also other feminist groups influenced by them, have excluded male supporters from membership. This exclusion seems eminently sensible, particularly while groups are in their formative stage, if women members are to develop their own solidarity, analysis and skills. Adams and Winston cite the apparent success of feminist ideas in Sweden, contrasting it with the limited achievement of the large and vocal women's movement in America, in order to question the need for separate women's organisations at all. But it is likely that such diffuse feminist pressure as exists in Sweden could only be effective in circumstances already highly propitious to feminist objectives. When circumstances are adverse and the need for feminist values most urgent, only a separate women's movement can ensure their articulation. The virtual absence of a feminist viewpoint in the economically 'advanced' countries of Eastern Europe must be closely connected with the political impossibility there of forming an independent women's organisation. In Third World countries, feminists are currently arguing about the need for an autonomous women's movement. At one discussion group, women from Latin America described how 'autonomy can politicise certain problems which have always been seen as private problems, experienced by every woman in isolation' and enables women to formulate and feel confident in stating their own demands (Davies, 1985, pp. 176–7).

On the other hand, insistence on separatism has at times precluded alliances, however tactical, with organisations of men or including men and this may be more regrettable. In the United States reformist feminist groups have been ready to collaborate on particular campaigns with a range of non-feminist allies, from all sides of the political spectrum. The most notable instance is during the fight to extend the deadline for the ERA, in 1978, when over 75 organisations including unions, civil liberties, religious and civic bodies were drawn into the coalition (Kolker, 1983, p. 219). Interestingly enough, many American feminists had second thoughts about the decision in 1980 to support candidates from either of the two main parties, so long as their position on feminist causes was sufficiently sound. The unambiguous opposition of the Reagan administration to feminist claims might indicate the need to support the campaign for a Democratic President (Katzenstein, 1984). Much more obviously in Britain and several other European countries, potential allies have been organisations, chiefly unions and parties, of the Left. There has been a recurrent debate, led by Marxist and socialist feminists, over the pros and cons of such an alliance. In Britain at the end of the 1970s the case was made forcefully, pointing to the growing influence of the non-workerist Left and of feminist values in the Labour Party. Wainwright argued that 'unless women's demands are integrated with the needs of these other groups then it is unlikely the women's demand will ever get the support necessary to take on the powerful vested interests they are up against' (1979, p. 5). But at this time the Left itself was in considerable disarray or 'fragments'. This led some to ask if women must wait upon the unification of the Left, whether indeed feminism must itself become 'the oil on the rusty wheels of socialism' (Cartledge, 1980). There were also fears that any attempt to forge such an alliance could precipitate a split within the women's movement (Wilson, 1980).

In the event no movement-wide alliance would have been possible but many socialist feminists did decide to work through the Labour Party, in bodies like the Women's Fightback Campaign for a Labour Victory and the Women's Action Committee (Coultas, 1981). But the partial success of this strategy created new dilemmas, with the proliferation of local government women's committees and equal opportunity units. These raised old anxieties about cooption (individual leaders being assimilated into the existing power structure), deradicalisation as women's projects compromised their original objectives in order to qualify for funds, and insufficient accountability.

In France we saw that feminists' dilemma under a socialist government in the early 1980s was still more acute. The Ministry of Women's Rights distributed funding and opportunities for feminist initiatives on an unprecedented scale even as feminist voices inside the Socialist Party were being silenced. As first sources of government funding dried up, then in 1986 a new conservative government took charge, French feminism seemed to be left high and dry, a warning against too close an alliance with the Left, however sympathetic and popular it may appear.

In fact the question of an alliance with the Left cannot easily be resolved (see also Randall, 1986a). In the long term, as Chapter 4 suggests, socialism (in the forms so far known) may be somewhat better for women than capitalism, although it may be more hostile to feminism. But I should argue that feminists should be more concerned with short-term considerations. Presently left-wing parties, and governments in Western Europe and the old Commonwealth at least, and for whatever instrumental reasons, are more likely to promote women politically and to pursue women's rights policies. During the recession it is also clear that many of the battles feminists face against cuts in welfare, education, employment and health services must likewise be battles of the Left. For these reasons, a degree of co-operation may be desirable but it should not be allowed to split the movement and most importantly it should not seek to *replace* an autonomous women's movement.

The fundamental strength and the fundamental weakness of the contemporary women's movement lie in the size and diversity of its actual, and potential, membership. In this context, the movement needs a radical core of ideas to provide its identity and unity, as well as some minimal organisational framework for continuity, co-ordination and strategy. Radicalism and organisation are not necessarily in conflict, but when a social movement's base is so heterogeneous, they almost certainly will be.

This leaves the movement apparently vulnerable to changes in the economic and political environment. On the other hand, if and when these changes stimulate a new surge of feminist militancy there will be a sufficiently fluid organisational and theoretical movement base to accommodate and sustain it.

6

Feminism and policy-making

The present wave of feminism has undoubtedly had an impact on policy; it has brought to the fore and redefined issues previously neglected, helped to secure major changes in official policy and ensured that these are at least partially implemented. In this chapter I want to focus on feminism's involvement in the detailed process of policy-making. What have been the most effective feminist tactics? How much can feminists achieve through this kind of political participation? To what extent does the adverse economic and political climate of the 1980s put in jeopardy successes of the 1970s and require different kinds of feminist action?

Where a few years ago there were only a few case studies of the process by which particular policies or decisions of concern to feminists were reached, and these generally confined to Britain and the US, there are now more sources to draw on. Case studies span a wider range of countries and there have also been more explicit attempts at cross-national comparison. These studies remain largely centred on the Western democracies but this is where in any case feminism to date has had most policy-making impact.

In order to explore the policy-making context, this chapter considers two rather different kinds of policy issue which have both been important targets of feminist activity, abortion and equal employment rights. While examining in greatest detail the determination of policy in these areas in Britain and America, I shall also look at the experience of other Western democracies, taking account of the contribution of the EEC. The final section specifically addresses the implications of the changing context of policy-making in the 1980s.

Abortion rights

Abortion emerged in the early 1970s as almost the definitive issue of contemporary feminism. For radical feminists it symbolised women's sexual and reproductive self-determination, but under their influence other feminists also came to recognise its importance for women's individual freedom of choice and effective participation in the public sphere. This was the issue around which the French, Italian and West German women's liberation movements really coalesced. Possibly with the sole exception of Sweden, with its early liberalisation of abortion law, Western feminist movements this time round have everywhere campaigned either to reform, or to defend and extend existing reforms in the law. If the issue of abortion has lost its central place latterly in the concerns of Western feminism, this is partly because abortion law has been liberalised. In Latin America, by contrast it is a main focus of the growing feminist movement.

If initially some conservative feminists were resistant – in 1967 for instance NOW split on the question – by the late 1970s a feminist opposed to the legal provision of abortion, though not necessarily without some restrictions, would have seemed almost a contradiction in terms. There have been disagreements about the necessary extent of reform, whether women should have 'abortion on demand'. As time has gone by, abortion has also ceased to appear such a morally or ideologically straightforward issue for feminists. In France it led feminists into a closer examination of what it meant to be a woman and potentially a mother (Duchen, 1986). In Italy, in particular, women engaged in the pro-abortion campaign recognised the complexities surrounding the issue. It seemed for instance that even where effective means of contraception were available, many women needed abortions, suggesting that they still felt guilty about having sex for pleasure rather than to procreate (Caldwell, 1986). Socialist feminists have expressed misgivings about basing the demand for abortion reform on women's individual 'right to choose'. As Himmelweit points out, such a claim appears to condone women's relegation to a private sphere, at the same time as feminists in other ways are challenging it.

Are we implicitly accepting that separation of production and reproduction into the social and the private? Are we accepting that under socialism, or whatever name we give the society we are working for, production will be planned, ever so democratically but still planned for the benefit of all, but reproduction will remain a private, individual decision and right?

She concludes, however, that in capitalist society, it is necessary to claim whatever individual freedoms one can, and that in the absence of a mechanism equivalent to the market to regulate decisions about reproduction, freedom of choice in this area could actually help to undermine the power of capital (Himmelweit, 1980, p. 68). Similarly, Jagger argues that a woman's right to choose 'is not derived from some obscure right to her own body; not is it part of her right to privacy. It is a contingent right rather than an absolute one, resulting from women's situation in our society'. Above all, it is because 'women's lives are enormously affected by the birth of their children, whereas the community as a whole is affected only slightly' that they should decide. In a different society, in which the community assumed major responsiblity for the welfare of mother and child, that community should likewise share the right to choose (Jaggar, 1976, p. 356). Most recently criticisms have been made of the exclusivity of a focus on abortion rights. Access to abortion should be only one aspect of women's right to choose. One development prompting these criticisms has been the emergence of more sophisticated 'reproductive technology', raising new questions about the acceptability of 'in vitro' fertilisation for instance and surrogate motherhood. More decisive have been the arguments of Third World feminists that methods of preventing conception – contraceptive devices, abortion, sterilisation – have been introduced insensitively, incompetently or through outright coercion, in their own countries. The conclusion is that feminists should campaign for reproductive rights as a whole, instead of just the narrow issue of abortion. As we shall see, however, the issue of abortion itself is far from resolved or settled. Even in countries where abortion law has been reformed, the terms of the reform are open to constant challenge and renegotiation.

Although abortion may nowadays seem a more complex issue for feminists than a decade previously, most would still support abortion reform. The real difficulties with the issue of abortion, from a feminist standpoint, is that others do not perceive it as a question of women's rights or autonomy and many have bitterly opposed liberalisation of abortion policy. Indeed, much of the battle over abortion rights has been precisely about how the issue is defined. Abortion policy has first reflected, particularly in state socialist societies, the state's interest in regulating population growth so as to satisfy labour and defence needs. Admittedly in Britain and the United States, such policies have been little in evidence over recent years and would seem to contradict prevalent liberal values (Riley, 1981). In France, arguments about the declining birth-rate – 'The fall of Rome, where abortion was widely practised, was made inevitable by the decline in its birthrate' – were mobilised in parliamentary debates on the 1975 Act (Mossuz-Lavau, 1986, p. 91) and may even have influenced the Socialist government in the early 1980s.

But abortion has also been defined as a medical issue, or as a legal issue, in both cases according it a technical or apolitical character. Most seriously for feminism, it has been seen as a moral issue, one in which the pronouncements of religious leaders must be binding for their followers. In the West, the moral argument against abortion has been articulated and orchestrated above all by the Roman Catholic Church. While the Church always disapproved of abortion, as evidence of sexual indulgence, the real pressures to outlaw abortion in the nineteenth century came as we saw from the increasingly assertive medical profession, using primarily arguments about the danger to women's health. It is in the present century that the Catholic case against abortion has come to centre on the right to life of the unborn child. The Catholic Church now officially maintains that life begins at the moment of conception. Earlier Catholic theologians did not all share this view. Pope Gregory XIV for instance condoned abortions up to forty days in a pronouncement of 1591. Only in 1869 did Pope Pius IX forbid all abortions and this position has been regularly reaffirmed. The 1974 Declaration on Procured Abortions states 'The First Right of the Human Person is his life. Never, under any pretext may a woman resort to abortion. Nor can one exempt women from what nature demands of them' (Bishop, 1979, pp. 66–7). The right to life of the unborn child has proved a highly emotive theme and it would certainly be unfair to dismiss it as the rationalisation of misogynists but it is worth pointing out that many of its proponents simultaneously support capital punishment and oppose pacifism (Richards, 1980, pp. 216–320). In so far as abortion has been successfully projected as a moral issue, the possibility of compromise has been reduced. If compromise is reached this is likely to be provisional, waiting on a major shift in the relevant balance of power.

Abortion thus does not sit comfortably in conventional typologies of political issues which tend to assume a kind of jostling of 'interests'. Nevertheless many authors, including myself, have used the classification suggested by Lowi (1964), which distinguished between kinds of policies in terms of their effects on those they are directed towards. On the one hand, 'regulatory' policies can regulate how individuals or groups may use the resources they have, while 'redistributory' policies entail some redistribution of resources, usually between broads social classes of 'haves' and 'have nots'. There is some argument as to whether abortion can be fitted into this framework (see in particular Outshoorn, 1986). It seems to me that abortion *is* in the first instance a regulatory issue, though following Tatalovich and Daynes (1981) it may be reasonable to qualify this by saying that it a specific variant of regulatory issue in which the kinds of economic self-interest Lowi's model tends to assume, are not so salient. As a regulatory issue it is marginal to the concerns of the main class-based national political parties. However the implementation of abortion reform does have redistributory implications when the state is required to provide free or subsidised abortion facilities. These have loomed larger once feminists have secured liberalisation of abortion law.

Abortion reform in Britain

In Britain we have seen (p. 161), the battle to legalise abortion dates back at least to the formation of ALRA in 1936 and the first legislative initiative was in 1952, Reeve's Private Member's Bill. All subsequent abortion Bills have been either Private Members' Bills or introduced under the '10-minute rule', because the parliamentary parties have considered them too controversial and inappropriate for inclusion in their legislative programmes.

As such their progress has been perilous. Private members compete by ballot to introduce Bills on one of the approximately sixteen days set aside for them in each parliamentary session. If lucky, they still face the danger that their Bill will be 'talked out' in the Second Reading, and the further difficulty, after it has been to

Committee, of getting it through the final Report Stage in the limited time allotted. Indeed, Marsh and Chambers conclude that unless it is dealing with a narrowly technical and uncontroversial issue, a Private Member's Bill will only get through Parliament with the active support of the Government, which can award extra time (Marsh and Chambers, 1981, p. 187). Bills introduced under the 10-minute rule are not even guaranteed a second reading.

Steel's successful Bill in 1967 prevailed almost despite medical opinion, at a time when public opinion polls indicated popular support for some reform of the law but probably less than was actually legislated. Though the lobbying by ALRA and the thalidomide scandal assisted, it was developments within Parliament itself that were decisive. Lord Silkin's successful abortion Bill in the House of Lords provided a valuable precedent. In the House of Commons, the sympathetic Labour Government gave the Bill extra time, while on the crucial vote on whether to proceed to a Third Reading, 234 supporting votes came from Labour MPs, twenty from Conservatives and 8 from Liberals. This favourable parliamentary attitude did not simply reflect the existence of a Labour majority. It was also due to the advent to the House in 1964 of many younger, highly educated middle-class MPs, who favoured such social reforms as the abolition of capital punishment and the legalisation of homosexuality.

The 1967 Act itself represented a compromise. It authorised abortion up to twenty-eight weeks of pregnancy, in cases where two registered doctors agreed that otherwise the life or health of the mother or other children would be at risk, or that the baby was likely to be handicapped. But a clause allowing abortion if the pregnant women would be severely overstrained as a mother, which had been in the original Bill, was dropped. A provision was added entitling doctors and nurses to refuse to take part in abortions on grounds of 'conscience'. Commentators seem agreed that Steel was tactically correct to accept this compromise. Even so, Greenwood and King stress the Act's limitations, suggesting that those who drafted it only expected it to be used by 'problem', and not 'normal', women. The subsequent demand for abortion took them by surprise (Greenwood and King, 1981, p. 178).

Steel's Bill also provoked a backlash. It prompted the formation of SPUC (Society for the Protection of the Unborn Child), headed by Phyllis Bowman. Initially Roman Catholics were excluded, but

Bowman subsequently converted to Catholicism and many of SPUC's membership by the late 1970s were Catholic, though also including Russian Orthodox, Buddhists, Evangelicals and Baptists. In 1980 overall membership was estimated at 26,000 and by January 1984 SPUC claimed 30,000 members (Lovenduski, 1986b). Marsh and Chambers suggest that SPUC has concentrated on mobilising opinion – often through the pulpit – in the constituencies, and only to a limited extent cultivated direct links with MPs. A more extreme breakaway, LIFE, was formed in 1970, and it has been even less concerned to lobby individual MPs. Its main emphasis instead has been on counselling pregnant women not to have abortions and providing practical help for those accepting their guidance. During 1981, however, it began to emerge as a more campaigning organisation, initiating a number of court cases concerned with abortion and the 'right to life' of foetuses which may be severely deformed. It has also pursued a distinctive strategy of setting up national groups representing particular sectors of its membership such as LIFE NURSES, LIFE LABOUR. By 1979, LIFE claimed an overall membership of around 20,000. One further feature of these organisations worth noting is that they have been much better financed than bodies campaigning for abortion.

Between 1967 and 1983 there were no less than nine attempts to introduce restrictive amendments to the Act. The first four got nowhere. In 1971, the Health Minister appointed a Parliamentary Committee under Mrs Justice Lane to examine the administration of the Act. After hearing detailed evidence for over two years the Committee reported its substantial apporval for the Act, though it favoured a reduction of the abortion time-limit from 28 weeks to 24. It was particularly impressed by the views of the British Medical Association and Royal College of Obstetricians and Gynaecologists which had both come round to the Act, through having to implement it.

But in the meantime SPUC launched an effective campaign in the constitutencies which won media support, especially following publication in 1974 of *Babies for Burning*, a sensationalised and in places fictional account of abuses under the Act. This strategy influenced public opinion and, most of all, the attitudes of many Labour MPs who had originally supported the Act. When James White in 1975, submitted his Private Member's Bill which would have severely reduced access to legal abortion, the vote of 203 to 88 to give it a Second Reading, though in part tactical, also reflected a genuine shift in Parliamentary opinion.

White's Bill in turn galvanised the pro-abortion lobby. Although the first Women's Liberation Conference, held in Oxford in February 1970, had adopted as the movement's third demand 'Free contraception and abortion on demand', activities to support this demand had been localised and sporadic. When ALRA called a meeting in 1975 to counter White's Bill, the response was enthusiastic. The resultant National Abortion Campaign (NAC) was soon organising a militant campaign throughout the country for 'abortion on demand'. In July, NAC mounted a demonstration of around 20,000 – the 'biggest demonstration on a women's issue since the suffragettes' (Marsh and Chambers, 1981, p. 47). It also fostered links with trade unions and the Labour Party. Lovenduski (1986b) describes how NAC activists in the trade unions formed 'networks' co-operating to keep the issue of abortion on their union agenda. Blue-collar unions were more resistant than white-collar such as the National Union of Employees (NUPE) and the National Association of Local Government Officers (NALGO). NAC members also sought to involve local trade unionists in their meetings and campaigns and to persuade national unions to affiliate to the national campaign. At the same time NAC encouraged local Labour parties to set up their own branches of a national Labour Abortion Rights Campaign (LARC). In the event White's Bill did not go beyond a Second Reading because the Minister of Health persuaded its sponsors that the matter should be referred to a Select Committee. Possibly this reflected the Minister's interest in defusing the issue. At any rate, the Bill had by now set off a powerful reaction.

NAC had from the start assumed a radical stance on the issue of abortion. In 1976 a Co-ordinating Committee in Defence of the 1967 Act (Co-ord) was set up, whose aims, as its title suggests, were more modestly defensive and which was to act as an umbrella organisation. By 1980 it co-ordinated the campaigns of 56 member organisations. At the same time, as we have already seen, a number of Labour women MPs, including Jo Richardson and Oonagh Macdonald, were beginning to work more closely together to defend abortion reform in Parliament.

Following White's Bill, two further attempts to amend the Act, by William Benyon and Bernard Braine respectively, were again unsuccessful. Benyon's Bill in 1977, did draw on findings from the report of the Select Committee set up in response to White's Bill, and was the first amendment Bill to reach Committee stage. But the pro-abortion members of the Committee were well-briefed and learning fast the tactics of delay, and the Bill ran out of time.

When in May 1979 John Corrie drew first place in the Private Member's ballot, it seemed for a time that his Bill, which would again have radically reduced access to legal abortions, would succeed. At Second Reading the vote in its favour was 242:98, meaning that its supporters predominated in the Standing Committee to which it was sent. The Bill's eventual defeat was a result both of the effectiveness of the opposition campaign and of its proponents' mismanagement. Pro-abortionists on the Standing Committee included seasoned campaigners like Jo Richardson and the skilled parliamentarian, Ian Mikardo. They were well primed by Co-ord. Furthermore, though attempts to get the Parliamentary Labour Party to impose a three-line whip were unsuccessful, since the 1977 Annual Conference it had been official policy in the Party at large to defend the 1967 Act. Joyce Gould, Chief Women's Officer of the Labour Party, watched over and briefed Labour MPs. At the same time, outside Parliament, NAC launched a Campaign Against Corrie which helped to counteract the constituency activities of the anti-abortion lobby. An official Trades Union Congress march against the bill in October attracted an estimated 100,000 marchers, 'widely believed to be the largest ever pro-abortion rights march' (Lovenduski, 1986b, p. 61). Corrie's Bill was badly drafted, and drew damaging criticisms from the British Medical Association. The different groupings within the anti-abortion lobby were divided on objectives and poorly co-ordinated. Corrie himself compromised too little and too late to save the Bill, which ran out of time and was formally withdrawn on 25 March 1980.

After Corrie, pro-abortionists for a time believed they had finally routed the anti-abortion lobby (Francome, 1984, p. 180) but in fact the issue was not resolved and still remains a likely source of further conflict. In December 1982 Lord Robertson introduced a further amendment restricting the Act's provisions, in the House of Lords, though this did not get far. Marsh and Chambers argue that it is easier to defend the law than change it, so that only a major shift of public, and especially Parliamentary, opinion could lead to radical revision of the Act. Defenders of the Act none the less need to maintain their vigilance. There were fears for instance in 1985 that Enoch Powell's Private Member's Bill to outlaw the use of human embryos for research and in vitro fertilisation could form the basis for a new attack on abortion (South, 1985).

But the real threats to abortion provision now come from changes in the regulations governing its administration, regional variations in implementation and from national health cuts. In January 1982 the introduction of new forms to certify the need for abortion was one such administrative constraint (*The Guardian*, 23 January 1982). By 1985 pressure was mounting to reduce the maximum term within which an abortion could be carried out from 28 to 24 weeks of pregnancy. Following recommendations from both the British Medical Association and the Royal College of Gynaecology, the government decided not to seek new legislation but to make this a condition of licensing private abortion clinics. In themselves these measures may not be too serious (opinions are divided on how far reduction of the maximum term is a damaging restriction) but do indicate the scope for government reinterpretation of the Act.

Since the law allows doctors considerable discretion, there are also marked variations in the availability of NHS abortions in different areas of the country. Such variations are doubtless compounded by the effect of health cuts. The National Abortion Campaign has been committed in the longer run to the principle of abortion on demand. A possible start in this direction was the Bill to make NHS abortion facilities mandatory, introduced in July 1981, under the 10-minute rule. It was defeated by 215 to 139 votes (Parker, 1981). But the more immediate problem has been reduced availability. Abortion day-centres, urged as a remedy for regional disparities in provision, were slow to appear and are now being threatened with closure. NAC, just surviving the split in 1983 when a section broke away to form the Women's Reproductive Rights Campaign, has sought to regalvanise local activity around the need ' to expand national health provision.

Abortion reform in the United States

The process of abortion reform has been rather different in the USA. While liberalisation of the law and its interpretation has gone further, this legal victory is less secure and implementation has been even less satisfactory. This is firstly because the conflict has been more polarised, with pro-abortionists since the late 1960s demanding 'abortion on request', and anti-abortionists opposed to abortion on any grounds. But the policy process has also been distinctively shaped by the decentralised character of American politics, and especially by the impact of federalism and the courts.

Up to the 1960s, we have seen, abortion was illegal. Its emergence as a major political issue in that decade was not due to feminist pressure. Rather it reflected lawyers' concern that abortion was still a punishable offence, doctors' changing attitude to abortion as well as their resentment of legal interference in decisions they felt should be based on professional medical opinion, and broader changes in public opinion.

In 1959, the American Law Institute drafted a model Bill, proposing a reform to existing laws that would allow abortion on conditions very similar to the Steel Act. It was endorsed by the powerful American Medical Association, as well as the American Civil Liberties Union (ACLU) and formed the basis for laws subsequently passed in five states. By this time, however, the new radical feminists were beginning to argue that the law should not be reformed but repealed. Their case was assisted by ample evidence that the reforms so far enacted had not greatly improved access to legal abortion. Moreover by the late 1960s, under the sponsorship of the ACLU, abortion laws were being challenged in the courts; this culminated in the decision of a court in Washington DC that its abortion law was unconstitutional. In 1969 Lawrence Lader founded the National Association for the Repeal of the Abortion Laws (NARAL which, following the 1973 Supreme Court decision came to stand for National Abortion Rights Action League), the major American pressure group for the repeal of the abortion laws. It was against this background that New York State's legislature in 1969 rejected a Bill to reform abortion law, but in 1970 legislated for abortion on request up to twenty-four weeks of pregnancy.

The major national initiative was taken by the Supreme Court. American political scientists disagree over the Supreme Court's general role in policy-making. Writers like Dahl have suggested that it usually acts in concert with the dominant national political coalition, while others, citing (for instance) its role in advancing civil rights in the 1960s, argue that it can anticipate and even mould dominant political values. The Burger Court, whose Chief Justice,

Warren Earl Burger, was appointed by Nixon in 1969, might seem an unlikely champion of women's rights, but Goldstein suggests that it 'has done more to enhance the freedom of American women than any single policy-making body in history' (Goldstein, 1979, p. 105). Its decisions on abortion were central to this contribution. Cook tries to identify the broader values underlying the Court's attitudes to women. She finds that votes in the Court on women's roles were more closely correlated with its members' orientation to civil liberties than with their views on regulating the market or on equality (Cook, 1977). Thus, in their treatment by the Supreme Court, women were perhaps the beneficiaries of the civil rights movement.

On 22 January 1973, the Supreme Court made two rulings on abortion. In Roe *v.* Wade, it argued, on grounds anticipated in the 1965 ruling on contraception, that the right of privacy under the Fourteenth Amendment should cover a woman's decision on whether to have an abortion: in the first trimester this would be a decision solely for the woman and her doctor, in the second the state could interfere if the woman's health was at stake, and in the third it could even forbid abortion, in the interests of the future child. In Doe *v.* Bolton, the Court ruled that the consent of the woman's husband or parents was not needed. Cumulatively these rulings went further towards the legalisation of abortion than Britain's 1967 Act. Yet their sequel has been disappointing. Under pressure from the vehement anti-abortion lobby, both the Supreme Court and Congress have modified the original legal guidelines. This has only reinforced the inadequacy of their implementation.

One reason for the success of the campaign to legalise abortion was that, to begin with, opposition was divided and disorganised. The anti-abortion movement originated in 1970 in New York State, where it was closely associated with the Catholic Church, but did not assume its present form, with a more autonomous and structured organisation, in the National Right to Life Committee until after the 1973 Supreme Court decision. The Roman Catholic hierarchy has continued to provide much of the leadership. In 1975 the Conference of Catholic Bishops pledged itself to help organisations campaigning for a constitutional amendment against abortion, though it chose not to campaign in its own right. Hayler suggests, however, that the movement's supporters have been distinguished as much by the degree of their religious commitment and by their generally conservative approach to political and moral questions as by any particular religious affiliation (Hayler, 1979).

Emergence of the anti-abortion lobby paralleled and overlapped that of the New Right, the increasingly effective reassertion of radical right politics and moral conservatism discernible in America, especially in the mid-West and South, from the mid-1970s. Durham dates the formation of a New Right strategy from 1974, with the coming together of four longstanding right-wing activists, including Richard Viguerie, former executive secretary of the Young Americans for Freedom and founder of a direct-mail company which by the use of advanced technology and extensive mailing-lists was able to reach millions of potential supporters with conservative literature' (Durham, 1985, p. 180). They founded organisations to fund and lobby sympathetic Congressional candidates and target a 'hit-list' of liberals, the best known of these organisations being the National Conservative Political Action Committee (referred to as Nik-Pak). They also sought to draw into their ambit existing conservative organisations, including the NLRC, and to tap the reservoirs of religious fundamentalism and moral conservatism through what has become known as the pro-family movement. In the latter context they facilitated the launching of three new organisations in 1979, of which the most prominent has been the Moral Majority led by the TV preacher, Jerry Falwell. Interpretations differ as to whether, as Durham seems to imply, the New Right has used issues of family and sexual morality to make a link with and popularise its real objectives in the areas of defence and economic policy, or whether these moral questions are indeed central and what distinguishes today's New Right. What is less in doubt is that opposition to abortion has become a vital rallying-point; according to one observer, by the end of the decade it had become 'the New Right's Number One Priority' (St Clair, 1981, p. 32).

There are two main anti-abortion organisations. The NLRC by June 1977 claimed an active membership of eleven million, organised in 3000 local chapters (Palley, 1979), and by 1981 thirteen million. It has been less ready to compromise than SPUC in Britain, but like SPUC has concentrated on mobilising grass-roots public opinion. Members of national and state legislatures have been inundated with letters from their constituencies. During the 1980 national elections, the NLRC identified its own hit-list of Congressmen, according to Francome with some success. The other organisation, March for Life, is smaller and more extreme (Francome, 1984).

Opposition to abortion was already sufficiently vocal to persuade Congress to pass, in 1976, the 'Hyde Amendment' to an Appropriations Bill. This proscribed the use of federal funds to provide abortions for poor women, within the Medicaid programme, unless they were deemed medically necessary. In 1977, the Supreme Court further ruled, by six votes to three, that the states were not obliged to pay Medicaid benefits for 'non-therapeutic' abortions. The result was considerably to reduce the availability of legal abortion for working-class and black women. According to Hayler, 'federally funded abortions for low-income women dropped from an estimated 250,000 annually to about 2,400 in 1978' (Hayler, 1979, p. 320). A report published by the Planned Parenthood Federation of America, shortly after the 1977 Supreme Court ruling, showed that publicly financed abortions had been abolished in more than twenty states. Only in fourteen, including the great metropolitan regions, were they easily obtained, indeed possibly more easily than in Britain (Palley, 1979). As a final blow, in May 1981, Congress removed the exemption from the provisions of the Hyde Amendment of victims of rape or incest.

Another favoured strategy of the anti-abortion movement has been to seek an amendment to the US Constitution outlawing all abortions. The most extreme version, sponsored by Senator Jesse Helms, claimed the 'paramount right to life', beginning even before conception, with fertilisation. Despite the support of the Republican Party in principle, and of many southern Democrats, these attempts have not so far succeeded. Partly in recognition of the difficulties, in 1982 Senator Hatch proposed a seemingly more modest amendment that would simply state 'The right to abortion is not secured by this Constitution', thereby allowing Congress and state legislatures to prohibit abortion if they so chose, but failed to win sufficient support.

There has been of course a third tactic, though not one condoned by the main anti-abortion lobby, which is physically to attack abortion clinics. Such attacks have been reported from the late 1970s but reached a peak around 1982. These can hardly directly have assisted the anti-abortion lobby – even Reagan felt obliged to deplore them – but they did have some demoralising effect on the pro-abortion campaigners.

In general though these offensives have triggered new exertions from the pro-abortion camp. NARAL by 1981 had an official membership of 125,000 and worked with a wide spectrum of groups, the most important of which were NOW and Planned Parenthood but including several religious associations, two of them Catholic. By 1983 the pro-abortion coalition included about 30 groups (Kolker, 1983).

The election of Reagan as President in November 1980 gave heart not only to the New Right, which after some prevarication had come to see him as their best hope, but to the anti-abortion campaign. Reagan has repeatedly stated his support for pro-Life objectives. All the same messages from his own administration have been mixed and the anti-abortionists have not had it all their own way. In 1981 Reagan appointed Sandra Day O'Connor, known to favour abortion rights, to the Supreme Court. On the other hand, following his inauguration for a second term, in 1985 Reagan directed the Justice Department to file a brief with the Supreme Court aimed at getting it to review the Roe versus Wade ruling. In January 1986 he reaffirmed his intention of working to overthrow the Supreme Court's 1973 decision but in June the Court itself expressed its continuing commitment to that decision by striking down a Pennsylvania law that contradicted it, albeit by the narrow margin of five votes to four. Quite clearly as in Britain the issue of abortion is not resolved.

Abortion reforms: some comparisons

In comparing the British and American experience it is clear firstly that the pro-abortion movements operate within quite different governmental frameworks. In Britain the appropriate focus of pressure activity was obvious – Parliament – though within it, the House of Lords played a valuable 'incubatory' role. What really mattered was the climate of Parliamentary opinion. In the United States, a number of points for pressure were possible: state legislatures, Congress, the courts. When one of these was favourable, for instance the New York State legislature or the Supreme Court, it could be used to take the fight further. But in the longer run, this decentralisation of authority placed great obstacles in the way of significantly changing national policy on any other basis than 'creeping consensus'.

In the second place, party politics play less part in the American than in the British legislative process. Abortion is not strictly a party political issue even in Britain; no party whip has officially been imposed. Consequently MPs have been more open than usual to extra-Parliamentary lobbying and especially pressures from their constituencies. Even so, MPs' voting accorded closely with their party membership, there was a strong 'unofficial' whip in the PLP and the Labour Government gave Steel's Bill extra time. In America, abortion has been much less a party political matter, although since 1976 the Republican national platform has called for a ban on abortion while the Democratic platform has opposed this and although in Senate votes, Democrats, specifically northern Democrats, has been less inclined to support a constitutional amendment. The absence of party discipline in practice has meant that both Congressmen and state legislators have been more susceptible to pressures from lobbies, and above all from their constituents.

Both in Britain and in the United States, implementation of legal changes has posed separate problems. However, these have been most acute in the United States. There, continuing questioning of the need for public expenditure on social facilities combines with the doctrine of 'States' Rights', which was enjoying a mild revival in the 1970s and permits individual states enormous discretion in matters of social policy.

At this point it will be useful to bring in the findings of recent research in a number of West European countries, which shed additional light on the factors which favour and obstruct abortion law reform. In particular they further illuminate the impact of party politics and of Roman Catholicism.

Britain and the United States are both generally thought of as two-party systems, even though recent changes, notably the emergence of the Alliance, have called this designation into question in the case of Britain and the American system is so decentralised that some have preferred to think of it as a four or fifty party system. In most West European countries, multi-party systems prevail, with such parties ranged along a left–right axis but also often incorporating religious or ethnic cleavages. In some ways the Netherlands, discussed by Outshoorn (1986) presents the paradigm case. Into the 1960s the classic interpretation of Dutch society was that it consisted of three subcultures or pillars ('verzuiling') – Catholic, Protestant and secular, the last subdivided into socialist and liberal wings. The party system reflected these divisions producing a complex but essentially 'balanced' pattern in which no one party or sector predominated. Elaborate 'rules of the game' had evolved within the political élite resulting in a form of consensus policy-making.

One characteristic of this 'politics of accommodation' was that by tacit consent political leaders avoided where possible issues likely to undermine consensus and open up underlying divisions, such as abortion. By the turn of the century abortion had been virtually banned, as in other Western countries and when in the 1960s more liberal attitudes began to indicate some reconsideration of this prohibition, it was the medical profession which reopened and tended to dominate the debate, with progressive doctors demanding reform and themselves performing illegal 'therapeutic' abortions. The ruling coalition of liberals and the three main confessional parties hoped to leave redefinition to the physicians, that is to treat it as a technical matter but the doctors disagreed amongst themselves and one group, the Foundation for Medically Responsible Interruption of Pregnancy (Stimezo) began to offer abortion services, based in private clinics, virtually on demand. In 1970 the government appointed a commission of enquiry – 'A time-honoured method of dealing with an issue touching the religious cleavage, an example of both the politics of postponement and depoliticization' (Outshoorn, 1986, p. 19) but by now the women's liberation movement, in the form of the Dolle Minas, was beginning to challenge existing definitions of the issue in favour of one that acknowledged women's right to be 'Boss over one's own body'. Reluctantly the government introduced a bill outlining very modest reforms which, however, lapsed when the coalition itself came unstuck not on this issue simply but as part of a growing crisis in the old formula of political coalition. The new government, including this time Labour and two confessional parties, was still less able to agree an acceptable abortion policy, leaving the way open for a much broader public argument: women's liberation groups came together with women in trade unions, left-wing parties and gay rights organisations in We Women Demand (WVE) in 1974, with opposition centred in the Committee to Save the Unborn Child (CROK) led by orthodox Protestants.

As Outshoorn writes, 'the continual pressure of the CROK and the WLM broke down the politics of postponement' (1986, p. 21).

A Private Member's Bill to reform the abortion law failed when the government allowed a free vote and liberals feared to alienate their potential future coalition partners in the confessional parties. The 1977 General Election, however, brought in a coalition of liberals with a new Christian Democratic Party based on a merger of the three main confessional parties, and marked the reassertion of the old élitist consensual politics, around a more tenable and stable party alignment. This coalition finally felt strong enough to push through a bill on the abortion issue which otherwise was clearly not going to go away. Moreover while the bill sought to hedge abortion provision about with procedural hurdles, it did not in fact specify any limitations on acceptable grounds for abortion.

Overall then the political élite had been forced to come to terms with changes in public attitudes to abortion and in abortion practice, though by the time the new law came into effect at the end of 1984, it made little difference to that practice itself. The example of the Netherlands suggests that coalition governments in multi-party systems are often even more reluctant than leadership in two-party systems to take up a polarising, non-incremental issue like abortion and that when they do the result may be deadlock. The issue of abortion contributed to the fall of the Dutch government in 1977 and similarly has helped to bring down governments in Italy, West Germany and Belgium.

While then Italy provides a further example of the interaction of the abortion issue with the dynamics of multi-party politics, its special interest lies in the conflict between the powerfully entrenched Catholic Church and a well-established socialist tradition out of which emerged, as already noted, one of the strongest contemporary feminist movements. Italy's 1931 Penal Code made abortion punishable by imprisonment. The same Code, until 1971, forbade the sale or advertisement of contraceptives. In these circumstances, and given ignorance or religiously inspired disapproval of other forms of birth control, illegal abortions became in practice the main resort. They were variously reckoned to run at the rate of 800,000 to three million a year!

As we have seen, the Church's line on abortion has been uncompromising. Its 'statements on sexuality and the family represent the most significant proportion of its public statements to the faithful. It is a central doctrinal area and one through which the Church is intent on reinforcing and extending its control' (Caldwell,

1981, p. 51). In Italy, the Roman Catholic Church exercises political influence in a number of ways. The first is through the party system. Since 1948, the (Catholic) Christian Democrats have been in power. The major opposition party, the Communists (PCI), long before this link became explicit in the famous 'historic compromise' of 1973, had learned to respect Catholic interests. Until the 1970s, all the political parties feared to challenge the Church on a matter over which it claimed sole jurisdiction. Secondly, the Church itself runs a wide range of community services at local level. This has hindered the development of a secular welfare state and provides a valuable means of reinforcing traditional Catholic values.

Abortion was an obvious and urgent issue for second-wave feminism. Here it is important to remember (and in contrast to the Irish Republic to be discussed shortly) that the Italian women's liberation movement drew much of its strength and vitality from the prior existence in Italy of a more secular and egalitarian tradition, with a solid base of support at least in the north, which, even if unwilling to challenge Catholic social morality directly, represented an alternative political perspective. Coming out of this background, albeit rebelling against it, the new women's movement was capable of taking the church on.

Two bills, in the early 1970s, designed to legalise therapeutic abortion, failed to reach discussion stage. In the meantime, however, radical feminist arguments began to impress members of the Socialist Party and the civil-libertarian Radical Party, though the PCI was still resistant. The year 1973 saw three new initiatives: the Constitutional Court was asked to reinterpret the law, collection began of the half million signatures needed for a referendum and a socialist deputy introduced a Bill to legalise abortion. Its provisions were extremely limited but still provoked the condemnation of the Council of Italian Bishops. At the same time, while some feminists worked within left-wing parties and trade unions or with them in the co-ordinating committees, others emulating the French example, were setting up their own self-help abortion service, both the Italian Centre for Abortions and Sterilizations (CISA) in which the Radical Party and the MLD were prominent and rather less established, more informal networks.

By 1975 the political parties were forced to recognise that the abortion issue would not go away. The requisite number of signatures for a referendum had been collected. The Constitutional

Court had ruled that therapeutic abortions were legal. With the general elections of 1976, which increased the representation of the PCI, a pro-abortion majority prevailed in the lower House. The Bill that it approved in January 1977 was none the less delayed for six months by the more conservative Senate and further delayed by a series of amendments tabled by the Christian Democrats.

The new law, passed in June 1978 allows women over 18, with minimal procedural difficulty, to obtain an abortion during the first three months of pregnancy. As such it is 'one of the most advanced in West Europe' (Caldwell, 1981, p. 49). In 1979, according to official records, 188,000 legal abortions were performed, in 1983 233,976. There have none the less been serious problems of implementation, first because although a law of 1975 committed the government to setting up state family planning and health centres, these have been too few in number, especially in the south, where women have had to continue relying on illegal abortions. Hospital abortion facilities are also inadequate but the law does not extend the right to conduct abortions to the private sector (a referendum initiated by the Radical Party in 1981 that would have allowed this was defeated). The Act further includes a conscience clause exempting doctors from the obligation to perform abortions. Since a good majority of doctors in Italy are Catholic, following an intensive campaign by the Church in 1979, 72 per cent were claiming this exemption. In 1983 the corresponding figure was still over 59 per cent.

The impact of the Catholic Church in Italy then was both to delay and to polarise conflict over abortion. Given the strength of a left-wing tradition and of the women's liberation movement, the Church could not ultimately prevent abortion law reform. A national referendum in 1981 showed 68 per cent of voters in favour of the abortion law and a second referendum proposal to restrict the law, moved by the Roman Catholic Movement for Life, was unsuccessful. The campaign for abortion rights had also, as in the Netherlands, faced considerable resistance even from left-wing parties but was then able to make use of unstable party alignments in the early 1970s to persuade party politicians they could not afford to ignore the issue. As in Britain and the Netherlands, campaigners did succeed eventually in mobilising valuable support in unions and parties of the Left. Though unable to prevent the Act, however, the Church has continued to undermine its implementation.

The real difference between Italy and the Irish Republic, as far as abortion policy is concerned, is that in Ireland the Catholic Church has faced no significant challenge to its moral hegemony from an alternative secular or socialist cultural tradition. While other Western countries have more or less gradually moved to liberalise their abortion law, the Referendum of September 1983 resulted in a Constitutional Amendment which actually reinforces the existing ban (see Randall, 1986b). While the amendment cannot simply be interpreted as evidence of increasing anti-abortion sentiment and was itself a response to growing pressures for liberalisation, these still have a very long way to go.

Ireland is still governed by the 1861 British Offences Against the Person Act. In the past women had to risk backstreet abortions though with the easing of restrictions inside Britain increasing numbers have come to England for abortions. By 1981 these were officially reckoned to run at 3604 a year, though this is almost certainly a considerable underestimate.

Irish second-wave feminism emerged in the early 1970s and did not initially take up the issue of abortion. By the mid-1970s feminists were providing a referral service which did contribute to the increase in Irish women's abortions in England. None the less they posed little threat to the existing ban in Ireland. What motivated proponents of the Amendment seems rather to have been both the belief that Ireland must be used to stem the international tide of abortion liberalisation and the shrewd recognition that the abortion issue would be an ideal rallying ground against the slow but steady erosion of traditional Catholic values in Ireland.

The Pro-Life Abortion Campaign launched in April 1981 drew on numerous lay Catholic associations, the medical profession and the Irish branch of SPUC. Within three weeks it had the agreement of the two main party leaders to hold a referendum. This was because the balance of power was so close (between then and the Referendum there were no less than three changes of government) and because historically the parties formed around a split on the national question and were otherwise remarkably similar in terms of social base and 'catch-all' policies. Neither could afford to offend an overwhelmingly Catholic electorate.

In fact the leader of Fine Gael, Garrett Fitzgerald, under pressure from liberals in his own party and their coalition partners, the small Labour Party, and afraid such an amendment could jeopardise his own 'Crusade' to make the Irish Constitution more secular and thus acceptable to the North, did subsequently attempt to introduce a revised wording for the proposed amendment. But he felt unable to declare open battle either in the Parliamentary stage of the Referendum process or in the three final weeks leading up to the Referendum itself, though he did eventually advise the public to vote against. Irish feminists had been completely taken unawares by PLAC but swiftly mounted their own Anti-Amendment Campaign (AAC) launched in June 1981, keeping a low profile behind sympathetic lawyers, doctors and clerics. They judged it wisest not to concentrate their arguments on abortion rights at all but on medical and legal technicalities (these tactics caused one section, favouring a more direct and as they felt less élitist approach, to break away). The AAC faced an extremely ruthless and effective pro-amendment campaign, which drew on the experience and funds of American organisations; local Catholic clergy and SPUC members mobilised support from the parish pulpit. The eventual result, a vote in favour of the Amendment of roughly two to one, rising to almost 100 per cent in some western rural areas, was no surprise and though some argued the high abstention rate of 45.4 per cent indicated a silent 'no' vote, a more systematic analysis suggests (Walsh, 1984) that a higher turnout might have increased the pro-amendment majority.

Equal rights policy-making

Campaigning for equal rights, particularly for equal employment rights and, in the United States, around the Equal Rights Amendment, has been another major area of feminist activity in Britain and the United States. At the same time it offers a number of striking contrasts to abortion reform. Feminists have been less agreed on its importance and it has been less universally a priority of national feminist campaigns. On the other hand, there has been little opposition to legislation for equal economic rights from the late 1960s onwards (excluding the more broadly couched Equal Rights Amendment) where this has been pursued with determination. The real difficulties have come in the implementation stage, difficulties so severe as to raise doubts as to the value of the whole exercise.

Equal rights feminism was a vital component of the nineteenth century movement; its waning in many ways constituted the lull that followed. With second wave feminism, the campaign for equal rights revived, especially in the United States. Through organisations like NOW it has arguably developed into a more far-reaching demand for genuine equality of opportunity. It is none the less equated by revolutionary feminists with a suspect reformism. With some justification they see it as primarily serving the interests of already privileged professional women. They accuse it of using the rhetoric and political mechanisms of liberal-democracy, so helping to shore up the system. Elshtain, though not herself a revolutionary feminist, has expressed the dilemma well: 'A problem rarely considered by the equal opportunity feminists is the manner in which *individual* women and blacks are incorporated within the system and whether such piecemeal inclusion of individuals from previously excluded groups then implicates these individuals (barring other forms of social reconstruction) in institutionalised class, sex and race inequality and thus serves to further legitimise the notion of merit as the basis for inequality of respect and treatment' (Elshtain, 1975, p. 469).

Radical feminists in any case prefer to pursue issues that raise the physical basis of women's oppression. Socialist feminists have been more prepared to campaign for equal pay and the advancement of women in trade unions, so long as these are understood as transitional objectives (see, for instance, Rowbotham, 1973, pp. 100–1). Though more revolutionary forms of feminism have helped to make acceptable the comparatively moderate demands of equal rights feminism, their direct support has been qualified.

Nor have all reformist feminists been in favour of an equal rights strategy. In the previous chapter we saw that those whom Banks describes as welfare feminists opposed in particular the campaign for an Equal Rights Amendment, because it would undermine protective legislation they believed vital to the interests of (potential) mothers and working-class women. The League of Women Voters continued to oppose the ERA until 1972, though by now it is endorsed by virtually all the reformist American feminist organisations (Boles, 1979). In Britain, too, many women trade unionists have continued to favour protective legislation.

The pursuit of equality of economic opportunity has led in the 1970s to a fuller recognition that campaign objectives must extend beyond legislation for equal pay and against sex discrimination, to take account of women's role in the family, through for instance provision for maternity (and paternity) leave and child care. Otherwise as Lewis writes, 'when equal opportunities are extended to individuals who because of the additional burden of their family responsibilities are not in a position to start equal, the rights gained are likely to be formal rather than substantive' (Lewis, 1983a, p. 2). Similarly, since women tend to be concentrated amongst part-time workers, many have argued energies should be focused on improving conditions for all part-time workers. In these and other ways, the original goal of equal employment rights has opened up ever wider ramifications, but agencies and feminist groups have not always agreed on either the range of issues they should be tackling or which should be given priority.

The cause of equal economic opportunity has also given rise in recent years to demands for positive discrimination, over some transitional period, in favour of women. Proposals range from exhortation and encouragement, through 'affirmative action programmes', to quota systems (allocating a fixed proportion of posts or benefits to women) and preferential hiring (selecting a woman applicant if she is as well qualified as in any others or, in some cases, even if she is not quite so well-qualified in other respects as the best-qualified applicant). Advocates of positive discrimination justify it either as compensation for past injustice to women, individually or as a group, or as necessary for the achievement of a future equal society (Thalberg, 1976). But again not all reformist feminists approve of positive discrimination. From a classical equal rights position some argue that it is unfair to men. They also question its effectiveness as a strategy, pointing out that it may lower the credibility of women who benefit from it (see, for instance, Segers, 1979, pp. 336–7).

If the contemporary women's movement remains divided on the question of equal rights, by the same token feminists in different countries vary in the emphasis they accord the issue. The campaign for equal rights has been most lively in the United States. In Britain, legislation for equal pay and against sex discrimination owes less to organised feminism, though groups like Rights of Women and the Rights for Women Unit of the National Council for Civil Liberties have been founded to defend and build upon it.

In other West European countries also, autonomous feminist groups have generally shown little interest in these issues, though feminists moving into political parties and trade unions have pushed them more vigorously, in Scandinavia and, from the late 1970s, in Italy and France.

Yet explicit opposition to demands for equal pay and employment opportunities has in no way matched the vehemence of reaction to abortion reform. This is again because of the kind of issue it is. It is firstly perceived and couched in terms of equality of opportunity that have become central to the philosophy of liberal capitalism. Though feminists similarly advocate abortion reform on grounds of individual rights, they are countered by the moral principle of the right to life. No such effective counter-principle can be mobilised against equal economic opportunity. Secondly, although the issue is implicitly redistributive in that it ultimately requires transfer of resources from men to women, its effects are disaggregated. Both unions and employers' organisations will be involved in the decision process, but it is individual firms and workers who eventually pay for it. Legislators therefore will not necessarily be under pressure from either business or labour to resist legislation for equal economic rights which they themselves publicly support.

Resistance comes instead when attempts are made to implement such measures, in so far as they are seen to threaten the interests of the male workforce. Without constant feminist pressure, implementation agencies remain under-resourced and overly cautious. Local unions and individual employers are reluctant to co-operate. Women are inadequately informed of their rights, or simply afraid to come forward. Still more fundamental obstacles are the widespread and entrenched segregation of women's jobs and women's continuing domestic responsibilities. Economic recession serves to exacerbate these already formidable obstacles.

Equal pay and employment opportunities in Britain

In Britain, we have seen, the demand for equal pay legislation dates back a long time. Indeed, as Banks writes, 'within the women's trade union movement . . . the fight for equal pay was never really abandoned' (Banks, 1981, p. 177). With the decision to phase it in within the non-industrial public sector by 1963, pressure from outside Parliament abated somewhat. In 1964, however, the Labour Party's manifesto committed a future Labour Government to equal pay for equal work. Duly elected, the Labour Government consulted with the CBI and the TUC, before in 1969 Barbara Castle announced legislation for equal pay to take effect after five years, in 1975.

The Government's Bill went through Parliament with remarkably little difficulty. This is because it was in line with Conservative Party thinking; Robert Carr welcomed it for the Opposition. No important amendments arose from the committee stage. However, attendance at parliamentary debates was sparse, in contrast to the high turnout at more recent debates on the abortion issue.

The Act required that women receive equal pay with men in comparable or equivalent occupations, with various significant exceptions. Individuals should complain initially to representatives of the Advisory, Conciliation and Arbitration Services (ACAS), then to Industrial Tribunals, and in the last instance to Employment Appeal Tribunals, all of these bodies being part of existing industrial relations machinery.

One of the few major criticisms made in Parliament of the Equal Pay Act was that it did not go far enough; its provisions could easily be avoided so long as discrimination was allowed in other aspects of employment. In some ways therefore the Sex Discrimination Act was the logical corollary of the Equal Pay Act. Though the first Private Member's Bill on sex discrimination was only introduced by Joyce Butler in 1967, Private Member's Bills submitted in each of the succeeding four years attracted growing support. The last of these, introduced in 1972 by Willie Hamilton, was the basis for a Bill placed by Baroness Seear before the House of Lords. It was there referred to a Select Committee empowered to call for evidence of sex discrimination and for advice on effective legislative countermeasures. In 1973 the House of Commons also established a Select Committee to examine this Bill. In that same year, the Conservative Government announced it would bring in its own legislative proposals, including the creation of an Equal Opportunities Commission, which would however be restricted to a largely advisory role.

In February 1974 a new Labour Government was elected which

produced its own, more radical, White Paper. Following the October 1974 General Election, the Labour Government introduced a Bill, which went even further than the White Paper, to include 'indirect' discrimination. Again there was minimal opposition in principle to the proposals – two notable exceptions being the (then) Conservative MPs, Ronald Bell and Enoch Powell – and amendments to the Bill arising from Committee or adopted in the Report Stage were a matter of detail only.

The Sex Discrimination Act aimed to eliminate sex discrimination in employment, but also education, housing and goods, facilities and services, areas largely excluded from the Conservative proposals. It defined as 'unlawful' not only 'direct' discrimination, when an individual is unfairly treated on grounds of sex, but 'indirect' discrimination, when a substantial proportion of one sex does not conform to a criterion for treatment which is strictly irrelevant, and also victimisation of anyone appealing against discrimination under the Act. Specifically in the field of employment, the Act covered recruitment, promotion and training in an establishment employing more than five workers, with certain exemptions. It provided for appeal by individuals to Industrial Tribunals or County Courts, but also established the Equal Opportunities Commission, with far-reaching powers to investigate and, through the courts, correct infringements of the Equal Pay Act and the Sex Discrimination Act, on behalf of outside groups or on its own initiative. It would also advise individual complainants.

If, at the beginning of the 1960s, equal pay was hardly a burning issue and sex discrimination was not on the political agenda at all, how can we explain the transformation of attitudes that secured such easy passage of both Acts in the 1970s? One element was the direct and indirect, impact of extra-parliamentary groups. The TUC pressed for equal pay legislation all through the 1960s. In part this reflected steady pressure from militant women trade unionists and the growth of union membership among women; it was primarily due, however, to the unions' continuing concern to prevent the wages of women workers from undercutting men's. Though second wave feminism emerged too late to influence equal pay, it undoubtedly contributed indirectly to the change in political attitudes in the early 1970s. Specific women's organisations, such as the National Joint Council of Women Workers' Organisations and the Equal Pay and Opportunities Campaign (EPOC), lobbied

Parliament and provided the House of Lords Select Committee with valuable evidence. Rendel even suggests that their 'effective public demonstrations', especially those of Women in Media, forced the Conservative Government, as a 'rearguard defence', to submit its own proposals in 1973, but this probably exaggerates Conservative opposition to sex discrimination legislation in the first place (Rendel, 1978, p. 900).

It can be argued that the extra-parliamentary lobby was, however, relatively weak and that what mattered was MPs' willingness to pay it attention. The change in MPs' attitudes can, as with abortion be partly attributed to the new climate of 'social reformism' in the House. More precisely Meehan suggests this entailed a changing view of who the recipients of policy should be. Although political values in twentieth-century Britain might, as in America, be broadly characterised as 'Liberal democratic', they have, particularly in the case of the Labour Party, been refracted through a more collectivist and social-class centred model of politics. The Labour Party was uncomfortable with the individualist premise of equal rights policy;indeed Richard Crossman's diaries indicate the Cabinet was split on the question of equal pay. But it was becoming clear that the welfare state was not equally benefiting all its members and by the early 1970s there was much wider acceptance for the view that 'it was proper to protect particular and readily identifiable groups'. This was first and most seriously applied to race relations, which then established a precedent for its extension to women (Meehan, 1985, pp. 84–5).

They were also specifically affected by the new wave of feminism as diffused via public, and élite, opinion. Vallance is inclined to play down the role of individual women MPs. Certainly they did not rally so single-mindedly to this cause as to defend the Abortion Act. She even suggests that some of them cynically perceived the legislative proposals in 1975 as a hollow gesture towards International Women's Year (Vallance, 1979, p. 41). Even so, longer-standing advocates of women's rights, such as Dame Irene Ward and Renée Short, joined forces with newer members like Jo Richardson, Maureen Colquhoun and Sally Oppenheim to maintain the pressure within Parliament for sex discrimination legislation.

Two further considerations weighed with Parliament, or at least the Government. The first was the perceived need to comply with ILO and EEC provisions. One additional reason for TUC pressure for Equal Pay legislation was that otherwise it could not ratify Convention 110 of the International Labour Organisation accords. More urgently, both Labour and Conservative Governments were committed to British entry to the Common Market. The treaty of Rome incorporated the principle of equal pay, and EEC Directives in 1975 and 1976 required member states to report on measures they had taken to promote equal pay and other aspects of job equality. These EEC pronouncements without doubt helped spur the Government to action.

The second consideration has already been touched on in the context of the move towards group as opposed to class-oriented policy-making – the issue of racial discrimination. Not only did those who framed the Sex Discrimination Act draw upon British, and also American, experience of race relations legislation. It has also been further suggested that in the Labour Government formed in February 1974, Roy Jenkins as Home Secretary intended to use sex discrimination legislation as a model for revising existing race relations machinery (Byrne and Lovenduski, 1978). This is one reason why the Labour Government's White Paper was more radical than either EEC requirements or the Conservative Party's proposals of 1973.

In view of the speed and consensus characterising passage of the two Acts, their implementation has been a distinct anti-climax. In 1980, one study concluded, 'There are no notable signs that deeply entrenched patterns of discrimination, which serve to perpetuate job segregation and unequal pay, have been disturbed by the new laws' (Robarts, 1981, p. 10). The Equal Pay Act, at least initially, had more impact than the Sex Discrimination Act. One appraisal of their implementation in 1979 argued that, even taking account of the equalising effect of inflation, a sizeable reduction in sex pay differentials, especially among blue-collar workers, must be attributed to the Equal Pay Act (Snell, 1979). Subsequently the differentials began to widen anew, so that the EOC's Annual Report for 1980 showed that in the previous year female employees' average hourly earnings were 73 per cent of men's, an actual drop from the peak of 75 per cent achieved in 1977. The Report concluded that 'since 1977 improvements in women's earnings as a result of Equal Pay legislation have ceased' (EOC, 1981, p. 70). Women's pay as a proportion of men's has remained around this level ever since. It is less easy to measure improvements due to the sex Discrimination Act. But in general commentators seem agreed that both the number and outcome of cases brought under it have been disappointing. From 243 cases brought in 1976, 51 per cent of which were 'conciliated' and 10 per cent upheld by the tribunal, the rate declined to 171 in 1978 with 71 per cent conciliated and 30 per cent upheld. There has been some recovery since in the number of cases brought but the rate of success in tribunal hearings has not risen over 26 per cent (Atkins, 1986, p. 59).

One part of the explanation for these unsatisfactory results lies in the way the acts were framed. They are firstly limited in their coverage: there are a number of important exemptions, complaints can only be brought by and on behalf of individuals, the burden of proof is on the complainant rather than the alleged discriminator, and no legal aid is available for tribunal cases. In addition it is not always clear which of the two Acts apply. Finally, under the Equal Pay Act, it is often difficult to demonstrate the comparability of women's work.

There have been further weaknesses in the implementing machinery. The Industrial Tribunals, already overloaded with other work, have been reasonably helpful in equal pay cases, but have often seemed unsympathetic or, as Meehan phrases it, not 'at home with' cases brought under the Sex Discrimination Act (Meehan, 1982, p. 15). She singles out two particularly problematic features of the tribunals. First is their 'tripartite' composition, each consisting of a legally trained person in the chair and two lay members nominated by the CBI and TUC respectively, which has reduced the likelihood that it will include either a woman or someone sympathetic to the feminist viewpoint. Secondly their supposed informality rather than assisting applicants means that they cannot know in advance the unwritten rules which inevitably do exist and govern proceedings (Meehan, 1985, p. 148). Implementation of the Sex Discrimination Act pivots even more on the role of the EOC which, until recently, has been widely criticised for its excessive caution. Initially this was due to its inundation with queries from individual complainants which it was statutorily obliged to answer. Its budget has also been inadequate. But it has been mainly hampered by the attitudes of its fifteen Commissioners, appointed by the Government to represent the civil service, business and labour, as is customary with such bodies, and of whom it was stated in 1978, 'few if any can be said to have a professional interest in the feminist cause and none . . . took a leading part in sponsoring the legislation' (Byrne and Lovenduski,

1978, p. 162). At the same time, in keeping with the ethos of British civil service neutrality, the commissioners have been reluctant to delegate decision-making to staff. As a result although the EOC has undertaken or commissioned extensive and valuable research, issued useful publications and advised government on necessary changes in the law, it has been much less willing to use its substantial powers of enforcement. Though authorised, under provisions in the 1976 Race Relations Act, to issues code of practice to individual employers, by 1984 only eight formal investigations had been carried out and no codes of practice issued as a consequence.

Two other institutions have played a subsidiary part in implementing the Acts. The Central Arbitration Committee – part of the general industrial relations machinery – has proved relatively helpful but is only able to act when the terms of collective agreements are referred to it by either employers or unions. The ostensible role of ACAS (Advisory Conciliation and Arbitration Service) has been to help resolve disputes before they go before a tribunal, but they do not have a good record of advice to applicants under the Equal Pay and Sex Discrimination Acts (Gregory, 1982).

Partly because of these shortcomings, there has been continuing ignorance of this legislation, especially amongst trade unions and women employees themselves. Moreover many employers have found ways to get round the Acts, such as segregating women's work, while would-be women claimants have often received little assistance by their unions, particularly at shop-floor level. The onset of economic recession has exacerbated difficulties: to quote the EOC, 'It can fairly be said that in the entire post-war era, there has not been a five-year period more unhelpful and less propitious in which to embark on the task of promoting equal opportunities for women' (EOC, 1981, p. 1).

And yet developments in the 1980s have shown both heartening and depressing aspects. On the one hand, chiefly under pressure from the EEC, there has been an improvement in the legislation itself as it relates directly to employment and in the way it can be applied. There have been the new opportunities associated with 'municipal feminism' and the beginnings of moves to combat sexual harassment at work and to adopt affirmative action programmes. On the other hand the value of these changes has been limited by the continuing inadequacy of implementing machinery, the failure of legislation to take sufficient account of women's special circumstances and the impact of recession and Conservative government policies, that directly weaken employment protection and benefit entitlement and indirectly reduce childcare provision.

Perhaps the single most auspicious development has been in the scope and binding force of EEC equality policy. Here a brief account of the political background is needed. As Hoskyns (1985) describes, the Treaty of Rome is basically a document about economic structures and policy. Its 'social' policy is mainly contingent on this, designed to facilitate labour mobility, to ensure fair competition between member states by standardising labour costs, although also to cushion workers from the worst effects of change and improve working conditions. Thus sex equality was originally seen primarily in terms of enabling women to compete freely in the labour market. By the 1970s, however, feminist lawyers were beginning to bring cases to test the implications of the equal pay provision. The Council of Europe was itself giving more attention to social policy, including policy towards women, as part of the attempt to give the Community 'a more human face'. The Social Affairs Directorate (DGV) was charged with drafting a Social Action Programme, which in turn delegated to an *ad hoc* group the drafting of two important Directives. It should be explained that EEC Directives are not directly binding, as Regulations are, but bind member states on the results to be achieved.

A pivotal role at this stage was played by Jacqueline Nonon, a French career civil servant in the DGV who brought onto the *ad hoc* group a number of women with particular knowledge and interest in the field of women's employment. Their impact was clearest in the second Directive, on Equal Treatment, although even then the group's first draft was considerably amended by the Council's Social Affairs Working Group, all of whose high-ranking members were men.

Article 119 of the treaty of Rome ruled that equal pay should be given for equal work. This went further than in the British legislation which as we have seen specified the same or comparable work. The 1975 Directive on Equal Pay elaborated 'equal work' as meaning work of equal value, which greatly enhanced the possibility of demonstrating comparability. In Britain, the EOC had long pressed for a revision of the Equal Pay Act in line with EEC wording. In March 1980, Wendy Smith won an appeal to the European Court of Justice for her claim for pay equal to that earned by the man who held her job before her, where the implications of the British Act had been insufficiently clear. Eventually in February 1983 the British Government announced the revision of the Equal Pay Act in conformity with this ruling, though it was not to come into effect until May 1984. Since then there *has* been a notable increase in the number of cases brought under the Act but it is not yet apparent whether more will be upheld.

The Equal Treatment Directive of 1976 understood sex discrimination much more broadly than the British Act, providing that 'there shall be no discrimination whatsoever on grounds of sex either directly or indirectly by reference in particular to marital or family status'. It covered access to employment and vocational training, and 'working conditions', though the content of this term was left vague. As a consequence, although the Commissioners intended it to include such matters as parental leave, most member states including Britain, have chosen not to define working conditions. A further weakness is that the Directive allows for exceptions or 'derogations' to the principle of equal treatment. The British Government produced the longest list of derogations of any member state, including within it all women working in firms or establishments with less than five employees (Vallance and Davies, 1986). In fact the European Court of Justice ruled against this particular exception in 1982. Subsequently the British Government has submitted a new Sex Discrimination Bill, which by November 1986 was still going through the House of Lords, which does extend the scope of legislation to cover women in small firms and domestic employment. The Bill also raises the female retirement age to 65, as it is for men in keeping with another ruling of the European Court, this time under the 1978 Directive on Social Security which came into effect in 1984.

Overall then the EEC Directives have been invoked to expand the scope of equal pay and sex discrimination legislation in Britain, despite the frequent resistance of the Government itself. Also valuable has been the proliferation of women's committees, equal opportunity units and officers, and women's rights units in Labour-controlled local authorities, beginning with the GLC's Women's Committee established in 1982. Its example was eventually followed by nine London boroughs and twelve other urban authorities outside London by the autumn of 1984. This development was associated with the coming to power of what Gyford (1985) calls the 'new urban left'. Flannery and Roelofs (1984) suggests that it was most far-reaching in London, where feminist councillors them-selves played a key instigating role, while in Sheffield and Leeds, for instance, equal opportunity machinery was initially a response to racial tensions and feminists pressures from outside the councils. This was in turn largely because the 'new urban left' made less headway in northern constituency parties. Even David Blunkett has been frequently quoted for 'not wanting the women's issue to sap the energy of the class struggle generally' (cited by Gyford, 1985, p. 51).

The various women's committees have come under considerable criticism from revolutionary feminists. Many committees have attempted to introduce elements of 'feminist democracy' into the decision-making process, organising large public meetings to dis-cuss their agenda, but the resultant chaos and conflict has some-times been incapacitating and they have still been accused of élitism and self-interest. The GLC's Committee was certainly the most ambitious. Interestingly enough, it had not been envisaged in the 1981 Labour Manifesto but was set up subsequently following the case made by Councillor Valerie Wise in particular that there needed to be a single body responsible for co-ordinating women's employment policy, otherwise fragmented across the council's different committees. By 1984 the Committee had a staff of 96 and in the period April–December 1983 it funded 227 women's projects to a total of £4.5 million. Writing for *Spare Rib* Loretta Loach (1985, p. 21) felt bound to conclude 'the Women's Committee has unquestionably benefited women in London'. But in March 1986 the GLC and its Committee were wound up by the Conservative Government. It is not yet clear whether the (Labour) Association of London Authorities will be able to sustain some of the work of the Women's Committee support unit but it is certain that many of the projects it helped to fund will face severe financial difficulties (*Spare Rib*, March 1986).

Another line of advance, recommended by the NCCL's Rights for Women Unit, is the development of 'affirmative action' programmes. This proposal is strongly influenced by experience in the United States, where as we shall see such programmes have multiplied and achieved some undoubted successes. In Britain such a scheme is particularly dependent on the co-operation of the unions (Robarts, 1981). A promising move in this direction was the

TUC's endorsement, at its 1981 Conference, of proposals submitted by the Women's Conference for a Positive Action Programme. One strand of this strategy is through contract compliance measures, that is that government(s) should award contracts to private firms only on condition that they provide details of their record of female employment and agree to affirmative action programmes. The NCCL Women's Rights Unit has set up a number of pioneering affirmative action projects in the private sector but this approach has yet to be taken up by the national government.

One further advance has been in gaining recognition that sexual harassment at work is an aspect of discrimination. In July 1985 Ms Dora Kantara won her case against a private hospital in Ealing, under the Sex Discrimination Act, claiming she had been sexually harassed. Later that year Women Against Sexual Harassment was established, with the primary objective of providing legal advice.

Though I have dwelt first on these encouraging developments, it has to be recognised that there are now mounting obstacles in the way of women actually availing themselves of these theoretical employment rights. Above all it has become clearer with the growing recession that the question of women's employment opportunities cannot be separated from that of their mothering and family responsibilities. As Lovenduski writes (1986a, p. 259), 'a sex equality policy which does not recognise that family and welfare are important components of women's opportunities is doomed to eventual failure'. The Equal Pay Act and even the Sex Discrimination Act with its inclusion of the concept of indirect discrimination, are too narrowly conceived. Since the brief of the EOC is coterminous with these Acts, it does not extend for instance to benefit entitlement or parental leave. In the meantime the Government in 1980 limited the employment protection provided to women taking maternal leave, under the 1976 Employment Protection Act, to those who had been two years or more in their present employment (though the Employment Appeal Tribunal in 1985 ruled, in *Hayes* v. *Malleable Working Men's Club*, that it was unlawful to dismiss a pregnant woman who had only been employed for five months). In 1982 a new 'availability for work' form, UB671, was introduced requiring women with children to indicate in advance how they would provide childcare if offered a job and by implication making this a condition of their eligibility for unemployment benefit. Simultaneously local authority nursery school provision, never extensive has been further eroded, beginning with the

1980 Education Act, and there has been a similar attack on the provision of school meals (Gardiner, 1983).

As a corollary of their continuing domestic responsibilities, women are concentrated disproportionately in part-time work and it has again become increasingly clear that in order to make a real impact on women's employment opportunities, the overall conditions of part-time employment must be improved. In 1983 the EEC produced a draft Directive that would entitle part-time to the same rights pro rata as full-time workers, but the governments of several member states, of which Britain was one, were not prepared to ratify it.

At the same time the machinery for implementing equality policy has continued to be inadequate. As a result of government cuts, the EOC was obliged to reduce its staff from 400 to 148 (*The Guardian*, 10 July 1980). There were signs that the commissioners themselves, following changes in the membership to include feminists like Ann Robinson and Sandra Brown, were taking a more aggressive stance but they still refused for instance to support Ms Kantara's sexual harassment case although in the event it was upheld. The NCCL Women's Rights Unit which was always tiny has been left in severe financial straits following the abolition of the GLC which provided much of its funding.

In 1983 Jo Richardson presented a Private Member's Bill on Sex Equality to the House of Commons, aimed at tackling many of these problems. It sought first the amalgamation of the Equal Pay and Sex Discrimination Acts, to eliminate confusing overlap and allow the concept of indirect discrimination to be applied to pay. Under the Bill, part-time workers would be able to claim equal pay proportionate with full-time. The jurisdiction of the EOC would be extended to cover such matters as parental leave. Sexual harassment at work would be illegal. Finally the Bill would have obliged both government departments and all employers of over 100 workers to operate equal employment policies. Though women's organisations did campaign around the Bill, it was defeated by 198 votes to 118.

Equal pay and employment opportunities in the United States

If over the last decade the development of abortion policy has seemed more promising in Britain than in the United states, in the area of equal pay and employment opportunity it has been the other way round. Legislation was secured earlier and at least as easily as in Britain. Implementation, in the sense of actions taken to apply the legislation, has been more vigorous. It is of course more difficult to estimate and compare the actual results. The gap between men and women's earnings has been greater than in Britain and has in fact widened since the 1960s, hovering at around 60 per cent since 1973. But the degree of occupational segregation, which formerly exceeded that in Britain is now less, even though absolute numbers of women breaking into traditional male occupational strongholds remain small (Meehan, 1985). It is not clear, however, how far government policies have contributed to these differences.

The first national Equal Pay Act in America was passed in 1963, with minimal dissension. Equal pay had been one issue on which equal rights and welfare feminists could agree since the 1920s. At least since the Second World War, many unions had added their pressure, to prevent women's wages from undercutting men's. Employers, as represented by the National Association of Manufacturers, had earlier resisted equal pay but by 1963 accepted it in principle. Indeed, a number of states had already passed their own Equal Pay Acts.

The Act prescribed 'equal pay for equal work', a somewhat broader criterion than in the later British legislation. As in Britain, significant exceptions were admitted; most notably, since it was passed as an amendment to the Fair Labour Standard Act, it was restricted to the 61 per cent of wage and salary earners covered by that Act, until a further amendment in 1972. On the other hand, it provided anonymity to complainants and was to be administered by the Wages and Hours Division of the Department of Labor.

As already noted, the Equal Pay Act is generally reckoned, in its own terms, a success. The Department of Labor has been vigilant for violations of the Act, speedy in handling cases and ready whenever necessary to take legal action. The courts in turn have interpreted the Act generously. Despite this impressive record, however, after eight years the median rate of women's pay in comparison with men's remained at 70 per cent, indicating in part the limitations of an equal pay policy on its own without an effective employment opportunity policy to back it up. Another eight years on, it had only increased to 72 per cent.

If equal pay was the beneficiary of labour politics, equal opportunity began as a by-product of race relations. Though the

President's Commission on the status of Women was beginning to highlight sex inequalities, the addition of the criterion of 'sex' to Title 7 of the Civil Rights Act, which outlawed discrimination in employment, was not the culmination of any specific feminist campaign. In fact, the welfare feminists of the Women's Bureau opposed it. According to Robinson, 'Credit for inserting "sex" into Title 7 must be shared between Martha Griffiths and Howard W. Smith, a strange collaboration of shrewd legislators' (Robinson, 1979, p. 415). Smith, who proposed the addition, was a 'Dixiecrat' and hoped thereby to divide the Bill's supporters. Griffiths, with the near unanimous support of other Congresswomen, seized the opportunity to get the amended Title 7 through the House. It also survived the Senate; Robinson suggests that opponents of the Civil Rights Act 'by broadening the law's focus hoped to weaken its effects for blacks', while civil rights advocates, though viewing the inclusion of 'sex' as a distraction from the Bill's real purpose, feared the loss of momentum that could result from resisting it, and hoped that in the implementation stage the 'sex' provision 'could safely be swallowed' (ibid., p. 419). The implications of the Bill for women were thus little discussed in Congress, and then as a subject of much mirth.

Though women were able to ride on the coat-tails of civil rights legislation, they also suffered from its limitations, the result of the deeprooted opposition to it within Congress. Title 7's coverage excluded employment in local government and in education. It established an Equal Employment Opportunity Commission that actually had fewer formal powers than the British EOC for which it was later to be the model. By the time Congress had modified the Kennedy administrations's original proposals, the Commission even lacked enforcement powers.

At the outset, the inclusion of 'sex' in Title 7 was accompanied by minimal political interest. Only one of the five EEOC Commissioners first appointed was a woman, a black who resigned after a year because of the Commission's lack of interest in helping women. In addition, the Commission was rapidly overloaded with work and inadequately funded. Yet Title 7 paved the way for major policy advances in equal employment opportunities for women.

The fundamental reason for these policy advances was the emergence and organisation of the women's liberation movement. Feminists working within the Commission encouraged women to bring their complaints to it, constituting already 25 per cent of all complaints in the first year. Freeman suggests that they also privately encouraged the organisation of the feminist lobby, the beginnings of NOW (Freeman, 1975). As the women's movement gained in strength and influence, Commissioners more acceptable to it were appointed. The Commission investigated and publicised women's employment rights, which had hitherto received little attention. 'Gradually, between 1968 and 1971, the Commissioners converted Title 7 into a magna carta for female workers, grafting to it a set of rules and regulations that certainly could not have passed Congress in 1964, and perhaps not a decade later, either' (Robinson, 1979, p. 427). In addition to issuing rigorous Guidelines against Sex Discrimination in 1969, that same year it ruled that laws 'protecting' women from certain kinds of employment contradicted Title 7, and by 1970 it was defending the right to maternity leave.

But given the growing leverage of feminism, advances were also assisted by the expansion of federal policies to promote equal opportunities for blacks, both because the EEOC was given enforcement powers in 1972, and because these policies were precedents that could then be applied to women. In 1965 President Johnson, alarmed at worsening race relations, called, in Executive Order 11246, for the establishment of an Office of Federal Contract Compliance, whose task was to ensure that all federal contracts not only forbade racial discrimination but included a pledge of affirmative action to promote equal opportunities. In 1967, prompted by the new Interdepartmental Committee on the status of Women which had itself been lobbied by a number of feminist organisations, the Federal Government, in Executive Order 11375, extended these terms to cover sex discrimination. Not only did this Order, in this way encourage equal opportunity for women in private employment, it extended the same conditions to women at all levels of *federal* employment. This was strengthed, in 1969, by a further Executive Order which spelled out what the new Federal Women's Programme of affirmative action should entail. Under affirmative action programmes, the employer is now required first, to produce an equal opportunity policy statement, and then to appoint someone to direct an affirmative action plan, which includes identifying 'under-utilised' sources of recruitment and setting time-tabled goals for future recruitment of women. Next, the employer has to decide what changes in employment practices are needed to achieve those goals, and lastly to institute a system for monitoring progress; if all this is done, the employer is reckoned to show 'good faith'. Finally in 1972, a year when Congress passed a bumper harvest of measures favourable to women, the combined pressure of the women's movement and the Civil Rights movement procured not only greater enforcement powers for the EEOC but expansion of Title 7 to cover employment in local government, education and unions.

The third factor was the generally sympathetic attitude of the courts. A series of claims pursued under Title 7 were upheld by appellate courts. In the first such case to reach the Supreme Court, in 1971, the Court ruled that the refusal to hire women with pre-school children contradicted the requirement of the Civil Rights Act 'that persons of like qualification be given employment opportunities irrespective of their sex'. A particularly contentious aspect of affirmative action programmes has been the setting of quotas for 'minority' groups. In the famous Bakke case, of 1978, the Supreme Court upheld the claim of a white American engineer against the university which had refused him a place while admitting less qualified black students, if only by five votes to four. Yet a year later in July 1979, in *Kaiser Aluminum* v. *Weber*, the Court supported a voluntary quota scheme.

As already stated, it is difficult to gauge the precise consequences of these various initiatives. Even once the EEOC had accepted that half its energies should be directed to equal employment opportunities for women, and then acquired powers powers of enforcement, its work was impeded by the tremendous backlog of cases. None the less in January 1973 it concluded perhaps its most successful case, against the largest corporation in the world, the American Telephone and Telegram Corporation, as a result of which $15 million was distributed in compensation for discriminatory practices amongst 13,000 female employees, and an affirmative action programme was introduced. The Office of Federal Contract Compliance was initially hampered by its dependence for actual implementation on eighteen different government agencies. From 1970, under pressure from the feminist organisation WEAL (Women's Equality Action League: see p. 225), it gradually took steps to apply Executive Order 11375 to employment in higher education.

Still by the late 1970s, there was a widespread scepticism amongst liberal feminists as to what had been achieved. Despite the Federal Women's Programme, between 1969 and 1975 there was minimal change in either the overall numbers of women in white-collar federal employment or their representation within senior service grades (Murphy, 1973; Freeman, 1975). A Supreme Court ruling in 1977 that 'a bona fide seniority plan does not infringe Title 7' was inauspicious, argued Sachs and Wilson. 'It leaves recently hired women . . . in a precarious position if lay-offs are forced by a sluggish economy' (Sachs and Wilson, 1978, p. 215). Yet Robarts insisted 'very real benefits have accrued to women directly affected by affirmative action programmes' (1981, p. 4) and Meehan found there was much greater public acceptance of the legitimacy of women's claim to equal employment opportunities in the United states than in Britain: 'Employers vie with each other in public at least, over their equal opportunity policies' (Meehan, 1982, p. 14).

The Equal Rights Amendment

It is necessary to consider at this stage the equal rights amendment campaign, running in tandem with the equal employment initiatives discussed so far. Though such an amendment would have implications for employment policy its remit obviously runs much wider. It has further relevance for the making of equal employment policy, however, in that by the late 1970s it was becoming *the* central focus of liberal feminist energies, seen perhaps as more promising than piecemeal legislation and judicial pronouncements.

The ERA is then a broader civil rights issue than simply equal employment, and furthermore does not have specific redistributory implications. On the one hand this increases its consonance with liberal values, on the other its open-endedness has been interpreted by its opponents as a threat to traditional American values, particularly the family. Boles points out that the ERA is also an all-or-nothing demand, offering little scope for compromise (Boles, 1979).

As we saw, the ERA proposal was first formulated by the National Woman's Party. With the achievement of suffrage, the Party conducted a survey which showed considerable legal discrimination against women, particularly in the areas of property, child guardianship and divorce (Banks, 1981, p. 156). It submitted the proposed Equal Rights Amendment to Congress in 1923 and then every following year until 1971. Although most feminist organisations including the League of Women Voters, the Women's Joint Congressional Committee and the Women's Bureau objected to the Amendment because it seemed to undermine protective legislation, the National Woman's Party was not entirely alone. By the 1930s it had the support of the influential National Federation of Business and Professional Women's Clubs (NFBPWC) and the National Association of Women Lawyers (Banks, 1981, p. 207).

In 1940 the Amendment was endorsed by the Republican Party, and in 1944 the Democratic Party. Already in 1945 it was approved for the first time by the House of Representatives, but opposition was still too entrenched for it to proceed further. Though in 1950 and in 1955 it even passed the Senate this was with the addition of the unacceptable 'Hayden rider' requiring that the amendment 'shall not be construed to impair any rights, benefits or exemptions now or hereafter conferred by law, upon persons of the female sex' (see Freeman, 1975, p.211). It was the upsurge of feminism at the end of the 1960s that gave the ERA its real chance.

What *is* the Equal Rights Amendment and why do its supporters believe it to be so essential to sexual equality? It is proposed as an amendment to the American Constitution and was originally worded: 'Men and women shall have equal rights throughout the United States and every place subject to its jurisdiction'. Since 1943 the wording has been changed to 'Equality of rights under the law shall not be denied or abridged by the United States or by any State on account of sex'.

One obvious advantage of such an Amendment would be its symbolic force. As Greenberg writes, 'From a moral standpoint, a constitutional amendment is the highest sanction in our legal system' (Greenberg, 1977, p. 1). It became a rallying focus for the new feminist movement, rather like suffrage was in the nineteenth century, though with the same dangers. The crucial argument for the ERA is that it would provide a more effective and uniform basis for establishing women's equal rights in law. Legislative advance has been slow and shaky. In particular the courts, which have assumed a central role in interpretation and therefore implementation, have yet firmly to establish the principle that sex is an irrelevant distinction in applying the law. The closest they came to setting such a precedent was in 1974 when, in *Frontiero* v. *Richardson*, four of the nine Supreme Court Justices maintained that 'statutory distinctions between the sexes often have the effect of invidiously relegating the entire class of females to inferior legal status without regard to the actual capabilities of its individual members' (cited by Sachs and Wilson, 1978, p. 213).

While there is no nationally established principle of sex equality, and while the courts are so influential in constructing the law, interpretations of women's rights vary enormously not only within federal law but from state to state. For instance some states still exempt women from jury service. In South Carolina a married woman still has no rights to matrimonial property during marriage or rights to more than one-third of it if widowed. The alternatives to an Equal Rights Amendment to deal with this situation are discussed by Sachs and Wilson (1978). One is to continue to seek favourable laws and court judgements, a 'piecemeal approach', but, as they comment, 'Piecemeal legislation reform began almost one hundred and fifty years ago with the Married Women's Property Acts. It could drag on for another one hundred and fifty and still not achieve full equality for women' (ibid., p. 222). Another option is to argue that equality of the sexes before the law is already implied in an existing clause of the Constitution. The most likely candidate is the clause in the Fourteenth Amendment providing 'equal protection' of the laws. But the courts have shown no inclination to interpret the clause in this way and much legal opinion is in any case against further manipulation of the Fourteenth Amendment. So neither alternative seems too promising.

Advocates of the ERA can further cite the advantages that have accrued to women in the sixteen states which have already passed their own version of an Equal Rights Amendment. Brown *et al.*, for instance, finds that while the number of cases brought under state ERAs is not yet large, 'the results on the whole have been very favourable' (Brown *et al.*, 1977, p. 29).

If the feminist arguments for an ERA are persuasive, the procedure for a Constitutional Amendment is daunting. Amendments can be introduced, in theory, by either Congress or two-thirds of the states, though in practice it has always been by Congress. Congress must then ratify the proposed amendment by a two-thirds majority of both Houses, before submitting it to the states. Three-quarters of the states, or their legislatures, must approve and although there is no time-limit set down for this process in the Constitution, convention prescribes seven years.

Notwithstanding, it seemed as the 1970s opened as if nothing could stop the ERA.

An important step in the growth of feminist support for the Amendment was in 1967 when NOW incorporated it into its programme. This provoked the withdrawal of NOW's United Auto Workers contingent though they rejoined two years later. At the same time less militant feminist organisations were coming round. This is partly because Title 7 of the 1964 Civil Rights Act already by implication invalidated states' protective legislation. Research was also exposing how state labour laws often restricted rather than protected women (Freeman, 1975, p. 212). In 1969 the Women's Bureau, under its new Director, Elizabeth Koontz, declared its support for the Amendment, an endorsement echoed by both the Citizens' Advisory Council on the Status of Women, set up by Kennedy in 1963, and Nixon's Task Force on Women's Rights and Responsibilities, established in 1969. The massive women's strike on 26 August 1970, which commemorated the fiftieth anniversary of the Nineteenth Amendment and demanded an ERA, was a highpoint in the unity and effectiveness of the new feminism.

The House Judicial Committee had been sitting on the amendment proposal for twenty years. Against this background of swelling feminist support, Congresswoman Martha Griffiths was finally able to dislodge it. Specifically, Freeman suggests that she called in a number of favours owed her by particular Committee Chairmen. She also helped form a National Ad Hoc Committee for the ERA amongst Congress employees which, together with the NFBPWC, mounted a formidable lobby of Congress. Once out of the Judicial Committee, the Amendment had an easy passage in the House but the Senate continued to resist.

Meanwhile the ERA campaign steadily gathered momentum. Embracing radical feminist groups, women in government and more than fifty national organisations including Common Cause and Americans for Democratic Action, it lobbied in person and also, according to Freeman, sent some key Congress members over 1500 letters a month. In October 1971 the House again passed the ERA, by an overwhelmingly majority. In March 1972, despite the ingenious efforts at obstruction of Senator Sam Ervin in the Judiciary Committee's Sub-Committee on Constitutional Amendments, the Senate approved it by eighty-four votes to eight.

Why, after fifty years of neglect, did the ERA suddenly receive such whole-hearted endorsement from the national legislature? The main reason was pressure from the women's movement, most of all direct pressure, but also its indirect influence on the climate of public opinion: polls indicated by the beginning of the 1970s a majority in favour of extending women's rights (Boles, 1979). But this pressure had to win over the legislators. Freeman argues that the ERA appealed to them first because it was 'simple, straightforward, consonant with traditional American values', did not clash with partisan loyalties and did not cost anything. Second, the ERA could be said to fall into the category of civil rights policy-making. On such issues it has been suggested that the chief influence on Congress members is their constituencies. Here it is significant that the tremendous lobbying on behalf of the ERA was not matched by opposing forces, which were taken by surprise and disunited (Freeman, 1975, p. 216).

The Amendment still required states' approval. Boles finds it remarkable in view of the extent of support for the ERA in 1972 that states' ratification was not automatic. Certainly within three months nineteen, and within a year thirty, states had ratified. But thereafter things slowed down dramatically. By 1977 only 35 of the requisite 38 states had ratified and three of these subsequently rescinded their ratification, though the constitutionality of this action was in doubt.

Opponents of the ERA reacted swiftly to its passage through Congress. The most important national organisation has been Stop-ERA (the National Committee to Stop the ERA) formed late in 1972 and led by Mrs Phyllis Schafly, a former member of the John Birch Society. Already by the beginning of 1973 it claimed several thousand members and branches in 26 states, especially in the South and Mid-West. It was assisted by Jacquie Davidson's Happiness of Women, established in 1971, which, together with its offshoot, the League of Housewives, reported 10,000 members in all 50 states by the end of 1972 (Boles, 1979). But, the campaign was always supported by a number of right-wing organisations, such as the John Birch Society and the American Conservative Union; and, like abortion, the ERA came to be identified as a target issue by the New Right. Some ERA supporters suspected the FBI, insurance companies and the southern textile industries of financing their opponents, but without providing effective proof. But there is no doubt that opposition to the ERA was augmented by Viguerie's amazing letter-writing organisation, already referred to.

None the less, Boles suggests that opposition was mounted primarily at state level, with little national co-ordination. The emphasis of state campaigns was on persuading supporters to write to legislators and on influencing public opinion, rather than directly approaching the decision-makers. Though some of the arguments employed were apparently 'reasonable' – that the Amendment is too vague, unnecessary or inappropriate, even that this is a matter which individual states should decide for themselves – much of the opposition's case was more unscrupulously emotional. The ERA was depicted as a threat to family life and a sanction to homosexual marriage, unisex dormitories for children and unisex public lavatories. Women's potential eligibility for military service was also emphasised.

What kind of women campaigned against the ERA? Two studies converged in their finding that such women were typically housewives, less educated than Amendment supporters, politically conservative and religious (66 per cent of a Texas sample belonged to a fundamentalist church). Perhaps most striking was the finding that they had not, usually, been politically active before. It was the apparent threat to their values that had stirred them to such (unfeminine?) behaviour (Tedin *et al.*, 1977; Arrington and Kyle, 1978).

ERA proponents did not immediately grasp the seriousness of the opposition. The ERA Ratification Council, formed after Congress had approved the Amendment, was an umbrella coalition with no staff and a tiny budget. As it became clear that the process of ratification was slowing down, a new national coalition, ERA-America, was set up, which in January 1976 took offices in Washington DC. Even so, Boles wrote, 'it has not had the resources to play the central role envisioned and by 1978 serves primarily as a steering committee and clearing-house for information on the Amendment' (Boles, 1979, p. 66). On the other hand all the main national feminist organisations supported the campaign. According to Freeman, when NOW realised in 1978 that ratification would not be achieved by the 1979 deadline, it decided to give the issue priority though the proposal to go against all constitutional precedents in seeking deferral of the deadline originated with two feminist law students and was not taken seriously at first. Once persuaded, NOW's leadership sought both to mobilise mass support – 100,000 women took part in the ERA march in 1978 – and to convince legislators (Freeman, 1982). Representatives Elizabeth Holtzman and Margaret Heckler first agreed to take up the issue and Gertzog (1984) sees getting Congressional agreement to defer the deadline (though not by the seven years originally envisaged by NOW) as the one solid achievement of the Congress Women's Caucus, a question all its members could agree on.

Despite this breathing space, the pro-ERA lobby could not succeed in securing ratification in sufficient states by the new deadline of June 1982. By the beginning of 1982 still only 35 states had ratified; those remaining were mainly hard-core conservative at a time when conservative attitudes were tending to harden. Although the majority of American women now recognised the existence of sex discrimination, and 170 national organisations supported the ERA while only 25 had publicly declared themselves against it, the effective constituency campaign mounted by Stop-ERA which legislators felt obliged to heed, and the decentralisation of America's federal system, had conspired to create an impasse. In 1983 the Equal Rights Amendment was reintroduced in Congress to be defeated by six votes. One feminist observer was confident that 'there is little doubt that the eighties will see equal rights for all citizens written into the US Constitution' (Rawalt, 1983, p. 73) but such optimism already seems premature.

Failure to get ratification was an undoubted setback but feminists have continued to campaign for equal rights and specifically equal employment rights. Perhaps the central line of attack has been back with the issue of equal pay. Kahn and Grune (1982) describe the emergence of a national movement for pay equity by the late 1970s. The aim was to replace the definition of equal pay in the 1964 Act, whose possibilities as a basis for improving women's pay it was felt had been largely exhausted, by one requiring equal pay for work of comparable value. Title 7 of the Civil Rights Act, as expanded upon by the accompanying Bennett amendment, was designed to cover pay but despite a seemingly favourable Supreme Court ruling in June 1981, in *Gunther* v. *Washington*, it remained unclear what evidence was needed to demonstrate discrimination. Under President Carter, the EEOC, the Women's Bureau and the OFCCP all took up the question of pay equity and indeed the OFCCP was about to issue new regulations in 1980 when the Reagan administration came in and deferred them.

As the campaign developed a National Committee was founded in 1980, with representatives of 13 organisations on its ruling board, to co-ordinate the strategies of sympathetic labour organisations, Working Women and the Committee of Labour Union Women, feminist lawyers and others. In response an organised opposition emerged; many unions have objected to the campaign and employers have formed an Equal Employment Advisory Council to pool their collective experience of resistance to equal employment policies. Even so by 1985, 46 of the 50 states were acting on the comparable worth formula, in some form.

Although pay equity has aroused opposition it is still far less controversial than the ERA and seems representative of the current pragmatic approach of liberal feminism. Even less contentious appears to be the economic equity package being introduced into Congress by the Caucus for Women's Issues, as the Congress-women's Caucus is now known, and designed to correct discrimination in areas such as insurance, retirement, tax law, employment and health care.

But as in Britain, recession and the Reagan administration's policies have convinced some reformist feminists that the question of employment equality has to be tackled more broadly. As mentioned in Chapter 1, there is growing concern at the 'feminisa-tion of poverty' and the corresponding realisation that activities need to address the specific problems of poorer women. It is in this direction, for instance, that Wider Opportunities for Women has moved, either themselves providing training and re-employment programmes or putting pressure on government bodies to do so (Fleming, 1983). Likewise many feminists have grasped the inter-dependence of women's employment prospects and their domestic responsibilities. They have become interested in alternative ways of structuring work (see Stoper, 1982). In particular there have been experiments, sanctioned by Congress or individual state legisla-tures, with forms of flexi-time or expansion of categories of part-time work, though feminists understand that these will not of themselves resolve women's underlying disadvantages.

Equal employment policy-making: comparative perspectives

How does policy-making for equal employment compare in Britain and the United States? In each case the process has been shaped by the context of government and political institutions. As in the abortion question, pressure for legislation in Britain centred upon Parliament, though also, through the TUC, directly on Government itself, while in the United States it focused on state legislatures initially, on Congress, the Presidency and the courts. At this legislative stage, however, differences in the two party systems were *more* significant than for abortion reform. In Britain equal opportunity was a party political issue in that both parliamentary parties espoused it, though it was not an object for inter-party conflict. As a consequence, extra-parliamentary lobbying was much less important than in the United States.

But differences in institutional context were most crucial in the elaboration and implementation of policy. One reason for this is that British policy consciously drew on American precedents; in particular the EOC was based on the EEOC. Meehan suggests that this institutional transplant did not 'take' successfully because of two specific differences in British and American governmental tradition, the role of the judiciary and the ethos of the bureaucracy. The mechanisms adopted to promote equal opportunity relied heavily on adjudication. But while the United States expects its courts to make policy through interpreting the law, in Britain no such explicit tradition exists. This is one reason why British courts, including the tribunals, have been more cautious, even half-hearted, in applying the acts, especially the Sex Discrimination Act. Two further features of the American legal system were missing in Britain: the ability of courts to refer to Congressional debate to clarify the intent behind legislation and the right to present cases on behalf of a class of individuals, not just one individual (Meehan, 1982, pp. 14–15).

Secondly, the United States governmental bureaucracy is much more explicitly 'political' than Britain's. The EEOC, as initially set up, was weak, yet through the militancy of its client group – the blacks – it became an innovative force. Most importantly, individual women within it helped to galvanise an effective women's lobby which then demanded and legitimised a more aggressive stance on sex equality. The EOC's statutory powers were greater. But first the initial composition of the Commission reflected 'corporatist' interests with little feminist input. Second, it inherited the British assumption of a sharp divide between the 'democratically' selected policy-makers and the 'neutral' staff. Byrne and

Lovenduski suggest that this neutrality may be a defensive response to 'adversarial politics', to the alternation in power of parties with opposing programmes (Byrne and Lovenduski, 1978). But Meehan points out that in practice there has been little difference in the way Labour and Conservative Governments treat the EOC. As a result of this combination of timid Commissioners and the expectation of staff neutrality, many staff members who were more feminist than the Commissioners felt frustrated and turnover rates were extremely high. But neither individual Commissioners, nor until recently, staff members, sought more seriously to mobilise a feminist lobby, preferring to cultivate contacts within governing bodies.

We can draw a further contrast between equal employment and abortion policy-making in terms of the interests mobilised around them, in the two countries. The primary groups mobilised by the abortion issue, other than women themselves, are the Church and the medical profession. In both Britain and the United States the main medical associations eventually threw their weight behind abortion reform, though it is suggested less because of their belief in women's right to choose than because they resent interference from whatever quarter in their own professional right to decide (see Shapiro, 1982).

As an ultimately 'redistributory' issue, equal opportunity is of concern to organised business and labour. The support of labour was vital in both countries to the passage of equal pay legislation. By the 1960s, neither business nor labour organisations at national level opposed the principle of equal opportunity, but in the United States pressures from business interests helped to water down the original proposals for Title 7 and the US Chamber of Commerce later opposed the strengthening of the EEOC. We have also noted the hardening of employers' opposition to pay equity in the 1980s. At the local level, both business and unions have often been unco-operative in implementing the legislation in both countries. This reflects the ambivalence, at best, of the male-dominated unions towards measures that can only improve women's employment opportunities at the expense of men's. Though employers in the long run might profit from more competition within the workforce, in the short run they want to minimise friction.

In both the United States and Britain, equal pay, and even equal opportunities, were legislated for without active feminist pressure. Though there was little danger of outright repeal, feminists had to campaign for effective implementation. Here, arguably, American feminists have been more successful than British. In particular, Britain has failed to evolve the kind of policy network between feminists inside government and women's organisations outside that has become so conspicuous in the United States since the mid-1960s. Even now that the EEC has, through its Directives and related measures, provided a valuable new lever for women's employment rights, British women's organisations have been slow to make use of it (Meehan, 1985). This is partly due to the different administrative styles of the implementing agencies, but also to the absence of a substantial contingent of reformist feminists in the British women's movement.

Finally, in equal opportunity policy-making, the implementation stage is even more important than for abortion reform. No doubt the legislation on its own has some educational and legitimising effect, but without effective implementation it may simply reinforce women workers' general cynicism. In both countries legislators have underwritten the principle of equal opportunity largely because it costs them nothing and accords with the dominant political ideology. They have also tacitly recognised vested economic interests by leaving implementation with agencies that have each, initially and in their different ways, been severely handicapped. The difference between the two countries has perhaps depended on what politically active feminists could salvage.

Though equivalent detailed case-studies of the *process* of equal employment policy-making in other Western democracies are not yet available, it is possible to make some further comparisons with other West European countries. All EEC member states have of course been under pressure to comply with its Directives, but they have differed widely in the character of their pre-existing policies and implementing machinery as well as in their response to that pressure.

In France, the most far-reaching initiatives were associated with the Ministry of Women's Rights, under Yvette Roudy, 1982–3. New laws required employers to produce annual reports on the comparative positions of male and female employees, and in establishments of over 300, to prepare action programmes. In 1984 an equal opportunities commission (*Conseil Supérieur de l'Ègalité Professionelle entre les Hommes et les Femmes*) was established to monitor adherence to these laws. In Italy, legislation in the 1970s was designed to bring employment law into line with EEC requirements but its implementation has been left primarily to the collective bargaining process, a pattern reinforced by the delegation of many economic planning functions to regional bodies. In 1984 the Ministry of Labour set up a national committee for equal opportunities. West Germany was slow to react to EEC measures and a law passed in 1980, to promote equality in the labour market, was widely held to be inadequate. At regional or *Länd* level, equal rights agencies, beginning with Hamburg's, formed in 1979, have been judged more effective but still lack sanctions. On the other hand in the Netherlands 'a sex equality apparatus was established during the 1970s and early 1980s which is today the most extensive and comprehensive in Europe' (Lovenduski, 1986a, p. 276). Its progress even so has not been entirely smooth; the Secretary of State appointed to co-ordinate policy in 1977, Mrs Kraaijeveld, rapidly antagonised much of the women's movement by her approach to her responsibilities.

Indeed, in all EEC countries, equal employment policies have been adopted and some implementing machinery established. Only in Britain, Ireland and France have specific equal opportunities commissions been instituted. Britain's is theoretically the most powerful, but it is generally agreed that Ireland's has been the most effective. Yet throughout the EEC, results have been extremely disappointing with relatively few cases brought under the legislation, the difficulty of overcoming inertia of entrenched interests and institutions and a general reluctance on the part of employers to go much further in the direction of positive action (Lovenduski, 1986a; Vallance and Davies, 1986).

As usual the picture in Scandinava, though by no means ideal, offers a number of contrasts. Here by and large policy is based on a more positive model of equal employment objectives, as opposed to the generally 'negative' emphasis on preventing sex discrimination in the rest of Europe. We have already noted that trditional reformist feminism retained its vitality through the inter-war years. By the early 1960s women's sections, especially in social-democratic parties, were pressing for more effective equality policy. They were greatly assisted by the fact that from the 1950s these countries had been experiencing a labour shortage and consequently trade unions were early on willing to take up issues of women's employment opportunities and moreover to concede that this meant tackling the question of their domestic role. In fact in the 1970s there was little recourse to legislation as such. Equality Councils were established between 1972 and 1976 in all five Nordic countries but within these employers and unions were fully represented and it was they who, in collective agreements, incorporated the Councils' recommendations. Following the fall of the Social Democratic government in Sweden in 1976, there was some departure from this approach. Under its successor centrist government, in 1979 an Act was passed on Equality between Men and Women, which contained measures to prevent sex discrimination, to be enforced mainly by the Labour Court, but also rules requiring employers to promote equality of opportunity. Implementation of these positive programmes was made the responsibility of an Equal Opportunities Ombudsman and an Equal Opportunities Commission, but could not overrule existing collective agreements between unions and employers' organisations.

As Eduards *et al.* (1985) comment, assessments of the effects of these policies are still relatively few. Women in Scandinavia are also feeling the impact of recession; unemployment rates have risen more rapidly than for men. Even so equal employment policies appear to go much further than in most Western countries in recognising the need to provide not simply equal treatment for women as individuals but compensating special treatment in terms of positive action and measures to alleviate and redistribute domestic responsibilities.

Feminism and policy-making in the 1980s

While one conclusion of this chapter must be that feminism in the 1970s extracted real and valuable resources and powers from policy-makers, the process was slow and arduous, and as constantly reiterated in these pages, feminists have encountered a much more hostile environment in which to pursue their policy demands in the 1980s. This is primarily due to economic recession which has undermined women's economic opportunities and more generally narrowed their life options, disheartened and perhaps deepened divisions amongst feminists and increased government reluctance to implement equal rights policies. Added to this, a political backlash has coalesced, most visibly in the United states where opposition to the ERA and abortion have been central planks not only of the Moral Majority but of the New Right and have found some echoes in the policies of the Reagan administration. This political reaction bases its arguments around the sanctity and vulnerability of the family. Such a theme can also be discerned in some of the analysis of the British New Right. David cites Ferdinand Mount, whose book, *The Subversive Family*, attacks feminist approaches to the family (though it does also oppose state intervention designed to sustain family life). He advised the Cabinet's secret Family Policy Group, some of whose recommendations were leaked to the press in 1982 and appeared to favour returning caring responsibilities to the family and encouraging mothers to stay at home (David, 1986, p. 152). I remain unconvinced, however, by any claim either that anti-feminism is somehow the distinctive ingredient of New Right ideology in Britain or that these attitudes permeate the Conservative government, as suggested for instance by Tusscher (1986) and David (1986). As I have shown successive measures under the present Conservative government have undercut women's rights but that has not necessarily been their central objective. Patrick Jenkin has been much quoted for declaring 'If the Good Lord had wanted us to have equal rights to go out to work, he wouldn't have created men and women' (cited by Gardiner, 1983, p. 195) but other Ministers appear more committed to the principle of equality of opportunity.

This is still scant comfort to feminists witnessing the seemingly irresistible erosion of the legislative advances painfully won or defended through the 1970s. Naturally many have questioned the point of pressing for further legislative change. Sex discrimination law has been particularly disappointing. Anti-discrimination law of any kind is notoriously difficult to frame and implement, since it goes 'beyond and behind the equal and universal subject of private law to confront the sociological reality of inequality between individuals and groups' (Cotterell, cited by Vallance and Davies, 1986, p. 115). Yet if policy does fail to go beyond formal equality for women as individuals to tackle the systematic sources of inequality in their 'dual' role, it will make very little real difference to women.

This brings us back to the question of the best strategy or strategies for feminism, which is one of the issues to be taken up in the Conclusion.

Conclusion

This book has made no claim to offer a single, unified interpretation of the relationship between women and politics. Its primary aim has been rather to introduce readers to this complex and often emotive question, and to the wide-ranging debate that surrounds it. All the same, some interim conclusions have emerged.

I suggested initially that political science and feminism can learn from each other. First, we have seen some of the ways in which political science can learn from feminism. This is not to say that feminism itself is a single, coherent and comprehensive world-view, or even that it has the potential to become one. But the various perceptions that feed into it can supplement, even correct for, the male bias, and its conceptual consequences, of traditional political science.

Political science has been obliged to pay more attention to the role of women in public politics. The facile sterotypes of women's participation in grass-roots politics have been modified, and in some instances confounded. Women, it turns out, do not necessarily vote at lower rates than men, particularly when account is taken of such intervening variables as age and education. Sex differences in participation rates for other forms of conventional politics, though still apparent, are not immutable but tend to narrow over time and are in many respects negligible in the United States. Moreover women play a significant, if unquantified, part in less conventional political activities: 'ad hoc' actions, 'community action' from the late 1960s, industrial action, the peace movement, revolutionary, nationalist and even 'terrorist' politics, as well as indirectly through women's associations and, in traditional societies, more informal modes of political influence.

Though husbands may still disproportionately mould their wives' political behaviour, there is much less evidence to suggest that daughters follow their fathers. More importantly, the cliché of female conservatism has been exposed as both conceptually unsubtle and, even where it refers simply to voting for conservative parties, no longer always true. Indeed in the United States, Scandinavia, and possibly Britain a 'gender gap' in the opposite direction shows signs of emerging. Women's tendency to personalise politics is now being questioned, while, in so far as women are still found to be more moralistic than men, feminists point out that this does not automatically signify political naïveté. The assertion that women are more apolitical than men appears more tenable, but even then it is suggested such an observation assumes an unjustifiably narrow conception of politics.

Though some ostensibly feminist accounts echo traditional political science in emphasising socialisation as the explanation for women's political behaviour, others have demonstrated the importance of situational and even structural constraints. A few have also shown how the present character of public politics itself deters women from grass-roots participation.

If, prior to second wave feminism, women's under-representation within political leadership was already obvious, it is only now that the full extent of this under-representation is being measured and regarded as a 'problem'. As more data appear, it becomes increasingly clear that women's presence varies inversely with the power attached to political office. At the same time, women do very much better in certain countries, notably those of Scandinavia, than in others. What must also be acknowledged is the slow but steady increase in the rate at which women attain political office almost everywhere – with the British and US national legislatures a disturbing exception – and in the numbers of women in political roles and occupations which provide a reservoir for leadership recruitment.

Some feminists again emphasise the effects of childhood socialisation on women's political achievement, but others, to my mind more usefully, stress situational constraints and more especially the consequences, given the present division of labour between the sexes, of motherhood. On the other hand, features of existing political institutions themselves are probably as important as deterrents. The institutionalisation of politics already poses problems for women still tethered to a private domain and role. Criteria for eligibility, the step-ladder process of political advancement, anticipation of male bias and even outright discrimination continue to militate against women. Finally, we have learned more about the behaviour of women politicians. Where earlier they were seen as 'naturally' cut out for feminine responsibilities, now it often appears that there is little significant difference in the style and orientation of male and female politicians, when they are free to choose.

In these ways political science has had to revise its assumptions about women's conventional political participation. Feminism has also been one source of pressure to examine less conventional political activities. But further, under the impact of radical feminism, political science's conception of what politics actually is has been challenged.

Feminism has helped to point up the limitations of viewing politics purely as a self-conscious activity. In elaborating the notion of male dominance, or patriarchy, and despite weaknesses in the way this notion to date has been theorised, women have drawn attention to the importance of power relationships – in this case between the sexes – as the framework for more explicit political processes. Women's political participation simply cannot be understood, for instance, without some appreciation of the 'systematic' nature of male dominance.

The most distinctive feminist criticism of conventional political thinking, however, has been of the assumption that there are two separate spheres, one private and apolitical, the other public and political. This does not necessarily mean denying the practical and ideological force of the assumption. As we have seen, it has been used ideologically to justify women's exclusion from public politics, while women's actual confinement to a narrow domestic sphere has been a major brake upon effective political participation. At the same time the public-private convention has masked the crucial interdependence of these spheres. Not only have women's private roles limited and largely defined their public contribution, but public policies have confirmed their 'private' obligations. Even now, throughout most of the world, though with partial exceptions such as Sweden, East Germany and Cuba, public policies assume and reinforce women's primary responsibility for the care of young children and the home. Similarly, public policies seek to regulate women's fertility and sexuality. Access to abortion is still restricted, and contested, in Britain and the United States; effective and moderns means of birth control are still in short supply in most state socialist countries.

Feminism, then, has not simply broadened our picture of women's political participation. It points to important conceptual limitations of the discipline. Carroll none the less remains sceptical of the extent to which its more radical criticisms have yet been absorbed by mainstream political science, or even by many self-styled feminist political scientists themselves (Carroll, 1979). Lovenduski also argues that 'in what is one of the minor tragedies of contemporary scholarship, an absorption of a rather constrained branch of women's studies by a one-dimensional academic discipline has taken place'. Compared with, say sociology she suggests that feminist consciousness made a relatively late appearance in political science. Reflecting this late start, and also perhaps the status insecurity of women political scientists, feminist scholarship within the discipline has itself tended to concentrate on exposing sexism in earlier work and gathering new data within parameters still largely ordained by tradition (Lovenduski, 1981, p. 83). Writing in the mid-1980s, Meehan still found political science lagging behind 'in dealing with questions about women's rights and roles' (Meehan, 1985, p. 121).

In keeping with these comments, we have found that studies of less conventional aspects of women's political participation were undertaken not typically by political scientists but by sociologists or anthropologists. Most discussion of the impact of public policy on women is amongst historians, students of social policy and lawyers. Even feminism, as a political movement, has received little attention from political scientists, with the notable exception of Freeman (1975). The influence of feminist thinking is probably greatest in the area of political philosophy and political thought (see, for instance, Okin, 1980; Elshtain, 1981; Jaggar, 1983). Overall, however, feminism is changing political science only very slowly.

As a corollary, there remain major lacunae in the study of women and politics, which it is to be hoped future political science research, by feminists, but also by men, will remedy. Too little is known of women's participation in such conventional forms of grass-roots politics as interest groups, and much too little is known of their unconventional political activities as a whole. Too great an emphasis has been placed on women's under-representation in

national legislatures and not enough on their role within bureaucracies and corporate organisations. In the last few years more studies
have appeared that compare or generalise from public policies
towards women and the process by which they emerge (notably
Meehan, 1985; Lovenduski and Outshoorn, 1986) but much further
work in this area remains.

The lessons of political science for feminists are in some ways less
obvious than vice versa. It is not so much what political science
explicitly says as its focus and perspective that feminism could
usefully incorporate. Most of all, political science assumes the
importance of public politics and provides a framework for
analysing it.

Given the convention of a distinct and apolitical private sphere
with which women have been associated, political science might
seem to imply that public politics mattered primarily for men. But
the preceding pages have shown how in practice policy-making has
significantly shaped *women's* status. In nineteenth-century
England, laws and policies surrounding a woman's rights in
marriage, fertility and sexuality, her role as mother and home-
maker, and income, education and employment possibilities,
together conspired to enforce her dependence upon men and
responsibility for care of children and the home. Subsequent policy
changes have reduced her direct dependence upon men – though
the state has taken on some aspects of the husband's role. They have
increased her control of her own fertility and sexuality. But they
have yet substantially to challenge her primary domestic role.
Indeed, Brophy and Smart, examing innovations in family law in
the early 1970s, argue that the were still predicated upon women's
responsibilities as mothers (Brophy and Smart, 1981). In Britain
and elsewhere, improvements in women's status have resulted less
from any recognition of women's 'rights' than from such overriding
considerations as the health and welfare of children and, related to
that, the 'quality' of the population, the stability if not of the
individual family then of the 'family-household system', and the
personnel requirements of economy and defence. In many Third
World countries they have also been shaped by attitudes to the West
and 'westernisation'. Male-dominance of policy-making has furthermore ensured that the changes demanded by such priorities in no
way jeopardise, even during war or revolution, men's privileged
position.

It is in this context that feminists need to care about the under-representation of women in public politics. Political science nowadays documents more fully the scale of that under-representation. It also helps to identify some of the more immediate ways in which women's political presence could be increased, through quota systems, adoption of the party-list system of proportional representation, women's caucuses and so forth (see pp. 145–51). Admittedly, stepping up female numbers is not enough since women politicians, it appears, are not necessarily more feminist than men. But Vallance has for instance shown how, against the background of a vigorous women's movement, in Britain during the 1970s, women MPs were able to secure important gains for their sex in a number of policy areas (Vallance, 1979). Similarly Vallance and Davies (1986) have demonstrated the impact of a, relatively, strong female presence in the European Parliament on policy for women.

This raises the issue of reform versus revolution that has exercised the contemporary women's movement. The analysis of the previous chapter makes clear that 'reformist' feminist politics wins no dramatic victories. Specifically, progress in Britain and the United States, in the areas of abortion policy and equal rights and employment opportunity, is modest and precarious. On the other hand, without reformist politics would any progress have been made at all? Even given the supporting groundswell of women's liberation, as well as changing priorities in public policy, it needed reformist feminism to make the most of the opportunities as they came. If women's position is deteriorating now, we do not know how much worse it would be, if feminist activists and politicians were not continuing to try to monitor and resist backsliding.

At a more abstract level, there *is* a case for saying that the kinds of changes in social organisation that could truly 'liberate' women would require a virtual revolution. Advanced capitalism may well be dependent upon the family–household system, and women's traditional role within it, to reproduce the social order that maintains it – though this seems largely true of existing state socialist societies also. Revolutionary feminists may argue that no real reform can be achieved within the present system, because the gain of one underprivileged group can only be at the expense of another, or that reforms are only sufficiently effective to prolong the life of an oppressive regime by making it superficially more acceptable (see Harding, 1976). However, reform and revolution are not necessarily incompatible. Simone de Beauvoir wrote in response to the similar debate within the French women's movement: 'In my opinion, extracting reforms from government can be a step on the road to revolution, so long of course as one does not leave it at that but makes these reforms the basis for further demands' (1977, p. 11). This may be particularly true, as far as feminist objectives are concerned. A purely feminist revolution – for instance, along the lines sketched by Firestone – is difficult to conceive and certainly a very long way off. If, on the other hand, feminists envisage women's liberation within the context of a broader social revolution, then, given the male-dominated character of existing society, including all institutions and groupings of the Left, they will be much better able to establish the legitimacy and centrality of their programme if feminist values have already been widely accepted and women's status strengthened.

It is possible therefore that, especially for feminists, the choice between reform and revolution is not as fundamental as is sometimes made out. At the same time the arguments and findings reviewed in this book point to three further dilemmas for the women's movement which may require more attention. One is that as the numbers of women drawn into feminist activities or ways of thought grow, as also our knowledge of the condition of women in differing regions and social groupings become more detailed, so we are forced to face the immense variety of women's experience and the limitations of a single, simple feminist analysis or strategy. It seems there is no going back to innocence, we have to welcome and incorporate this diversity but somehow hold on to what as women we have in common. Organisationally this is made easier by the movement's extreme decentralisation and structural versatility.

In view of this first problem, options regarding the second, the best immediate political strategy, are already limited. But I have argued that the cause of women and feminism currently appears to be best advanced in some kind of alliance with the Left. Despite its all too frequent male chauvinism, especially in the past, despite the hostility of state socialist systems to feminism, at present whether one is concerned with the promotion of women in political parties or as parliamentary candidates, measures to improve women's representation in senior bureaucratic and local government posts, government policies and funding to further women's rights in such areas as employment, childcare, abortion or rape, alliance with the

Left appears to hold out the best practical opportunities. But this emphatically does not mean dissolving autonomous feminist organisations or relinquishing separate feminist identity. The experience of feminists in France is all too recent a warning of the risks this would entail.

If the Left, nowadays, is more responsive to feminist demands, it has still been particularly slow to grapple with the fundamental issue of women's association with mothering and domestic responsibilities. In assessing different theories of male dominance, I argued that due weight should be given to biological sex differences, even though these could not be understood on their own as either 'causing' or justifying sex inequality. In particular, men have been able to define women's social role on the basis of their reproductive functions. Women have been consigned primarily to the domestic sphere with all the implications that follow for their public role. Women's responsibility for small children is perhaps the key constraint on the 'supply' of women for leading political positions, determining both the age at which they become available and the qualifications they bring. On the other hand, the most consistent and enduring consequence of public policy for women has been to shore up their mothering role.

The way that society – or perhaps, one should say, men – have linked women's part in biological reproduction with child-rearing faces feminists with their third, and possibly their most crucial dilemma, with the need to understand both what they want and how to get it. They can firstly decide to glorify women's mothering propensity, an approach that seems to be gaining popularity amongst both 'cultural' radical feminists and conservative feminists. Either this becomes the basis of a pro-woman, separatist philosophy and strategy, or, as Friedan (1983) now urges, the beginning of a return to the family as the essential site of what is good in society and a new more understanding partnership with men (shades of Beveridge?). This latter line in particular seems to me potentially dangerous, given the present economic and political climate. It over-estimates the extent to which feminist values have been absorbed by society at large and under-estimates the threats to feminist achievements in the 1980s.

Alternatively women can react sharply against the limitations of a mothering role, protesting that they are potentially the same, and as good as, men (currently) are. This was the response of many radical feminists in the early phase of second-wave feminism, for instance in the United States and France (see Duchen, 1986; Eisenstein, 1984) but it soon became apparent that it was avoiding the central issue. To deny motherhood, as Hein (1976) argues, is to accept men's low evaluation of women's traditional activities. Or, as Oakley asks, 'Are having and rearing children and a sense of emotional connection with, and responsibility for others, capacities that women must be liberated from in order to become human – that is, to become equal to men?' (1979, p. 394). Still more fundamentally, we must assume that women will go on having children, that the future of society requires it and most men and women want it. Women's liberation has to encompass this and build it into any realistic strategy.

Which may suggest a third option that prescribes 'androgyny' or role-sharing, both in domestic and public life. In so far as this is the most promising approach, there are still problems about how to realise it. Adams and Winston argue that the vital immediate question is how to respond to women's dual role. They believe that, while the long-term solution is to draw men into domestic role-sharing, in the meantime women's status can only be raised by enabling them to compete more successfully in the 'male' public sphere. It must be made easier for women to combine domestic responsibilities with outside employment through maternity leave, child-care provision, liberal birth-control policies and the like. As the value of women's contribution both to public life and to the family purse is incontrovertibly established, so men will come under increasing pressure to share domestic chores. One snag, as they concede, with this approach, is that in the short run it will serve to lower still further the status of child care and housework, making them less not more attractive to men (Adams and Winston, 1980). There is obviously a contradiction between women asserting the value of 'parenthood' and family life and their demanding public policies to reduce their domestic burden. But the valid criticism of this position (see for instance Banks, 1981, p. 237; Eisenstein, 1984) is that it still fails to transcend the existing range and structure of male and female activities and to envisage a different social and economic order in which the organisation of 'work', divisions between work and home, the nature of the 'family' could all be radically altered. As usual we must achieve a balance between being able to recognise the irrationality and waste of resources and human spirit embodied in the present system and, in the immediate, urgent present, working to improve women's options or prevent their further erosion.

Notes for further reading

Introduction

For a critique of male bias in political science see in particular Bourque and Grossholtz (1974); Carroll (1979); Evans (1980); Goot and Reid (1975); Iglitzin (1974); Jaquette (1974).

Chapter 1: Women's Place in Society

On the question of the universality of male dominance see Rosaldo (1974) and Goldberg (1979) and, on its relationship to other forms of oppression, Lees (1986). Problems with the concept of patriarchy are discussed by Beechey (1979) and in Barrett (1980). Sayers (1982) is a clear and interesting guide to the debate about the implications for women's status of biological sex differences, while the essays in Rosaldo and Lamphere (1974) are useful on cultural approaches, and Barrett (1980) is an especially competent survey of Marxist feminist theory.

Chapter 2: Women's Political Behaviour

The best, up-to-date sources on Europe are Lovenduski (1986a), and, for the Nordic countries, Haavio-Mannila et al. (1985), but for individual countries the essays in Lovenduski and Hills (1981b) are still very useful. Wolchik's essay on Eastern Europe remains particularly helpful, as does Hills (1981a) on Britain. Baxter and Lansing (1980) draw together much of the material on conventional forms of women's political participation in the United States. For Latin America, see Jaquette (1976), Aviel (1981) and Reif (1986).

Chapter 3: Women in Political Elites

Most informative, for Europe, are again Lovenduski (1986a) and Haavio-Mannila et al. (1985) but also Mossuz-Lavau and Sineau (1984). Hills

(1981a) and Vallance (1979) remain useful for Britain. Vallance and Davies (1986) provide a very thorough treatment of the European Parliament and for the US two helpful sources are Gertzog (1984) and the regular 'fact sheets' of the Center for the American Woman and Politics at the Eagleton Institute of Politics, Rutgers University.

Chapter 4: How Politics Affects Women

This chapter pieces together material from a great number of sources in order to make its argument. The analysis of Adams and Winston (1980) was a valuable starting-point. On specific countries, Lewis (1983c) is useful for Britain. Lapidus (1978) and Heitlinger (1979) provided much of the material for Eastern Europe. For China, two useful full-length studies of the impact of post-revolutionary policies on women are Davin (1976) and Croll 1978). For the section on policies in the Third World I found especially helpful Jayawardena (1986), Rogers (1983) and specifically on abortion, Francome (1984).

Chapter 5: The Politics of the Women's Movement

Banks (1981) offers an interesting account of first-wave feminism in Britain and the United States, with an excellent bibliography. In addition Evans (1977) provides a comparative treatment of the movement in Europe and Australasia, while Jayawardena (1986) examines its impact in countries of the Middle East and Asia. On contemporary feminism, Freeman (1975) is good on the United States for the period she covers, Bouchier (1983) provides an extensive analysis of the movement both in the US and Britain and Coote and Campbell (1982) are also helpful for Britain. For European movements, see Lovenduski (1986a), and specifically on France Duchen (1986) and West Germany Altbach *et al.* (1984). Davies (1985) offers some rather fragmented insights into feminism in the Third World and Ashworth (1982) looks at the international movement.

Chapter 6: Feminism and Policy-making

For abortion policy-making in Britain see Marsh and Chambers (1981), and for a comparative perspective, Lovenduski and Outshoorn (1986). Meehan provides a very thoughtful comparison of equal employment policy-making in Britain and the United States (1985). Vallence and Davies (1986) are useful on the EEC dimension and essays in Boneparth (1982) and Tinker (1983) give further background on policy-making in the US.

Bibliography

Adams, C. T. and Winston, C. T. (1980) *Mothers at Work* (New York and London: Longman).

Ahmed, L. (1982) 'Feminism and Feminist Movements in the Middle East, a Preliminary Exploration: Turkey, Egypt, Algeria, People's Democratic Republic of Yemen', *Women's Studies International Forum*, vol. 5, no. 2.

Ainad-Tabet, N. (1980) 'Participation des Algériennes à la vie du pays', in Souriau (ed.).

Alexander, S. (1976) 'Women's Work in Nineteenth Century London: a Study of the Years 1820–50', in Mitchell and Oakley (eds).

Allin, P. and Hunt, A. (1982) 'Women in Official Statistics', in Whitelegg *et al.* (eds).

Altbach, E. H. (1984) 'The New German Women's Movement' in Altbach *et al.* (eds).

Altbach, E. H., Clausen, J., Schultz, D. and Stephan, N. (eds) (1984) *German Feminism: Readings in Politics and Literature* (Albany: State University of New York Press).

Amundsen, K. (1971) *The Silenced Majority* (New Jersey: Prentice-Hall).

Andersen, K. (1975) 'Working Women and Political Participation, 1952–1972', *American Journal of Political Science*, vol. 19, no. 3.

Ardill, S. and O'Sullivan, S. (1986) 'Upsetting An Applecart: Difference, Desire and Lesbian Sadomasochism, *Feminist Review*, no. 23.

Arrington, T. S. and Kyle, P. A. (1978) 'Equal Rights Amendment Activities in North Carolina', *Signs*, vol. 3, no. 3.

Ashworth, G. (1982) 'International Linkages in the Women's Movement', in P. Willetts (ed.) *Pressure Groups in the Global System: The Transnational Relations of Issue – Orientated Non-Governmental Organisations* (London: Francis Pinter).

Atkins, S. (1986) 'The Sex Discrimination Act 1975: The End of a Decade', *Feminist Review*, no. 24.

Aviel, J. E. (1981) 'Political Participation of Women in Latin America', *Western Political Quarterly*, vol. 34, no. 1.

Bamberger, J. (1974) 'The Myth of Matriarchy : Why Men Rule in Primitive Society', in Rosaldo and Lamphere (eds).

Bandarage, A. (1984) 'Women in Development: Liberalism, Marxism and

Marxist-Feminism', *Development and Change*, vol. 15, no. 3.

Banks, O. (1981) *Faces of Feminism* (Oxford: Martin Robertson).

Barker, D. L. (1978) 'The Regulation of Marriage: Repressive Benevolence' in Wakeford and Yuval-Davis (eds).

Barnes, S. H. and Kaase, M. (eds) (1979) *Political Action* (Beverly Hills: Sage).

Barrett, M. (1980) *Women's Oppression Today* (London: Verso).

Barrett, M. and McIntosh, M. (1979) 'Christine Delphy: Towards a Materialist Feminism?' *Feminist Review*, no. I.

Barrett, M. and McIntosh, M. (1985) 'Ethnocentrism and Socialist-Feminist Theory', *Feminist Review*, no. 20.

Barrett, M. *et al.* (1986) 'Feminism and Class Politics: A Round-Table Discussion', *Feminist Review*, no. 23.

Bashvekin, S. (1985) 'Changing Patterns of Politicization and Partisanship Among Women in France', *British Journal of Political Science*, vol. 15, no. 1.

Baude, A. (1979) 'Public Policy and Changing Family Patterns in Sweden, 1930–1977', in Lipman-Blumen and Bernard (eds).

Baxter, S. and Lansing, M. (1980) *Women and Politics: The Invisible Majority* (University of Michigan).

Beck, P. and Jennings, M. K. (1975) 'Parents as "Middlepersons" in Political Socialization', *Journal of Politics*, vol. 37, no. 1.

Beckwith, K. (1985) 'Feminism and Leftist Politics in Italy: The Case of UDI-PCI Relations', *West European Politics*, vol. 18, no. 4.

Beechey, V. (1977) 'Some Notes on Female Wage Labour in the Capitalist Mode of Production', *Capital and Class* no. 3.

Beechey, V. (1979) 'On Patriarchy', *Feminist Review*, no. 3.

Beechey, V. (1983) 'What's So Special about Women's Employment? A Review of Some Recent Studies of Women's Paid Work', *Feminist Review*, no. 15.

Benston, M. (1969) 'Political Economy of Women's Liberation', *Monthly Review* vol. 21, no. 4.

Bentzon, K. (1977) 'Comparing Women and Men's Political Attitudes and Behaviour in Denmark', European Consortium for Political Research.

Berkin, C. R. and Lovett, C. (eds) (1981) *Women, War and Revolution* (New York and London: Holmes & Meier).

Bernard, J. (1979) 'Women as Voters: From Redemptive to Futurist Role', in Lipman-Blumen and Bernard (eds).

Bevs, T. H. (1978) 'Local Political Elites: Men and Women on Boards of Education', *Western Political Quarterly*, vol. 13., no. 3.

Bhavnani, K. and Coulson, M. (1986) 'Transforming Socialist-Feminism: the challenge of Racism', *Feminist Review*, no. 23.

Bishop, N. (1979) 'Abortion: the Controversial Choice', in Freeman (ed.).

Black, J. H. and McGlen, N. E. (1979) 'Male-Female Political Involvement Differentials in Canada, 1965–74', *Canadian Journal of Political Science*, vol. 12, no. 3.

Blay, E. A. (1979) 'The Political Participation of Women in Brazil; Female Mayors', *Signs*, vol. 5, no. 1.

Blondel, J. (1965) *Voters Parties and Leaders* (London: Penguin).

Boals, K. (1975) 'Political Science', *Signs*, vol. 1, no. 1.

Boles, J. K. (1979) *The Politics of the Equal Rights Amendment* (New York and London: Longman).

Boneparth, E. (1977) 'Women in Campaigns: From Lickin' and Stickin' to Strategy', *American Politics Quarterly*, vol. 5, no. 3.

Boneparth, E. (ed) (1982) *Women, Power and Policy* (New York: Pergamon).

Boserup, E. (1970) *Women's Role in Economic Development* (New York: St Martin's Press).

Bouchier, D. (1979) 'The Deradicalisation of Feminism: Ideology and Utopia in Action', *Sociology*, vol. 13, no. 3.

Bouchier, D. (1983) *The Feminist Challenge* (London: Macmillan).

Boulding, E. (1976) *The Underside of History: A View of Women Through Time* (Boulder, Colorado: Westview Press).

Bourque, S. and Grossholtz, J. (1974) 'Politics an Unnatural Practice: Political Science Looks at Female Participation', *Politics and Society*, vol. 4, no. 4.

Brennan, T. and Pateman, C. (1979) 'Mere Auxiliaries to the Commonwealth: Women and the Origins of Liberalism', *Political Studies*, vol. 27, no. 2.

Breugel, I. (1979) 'Women as a Reserve Army of Labour: a Note on Recent British Experience', *Feminist Review*, no. 3.

Bristow, S. L. (1980) 'Women Councillors – An Explanation of the Under-representation of Women in Local Government', *Local Government Studies*, vol. 6, no. 3.

Brooke (1978) 'The Retreat to Cultural Feminism' in Redstockings.

Brophy, J. and Smart, C. (1981) 'From Disregard to Disrepute: The Position of Women in Family Law', *Feminist Review*, no. 9.

Brown, B., Freeman, A., Katz, H. and Price, A. (1977) *Women's Rights and the Law: The Impact of the Era on State Laws* (New York: Praeger).

Brown, J. K. (1975) 'Iroquois Women: An Ethnohistoric Note', in Reiter (ed.).

Brownmiller, S. (1975) *Against Our Will: Men, Women and Rape* (London: Secker & Warburg).

Bunster-Burotto, X. (1986) 'Surviving Beyond Fear: Women and Torture in Latin America', in Nash and Safa (eds).

Butalia, V. (1985) 'Indian Women and the New Movement', *Women's Studies International Forum*, vol. 18, no. 2.

Butler, D. and Stokes, D. (1974) *Political Change in Britain* (London: Macmillan).

Butler, D. and Kavanagh, D. (1980) *The British General Election of 1979* (London: Macmillan).

Byrne, E. (1978) *Women and Education* (London: Tavistock).

Byrne, P. and Lovenduski, J. (1978) 'Sex Equality and the Law in Britain', *British Journal of Law and Society*, vol. 5, no. 2.

Byrne, P. and Lovenduski, J. (1983) 'Two New Protest Groups: the Peace and Women's Movements', in H. Drucker, P. Dunleavy, A. Gamble and G. Peale (eds) *Developments in British Politics* (London: Macmillan).

Caine, B. (1982) Feminism, Suffrage and the Nineteenth Century English Women's Movement', *Women's Studies International Forum*, vol. 5, no. 6.

Caldwell, L. (1981) 'Abortion in Italy', *Feminist Review*, no. 7.

Caldwell, L. (1986) 'Feminism and Abortion Politics in Italy', in Lovenduski and Outshoorn (eds).

Cambridge Women's Studies Group (ed.) (1981) *Women in Society: Interdisciplinary Essays* (London: Virago).

Campbell, A., Converse, P., Miller. W. and Stokes, D. (1960) *The American Voter* (New York: John Wiley).

Carroll, B. (1979) 'Political Science, Part I: American Politics and Political Behaviour', *Signs*, vol. 5, no. 2.

Carroll, S. J. (1984) 'Women Candidates and Support for Feminist Concerns: The Closet Feminist Syndrome', *Western Political Quarterly*, vol. 37, no. 2.

Cartledge, S. (1980) 'Together Again?', *Spare Rib*, November.

Cassell, J. (1977) *A Group Called Women: Sisterhood and Symbolism in the Feminist Movement* (New York: David McKay).

Castles, F. (1981) 'Female Legislative Representation and the Electoral System', *Politics*, no. 3.

Cavendish, R. (1982) *Women on the Line* (London: Routledge & Kegan Paul).

Chaney, E. (1979) *Supermadre* (University of Texas).

Charzat, G. (1972) *Les Françaises Sont-elles des Citoyennes?* (Paris: Denöel Gonthier).

Cherpak, E. (1978) 'The Participation of Women in the Independence Movement in Gran Colombo, 1780–1830' in Lavrin A. (ed.) *Latin American Women* (Westport: Greenwood Press).

Christy, C. A. (1985) 'American and German Trends in Sex Differences in Political Participation', *Comparative Political Studies*, vol. 18, no. 1.

Cockburn, C. (1977) 'When Women Get Involved in Community Action', in Mayo (ed.).

Constantini, E. and Craik, K. (1977) 'Women as Politicians: the Social Background, Personality and Political Careers of Female Party Leaders', in Githens and Prestage (eds).

Cook, B. B. (1977) 'Sex Roles and the Burger Court', *American Politics Quarterly*, vol. 5, no. 3.

Cook, B. B. (1979) 'Judicial Attitudes and Decisions on Women's Rights: Do Women Judges Make a Difference?', unpublished paper presented to International Political Science Association Round Table on Sex Roles and Politics.

Coote, A. (1979) 'Equality: A Conflict of Interests', *New Statesman*, 31 August.

Coote, A. and Campbell, B. (1982) *Sweet Freedom* (London: Picador).

Coote, B. (1985) 'Woman a One Per cent Class', *The Observer* 21 July.

Costa, M. D. and James, S. (1972) *The Power of Women and the Subversion of the the Community* (Bristol: Falling Wall Press).

Costain, A. N. (1982) 'Representing Women: The Transition from Social Movement to Interest Group', in Boneparth (ed.).

Coveney, L. *et al.* (1984) *The Sexuality Papers* (London: Hutchinson).

Coultas, V. (1981) 'Feminists Must Face the Future', *Feminist Review*, no. 7.

Crewe, I. (1979) 'Who Swung Tory?', *The Economist*, 12 May.

Croll, E. (1978) *Feminism and Socialism in China* (London: Routledge & Kegan Paul).

Currell, M. (1974) *Political Woman* (London: Croom Helm).

Currell, M. (1978) 'The Recruitment of Women to the House of Commons', unpublished paper to the UK Political Studies Association Conference.

Dahl, T. S. and Snare, A. (1978) 'The Coercion of Privacy: A Feminist Perspective' in Smart, C. and Smart, B. (eds) *Women, Sexuality and Social Control* (London: Routledge & Kegan Paul).

Dahlerup, D. and Gulli, B. (1985) 'Women's Organisations in the Nordic Countries: Lack of Force or Counterforce?', in Haavio-Mannila *et al.* (eds).

Daly, M. (1978) *Gyn/Ecology (The Metaethics of Radical Feminism)* (London: The Women's Press).

Darcy, R. and Schramm, S. (1977) 'When Women Run Against Men', *Public Opinion Quarterly*, vol. 41, no. 1.

David, M. (1980) *The State, the Family and Education* (London: Routledge & Kegan Paul).

David, M. (1986) 'Moral and Maternal: The Family in the Right', in R. Levitas (ed.) *The Ideology of the New Right* (London: Polity Press).

Davies, M. (ed.) (1985) *Third World: Second Sex* (London: Zed Books).

Davin, D. (1976) *Woman-Work: Women and Party in Revolutionary China* (Oxford University Press).

Davis, E. G. (1971) *The First Sex* (New York: G. P. Putnam).

De Beauvoir, S. (1977) 'Introduction' to de Pisan and Tristan (eds).

Decter, M. (1973) *The New Chastity and Other Arguments Against Women's Liberation* (London: Wildwood Howe).

Deere, C. D. (1986) 'Rural Women and Agrarian Reform in Peru, Chile and Cuba', in Nash and Safa (eds).

De Giry, A. (1980) 'Les Femmes et la Politique en Grèce', in Souriau (ed.)

De la Chungara, D. B. (1985) 'Women and Organisation' in Davies (ed.)

Delamont, S. (1980) *The Sociology of Women* (London: George Allen & Unwin).

Delazay, Y. (1976) 'French Judicial Ideology in Working-Class Divorce', in Barker. D. L. and Allen, S. (eds) *Sexual Divisions and Society: Pricess and Change* (London: Tavistock).

Delmar, R. (1972) 'What is Feminism?', in Wandor, M. (ed.) *The Body Politic* (London: Stage 1).

Delphy, C. (1977) *The Main Enemy* (London: Women's Research and Resources Centre Publications).

De Pisan, A. and Tristan, A. (1977) *Histoires du MLF* (Paris: Calmann-Lévy).

Devaud, M. S. (1968) 'Political Participation of Western European Women', *Annuals of the American Academy of Political and Social Science*, vol. 375.

Diamond, I. (1977) *Sex Roles and the State House* (New Haven and London: Yale University Press).

Diaz, G. (1985) 'Roles and Contradictions of Chilean Women in the Resistance and Exile', in Davies (ed.).

Dobash, R. E. and Dobash, R. (1980) *Violence Against Wives* (Newton Abbot: Open Books).

Dowse, R. and Hughes, J. (1971) 'Girls, Boys and Politics', *British Journal of Sociology*, vol. 22, no. 1.

Dowse, R. and Hughes, J. (1972) *Political Sociology* (London and New York: John Wiley).

Draper, P. (1975) '!Kung Women: Contrasts in Sexual Egalitarianism in Foraging and Sedentary Contexts', in Reiter (ed.).

Duchen, C. (1986) *Feminism in France: From May '68 to Mitterand* (London: Routledge & Kegan Paul).

Durham, M. (1985) 'Family, Morality and the New Right', *Parliamentary Affairs*, vol. 38, no. 2.

Duverger, M. (1955) *The Political Role of Women* (New York: UNESCO).

Edholm, F., Harris, O. and Young, K. (1977) 'Conceptualising Women', *Critique of Anthropology*, vol. 3, nos 9 and 10.

Edholm, F. (1982) 'The Unnatural Family', in Whitelegg *et al.* (eds).

Eduards, M. L. (1981) 'Sweden', in Lovenduski and Hills (eds).

Eduards, M. L. (1986) 'Equality Policy Contradictions – the Case of Sweden', unpublished paper presented for the European Consortium of Political Research at Goteborg.

Eduards, M. L., Halsaa, B. and Skjeie, H. (1985) 'Equality, how Equal?: Public Equality Policies in the Nordic Countries', in Haavio-Mannila *et al.* (eds).

Einhorn, B. (1980) 'Women in the German Democratic Republic: Reality Experiences and Reflected', unpublished paper presented to the UK Political Studies Association Conference.

Eisenstein, H. (1984) *Contemporary Feminist Thought* (London: Unwin).

Eisenstein, Z. (ed.) (1979) *Capitalist Patriarchy and the Case for Socialist Feminism* (New York: Monthly Review Press).

Elshtain, J. B. (1974) 'Moral Woman and Immoral Man: A Consideration of the Public-Private Split and its Political Ramifications', *Politics and Society*, vol. 4, no. 4.

Elshtain, J. B. (1975) 'The Feminist Movement and the Question of Equality', *Polity*, vol. 7, no. 4.

Elshtain, J. B. (1981) *Public Man, Private Women* (Oxford: Martin Robertson).

Elshtain, J. B. (1982) 'Feminism, Family and Community', *Dissent*, Fall.

Encel, S., Mackenzie, N. and Tebbutt, M. (1975) *Women and Society* (London: Malaby Press).

Engels, F. (1972) *Origin of the Family, Private Property and the State* (New York: Pathfinder Press).

Epstein, C. F. (1981) 'Women and Power: The Roles of Women in Politics in the United States', in Epstein and Coser (eds).

Epstein, C. F. and Coser, R. L. (eds) (1981) *Access to Power: Cross-National Studies of Women and Elites* (London: George Allen & Unwin).

Equal Opportunities Commission (1981) *Fifth Annual Report, 1980* (Manchester).

Ergas, Y. (1982) 'Feminism and the Italian Party System: Women's Politics in a Decade of Turmoil', *Comparative Politics*, vol. 14, no. 3.

Etienne, M. and Leacock, E. (eds) (1980) *Women and Colonization: Anthropological Perspectives* (New York: Praeger).

Evans, J. (1980) 'Women in Politics: A reappraisal', *Political Studies* vol. 28, no. 2.

Evans, J. *et al.* (eds) (1986) *Feminism and Political Theory* (London: Sage).

Evans, R. J. (1977) *The Feminists: Women's Emancipation Movements in Europe, America and Australasia, 1840–1920* (London: Croom Helm)

Evans, S. (1979) *Personal Politics: The Roots of Women's Liberation in the Civil Rights Movement and the New Left* (New York: Knopf).

Fawcus, S. (1981) 'Abortion and the Cuts', in Feminist Anthology Collective (ed.).

Feminist Anthrology Collective (ed.) (1981) *No Turning Back: Writings from the Women's Liberation Movement 1975–80* (London: The Women's Press).

Finch, S. *et al.* (1986) 'Socialist-Feminists and Greenham', *Feminist Review*, no. 23.

Finkelstein, C. A. (1981) 'Women Managers: Career Patterns and Changes in the United States', in Epstein and Coser (eds).

Firestone, S. (1970) *The Dialectic of Sex* (London: Paladin).

Flannery, K. and Roelofs, S. (1984) 'Local Government Women's Committees' in J. Holland (ed.) *Feminist Action 1* (London: Battle Axe Books).

Fleming, J. (1983) 'Wider Opportunities for Women: The Search for Equal Employment', in Tinker (ed.).

Flora, C. B. and Lynn, N. B. (1974) 'Women and Political Socialization: Considerations of the Impact of Motherhood', in Jaquette (ed.).

Francis, J. G. and Peele, G. (1978) 'Reflections on Generational Analysis: Is There a Shared Political Perspective Between Men and Women?', *Political Studies*, vol. 26, no. 3.

Francome, C. (1984) *Abortion Freedom: A Worldwide Movement* (London: George Allen & Unwin).

Fraser, A. S. (1983) 'Insiders and Outsiders: Women in the Political Arena', in Tinker (ed.).

Freeman, J. (1975) *The Politics of Women's Liberation* (New York and London: Longman).

Freeman, J. (1979) 'The Women's Liberation Movement: Its Origins, Organizations, Activities and Ideas', in Freeman (ed.).

Freeman, J. (1982) 'Woman and Public Policy: An Overview', in Bone-parth (ed.).

Freeman, J. (ed.) (1979) *Women: A Feminist Perspective* (California: Mayfield).

Friedan, B. (1963) *The Feminist Mystique* (London: Penguin).

Friedan, B. (1983) *The Second Stage* (London: Abacus).

Friedl, E. (1967) 'The Position of Women: Appearance and Reality', *Anthropological Quarterly*, vol. 4, no. 3.

Froggett, L. (1981) 'Feminism and the Italian Trade Unions: *L'Acqua in Gabbia*: A Summary and Discussion', *Feminist Review*, no. 8.

Gallagher, A. (1977) 'Woman and Community Work', in Mayo (ed.).

Gallagher, M. (1984) '166 Who Rule: The Dail Deputies of November 1982', *Economic and Social Review*, vol. 15, no. 4.

Gardiner, J. 'Women, Recession and the Tories', in S. Hall and M. Jacques (eds) *The Politics of Thatcherism* (London: Lawrence & Wishart).

Gardiner, J., Himmelweit, S. and McIntosh, M. (1980) 'Women's Domestic Labour', in Malos, E. (ed.) *The Politics of Housework* (London: Allison & Busby).

Gehlen, F. (1969) 'Women in Congress: Their Power and Influence in a Man's World', *Transaction*, vol. 6, no. 11.

Gehlen, F. (1977) 'Women Members of Congress: A Distinctive Role' in Githens and Prestage (eds).

Gelb, J. (forthcoming) 'Social Movement "Success": A Comparative Analysis of Feminism in the US and UK', in C. Mueller and M. F. Katzenstein (eds) *Changing Paradigms: New Theoretical Perspectives for the Women's Movements of Western Europe and the United States*.

Gertzog, I. N. (1984) *Congressional Women: Their Recruitment, Treatment and Behavior* (New York: Praeger).

Giele, J. Z. (1977a) 'Introduction: Comparative Perspectives on Women', in Giele and Smock (eds.)

Giele, J. Z. (1977b) 'United States: A Prolonged Search for Equal Rights', in Giele and Smock (eds).

Giele, J. Z. and Smock, A. C. (eds) (1977) *Women: Roles and Status in Eight Countries* (New York: John Wiley).

Githens, M. (1977) 'Spectators, Agitators or Lawmakers: Women in State Legislatures', in Githens and Prestage (eds).

Githens, M. and Prestage, J. (1977) 'Introduction', in Githens and Prestage (eds).

Githens, M. and Prestage, J. (eds) (1977a) *A Portrait of Marginality: The Political Behavior of the American Woman* (New York: David McKay).

Gittell, M. and Shtob, T. (1980) 'Changing Women's Roles in Political Volunteerism and Reform of the City', *Signs*, vol. 5, no. 3.

Goldberg, S. (1979) *Male Dominance: The Inevitability of Patriarchy* (London: Abacus).

Goldstein, L. F. (1979) 'Sex and the Burger Court: Recent Judicial Policy Making toward Women', in Palley and Preston (eds).

Goode, W. J. (1963) *World Revolution and Family Patterns* (Glencoe, Illinois: Free Press).

Goodin, J. M. (1983) 'Working Women: The Pros and Cons of Unions', in Tinker (ed.).

Goodin, R. E. (1982) 'Banana Time in British Politics', *Political Studies* vol. 30, no. 1.

Goot, M. and Reid, E. (1975) *Women and Voting Studies: Mindless Matrons or Sexist Scientism* (Beverly Hills: Sage).

Gordon, L. (1977) *Woman's Body, Woman's Right* (London: Penguin).

Gough, K. (1975) 'The Origin of the Family', in Reiter (ed.).

Gould, C. C. and Wartofsky, M. W. (eds) (1976) *Women and Philosophy* (New York: G. P. Putnam).

Greenberg, H. (1977) 'The ERA in Context: Its Impact on Society', in Brown *et al.*

Greenstein, F. (1965) *Children and Politics* (Yale University Press).

Greenwood, K. and King, L. (1981) 'Contraception and Abortion', in Cambridge Women's Studies Group (ed.).

Gregory, J. (1982) 'Equal Pay and Sex Discrimination: Why Women Are Giving Up the Fight', *Feminist Review*, no. 10.

Gruberg, M. (1968) *Women in American Politics* (Wisconsin: Acadaemia Press).

Gyford, J. (1985) *The Politics of Local Socialism* (London: George Allen & Unwin).

Haavio-Mannila, E. (1981) 'Women in the Economic, Political and Cultural Elites in Finland, in Epstein and Coser (eds).

Haavio-Mannila, E. (1981a) 'Finland' in Lovenduski and Hills (eds).

Haavio-Mannila, E. *et al.* (eds) (1985) *Unfinished Democracy: Women in Nordic Politics* (New York and Oxford: Pergamon).

Hall, J. (1981) 'West Germany', in Lovenduski and Hills (eds).

Halligan, J. and Harris, P. (1977) 'Women's Participation in New Zealand Local Body Elections', *Political Science*, vol. 29, no. 2.

Hanisch, C. (1978) 'The Liberal Takeover of Women's Liberation', in Redstockings.

Hamner, J. (1978) 'Violence and the Social Control of Women', in Wakeford and Yuval-Davis (eds).

Harding, S. G. (1976) 'Feminism, Reform or Revolution?', in Gould and Wartofsky (eds).

Hargadine, E. (1981) 'Japan', in Lovenduski and Hills (eds).

Hayler, B. (1979) 'Abortion', *Signs*, vol. 5, no. 2.

Hecht, D. and Yuval-Davis, N. (1978) 'Ideology without Revolution: Jewish Women in Israel', *Khamsin*, no. 6.

Hein, H. (1976) 'On Reaction and the Women's Movement', in Gould and Wartofsky (eds).

Heiskanen, V. (1971) 'Sex Roles, Social Class and Political Consciousness', *Acta Sociologica*, vol. 14, nos. 1–2.

Heitlinger, A. (1979) *Women and State Socialism* (London: Macmillan).

Hendessi, M. (1986) 'Fourteen Thousand Women Meet: Report from Nairobi, July 1985', *Feminist Review*, no. 23.

Hernes, H. M. (1984a) 'Women and the Welfare State. The Transition from Private to Public Dependence', in H. Holter (ed.) *Patriarchy in a*

Welfare Society (Norway: Universitetsforlaget).

Hernes, H. M. (1984b) *The Role of Women in Voluntary Associations and Organisations*, Part 3 of *The Situation of Women in the Political Process in Europe* (Strasbourg: Council of Europe).

Hernes, H. M. and Voje, K. (1980) 'Women in the Corporate Channel in Norway: A Process of Natural Exclusion?', *Scandinavian Political Studies*, vol. 3, no. 2.

Hernes, H. M. and Hänninen-Salmelin, E. (1985) 'Women in the Corporate System' in Haavio-Mannila *et al.* (eds).

Heron, E. (1980) 'The Mystique of Motherhood', *Time Out*, 21–27 November.

Higgins, P. J. (1985) 'Women in the Islamic Republic of Iran: Legal, Social and Ideological Change', *Signs*, vol. 10, no. 3.

Hightower, N. V. (1977) 'The Recruitment of Women for Public Office', *American Politics Quarterly*, vol. 5, no. 3.

Hills, J. (1978) 'Women in the Labour and Conservative Parties', unpublished paper presented to the UK Political Studies Association Conference.

Hills, J. (1981a) 'Britain', in Lovenduski and Hills (eds).

Hills, J. (1981b) 'Candidates, the Impact of Gender', *Parliamentary Affairs*, vol. 34, no. 2.

Hills, J. (1982) 'Women Local Councillors – A Reply to Bristow', *Local Government Studies*, vol. 8, no. 1.

Himmelweit, S. (1980) 'Abortion: Individual Choice and Social Control', *Feminist Review*, no. 5.

Holden, A. (1980) 'How the "Steel Magnolia" Blossomed in the White House: A Profile of Rosalynn Carter', *Observer Magazine*, 3 August.

Holland, B. (ed.) (1985) *Soviet Sisterhood* (London: Fourth Estate).

Hoskyns, C. (1985) 'Women's Equality and the European Community', *Feminist Review*, no. 20.

Hough, J. (1977) 'The Impact of Participation: Women and the Women's Issue in Soviet Policy Debates', in *The Soviet Union and Social Science Theory* (Harvard University Press).

Humphries, J. (1981) 'Protective Legislation, the Capitalist State, and Working Class Men: The Case of the 1842 Mines Regulation Act', *Feminist Review*, no. 7.

Hunter, E. (1979) 'A Woman's Place in in the House – or is it?', *New Statesman*, 22 June.

Husbands, C. (1986) 'Race and Gender', in H. Drucker, P. Dunleavy, A. Gamble and G. Peele (eds) *Developments in British Politics 2* (London: Macmillan).

Iglitzin, L. (1974) 'The Making of the Apolitical Woman: Femininity and Sex-Stereotyping in Girls', in Jaquette (ed.).

Iglitzin, L. (1977) 'A Case Study in Patriarchal Politics: Women on Welfare', in Githens and Prestage (eds).

Iglitzin, L. and Ross, R. (eds) (1976) *Women in the World* (Oxford and Santa Barbara: Clio Books).

Inglehart, M. (1981) 'Political Interest in West European Women: A

Historical and Empirical Comparative Analysis', *Comparative Political Studies*, vol. 14, no. 3.

Jackson, M. (1984) 'Sexology and the Social Construction of Male Sexuality', in Coveney *et al.*

Jacobs, M. (1978) 'Civil Rights and Women's Rights in the Federal Republic of Germany Today', *New German Critique*, no. 13.

Jaggar, A. (1976) 'Abortion and a Woman's Right to Decide', in Gould and Wartofsky (eds).

Jaggar, A. (1983) *Feminist Politics and Human Nature* (Sussex: Harvester Press).

Jancar, B. W. (1978) *Women Under Communism* (Johns Hopkins University Press).

Jaquette, J. (1973) 'Women in Revolutionary Movements in Latin America', *Journal of Marriage and the Family*, vol. 35, no. 2.

Jaquette, J. (1974) 'Introduction', in Jaquette (ed.).

Jaquette, J. (ed.) (1974) *Women in Politics* (New York: John Wiley).

Jaquette, J. (1976) 'Female Political Participation in Latin America', in Iglitzin and Ross (eds).

Jayawardena, K. (1983) 'The Feminist Challenge in the 18th Century', in Mies and Jayawardena

Jayawardena, K. (1986) *Feminism and Nationalism in the Third World* (London: Zed Press).

Jeffreys, S. (1984) "Free from All Uninvited Touch of Man": Women's Campaigns around Sexuality, 1880–1914', in Coveney *et al.*

Jennings, M. K. and Farah, B. G. (1980) 'Ideology, Gender and Political Action: A Cross-National Survey', *British Journal of Political Science*, vol. 10, no. 2.

Jennings, M. K. and Langton, K. P. (1969) 'Mothers versus Fathers: The Formation of Political Orientations among Young Americans',*Journal of Politics*, vol. 31, no. 2.

Jennings, M. K. and Niemi, R, G. (1971) 'The Division of Political Labour Between Mothers and Fathers', *American Political Science Review*, vol. 65, no. 1.

Jenson, J. (1985) 'Struggling for Identity: The Women's Movement and the State in Western Europe', *West European Politics*, vol. 18, no. 4.

Jones, H. J. (1975) 'Japanese Women in the Politics of the 70s', *Asian Survey*, vol. 15, no. 7.

Kahn, W. and Grune, J. A. (1982) 'Pay Equity: Beyond Equal Pay for Equal Work', in Boneparth (ed.).

Katzenstein, M. F. (1978) 'Towards Equality? Cause and Consequence of the Political Prominence of Women in India', *Asian Survey*, vol. 18, no. 5.

Katzenstein, M. F. (1984) 'Feminism and the Meaning of the Vote', *Signs*, vol. 10, no. 1.

Kearney, R. N. (1981) 'Women and Politics in Sri Lanka', *Asian Survey*, vol. 21, no. 7.

Kelley, J. and McAllister, I. (1983) 'The Electoral Consequences of Gender in Australia', *British Journal of Political Science*, vol. 13, no. 3.

Kelley, R. M. and Boutilier, M. (1978) *The Making of Political Woman: A Study of Socialization and Role Conflict* (Chicago: Nelson Hall).

Kincaid, D. D. (1978) 'Over his Dead Body: A Positive Perspective on Widows in the US Congress', *Western Political Quarterly*, vol. 31, no. 1.

King, E. C. (1977) 'Women in Iowa Legislative Politics', in Githens and Prestage (eds).

Kinsley, S. (1977) 'Women's Dependency and Federal Programs', in Chapman, J. R. and Gates M. (eds) *Women Into Wives: The Legal and Economic Impact of Marriage* (Beverly Hills: Sage).

Kirkpatrick, J. (1974) *Political Women* (New York: Basic Books).

Klein, E. (1984) *Gender Politics* (Harvard University Press).

Kolker, A. (1983) 'Women Lobbyists', in Tinker (ed.).

Kuhn, A. and Wolpe, A. (eds) (1978) *Feminism and Materialism* (London: Routledge & Kegan Paul).

Kyle, P. and Francis, M. (1978) 'Women at the Polls: The Case of Chile, 1970–71', *Comparative Political Studies*, vol. 11, no. 3.

Lafferty, W. (1978) 'Social Development and Political Participation: Class, Organization and Sex', *Scandinavian Political Studies*, vol. 1, no. 4.

Land, H. (1980) 'The Family Wage', *Feminist Review*, no. 6.

Lane, R. (1959) *Political Life* (Glencoe, Illinois: Free Press).

Lapidus, G. W. (1978) *Women in Soviet Society* (University of California Press).

Lawrence, E. (1977) 'The Working Women's Charter Campaign', in Mayo (ed.).

Lawrence, J. (1985) 'Feminist Leaders See Change Coming in Women's Movement', *The Kentucky Advocate*, 23 June.

Lazarsfeld, P. R., Berelson, B. and Gaudet, H. (1968) *The People's Choice* (Columbia University Press).

Lee, M. M. (1976) 'Why Few Women Hold Public Office: Democracy and Sex Roles', *Political Science Quarterly*, vol. 91, no. 2.

Lees, S. (1986) 'Sex Race and Culture: Feminism and the Limits of Cultural Pluralism', *Feminist Review*, no. 22.

Leibowitz, L. (1975) 'Perspectives on the Evolution of Sex Differences', in Reiter (ed.).

Leis, N. (1974) 'Woman in Groups: Ijaw Women's Associations', in Rosaldo and Lamphere (eds).

Lepper, M. (1974) 'A Study of Career Structures of Federal Executives: A Focus on Women', in Jaquette (ed.)

Levy, D. G. and Applewhite, H. B. (1980) 'Women of the Popular Classes in Revolutionary Paris, 1789–1795', in Berkin and Lovett (eds).

Lewis, Jane (1979) 'The Ideology and Politics of Birth Control in Inter-War England', *Women's Studies International Quarterly*, vol. 2, no. 1.

Lewis, J. (1983a) 'Introduction', in Lewis (ed.).

Lewis, J. (1983b) 'Dealing with Dependency: State Practices and Social Realities, 1870–1945', in Lewis (ed.).

Lewis, J. (ed.) (1983c) *Women's Welfare: Women's Rights* (London: Croom Helm).

Lewis, Jill (1981) '"Women's Liberation Ltd" – The French Controversy',

Spare Rib, July.

Lewis, P. (1971) 'The Female Vote in Argentina, 1958–65', *Comparative Political Studies*, vol. 3, no. 4.

Liddington, J. and Norris, J. (1978) *One Hand Tied Behind Us: The Rise of the Women's Suffrage Movement* (London: Virago).

Likimani, M. (1985) *Passbook Number F. 47927: Women and Mau Mau in Kenya* (London: Macmillan).

Lipman-Blumen, J. and Bernard, J. (eds) (1979) *Sex Roles and Social Policy* (Beverly Hills: Sage).

Lipset, S. M. (1963) *Political Man* (New York: Anchor Books).

Little, K. (1973) *African Women in Towns* (Cambridge University Press).

Loach, L. (1985) 'Local Government: What have Women Got to Lose?' *Spare Rib*, February.

Lobban, G. (1978) 'The Influence of the School on Sex-Role Stereotyping', in Chetwynd, J. and Hartnett, O. (eds) *The Sex Role System* (London: Routledge & Kegan Paul).

London Women's Liberation Campaign for Legal and Financial Independence and Rights of Women (1979) 'Disaggregation Now! Another Battle for Women's Independence', *Feminist Review*, no. 2.

Loughran, C. (1986) 'Armagh and Feminist Strategy: Campaigns Around Republican Women Prisoners in Armagh Jail', *Feminist Review*, no. 23.

Lovenduski, J. (1981) 'Towards the Emasculation of Political Science', in D. Spender (ed.) *Men's Studies Modified* (Oxford: Pergamon).

Lovenduski, J. (1986a) *Women and European Politics: Contemporary Feminism and Public Policy* (Brighton: Harvester Press).

Lovenduski, J. (1986b) 'Parliament, Pressure Groups, Networks and the Women's Movement: the Politics of Abortion Law Reform in Britain (1967–83)', in Lovenduski and Outshoorn (eds).

Lovenduski, J. and Hills, J. (1981a) 'Conclusion', in Lovenduski and Hills (eds).

Lovenduski, J. and Hills, J. (eds) (1981b) *The Politics of the Second Electorate* (London: Routledge & Kegan Paul).

Lovenduski, J. and Outshoorn, J. (eds) (1986) *The New Politics of Abortion* (London: Sage).

Lowi, T. J. (1964) 'American Business, Public Policy, Case-Studies and Political Theory', *World Politics*, vol. 16, no. 4.

Lynn, N. B. (1979) 'American Women and the Political Process', in Freeman (ed.).

Lynn, N. and Flora, C. (1977) 'Societal Punishment and Aspects of Female Political Participation: 1972 National Convention Delegates', in Githens and Prestage (eds).

McCourt, K. (1977) *Working-Class Women and Grass-Roots Politics* (Indiana University Press).

McDonagh, R. and Harrison, R. (1978) 'Patriarchy and Relations of Production', in Kuhn and Wolpe (eds).

McIntosh, M. (1978) 'The State and the Oppression of Women', in Kuhn and Wolpe (eds).

McIntosh, M. (1979) 'The Welfare State and the Needs of the Dependent

Family', in Burman (ed.).

Mackerras M. (1977) 'Do Women Candidates Lose Votes?', *Australian Quarterly*, vol. 49, no. 3.

McWilliams, N. (1974) 'Contemporary Feminism, Consciousness-Raising and Changing Views of the Political', in Jaquette (ed.).

Manderson, L. (1977) 'The Shaping of the Kaum Ibu (Women's Section) of the United Malays National Organization', *Signs*, vol. 3, no. 1.

Marsh, A. and Kaase, M. (1979) 'Background of Political Action', in Barnes and Kaase (eds).

Marsh, D. and Chambers, J. (1981) *Abortion Politics* (London: Junction Books).

Mayo, M. (ed.) (1977) *Women in the Community* (London: Routledge & Kegan Paul).

Mazumdar, V. (ed.) (1979) *Symbols of Power: Studies on the Political Status of Women in India* (Delhi: Allied Publishers).

Mead, M. (1935) *Male and Female* (London: Penguin).

Means, I. N. (1976) 'Scandinavian Women', in Iglitzin and Ross (eds).

Meehan, E. (1982) 'Implementing Equal Opportunity Policies: Some British-American Comparisons', *Politics*, vol. 2, no. 1.

Meehan, E. (1985) *Women's Rights at Work: Campaigns and Policy in Britain and the United States* (London: Macmillan).

Meehan, E. (1986) 'Women's Studies and Political Studies', in Evans *et al.* (ed.).

Merck, M. (1978) 'The City's Achievement: The Patriotic Amazonomachy and Ancient Athens' in Lipshitz, S. (ed.) *Tearing the Veil* (London: Routledge & Kegan Paul).

Miliband, R. (1977) *Marxism and Politics* (Oxford University Press).

Mies, M. (1983) 'Marxist Socialism and Women's Emancipation: the Proletarian Women's Movement in Germany 1860–1919', in Mies and Jayawardena.

Mies, M. and Jayawardena, K. (1983) *Feminism in Europe: Liberal and Socialist Strategies* (The Hague: Institute of Social Studies).

Millet, K. (1972) *Sexual Politics* (London: Abacus).

Milne, R. S. and Mackenzie, H. C. (1958) *Marginal Seat, 1955* (London: Hansard Society).

Minces, J. (1982) *The House of Obedience: Women in Arab Society* (London: Zed Press).

Mitchell, J. (1974) *Psychoanalysis and Feminism* (London: Penguin).

Mitchell, J. (1976) 'Women and Equality', in Mitchell and Oakley (eds).

Mitchell, J. and Oakley, A (eds) (1976) *The Rights and Wrongs of Women* (London: Penguin).

Molyneux, M. (1979a) 'Women and Revolution in the People's Democratic Republic of Yemen', *Feminist Review*, no. 1.

Molyneux, M. (1979b) 'Beyond the Domestic Labour Debate', *New Left Review*, no. 116.

Molyneux, M. (1985) 'Family Reform in Socialist States: The Hidden Agenda', *Feminist Review*, no. 21.

Morgan, D. (1975) *Suffragists and Liberals* (Oxford: Basil Blackwell).

Moses, J. C. (1976) 'Indoctrination as a Female Political Role in the Soviet Union', *Comparative Politics*, vol. 8, no. 4.

Mossuz-Lavau, J. (1986) 'Abortion Policy in France under Governments of the Right and Left (1973–84)', in Lovenduski and Outshoorn (eds).

Mossuz-Lavau, J. and Sineau, M. (1981) 'France', in Lovenduski and Hills (eds).

Mossuz-Lavau, J. and Sineau, M. (1983) *Enquete sur les Femmes et la Politique en France* (Paris: Presses Universitaires de France).

Mossuz-Lavau, J. and Sineau, M. (1984) *Women in the Political World in Europe*, Part 2 of *The Situation of Women in the Political Process in Europe* (Strasbourg: Council of Europe).

Muni, S. D. (1979) 'Women in the Electoral Process', in Mazumdar (ed.).

Murphy, I. (1973) *Public Policy on the Status of Women* (Lexington Press).

Murray, N. (1979) 'Socialism and Feminism: Women and the Cuban Revolution', *Feminist Review*, nos. 2 and 3.

Nash, J. (1977) 'Women in Development: Dependency and Exploitation', *Development and Change*, vol. 8, no. 2.

Nash, J. and Safa, H. (eds) (1986) *Women and Change in Latin America* (Massachusetts: Bergin and Garvey).

Navarro, M. (1977) 'The Case of Eva Perón', *Signs*, vol. 3, no. 1.

Nelson, B. (1984) 'Women's Poverty and Women's Citizenship: Some Political Consequences of Economic Marginality', *Signs*, vol. 10, no. 2.

Nelson, C. (1975) 'Public and Private Politics: Women in the Middle Eastern World', *American Ethnologist*, vol. 1, no. 3.

Nielson, H. J. and Sauerberg, S. (1980) 'Upstairs and Downstairs in Danish Politics: An Analysis of Political Apathy and Social Structure', *Scandinavian Political Studies*, vol. 3, no. 1.

Norderval, I. (1985) 'Party and Legislative Participation among Scandinavian Women', *West European Politics*, vol. 8, no. 4.

Norris, P. (1985a) 'The Gender Gap in Britain and America', *Parliamentary Affairs*, vol. 38, no. 2.

Norris, P. (1985b) 'Women's Legislative Participation in Western Europe', *West European Politics*, vol. 8, no. 4.

Norris, P. (1986a) 'Conservative Attitudes in Recent British Elections: An Emerging Gender Gap?', *Political Studies*, vol. 34, no. 1.

Norris, P. (1986b) 'Women in Congress: A Policy Difference?', *Politics* vol. 6, no. 1.

Northcutt, W. and Flaitz, J. (1985) 'Women, Politics and the French Socialist Government', *West European Politics*, vol. 8, no. 4.

Oakley, A. (1972) *Sex, Gender and Society* (London: Maurice Temple Smith).

Oakley, A. (1979) 'The Failure of the Movement for Women's Equality', *New Society*, 23 August.

O'Brien, M. (1981) *The Politics of Reproduction* (London: Routledge & Kegan Paul).

O'Donovan, K. (1979) 'The Male Appendage – Legal Definitions of Women', in Burman (ed.).

Okin, S. M. (1980) *Women in Western Political Thought* (London: Virago).

O'Laughlin, B. (1974) 'Mediation of Contradiction: Why Mbum Women Do Not Eat Chicken', in Rosaldo and Lamphere (eds).

O'Neill, W. L. (1969) *The Woman Movement: Feminism in the United States and England* (London: George Allen & Unwin).

Ortner, S. (1974) 'Is Female to Male as Nature is to Culture?', in Rosaldo and Lamphere (eds).

Orum, A. M., Cohen, R. S., Grasmuck, S. and Orum, A. W. (1974) 'Sex, Socialization and Politics', *American Sociological Review*, vol. 39, no. 2.

Outshoorn, J. (1986) 'The Rules of the Game: Abortion Politics in the Netherlands', in Lovenduski and Outshoorn (eds).

Palley, H. A. (1979) 'Abortion Policy Since 1973: Political Cleavage and its Impact on Policy Outputs', in Palley and Preston (eds).

Palley, M. L. and Preston, M. B. (eds) (1979) *Race, Sex and Policy Problems* (Lexington: Lexington Books).

Papanek, H. (1977) 'Development Planning for Women', *Signs*, vol. 3, no. 1.

Parker, J. (1981) 'Facilitating in Britain', *Spare Rib*, September.

Parkin, F. (1968) *Middle Class Radicalism* (Manchester University Press).

Parr, C. (1983) 'Women in the Military', in Tinker (ed.).

Peers, J. (1985) 'Workers by Hand and Womb – Soviet Women and the Demographic Crisis', in Holland (ed.).

Perrigo, S. (1986) 'Socialist-Feminism and the Labour Party: Some Experiences from Leeds', *Feminist Review*, no. 23.

Petchesky, R. (1979) 'Dissolving the Hyphen: A Report on Marxist-Feminist Groups 1–5', in Eisenstein (ed.).

Pharr, S. J. (1977) 'Japan: Historial and Contemporary Perspectives', in Giele and Smock (eds).

Phillips, M. (1980) *The Divided House* (London: Sidgwick & Jackson).

Place, H. (1979) 'Sex Roles in Women's Employment Opportunities in New Zealand', unpublished paper presented to the International Political Science Association Round Table on Sex Roles and Politics.

Pomper, G. (1975) *Voter's Choice* (New York: Dodd Mead).

Pope, B. C. (1980) 'Revolution and Retreat: Upper-Class French Women after 1789', in Berkin and Lovett (eds).

Randall, V. (1986a) 'Women and the Left in Western Europe: a Continuing Dilemma', *West European Politics*, vol. 9. no. 2.

Randall, V. (1986b) 'The Politics of Abortion in Ireland', in Lovenduski and Outshoorn (eds).

Randall, V. and Smyth, A. (forthcoming) 'Bishops and Bailiwicks: Obstacles to Women's Political Participation in Ireland', *Economic and Social Review*.

Rawalt, M. (1983) 'The Equal Rights Amendment', in Tinker (ed.).

Redstockings (1978) *Feminist Revolution* (New York: Random House).

Reed, E. (1975) *Women's Evolution* (New York: Pathfinder Press).

Reif, L. L. (1986) 'Women in Latin American Guerilla Movements: a Comparative Perspective', *Comparative Politics*, vol. 18, no. 2.

Reiter, R. (1975) 'Men and Women in the South of France: Public and Private Domains', in Reiter (ed.).

Reiter, R. (ed) (1975) *Toward an Anthropology of Women* (New York: Monthly Review Press).

Reiter, R. (1977) 'The Search for Origins', *Critique of Anthropology*, vol. 3, nos. 9 and 10.

Rendel, M. (1978) 'Legislation for Equal Pay and Opportunity for Women in Britain', *Signs*, vol. 3, no. 4.

Rich, A. (1977) *Of Women Born* (London: Virago).

Richards, J. R. (1980) *The Sceptical Feminist: A Philosophical Enquiry* (London: Routledge & Kegan Paul).

Rights of Women Europe Group (1980) 'The EEC and Women – A Case Study of British and European Legislation on Equal Pay', unpublished paper presented to the UK Political Studies Association Women's Group Conference.

Riley, D. (1979) 'War in the Nursery', *Feminist Review*, no. 2.

Riley, D. (1981) 'Feminist Thought and Reproductive Control: the State and "the Right to Choose"', in Cambridge Women's Studies Group (ed.).

Robarts, S. (1981) *Positive Action for Women* (London: National Council for Civil Liberties).

Robinson, D. A. (1979) 'Two Movements in Pursuit of Equal Employment Opportunity', *Signs*, vol. 4, no. 3.

Rodrigues, A. (1985) 'Mozambican Women After the Revolution', in Davies (ed.).

Rogers, B. (1983) *The Domestication of Women* (London and New York: Tavistock).

Rosaldo, M. (1974) 'Woman, Culture and Society: A Theoretical Overview', in Rosaldo and Lamphere (eds).

Rosaldo, M. and Lamphere, L. (eds) (1974) *Woman, Culture and Society* (Stanford University Press).

Rose, J. (1983) 'Femininity and its Discontents', *Feminist Review*, no. 14.

Rose, R. (1974) 'Britain: Simple Abstractions and Complex Realities', in Rose, R. (ed.) *Electoral Behaviour* (London: Collier-Macmillan).

Rossi, A. (1965) 'Equality between the Sexes: an Immodest Proposal', in Lifton, R. J. (ed.) *The Woman in America* (Boston: Houghton Mifflin).

Rossi, A. (1971) 'Sex Equality: The Beginnings of Ideology', in Thompson, M. (ed.) *Voices of the New Feminism* (Boston: Beacon Press).

Rowbotham, S. (1972) 'The Beginnings of Women's Liberation in Britain, in Wandor (ed.).

Rowbotham, S. (1973) *Woman's Consciousness, Man's World* (London: Penguin).

Rowbotham, S. (1974) *Hidden From History* (London: Pluto Press).

Rowbotham, S. (1979) 'The Women's Movement and Organizing for Socialism', in Rowbotham et al. (eds).

Rowbotham, S. (1984) (interview with Jean McCrindle) 'More than Just a Memory: Some Political Implications of Women's Involvement in the Miners' Strike, 1984–85', *Feminist Review*, no. 23.

Rowbotham, S., Segal, L. and Wainwright, H. (eds) (1979) *Beyond the Fragments* (London: Merlin Press).

Rubin, G. (1975) 'The Traffic in Women: Notes on the "Political Economy" of Sex', in Reiter (ed.).

Rupp, L. (1977) 'Mother of the Volk: The Image of Women in Nazi Ideology', *Signs*, vol. 3, no. 2.

Sabrowsky, J. (1979) *From Rationality to Liberation* (Westport: Greenwood Press).

Sachs, A. and Wilson, J. H. (1978) *Sexism and the Law* (Oxford: Martin Robertson).

Safilios-Rothschild, J. (1974) *Women and Social Policy* (New Jersey: Prentice-Hall).

St Clair, D. (1981) 'The New Right: Wrong Turn USA', *Spasre Rib*, September.

Salaff, J. and Merkle, J. (1970) 'Women in Revolution: the Lessons of the Soviet Union and China', *Berkeley Journal of Sociology*, vol. 15.

Sanday, P. (1974) 'Female Status in the Public Domain', in Rosaldo and Lamphere (eds).

Sapiro, V. (1979) 'Sex and Games: On Oppression and Rationality', *British Journal of Political Science*, vol. 9, no. 4.

Savara, M. (1985) 'Report of a Workshop on "Women, Health and Reproduction"', in Davies (ed.).

Sayers, J. (1982) *Biological Politics* (London: Tavistock).

Schlaeger, H. (1978) 'The West German Women's Movement', *New German Critique*, no. 13.

Schmidt, S. (1977) 'Political Participation and Development: The Role of Women in Latin America', *Journal of International Affairs*, vol. 30, no. 2.

Schmink, M. (1981) 'Women in Brazilian "Abertura" Politics', *Signs* vol. 7, no. 1.

Schoenberg, S. P. (1980) 'Some Trends in the Community Participation of Women in their Neighbourhoods', *Signs*, vol. 5, no. 3.

Schultz, D. (1984) 'The German Women's Movement in 1982', in Altbach *et al.* (eds).

Scott, H. (1974) *Does Socialism Liberate Women?* (Boston: Beacon Press).

Seccombe, W. (1974) 'The Housewife and Her Labour Under Capitalism', *New Left Review*, no. 83.

Segers, M. C. (1979) 'Equality, Public Policy and Relevant Sex Differences', *Polity*, vol. 11, no. 3.

Seligman, L., Kim, C. and Smith, R. (1974) *Patterns of Recruitment* (Chicago: Rand McNally).

Sertel, Y. (1980) 'La Femme Turque dans la Vie Politique', in Souriau (ed.).

Shabad, G. and Andersen, K. (1979) 'Candidate Evaluations and Women', *Public Opinion Quarterly*, vol. 43, no. 1.

Shapiro, R. (1982) 'Life: A Doctor's Right to Choose', *Spare Rib*, January.

Sharara, Y. P. (1978) 'Women and Politics in Lebanon', *Khamsin*, no. 6.

Shover, M. (1975) 'Roles and Images of Women in World War I Propaganda', *Politics and Society*, vol. 5.

Sigelman, L. (1976) 'The Curious Case of Women in State and Local

Government', *Social Science Quarterly*, vol. 56, no. 4.

Siltanen, J. and Stanworth, M. (1984) 'The Politics of Private Woman and Public Man', in Siltanen and Stanworth (eds).

Siltanen, J. and Stanworth, M. (eds) (1984) *Women and the Public Sphere* (London: Hutchinson).

Silver, C. B. (1977) 'France: Contrasts in Familial and Societal Roles', in Giele and Smock (eds).

Silver, C. B. (1981) 'Public Bureaucracy and Private Enterprise in the USA and France: Contexts for the Attainment of Executive Positions by Women', in Epstein and Coser (eds).

Simms, M. (1981) 'Australia', in Lovenduski and Hills (eds).

Sinkonnen, S. (1977) 'Women's Increased Political Participation in Finland: Real Influence or Pseudodemocracy?', unpublished paper presented to the European Consortium of Political Research Workshop.

Sinkonnen, S. (1985) 'Women in Local Politics', in Haavio-Mannila *et al.* (eds).

Skard, T. (1981) 'Progress For Women: Increased Female Representation in Political Elites in Norway', in Epstein and Coser (eds).

Skard, T. and Haavio-Mannila, E. (1985a) 'Mobilization of Women at Elections', in Haavio-Mannila *et al.* (eds).

Skard, T. and Haavio-Mannila, E. (1985b) 'Women in Parliament', in Haavio-Mannila *et al.* (eds).

Skocpol, T. (1979) *States and Social Revolutions* (Cambridge University Press).

Skold, C. B. (1981) 'The Job He Left Behind: American Women in the Shipyards During World War II', in Berkin and Lovett (eds).

Slocum, S. (1975) 'Woman the Gatherer: Male Bias in Anthropology', in Reiter (ed.).

Smith, R. (1982) *Women in the Press*, Report prepared for the Equality Working Party of the National Union of Journalists.

Smock, A. C. (1977) 'Ghana: From Autonomy to Subordination', in Giele and Smock (eds).

Smock, A. C. and Yousseff, N. H. (1977) 'Egypt: From Seclusion to Limited Participation', in Giele and Smock (eds).

Snell, M. (1979) 'The Equal Pay and Sex Discrimination Acts: Their Impact in the Workplace', *Feminist Review*, no. 1.

Souriau, C. (ed.) (1980) *Femmes et Politique Autour de la Mediterranée* (Paris: L'Harmattan).

South, J. (1985) 'And at the End of the Day Who is Holding the Baby?', *New Statesman* 15 November.

Sowerwine, C. (1982) *Sisters or Citizens? Women and Socialism in France Since 1876* (Cambridge University Press).

Spender, D. (1980) *Man Made Language* (London: Routledge & Kegan Paul).

Stacey, J. (1983) 'The New Conservative Feminism', *Feminist Studies*, vol. 9, no. 3.

Stacey, M. and Price, M. (1981) *Women, Power and Politics* (London: Tavistock).

Statistics Sweden (1985) *Women and Men in Sweden* (Stockholm).
Stephenson, J. (1975) *Women in Nazi Society* (London: Croom Helm).
Stiehm, J. (1976) 'Algerian Women: Honor, Survival and Islamic Social-ism', in Iglitzin and Ross (eds).
Stiehm, J. (1979) 'Women and Citizenship: Mobilization, Participation, Representation', unpublished paper presented to the International Political Science Association Congress.
Stoper, E. (1977) 'Wife and Politician: Role Strain Among Women in Public Office', in Githens and Prestage (eds).
Stoper, E. (1982) 'Alternative Work Patterns and the Double Life', in Boneparth (ed.).
Stoper, E. and Johnson, R. A. (1977) 'The Weaker Sex and the Better Half: The Idea of Women's Moral Superiority in the American Feminist Movement', *Polity*, vol. 10, no. 2.
Tabari, A. (1980) 'The Enigma of Veiled Iranian Women', *Feminist Review*, no. 5.
Tatalovich, R. and Daynes, B. W. (1981) *The Politics of Abortion. A Study of Community Conflict in Public Policymaking* (New York: Praeger).
Tedin, K., Brady, D., Buxton, M., Gorman, B. and Thompson, J. (1977) 'Social Backgrounds and Political Differences between Pro- and Anti-ERA Activists', *American Politics Quarterly*, vol. 5, no. 3.
Tedin, K., Brady, D. and Vedlitz, A. (1977) 'Sex Differences in Political Attitudes and Behaviour: The Case for Situational Factors', *Journal of Politics*, vol. 39, no. 2.
Tension, E. (1981) 'You Don't Need a Degree to Read The Writing On the Wall', in Feminist Anthology Collective (ed.).
Thalberg, I. (1976) 'Reverse Discrimination and the Future', in Gould and Wartofsky (eds).
Thiercelin, R. (1980) 'Les Femmes Espagnoles et la Politique', in Souriau (ed.).
Threlfell, M. (1985) 'The Women's Movement in Spain', *New Left Review*, no. 151.
Tiger, L. (1969) *Men in Groups* (New York: Random House).
Tinker, I. (1976) 'The Adverse Impact of Development on Women', in I. Tinker, M. Bransen and M. Buvinic (eds) *Women and World Development* (New York: Praeger).
Tinker, I. (ed.) (1983) *Women in Washington* (California and London: Sage).
Tolchin, S. (1977) 'The Exclusion of Women from the Judicial Process', *Signs*, vol. 2, no. 1.
Toner, B. (1977) *The Facts of Rape* (London: Arrow).
Toubia, N. (1986) 'Arab Women's Call to Unveil the Mind', *Spare Rib*, October.
Tusscher, T. (1986) 'Patriarchy, Capitalism and the New Right', in Evans *et al.* (eds).
Uhlaner, C. J. and Schlozman, K. L. (1986) 'Candidate Gender and Congressional Campaign Receipts', unpublished paper.
Vallance, E. (1979) *Women in the House* (London: Athlone Press).

Vallance, E. (1984) 'Women Candidates in the 1983 General Election', *Parliamentary Affairs*, vol. 37, no. 3.

Vallance, E. and Davies, E. (1986) *Women of Europe: Women MEPs and Equality Policy* (Cambridge University Press).

Verba, S. and Nie, N. (1972) *Participation in America* (New York: Harper & Row).

Verba, S. and Nie, N. and Kim, J. (1978) *Participation and Political Equality* (Cambridge University Press).

Vibhuti *et al.* (1985) 'The Anti-Rape Movement and Issues Facing Autonomous Women's Organisations in India', in Davies (ed.).

Vickers, J. M. and Brodie, M. J. (1981) 'Canada', in Lovenduski and Hills (eds).

Wainwright, H. (1979) 'Introduction', in Rowbotham *et al.* (eds).

Wakeford, J. and Yuval-Davis,, N. (eds) (1978) *Power and the State* (London: Croom Helm).

Walsh, B. (1984) 'The Influence of Turnout on the Results of the Referendum', *Economic and Social Review*, vol. 15, no. 3.

Walter, E. V. (1969) *Terror and Resistance* (Oxford University Press).

Wandor, M (ed.) (1972) *The Body Politic* (London: Stage 1).

Wandor, M. (1981) 'Where to Next?', *Spare Rib*, April.

Watt, I. (1984) 'Industrial Radicalism and the Domestic Division of Labour', in Siltanen and Stanworth (eds).

Weber, M. (1981) 'Italy', in Lovenduski and Hills (eds).

Webster, P. (1975) 'Matriarchy: A Vision of Power', in Reiter (ed.).

Weinbaum, B. and Bridges, A. (1979) 'The Other Side of the Paycheck: Monopoly Capital and the Structure of Consumption', in Eisenstein (ed.).

Weiner, T. S. (1978) 'Homogeneity of Political Party Preferences between Spouses', *Journal of Politics*, vol. 40, no. 1.

Welch, S. (1977) 'Women as Political Animals? A Test of Some Explanations for Male-Female Political Participation Differences', *American Journal of Political Science*, vol. 21, no. 4.

Welch, S. (1978) 'Recruitment of Women to Public Office', *Western Political Quarterly*, vol. 31, no. 3.

Wells, A. S. and Smeal, E. C. (1974) 'Women's Attitudes Toward Women in Politics', in Jaquette (ed.).

White, C. (1980) 'Women and Socialist Development: Reflections on the Case of Vietnam', unpublished paper presented to the UK Political Studies Association Conference.

Whitehead, L. (1975) 'An Attempt to Rehabilitate "The State"', unpublished paper presented to the UK Political Studies Association Conference.

Whitelegg, E. *et al.* (eds) (1982) *The Changing Experience of Women* (Oxford: Martin Robertson, in association with the Open University).

Whyte, M. K. (1978) *The Status of Women in Pre-industrial Societies* (Princeton University Press).

Wickham, A. (1980) 'Engendering Social Policy in the EEC', *m/f*, no. 4.

Wilson, E. (1977) *Women and the Welfare State* (London: Tavistock).

Wilson, E. (1980) *Only Half-Way to Paradise: Women in Postwar Britain 1945–1968* (London: Tavistock).

Wolchik, S. (1981) 'Eastern Europe', in Lovenduski and Hills (eds).

Wolf, M. (1974) 'Chinese Women: Old Skills in a New Context', in Rosaldo and Lamphere (eds).

Wolin, S. (1960) *Politics and Vision* (Boston: Little, Brown).

Wolpe, A. (1978) 'Education and the Sexual Division of Labour', in Kuhn and Wolpe (eds).

Yishai, Y. (1979) 'Abortion in Israel: Social Democrats and Political Responses', in Palley and Preston (eds).

Yuval-Davis, N. (1980) 'The Bears of the Collective: Women and Religious Legislation in Israel', *Feminist Review*, no. 4.

Zald, M. N. and Ash, R. (1966) 'Social Movement Organizations: Growth, Decay and Change', *Social Forces*, vol. 44.

Index